The Collected

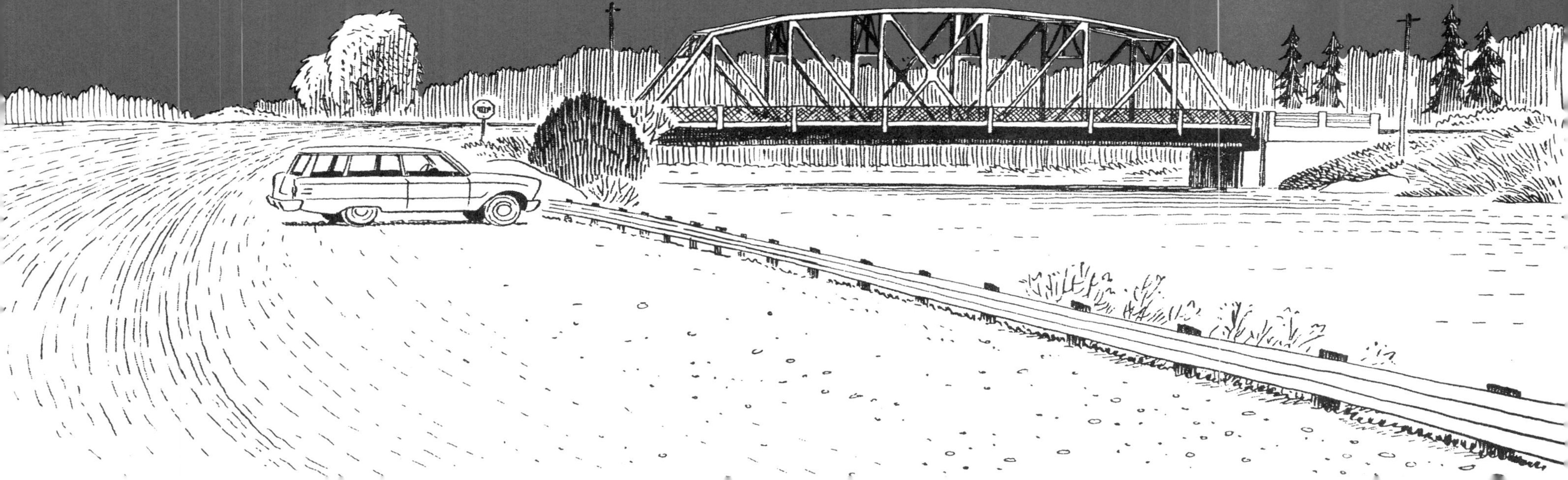

DOUGW

WRIGHT

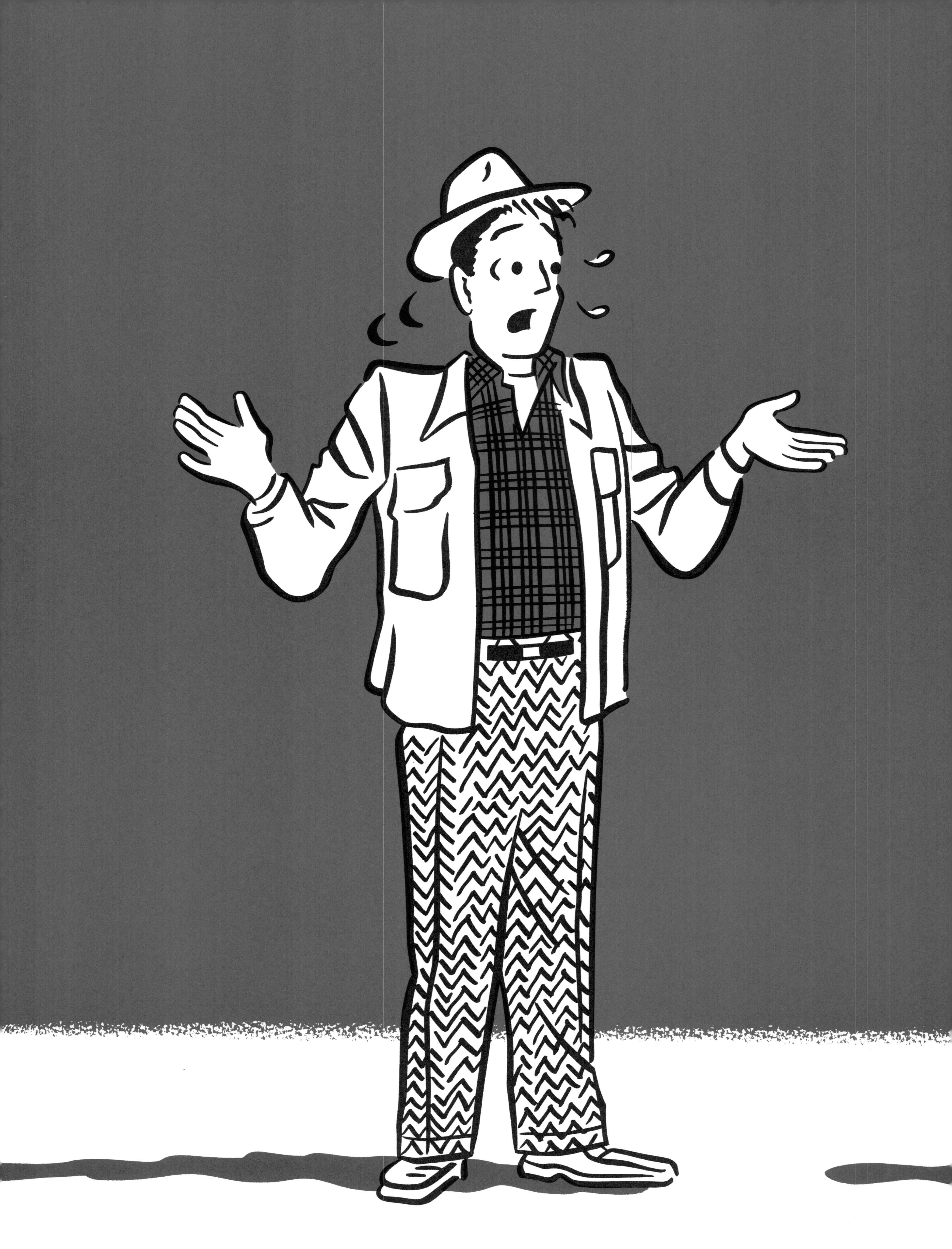

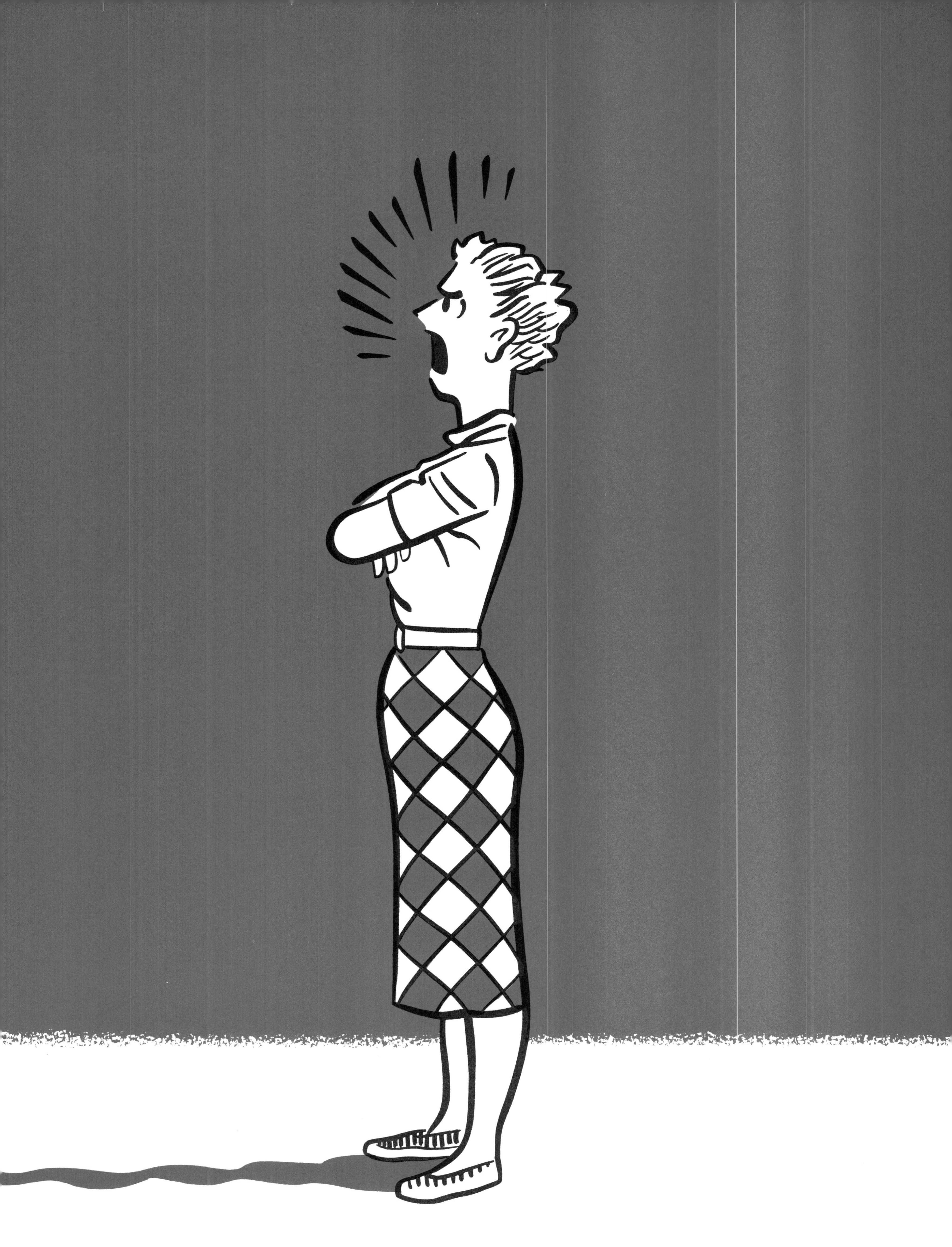

PUBLISHED BY:
Drawn & Quarterly,
Post Office Box 48056,
Montreal, Quebec,
Canada H2V 4S8
www.drawnandquarterly.com

First edition: April 2009. Printed in Malaysia.
10 9 8 7 6 5 4 3 2 1

Library and Archives Canada Cataloguing in Publication
Wright, Doug, 1917–1983
    The collected Doug Wright: Canada's master
cartoonist / edited by Seth, Brad Mackay; introduction
by Lynn Johnston.
ISBN 978–1–897299–52–4 (v. 1)
    1. Wright, Doug, 1917–1983. 2. Canadian wit and
humor, Pictorial. 3. Cartoonists––Canada––Biography.
I. Seth, 1962– II. Mackay, Brad, 1968– III. Title.
PN6790.C33W74 2009   741.5'971   C2008–905793–7

DISTRIBUTED IN THE USA BY:
Farrar, Straus and Giroux,
18 West 18th Street,
New York, NY 10011
Orders: 888.330.8477

DISTRIBUTED IN CANADA BY:
Raincoast Books,
9050 Shaughnessy Street,
Vancouver, BC V6P 6E5
Orders: 800.663.5714

Drawn & Quarterly acknowledges the financial contribution
of the Government of Canada through the Book Publishing
Industry Development Program (BPIDP) and the Canada
Council for the Arts for our publishing activities and for support of this edition.

Special thanks to Mary Johnston–Miller at Library and
Archives Canada in Gatineau, Quebec, for her invaluable
help in cataloguing the Doug Wright material and for aiding
our research on this book.

Visit Drawn & Quarterly's blog and website for news on
the release of the next volume of the Doug Wright series,
collecting material from 1963–1981.
www.drawnandquarterly.com/blog

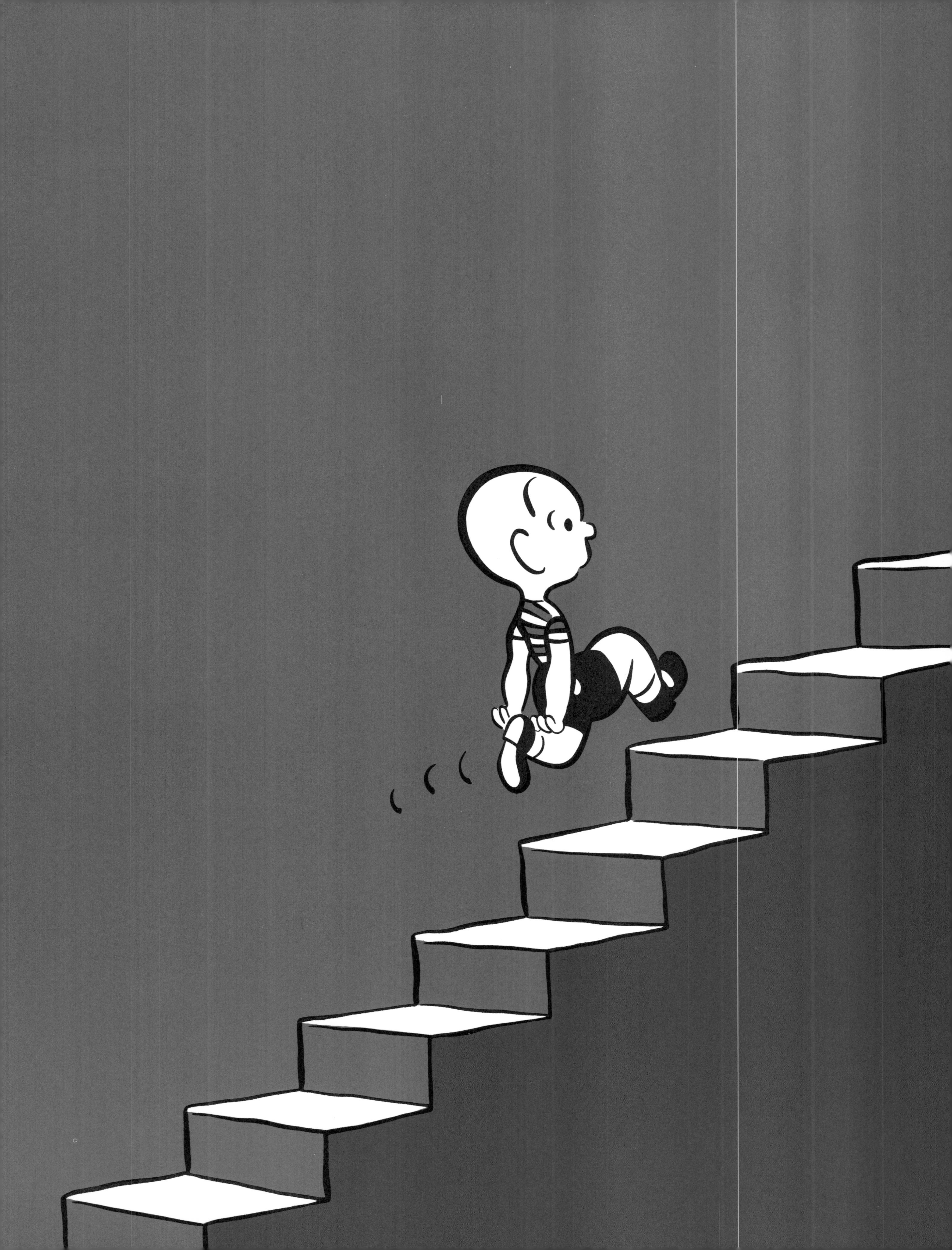

March 12, 1949.
THE STANDARD MAGAZINE. Nipper's first
appearance (though unnamed at the time).

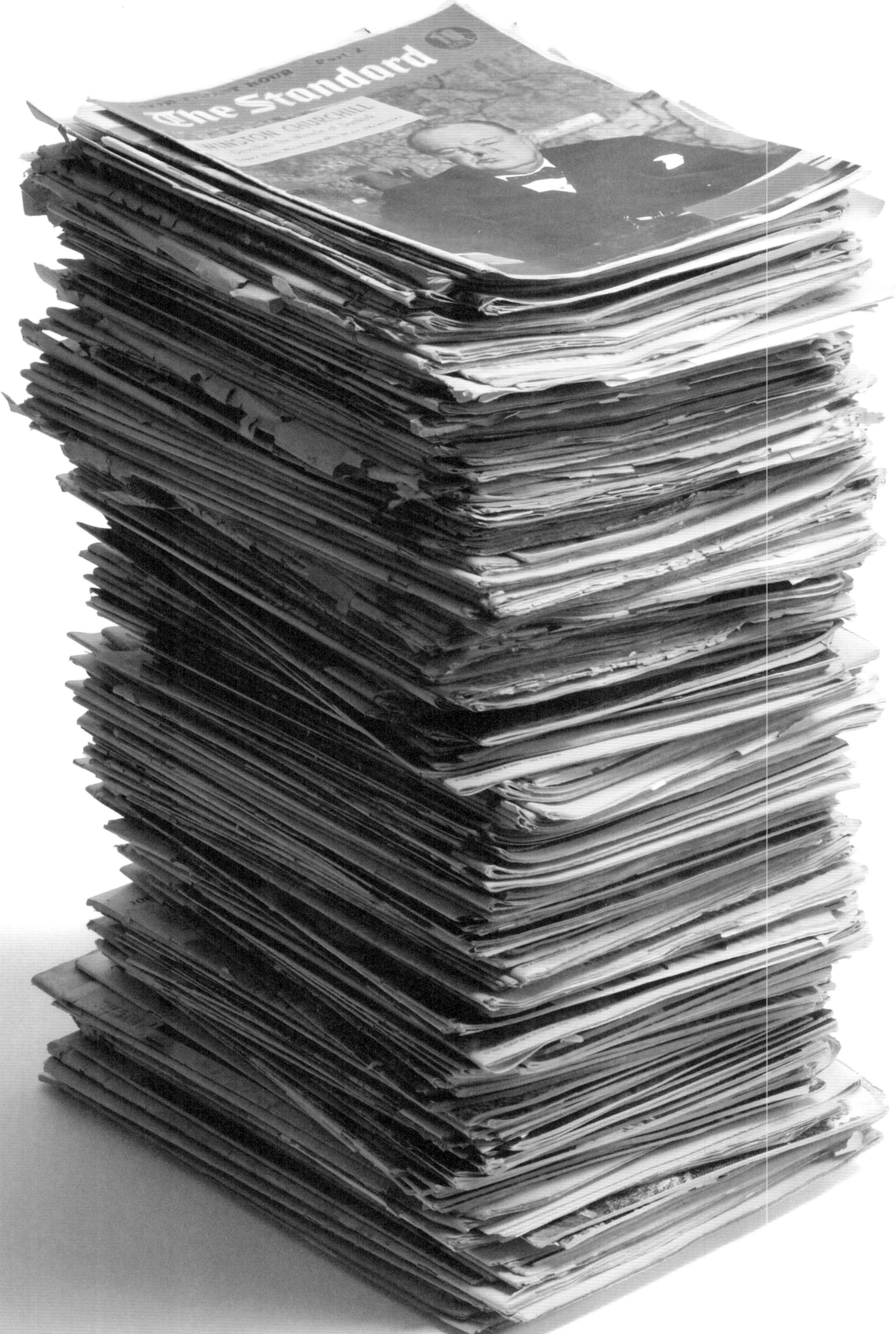
The Standard
WINSTON CHURCHILL

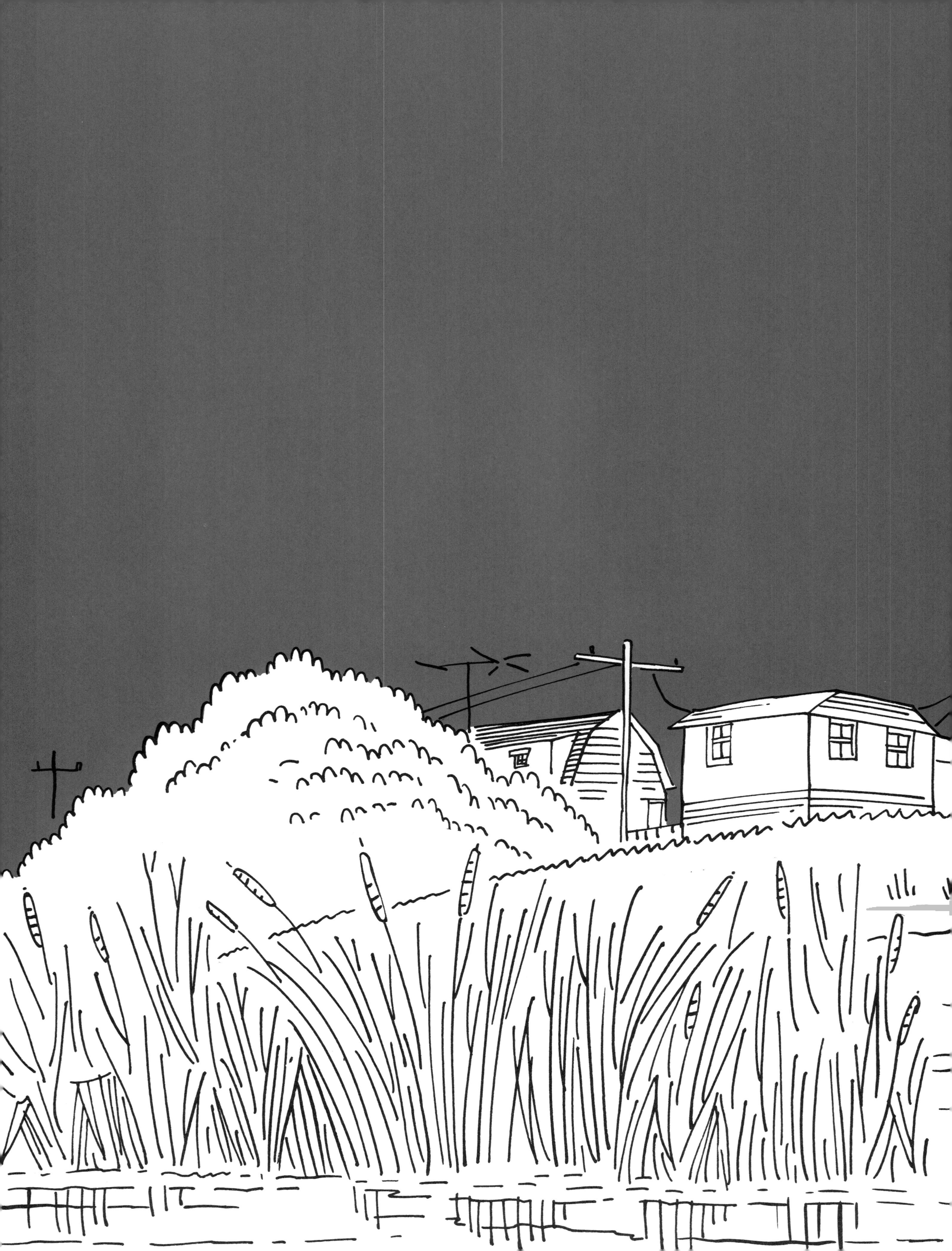

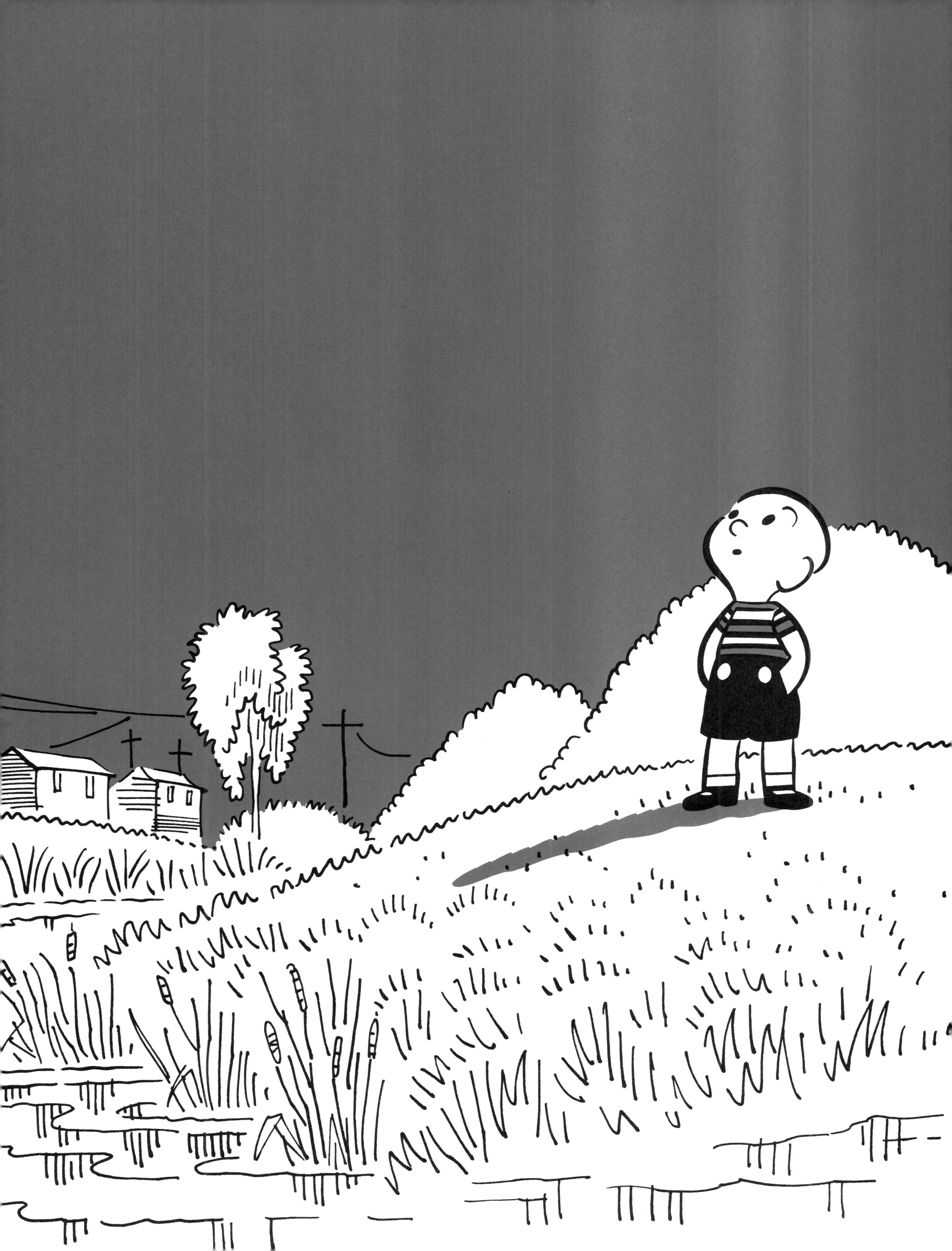

ABOVE: Flying officer DOUGLAS AUSTIN WRIGHT circa 1942 to 1945.
OPPOSITE: Self–portrait circa late 1930s.

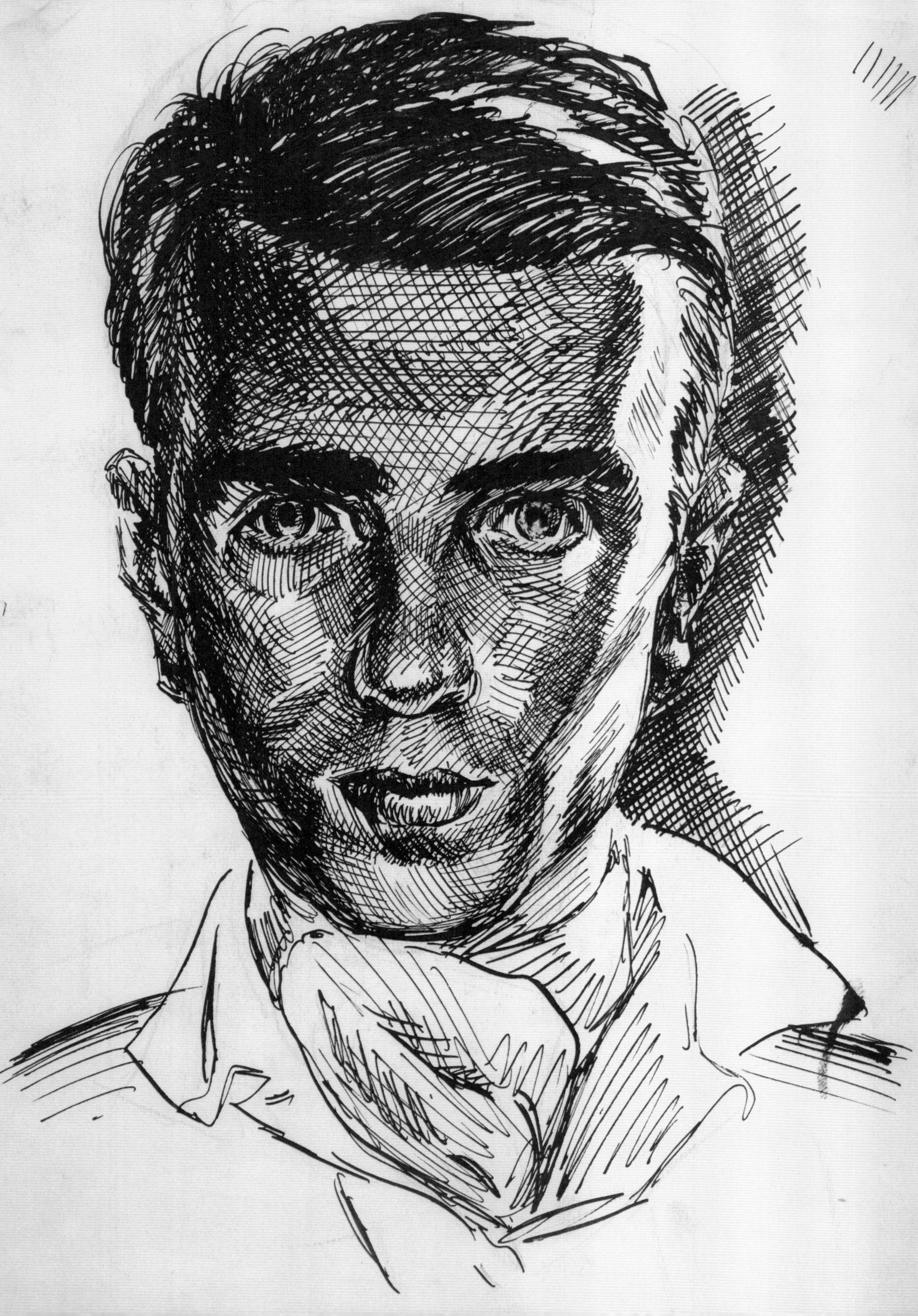

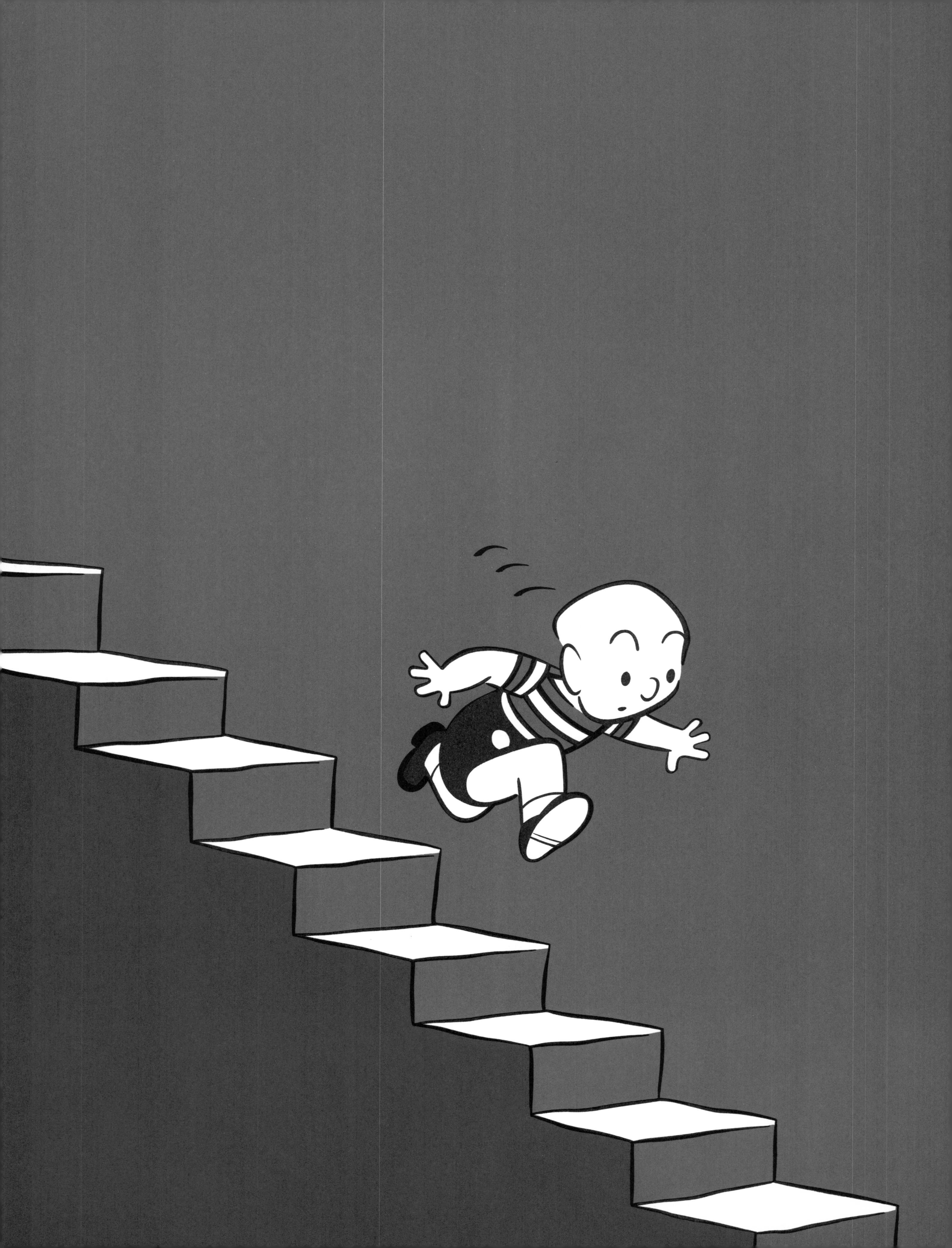

DEDICATED TO
PHYLLIS WRIGHT THOMAS
FOR HER UNWAVERING TRUST,
PATIENCE AND INVALUABLE ASSISTANCE
IN THE MAKING OF THIS BOOK.

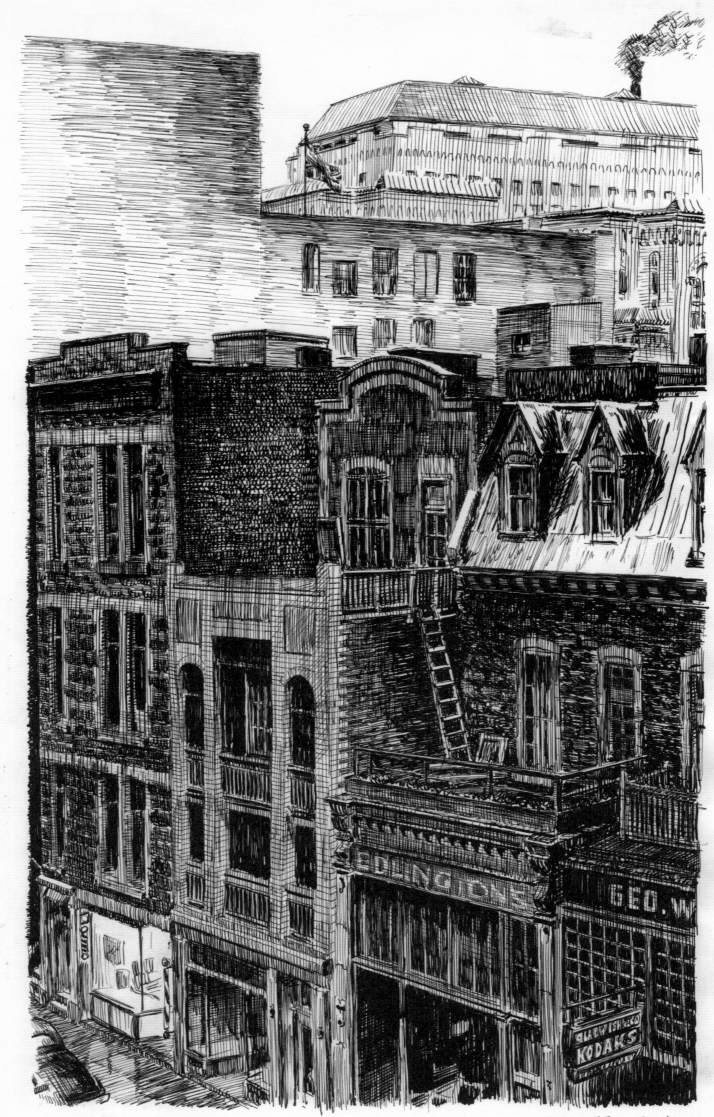

ARCHITECTURE – MANSFIELD ST.   DOUGLAS AUSTIN WRIGHT

THE VIEW FROM WRIGHT'S WINDOW
2005 Mansfield street, Apartment #10, Montreal,
circa 1938–40.

The Collected DOUG WRIGHT
CANADA'S MASTER CARTOONIST

1949 TO 1962

EDITED BY SETH
& BRAD MACKAY
DESIGNED BY SETH

DRAWN & QUARTERLY
MONTREAL

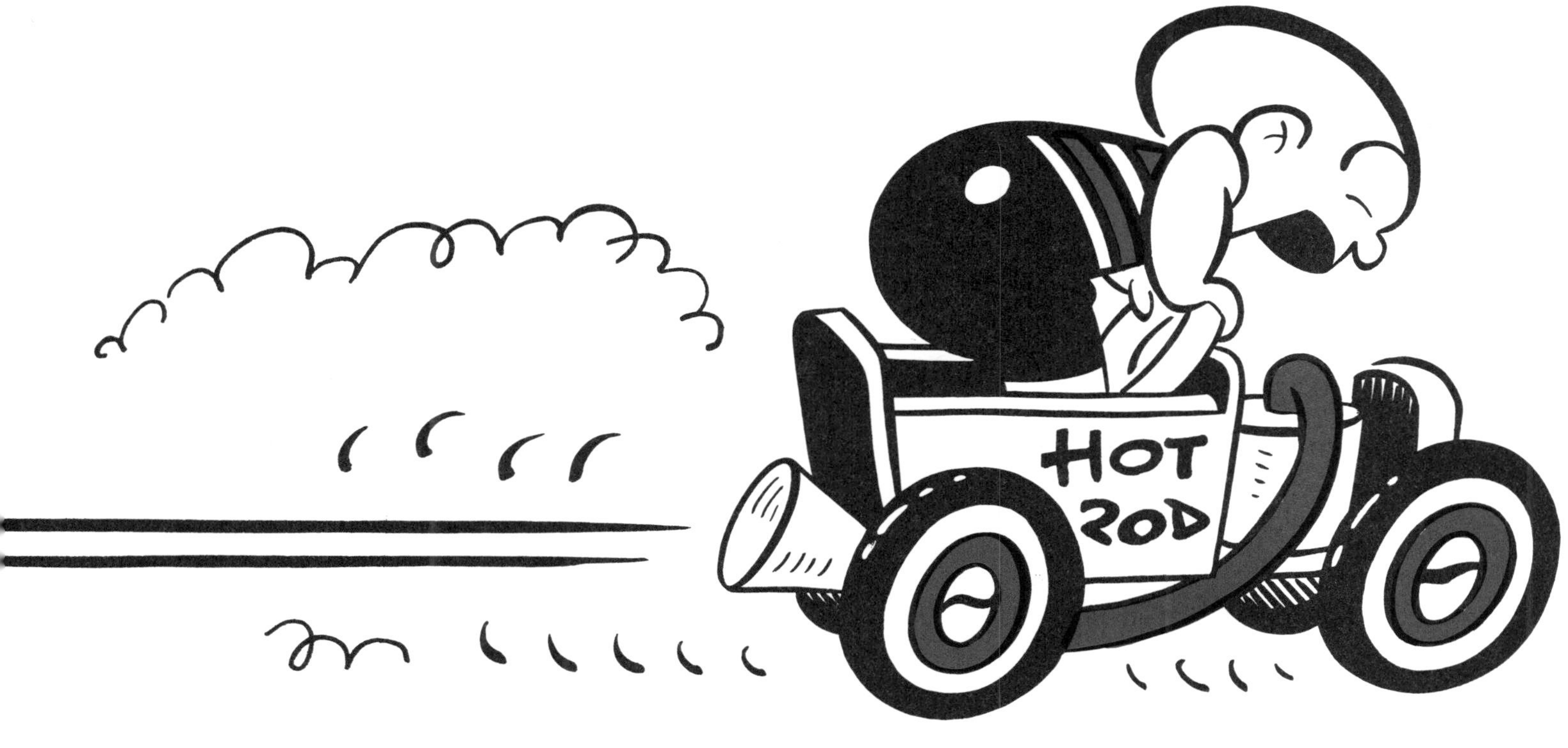
HOT ROD

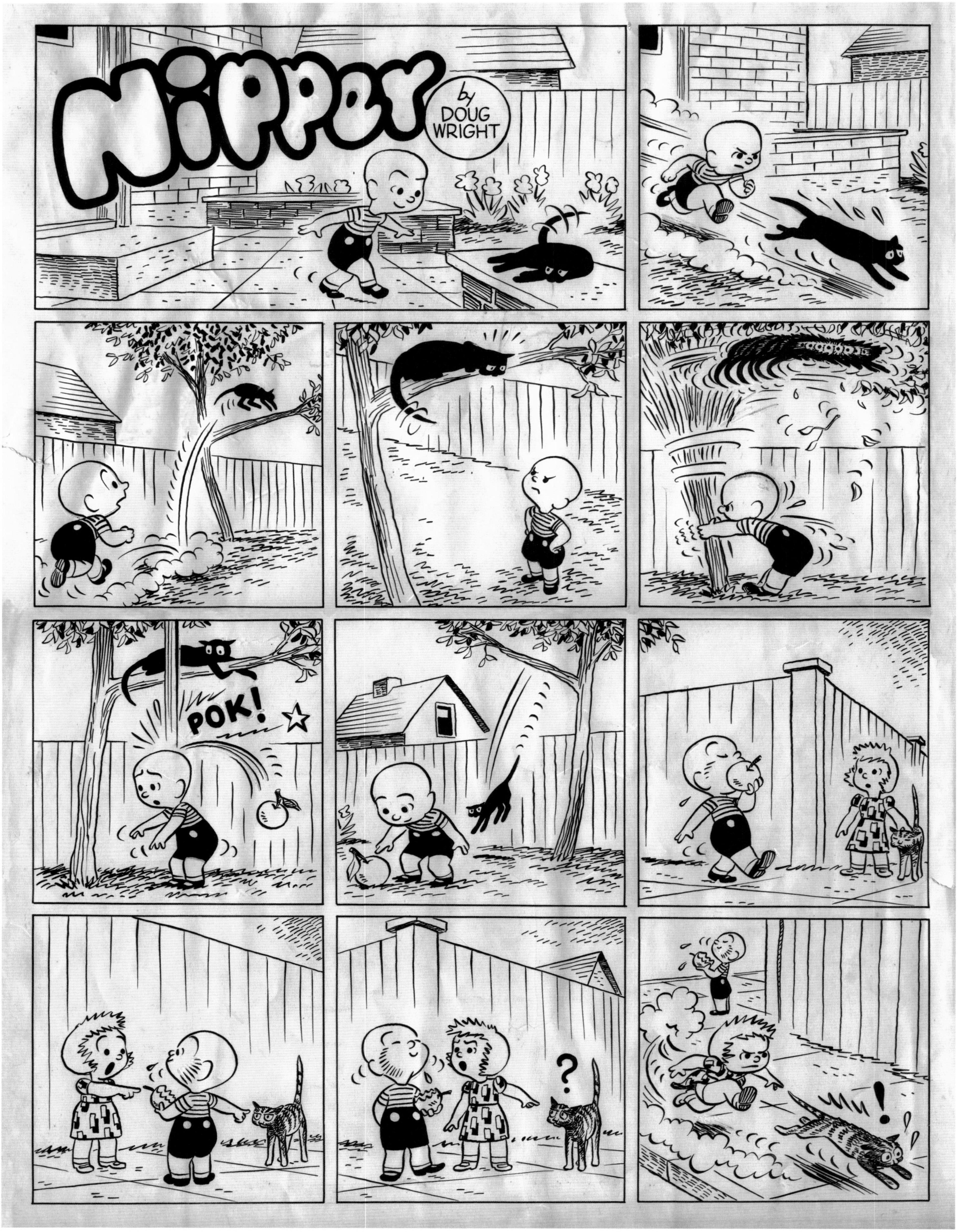

NIPPER
by DOUG WRIGHT
POK!
?

This large and very polished full page strip is quite likely part of a package of sample comics which Wright sent to the U.S. syndicates in the early 1950s.

INTRODUCTION
by LYNN JOHNSTON

{ **Creator of the internationally syndicated comic strip** FOR BETTER OR FOR WORSE }

When the paper came, my dad was the first to read the comics. He didn't just read them, he studied them and encouraged me to do the same. He was particularly fond of comic art that had structure and substance and the kind of subtle wit that brought the reader into the gag the way a storyteller tells a tale. Len Norris of the *Vancouver Sun* was one of his favourites, Doug Wright was another. When the *Star Weekly* came, he would turn to *Doug Wright's Family* and smile. "This is truly an art form," he told me. "It's not a cartoon as much as it's illustrated comic thought. This is comedy in its highest form. It's a performance, and a good performer involves the audience."

Doug Wright had the ability to draw extremely well and to time a situation with precision. His image sequences always had just enough information, just enough expression and just enough slapstick to make them truly believable and therefore truly funny. We identified with every situation from all points of view. There were no perpetual heroes, no perpetual villains, just real people living together, dealing with everyday concerns. *Doug Wright's Family* was everyone's family ... or we wished it was!!

He was smart, vulnerable, thoughtful, conscientious, observant, happy and kind. That was a given. He could not have done the work he did if he had not been profoundly sensitive and able to see things from another's point of view. His gentle and caring depiction of family life endeared his characters to everyone—and perhaps taught some parents to be just a bit more tolerant, to laugh at themselves a little more.

If he was an unwitting teacher of parenting skills, he was also a teacher of art. My dad made me aware of Doug Wright's attention to detail. If he drew a truck, it looked like a real truck! If he drew an office building, it had an architectural design and perfect perspective. He researched his material, which takes time and discipline!

In my room I had a desk and all the drawing supplies a kid could want. I loved to draw and I really loved to draw funny stuff. If I could make someone laugh, it was heaven. Drawing alone isn't enough to fulfill an aspiring cartoonist, much less an insatiable audience, and so the business of learning how to do comic art in sequence was something I wanted desperately to do. Having no schools or tutors at the time, someone with the same loose screws as I had went to the most obvious resources and studied the work of those we admired most. I joined my father at the kitchen table and mulled over the expressions on the faces of the *Katzenjammer Kids,* the simply outlined images in *Miss Peach* and laughed out loud at the way Len Norris drew policemen's feet (they always curled over the curb on the sidewalk). When the *Star Weekly* came, we two critics would turn to *Doug Wright's Family* and learn. I don't think I'd have had the basics needed to do a syndicated comic strip had it not been for Doug Wright. What he taught me was to think of the art as a performance. Pay attention to detail. Take the time to research everything from body language to backgrounds. See things from all of the characters' points of view. Don't overdo a gag, let the audience participate and get it for themselves. Be believable. Use your skills to do the best you can do at all times! Be consistent and be humble. Without humility, creativity like this cannot happen.

Sadly, it was after Doug's death that I had the privilege of communicating with his family. I would have liked to tell him how much his work meant to me. That he read and enjoyed *For Better or For Worse* was a joy. It's nice to know that one of my most respected teachers was pleased with my work!

NIPPER original for March 4, 1950.

MR. WRIGHT
BY BRAD MACKAY

{ "[NIPPER] was conceived by accident and born every week in agony." —Greg Clark }

I f you grew up in Canada during the 1960s or 1970s, then you likely need little introduction to Doug Wright or his masterpiece of Canadian cartooning, *Doug Wright's Family*. Created on the cusp of the 1950s under its birth name Nipper, the semi–autobiographical strip epitomized the competing joys and agonies of family life for millions of readers, and earned Wright a reputation as Canada's equivalent to Charles Schulz.

Like his American counterpart, Wright became an undeniable part of the cultural fabric of his country. *Doug Wright's Family* served as the inspiration for a generation of young Canadian cartoonists, including *For Better or For Worse's* Lynn Johnston, *Cerebus'* Dave Sim, *Louis Riel's* Chester Brown (whose first published work, at the age of 11, was an homage to *Doug Wright's Family*) and Guelph, Ontario's Seth—who was the driving force behind the very book you now hold in your hands.

Yet, unlike Schulz, in the years since Wright's death in 1983 his vast body of work has slowly—and excruciatingly—slipped into something of a cultural blind spot, where it has sat alongside a who's who of late, great Canadian cartoonists. Thankfully, the recent emergence of comics as a full–fledged member of the cultural canon has helped shine some light on the history of Canadian cartooning, one in which Wright played a major role.

A self–taught workhorse of an artist, Wright was renowned among other professional cartoonists for his expert draughtsmanship and spooky eye for detail[1]. These talents were well–exercised over the course of three decades and some 1,664 strips; each one revealing another aspect of a family ruled (and roiled) by two rambunctious and perpetually bald boys.

A family portrait served in weekly installments, *Doug Wright's Family* was a singular comics creation: sweet and unwavering in its honesty, it presented the parent–child relationship, with all of its pain and suffering intact. By confronting the realities of family life without flinching, Wright provided a much welcome counter–weight to the traditional family strip, which plied sentiment and raw sap for easy laughs. While *Family Circus* and *Dennis the Menace* (both of which *Nipper* predated) were tugging at your heartstrings, Wright was busy exploring the dark side of parenting in an attempt to answer the question all parents eventually end up asking themselves—"Why?"

His approach was deceptively simple. In Wright's work kids acted like kids, in all their uncensored, amoral glory. Whether they were wreaking abuse on the family pet, pouring cigarette butts into their dozing father's mouth or idly throwing rocks on unsuspecting adults[2], Wright presented the casual brutalities of childhood as an essential (and undeniable) fact of life, and his readers loved him for it. Of course, there were many heart–warming moments during the strip's 32 years—the best of which are included in this volume —but thanks to their proximity to the less–than–sweet, they typically came across as charming rather than cheap.

Wright's hard–earned skills and compulsive candour helped propel him to the upper echelon of Canadian cartooning in relatively short order. By the mid–1950s, *Nipper* was a household name, and Wright, with his wry grin and laconic humour, was a natural fit for the emerging media age, making regular TV appearances and appearing in celebrity endorsements. Yet, surprisingly, if it was up to Wright, *Nipper* would never have existed. Though it was destined to become his most enduring creation, *Nipper* began as an accident; a creative blunder that the then 30–year–old bachelor was quick to disown—even after it became a runaway success.

---

[1]Wright's ability to fill his work with minute telling details—from toasters and mailboxes to magazine racks and stairway railings—without cluttering up the composition, earned him the admiration and respect of other cartoonists. "He had an amazing way of making every line count," cartoonist Ben Wicks said in an obituary of Wright. "Nothing was ever wasted." Like musicians who can play any song by ear, Wright was gifted with the ability to draw anything he saw. His eldest son, Bill, summed it up nicely in an interview, "He just had something magic. Whatever he saw came out of his pen."

[2]I included this example to the effectiveness of Wright's dark art. During my research for this essay I was surprised to come across one strip, reproduced on the cover of a 1971 collection, that shows the two cartoon boys raining rocks over a river's ledge at a rest stop while their Dad smiles approvingly. When it's revealed that the rocks have been hitting two enraged fishermen below, the laughing boys flee to their car while their gobsmacked father is left to handle the situation. In the 30–odd years since I first witnessed this strip, I had come to believe that the cruel anecdote had actually taken place in my own family, with me and my older brother in the roles of the remorseless boys. A sure a sign as any of Doug Wright's formidable powers as a cartoonist.

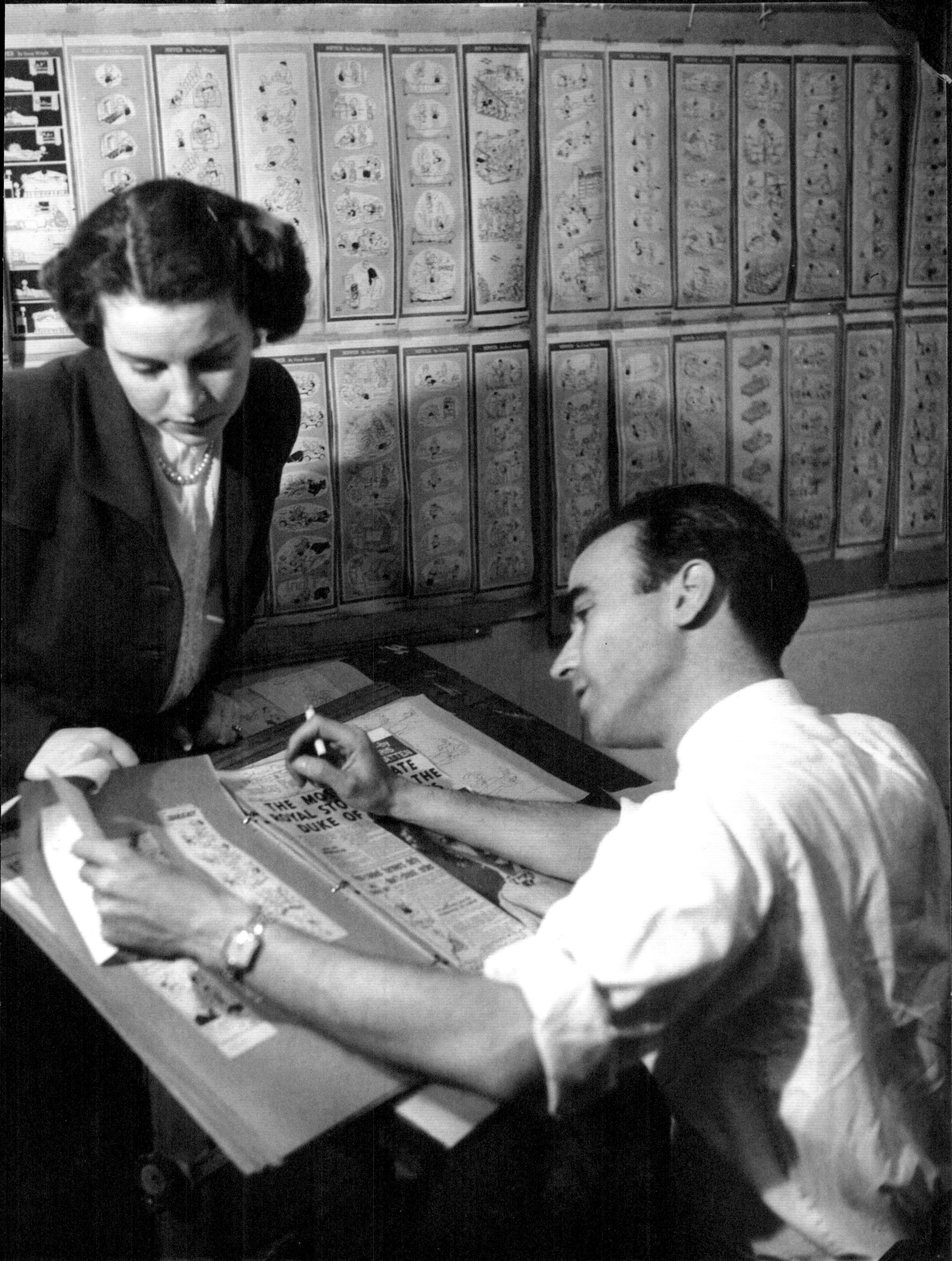

PHYLLIS SANFORD AND DOUG WRIGHT (engaged but not yet married) in Wright's office in the Sun Life Building, Montreal, 1952.

MARGARET AUSTIN WRIGHT and DOUGLAS AUSTIN WRIGHT, **circa 1920.**

Douglas Austin Wright was born in Dover, England on August 11, 1917, the first of two children to Marguerite Archibald and Alan Wright. His father, an Oxford–educated civil servant, spent his early 20s working in the Federated Malay States (present day Malaysia), where he rose to the position of First Class Magistrate, the British Commonwealth equivalent of a justice of the peace. When war broke out in Europe he requested a leave of absence and returned home to enlist in the British Army. As a 2nd Lieutenant in the East Surrey Regiment, Alan served throughout France before he was wounded in battle in the summer of 1916. He was sent to recuperate in Dover, a chief embarkation point for British troops. During his convalescence he met Marguerite ("Rita") Archibald, a woman from a well–to–do family. Born and raised in London, Rita had attended a finishing school in Brussels, and was also a talented pianist, trained by the celebrated performer and instructor, Max Pirani (who, years later, would establish the esteemed Music Teachers' College at the University of Western Ontario).

While no information exists about Alan and Rita's first meeting, it's clear that their mutual attraction was sudden and strong: they married only a few months later. After his recovery, Alan was promoted to Battalion Bombing Officer, a post that required that he remain in England. The newlyweds wasted little time starting a family, with their first child being born the following summer—about 12 months after their wedding. Sadly, the young family didn't have much time to spend together. When Doug was just two months old his father was further promoted—this time to full Lieutenant—and sent back into battle.

Alan Wright spent the next year fighting in Italy, France, and Belgium before he was killed in combat near the Belgian city of Ypres on Sept. 4, 1918, just two weeks after his son's first birthday and two months before the armistice. In the weeks before his death, Alan Wright's mind was clearly preoccupied with his first–born. He wrote a letter on August 8 (three days before his birthday) in which he wishes to Doug a happy "first anniversary" from "a dugout 2 ft. 6 x 3 ft. 6 x 10 ft. which smells of mould and stale air and rocks unpleasantly whenever a shell bursts within a hundred yards." A heart–breaking mix of sentiment and stoicism, the senior Wright's final letter offers up a series of life lessons to a son he feared he would never see again:

"Don't pull dog's tails, stroke cats the wrong way, catch bees on the window pane, or run after chickens

when their mother is about, as all these creatures have a nasty way of resenting undue familiarity."

"[Do] Live at peace with your neighbours, because Law is a rogue and a thief and War is the devil. Learn to love beauty and don't be put off with imitations...Be a man always and a great man some day, and if Daddy doesn't come home be a comfort and a pride to the best little mother in the world."

"May the sufferings of your parents smooth the way of life for you, my boy, and may you never know the horrors of civilized warfare."

With nearly one million Britons killed during the First World War and more than 1.5 million wounded, the Wrights were by no means alone in their grief. Still, the cruel timing of Alan's death must have weighed heavily. Rita was now faced with raising not only her young son by herself, but she was also two months pregnant with their second child; a daughter, Margaret Austin Wright, born the following spring. Despite her circumstances, she didn't seek out a new husband (indeed, she would never remarry) and seemed to have committed herself to providing as normal an upbringing as possible for her children.

Thanks to an army pension and support from her family and in–laws, Rita managed to set up a comfortable life for her young family in London. Her brother Ernie, a disabled bachelor, even stepped in as something of a father figure for Doug and Marge. The efforts were apparently not in vain. Family photos depict the pair as happy and carefree: both dressed as Indians battling each other with feather dusters; Marge smirking in a USS Malay sailor's cap; Doug dressed as a bobby mugging for the camera; and the entire family sunning themselves on the beaches at Eastbourne and Felpham, popular seaside resort towns. In fact, it's difficult to deduce what effect—if any—growing up without a father had on the adult Wright.

Of course it's unlikely that he retained any memories of his dad—a presumption that's supported by a close reading of Wright's personal journals, which contain no mention of Alan Wright. In addition, according to his wife and sons, Wright never discussed his father, or his death, with any of them. The only evidence that does exist is intriguing—if entirely circumstantial. Wright kept a stack of photos of his father (posing proudly with his infant son) in his personal

THIS PAGE: various "snaps" from the seemingly bucolic childhood of the Wright children, circa mid–1920s.

JUVENILE DRAWING, **date unknown.**

NOTEBOOK SKETCH, **circa early to mid–1930s.**

belongings along with a couple of copies of his final correspondence, one of which bears his hand-written notes. And even though Wright was close–lipped about personal matters when talking with reporters, in 1969 he broached the subject in an uncharacteristically forthcoming interview in the *Hamilton Spectator:*

"Dad returned home to England in 1915" [Wright] says, his shaggy eyebrows furrowing. "He joined the army, begat me in 1917, begat my sister in 1918 and got killed in one of those damn Sommes battles a month before the armistice. That bloody battle killed the flower of France and England."

Like many cartoonists, Doug Wright exhibited an early and absorbing passion for the pure act of drawing. According to his mother's accounts, Doug was using stray pieces of coal to scrawl on walls when he was one, and photos of him at the age of four show him sketching intently on his own pint–sized easel. His childhood subjects ranged from the expected (cars and comic strip characters) to the unorthodox, like a 1925 pencil sketch of a Greco–Roman bust—an unusual subject for a seven–year–old boy.

Rita Wright harboured a fierce pride for her first–born and encouraged Doug to pursue his innate talent at every turn. He once recalled when he was 10, bringing home a picture that an older boy at school had drawn to show it to his Mom. When he presented it to her he remembered her only comment being 'You could do better than that when you were four.'

With emotional backing from his mother, Doug pursued his artistic inclinations throughout his childhood and teen years, even at the cost of his formal education. By his own admission, Wright was a poor student and flunked out of high school in his final year. "My mother must have gone nuts trying to figure out what to do with me," he said[3]. To ease his mother's mind, Wright enrolled in the London County Council Art School in Wimbledon, England in an apparent effort to further develop his skills. But Wright and formal training proved a bad match. He dropped out after only three months, claiming that the instructors "were trying to change my style."

Though little of Wright's work from his brief art school period exists, what remains offers some insight into his teenage mindset. Sketches of female nudes, done during a life–drawing class, compete on the page with meticulous drawings of cars and comic strip characters—the true passions of his life at the time.

By 1936, at the tail–end of the Great Depression, Wright had little in the way of career opportunities. A high–school dropout with no formal art training and an unhealthy preoccupation with comic strips, the 19–year–old's future was bleak. But that autumn, he somehow managed to secure a position as an in–house artist at the London offices of the British appliance giant Electrolux. His time at the company was devoted to illustration work for staff newsletters and august publications like the Electrolux Refrigerator Bulletin, which was aimed at the company's sales force. He did manage to squeeze in the occasional comic strip, mostly makeshift affairs concerned with teaching door–to–door refrigerator salesmen how to deal with housewives and headstrong old ladies.

Despite his youthful concerns about protecting his 'style', his work at Electrolux lacks anything in the way of personal flair or panache. In fact, his personal work from his two years at the company seems indicative of an energetic and as–yet unformed artist who was seeking out a style of his

own. His sketchbooks contain everything from loose pencil sketches of street scenes to intricate pen–and–ink renderings of Josephine Baker and *Popeye.*

By the summer of 1938, Wright was bored and growing increasingly restless. He asked around the office about opportunities, and a co–worker mentioned that Sun Life—the largest insurance company in Canada—was on the lookout for illustrators. At $90 a month, the salary wasn't fantastic, but Wright's youthful wanderlust won out. Besides, his Aunt Lilly (his mother's sister) lived in Vancouver so he would always have somewhere to retreat to if the job didn't pan out. It's safe to say that Wright's decision was influenced by the fact that the job was at the company's headquarters in Montreal[4], arguably Canada's only cosmopolitan city at the time thanks to its notorious nightlife and European sensibilities. Montreal was also a relatively short train ride away from New York City, then a hub of the cartooning industry which Wright was angling to break into.

Despite their close bond, Rita Wright supported her son's desire to leave the country, though she had her own selfish motives. Keenly aware of Mussolini's recent invasion of Ethiopia and Hitler's sabre–rattling in Germany, she had become determined that Doug would not be sucked into the kind of bloody conflict that claimed his father. With him across the Atlantic, she secretly hoped that he might have a chance at avoiding service should war be declared. So with his mother's approval, Wright arranged a job in Sun Life's art department, and shortly after his 21st birthday, he departed on the Empress of Britain. On Sept. 27, 1938 he disembarked in Quebec City, and caught a train southwest to Montreal. Upon arrival, he rented a room in a boarding house on University street, then one of the city's main promenades. Any homesickness he may have felt was obviously allayed by the distractions offered up by his new life. He was living in the heart of one of the most sophisticated cities in North America, his room within walking distance of McGill University (which had a well–earned reputation as a party school even then) and the series of nightclubs, music halls and jazz clubs that lined nearby Saint Catherine street.

In a sprawling 21–page letter to his sister dated Nov. 19, 1938, Wright apologized for not writing sooner, explaining that "I practically lost my memory in the first three weeks here." His extracurricular hours were apparently spent navigating through the city's bars, clubs, hockey games, boxing matches, and "mess–strewn" parties attended by his fellow boarders, many of whom were students at McGill. "There's always somewhere to go instead of home," he summed up. His correspondence from this period was filled with newcomer's observations about the urban landscape and anecdotes marked by a clear, arch wit—qualities he would come to rely on in his future career. It also confirms his appreciation of comic strips, as both entertainment and art form. A long–time fan of E.C. Segar's rambunctious, big–hearted *Thimble Theater,* he writes about it and other popular features, like *Toonerville Trolley, Moon Mullins* and *Dick Tracy,* with a critical acumen that could only come from the mind of a true aficionado.

And like many comic fans, he was determined to make his own mark on the medium he loved. While his cartooning skills still needed some polish, he seemed to already possess the independent streak and loner sensibility shared by many in the profession. Barely a month into his tenure at Sun Life, his list of complaints was already long, ranging from petty office politics and his boss's cruddy

[3]Wright told this story several times throughout his life, though a certificate from the University of London seems to suggest that he graduated from the institution in 1934.

[4]When it opened its doors in 1931, the neo–classical Sun Life building was heralded as an architectural marvel around the world. Built in Montreal's Dominion Square, the 24–storey Beaux–Arts style headquarters made headlines for being the largest building in terms of square footage in the British Empire. During the Second World War, the vaults in its basement secretly held millions of dollars worth of gold, stocks and bonds belonging to the many European governments, and were rumoured to have been a safe haven for the British crown jewels.

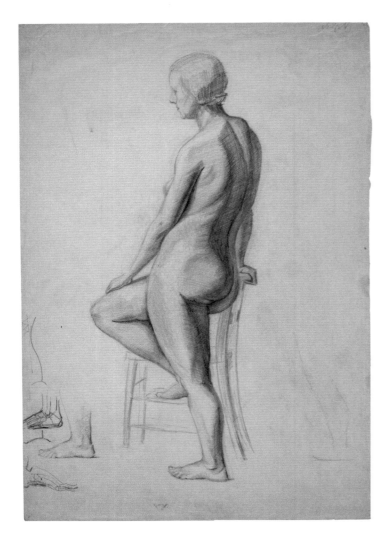

LIFE DRAWING, likely from London County Council School, 1935.

WARTIME SKETCH, circa early 1940s.

design sense to the quality of the work he was getting; "piddling jobs...all kinds of lettering and shit." As a result, Wright wasted little time trying to launch his cartooning career. According to a letter to his mother, by the winter of 1938 he had already made professional contacts and was trying to arrange a meeting with the editor of *Saturday Night* magazine about the possibility of contributing a few cartoons. He even mused about travelling south to take a stab at the legendary cartooning market represented by magazines like the *New Yorker* and the *Saturday Evening Post*. Unfortunately, his plans would soon be cut short as the outbreak of war overseas would put his youthful enthusiasm on hold.

OUR BOY "OZZIE"

In 1939, about a year after he had settled into his new life, Wright's mother and sister joined him in Canada. Doug abandoned his boarding house days in favour of a nearby apartment on Mansfield street that the three could share. But the close–knit family's reunion was short–lived. In September, Adolf Hitler's armies invaded Poland, which prompted Britain and France to declare war. A week later the Canadian Parliament voted to follow suit. Though Rita was still staunchly opposed to Doug entering the war effort, with Canada now preparing to send its own troops overseas he had only two options: enlist or risk being conscripted. After months of debate, he settled finally on a compromise that pleased his worried mother. Rather than sign up for active service right away, he enlisted in the reserve militia; a plan that ensured he would dodge any potential conscription legislation, while at the same time delay his being sent into battle. However, as the war dragged on, his hand was eventually forced: in June 1942 he enlisted in the Royal Canadian Air Force (RCAF)—a move informed by its relatively low risk of injury or death.

Despite his best efforts, danger had little trouble finding Wright. His budding career was cut short when, in the middle of his flight training, he crashed an Avro Anson fighter in a field in Manitoba. Fortunately he wasn't seriously injured, and after a brief recuperation (much of which he spent drawing) he was reassigned to a job as a RCAF navigation instructor at the No. 1 Central Navigation School in Rivers. It was here, in the small town west of Winnipeg, that the compulsive sketching of former–Flying Officer Wright caught the eye of an officer responsible for putting together a number of service magazines. The officer explained that he needed something light for his publications and Doug's cartoon sketches of British Air Force officers (the kind, Wright explained, "with big handle-bar mustaches, and battered hats and uniforms") seemed a perfect fit.

Wright quickly worked up some strips and sent them in. Within a few weeks *Lord Whiff of Grapeshot* by "Ozzie"[5] appeared in a magazine called *The Station*. Although technically not his first strip to be published (his makeshift cartoons for Electrolux hold this honour), Wright considered *Lord Whiff* his first published work as a working cartoonist. The four–panel strip was just what Canadian servicemen were hankering for. A send–up of stereotypical British airmen, it poked fun at their jutting teeth, raging pomposity and obsession with the "purfect cuppa" tea.

"I met a little tiny airman who had just bought a copy [of *The Station*] and was looking at my stuff," Wright recalled years later. "[He was] laughing so hard he didn't even see me salute." The first time Doug had ever witnessed anyone outside his own family laugh at one of his drawings, the experience hooked him on cartooning for good. Over the next few months, Wright cranked out work at the rate of a feverish schoolboy. Each of characters seemed to have a more outlandish name than the last; Booby Hatch, Lionel Gumbeater, W. Rockingham Underlip, Slipper Puss, Wack Pott, and A. Boddy[6], who was perhaps the strangest of his lot. A witless—and armless—private with a talent for being in the wrong place at the wrong time, A. Boddy held a special place in

Wright's heart. After the war he would resurrect the unusual, gloomy character in a series of strip proposals that tried to mine comedy from the sad sack's experiences reintegrating into civilian life. Unfortunately, Wright's efforts to market a strip about the comedic misadventures of what appeared to be a double–amputee war vet failed to catch fire.

A. Boddy is indicative of Wright's wartime oeuvre, which seemed to fall into one of two categories: the bizarre or the banal. Yet what it may have lacked in quality, it more than made up for with sheer diversity. Wright's body of work from his RCAF years has a refreshingly free–range feel to it, varying in both form (strips, editorial cartoons, one–panel cartoons and gag cartoons) and medium, from pen–and–ink to wash and even the occasional painted pieces. If not for the ever–present signature from "Ozzie," it would be impossible to guess that it all originated from the same hand. It was as if Wright consciously approached this period as a kind of professional workshop—a chance to try out various techniques and styles. Clewless McGoon, an aerial adventure strip, is clearly cast from the same mould as Milton Caniff's *Terry and the Pirates,*[7] complete with a colourful cast of supporting characters, like the lead's brash American cousin Typhoon McGoon.[7]

Wright also experimented with dialects, a staple of many classic cartoonists. His characters often spoke in vernaculars: from toffee–nosed Brit, to classic Yankee and Bronx. (There's a good chance that Wright borrowed this technique from Segar, who used it to tremendous effect with Doug's 'old fren', *Popeye* the sailor.) Though his work from this period pales next to a Segar or a Caniff, the opportunity to experiment with style and forms was formative for Wright. The breakneck pace he needed to maintain to meet his many deadlines, not to mention also teach his courses, surely served as foundation for the exhausting work ethic he would adopt in the future. (At the peak of his popularity in the 1960s and 70s, Wright kept a schedule that would likely make even the most disciplined contemporary cartoonist feel like a slouch. On any given week, he was responsible for three strips, a weekly editorial cartoon, and any number of illustrations and/or commissions—all on top of *Nipper/Doug Wright's Family*.)

Most important to Wright though, was the recognition his cartooning garnered. The RCAF marked his first genuine audience and his first brush with media attention. (Judging on his personal scrapbooks, Doug relished the attention; he pasted even the tiniest write–up he received in their pages.) "Our boy Ozzie" received a number of profiles in service magazines, and his work warranted attention from civilian media outlets as well. In Dec. 1944, the Canadian Press wrote a profile of Wright that ran in newspapers across Canada and in his native country.

In the end, Wright never achieved the level of fame of renowned war cartoonists such as Bill Maudlin (of *Willie and Joe* fame) or William "Bing" Coughlin, creator of Canada's war–time nebbish Herbie. Still, this period served as an invaluable training ground for his future endeavours.[8] Indeed, the

[5]This pseudonym was derived from Wright's middle name (Austin, or "Aussie"), which was a nickname that his mother gave him as a young boy. Most of his wartime work is signed this way (or as Austin Wright) though he would drop his pen–name after the war in favour of his proper name, Doug Wright—perhaps as a way of marking a turning point in his career. He would occasionally dust off his old nickname, like in the 1950s when he tried to pitch a daily version of Nipper (complete with word balloons) to an American syndicate under the title "Ozzie."

[6]The name was derived from an order commonly heard from commanding officers; "I need a body over here."

[7]I'm probably being too kind here. Clewless McGoon was a blatant, and perhaps knowing, imitation of Caniff's classic strip. It was also, according to Wright, a bit of a success. In February 1944, Clewless was published in Manitoba's *Drift Recorder,* which marked the first time one of his strips appeared in a civilian publication.

CLEWLESS McGOON PRELIMINARY, circa 1942–45.

VARIOUS WARTIME STRIPS which appeared in a variety of military publications, circa 1942–45.

ABOVE: Military publication cover, 1945.

LEFT: Wartime gag cartoon, circa 1942–45.

BELOW (this page and opposite): A gorgeously hand-illustrated resumé which Wright must have used in pursuit of work after being discharged from the RCAF in 1945.

proliferation of unit magazines—dozens of which were published across Canada—gave many famous cartoonists, including Duncan MacPherson, Merle "Ting" Tingley and Len Norris, critical first starts that they may not have had access to outside the war. In fact, long before he created *Mad* magazine, legendary cartoonist Harvey Kurtzman served as a U.S. Army illustrator during the war, while *The Spirit's* Will Eisner actually managed to build a lucrative business for his studio doing everything from newsletters and flyers to instructional comics and propaganda posters.

Wright's years in the service may have also helped plant the seed of one of his other great passions, his fascination with anything that moved, whether it was cars, trucks or planes. As a navigation instructor he was required to use diagrams and other visual aids in the classroom, but rather than rely on prepared ones Wright drew his own; a labourious task that demanded intense concentration and a mastery for perspective and scale–model accuracy. Thanks to his innate attention to detail, Doug excelled at the task, producing flawless schematics of bombers and fighter planes. His knack for drawing picture–perfect vehicles would make him a bit of an oddball among his peers. The average cartoonist shudders at the prospect of rendering highly technical drawings.[9] Over time, Wright's unique talent would become a professional calling card that led to lucrative commissions for trucking companies, a car culture–themed strip called *The Wheels* and a mail–order business dedicated to high–quality art prints of his drawings of old steam engines and vintage race cars.

Back in the summer of 1945, Wright's wartime stretch was coming to an end. On Aug. 7, 1945, three months after VE Day and a week before the surrender of Japan, Doug was discharged from the RCAF and sent back to civilian life. Though he entered the war with a single goal—to make it out alive—he left with far more than he expected. After three years, he was now a published cartoonist with a reputation and a bright future ahead.

Wright returned to his family and his old job in Montreal. Eager to put the drudgery of the office behind him, he wrote to Ham Fisher of *Joe Palooka* fame for career advice. Fisher's strip, about the adventures of an affable but dim–witted boxer, was an A–list title at the time with more than 900 newspapers to its name and nearly 50 million readers.[10] Impressed, Fisher suggested that Wright submit his work to the McNaught Syndicate, a New York–based firm that distributed such strips as *Toonerville Folks*, *The Bungle Family* and his own *Joe Palooka*. Since Wright had little to show outside of his war–themed strips, he headed back to the drawing board, dressed up his wartime characters in civilian clothes, and recast them in a series of urban–themed strips. In an effort to show off his range, he even threw in a few gag cartoons.

The following spring, Wright travelled to Manhattan and made the rounds, starting with the *New Yorker* and the *Saturday Evening Post*. But his attempts at gag cartooning—the bread-and-butter cartoons of American periodicals—fell horribly flat. "I just don't seem to have the formula for those one–panel, one–line gags," he said. In his remaining days, he also visited all the major syndicates,[11] including Fisher's. "Mildred Bellah was the editor then," Wright recalled. "and she must have already seen the work of dozens of ex–servicemen. She told me 'Wherever the hell you're from, go back and try to do something for them.'"

[8]Though his wartime work looks embryonic compared to his later work, Wright's efforts did make a lasting impression. After his death in the early 1980s, The Canadian Legion magazine ran a special feature on "Ozzie"'s career and stressed its pivotal role in boosting morale in the latter years of the war.

[9]Even Hergé, famed creator of *Tintin,* hired artists whose sole job was to draw the cars, trucks and planes in his celebrated strip.

[10]Debuting in 1928, *Joe Palooka* quickly became one of the most successful comic strips of the first half of the century. In fact, it was one of the first strips to be adapted into a feature film (with Jimmy Durante in the role of Joe's trainer), which, combined with merchandising opportunities, helped to make Fisher one of the original millionaire cartoonists. Doug was likely aware of this, so it's possible that by writing to him he may have been angling for a job with Fisher. If that was the case it's a good thing for Wright that Fisher didn't take the bait. Fisher is perhaps best known in cartooning circles for initiating a legendary feud with *L'il Abner's* Al Capp, his former assistant on *Joe Palooka*. Fuelled by accusations of plagiarism and sexual perversion, the two titanic egos kept the bitter and very public spat alive for more than 20 years. It reached its nadir in the early 1950s, when Fisher attempted to frame Capp by inserting pornographic imagery into *L'il Abner* strips and presenting them to a special meeting of National Cartoonist's Society as proof of his adversary's low moral character. When his deception was uncovered, the society banned the humiliated Fisher from it ranks. On Dec 27, 1955, he took his own life in his New York City studio.

With no leads, Doug heeded the syndicate editor's unvarnished advice and returned home. Though dispirited, he was lucky to be living in a city that was home to one of the most respected newspapers in the country, the *Montreal Standard*. Launched in 1905 as a Canadian version of the *Illustrated London News*, the *Standard* offered its readers a comprehensive (and occasionally dry) roundup of that week's news. By the 1940s it was far more family-oriented, with three fat sections bursting with feature stories, short fiction, advice columns, celebrity profiles, recipes and plenty of ads—by 1950 it had the highest advertising rates in the country.

In 1946 the *Standard* was in the middle of a newspaper war with the *Toronto Star's Star Weekly*, which had a circulation of more than 1 million, three times that of the *Standard*. Despite this, the *Standard* was considered by many, including journalists, to be the superior publication. It was home to a unique range of talent, which included the domestic guru Kate Aitken (a charming pre-cursor to Martha Stewart), and future short story writer Mavis Gallant, who divided her time writing feature stories, a radio column, and the occasional fiction piece. The magazine also featured a robust comics section ("The Best in Canada," if their ads were to be believed) that featured popular titles such as *Blondie, Little Orphan Annie, Steve Canyon, L'il Abner, Dick Tracy, Terry and the Pirates* and about 20 others. With nationwide distribution, a dedicated comics section, and commitment to new talent, the *Montreal Standard* was a smart target for an aspiring cartoonist.

A few months after he slunk back from New York, Doug dropped his portfolio off at the *Standard's* art department—only to have it politely rejected by art editor Dick Hersey. Though accomplished for a 29-year-old, Hersey explained that his characters were too one-dimensional for a general readership paper. Sadly, A. Boddy and his ill-conceived pals would never grace the same newsprint as the likes of Dagwood Bumstead and Daddy Warbucks.

Still, Hersey must have seen something in Wright because shortly after the discussion he started to feed him illustration work.[12] At first, it was largely black-and-white spot illustrations, but within the year, Wright was handed feature illustrations and the occasional covers. These half-page pieces were the perfect showcase for Wright's considerable talents; full-colour and packed (never cluttered) with tiny period-specific details. Seen even without the accompanying articles, his illustrations of office Christmas parties and urban crowd scenes manage to tell a story without the benefit of words.

Over the next two years, Doug juggled his freelance gigs with his responsibilities at Sun Life, which, though frustrating, definitely helped pay the bills.[13] In May 1948, Wright finally gathered his nerve and quit his day job to start his career as a full-time freelancer. Despite this, his ties to his old employer remained strong. Not only did he continue to do work for them on a freelance basis, but he set up his new office in his old building, in a small space that Sun Life management gave to him rent-free. As he would soon find out, his departure couldn't have come at a better time.

About a year before Wright's pivotal career move, cartoonist Jimmy Frise was in the middle of a major career move of his own. In the spring of 1947, Frise (pronounced "fries") moved his much-loved strip *Birdseye Center* from its long-running home in the pages of the *Star Weekly* to the rival

[11]It's worth noting that Wright didn't drop by any comic book companies during his trip. In 1946, Manhattan was home to dozens of shops and studios dedicated to producing content for the hundreds of comic books—from super-heroes and westerns to funny animals and romance—that jammed newsstands every month. At the time, the young medium was starving for artists, regardless of their talent, and have would have surely taken him in on the spot. The fact that Wright paid them no mind is proof positive of the seriousness of his intent; his heart and mind were clearly set on being a newspaper cartoonist, and the kid's stuff of comic books never factored into his career equation.

[12]If you're ever asked to make a list of the top Unsung Heroes of Canadian Cartooning, make a point to put Dick Hersey at the top. From the late 1930s through to the late 60s, the American-born artist and editor shepherded the early careers of many Canadian cartoonists and artists, including Wright, Oscar Cahen, Ed McNally, Harold Town and Duncan MacPherson. Among newspapermen, Hersey is considered the first editor to have relied on Canadian artists for illustration work. Prior to this, it was tradition for newspapers to use cheaper, second-run illustrations from American artists. His efforts were not lost on his stable of freelancers; MacPherson credited Hersey with keeping him flush during his early years, while Wright—who tended to keep to himself—considered Hersey one of his closest friends and confidants.

[13]Despite his frustrations, someone at Sun Life must have appreciated Wright's talent (or his growing disquiet) since he drew a number of cartoons dealing with humourous aspects of the insurance industry for employee newsletters published around this period.

ABOVE: A. Boddy also returns to civilian life in a (possibly) unpublished post-war strip, circa 1945.

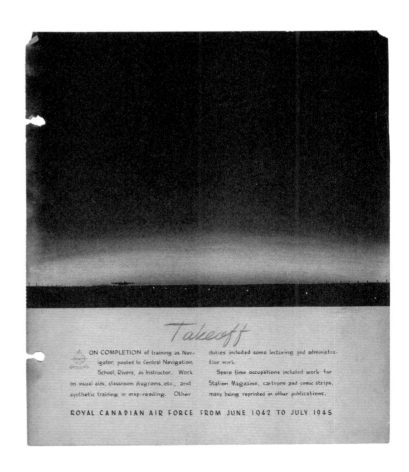

JUNIPER JUNCTION by Jimmy Frise, July 25, 1948.

JUNIPER JUNCTION by Doug Wright, May 11, 1949.

50-52

JUNIPER JUNCTION by Doug Wright, December 11, 1952.

HERE'S A REAL BIG EASTER EGG FER YOU, BUMPY — I DUG IT OUTA A PILE O' SAND DOWN BY TH' BOAT SHED T'DAY

MERCY, ARCHIE—WHAT KIND O' EGG IS THAT?

GEE! I HOPE IT IS! I'D LIKE T'HAVE A BABY SEA-SERPINT AN' TRAVEL 'ROUND SHOWIN' HIM AT FAIRS AN' STUFF!

HANG IF I KNOW — I'D SAY IT'S A SEA-SERPINT EGG — IF YOU B'LIEVED IN SEA-SERPINTS!

CRACK!

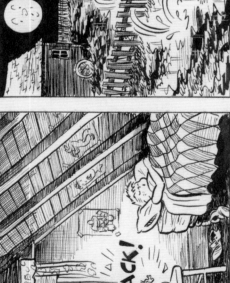

I DON'T THINK THERE EVER WAS ANYTHIN' IN IT — IT JES' CRACKED FROM TH' WARMTH IN TH' HOUSE

ENNYWAY, THERE'S ENOUGH HUNGRY MOUTHS IN THIS HOUSE T'KEEP ME BUSY WITHOUT HAVIN' A SEA-SERPINT T'FEED TOO!

JUNIPER JUNCTION by Doug Wright, April 20, 1949.

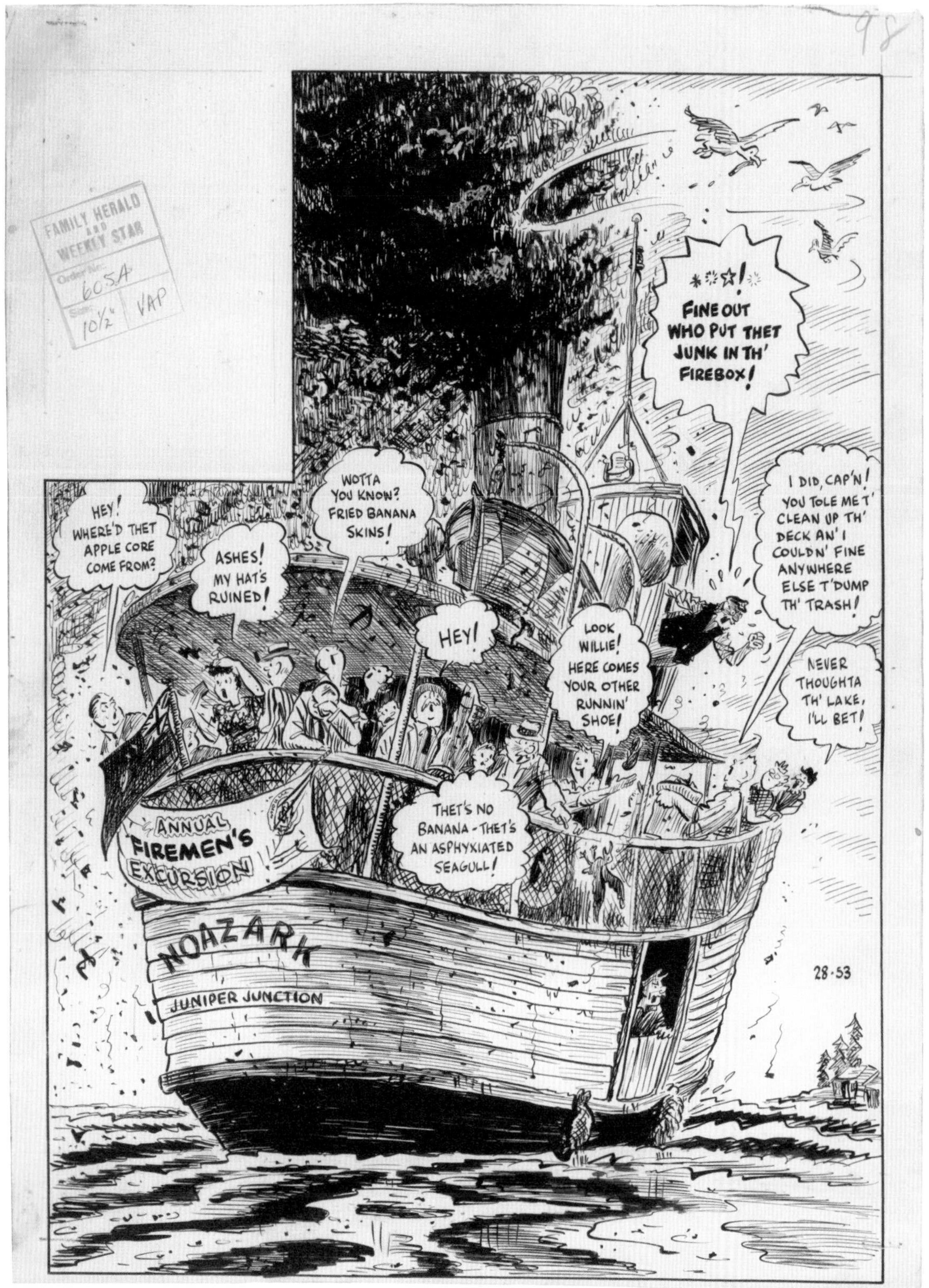
HEY! WHERE'D THET APPLE CORE COME FROM?
ASHES! MY HAT'S RUINED!
WOTTA YOU KNOW? FRIED BANANA SKINS!
HEY!
THET'S NO BANANA - THET'S AN ASPHYXIATED SEAGULL!
LOOK WILLIE! HERE COMES YOUR OTHER RUNNIN' SHOE!
*☼☆! FINE OUT WHO PUT THET JUNK IN TH' FIREBOX!
I DID, CAP'N! YOU TOLE ME T' CLEAN UP TH' DECK AN' I COULDN' FINE ANYWHERE ELSE T'DUMP TH' TRASH!
NEVER THOUGHTA TH' LAKE, I'LL BET!
ANNUAL FIREMEN'S EXCURSION
NOAZARK
JUNIPER JUNCTION
28-53
FAMILY HERALD AND WEEKLY STAR
Order No. 6054
Size 10½ VAP

JUNIPER JUNCTION by Doug Wright, July 9, 1953.

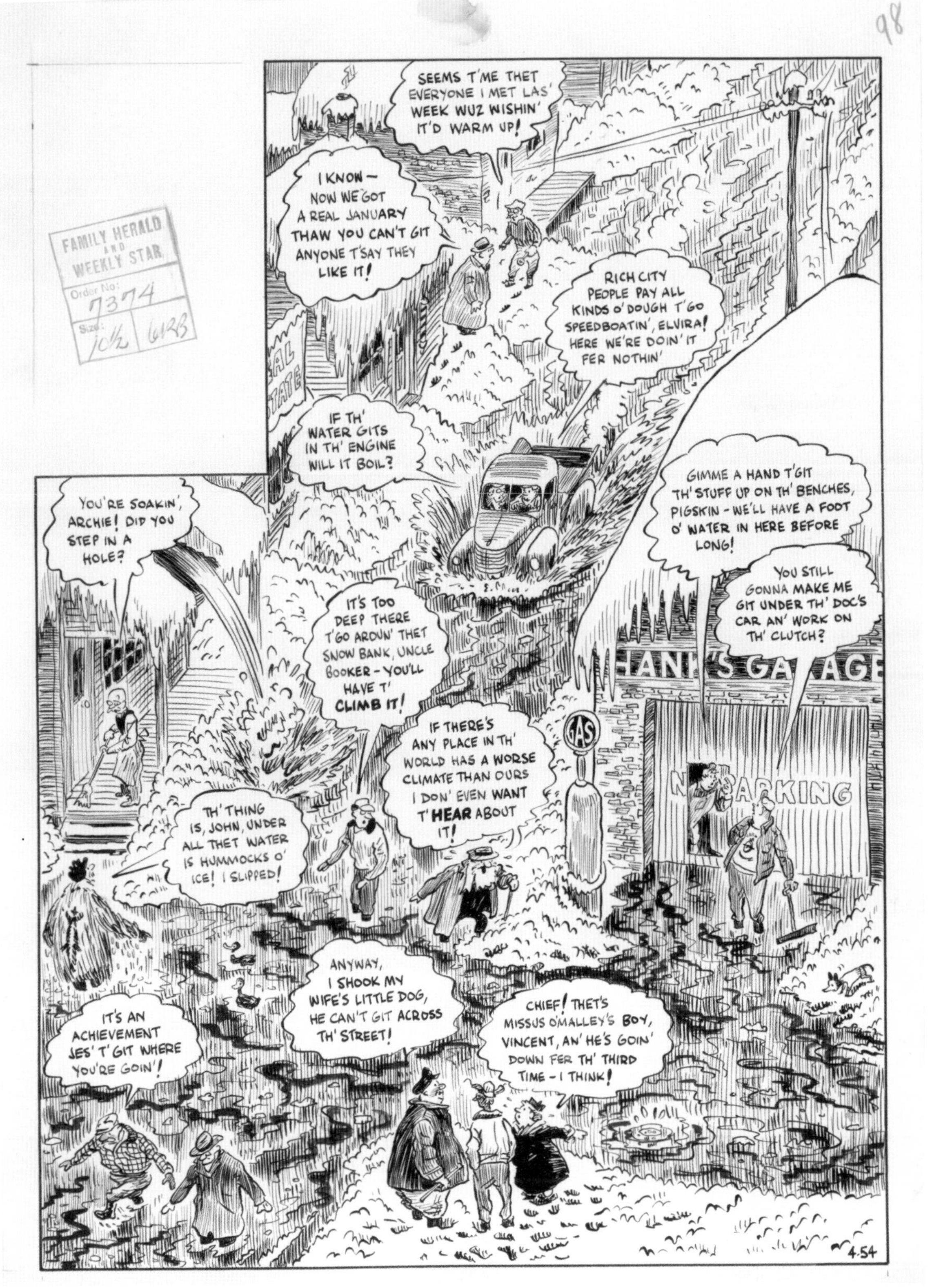
SEEMS T'ME THET EVERYONE I MET LAS' WEEK WUZ WISHIN' IT'D WARM UP!
I KNOW - NOW WE GOT A REAL JANUARY THAW YOU CAN'T GIT ANYONE T'SAY THEY LIKE IT!
RICH CITY PEOPLE PAY ALL KINDS O' DOUGH T'GO SPEEDBOATIN', ELVIRA! HERE WE'RE DOIN' IT FER NOTHIN'
IF TH' WATER GITS IN TH' ENGINE WILL IT BOIL?
YOU'RE SOAKIN', ARCHIE! DID YOU STEP IN A HOLE?
IT'S TOO DEEP THERE T'GO AROUN' THET SNOW BANK, UNCLE BOOKER - YOU'LL HAVE T' CLIMB IT!
GIMME A HAND T'GIT TH' STUFF UP ON TH' BENCHES, PIGSKIN - WE'LL HAVE A FOOT O' WATER IN HERE BEFORE LONG!
YOU STILL GONNA MAKE ME GIT UNDER TH' DOC'S CAR AN' WORK ON TH' CLUTCH?
HANK'S GARAGE
GAS
IF THERE'S ANY PLACE IN TH' WORLD HAS A WORSE CLIMATE THAN OURS I DON' EVEN WANT T' HEAR ABOUT IT!
TH' THING IS, JOHN, UNDER ALL THET WATER IS HUMMOCKS O' ICE! I SLIPPED!
IT'S AN ACHIEVEMENT JES' T' GIT WHERE YOU'RE GOIN'!
ANYWAY, I SHOOK MY WIFE'S LITTLE DOG, HE CAN'T GIT ACROSS TH' STREET!
CHIEF! THET'S MISSUS O'MALLEY'S BOY, VINCENT, AN' HE'S GOIN' DOWN FER TH' THIRD TIME - I THINK!
4-54
FAMILY HERALD AND WEEKLY STAR
Order No. 7374
Size 10½ 6123

JUNIPER JUNCTION by Doug Wright, January 28, 1954.

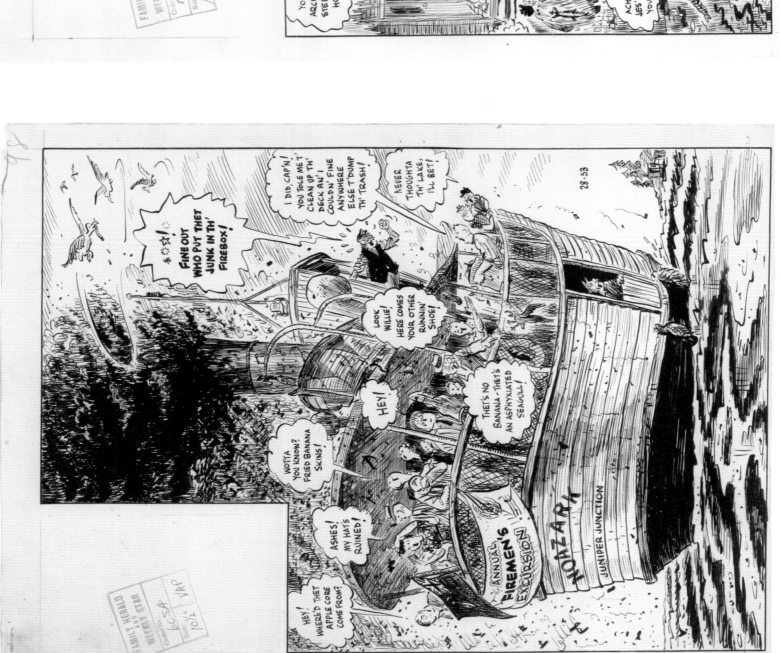

JUNIPER JUNCTION by Doug Wright, April 7, 1962.

Montreal Standard. Then the dean of Canadian newspaper cartooning, he was motivated by a number of factors, including the paper's refusal to run his weekly strip in full colour (a major barrier to breaking through into the U.S. market) and the management's shoddy treatment of its employees, including his friend and collaborator Greg Clark.

In his late 50s, Frise was a model of the successful cartoonist. Ambitious, self–taught and universally admired, he had overcome a potentially disabling injury in the First World War[14] to create one of Canada's most popular comic strips.

Frise started at the *Toronto Star* as an illustrator, and got his big break in January 1919, when his first regular feature debuted in the paper. Titled *At The Rink,* the one–panel cartoon seemed to be a concerted attempt to replicate a popular American feature by W.E. Hill, *Among Us Mortals,* which had been appearing in the paper for the past 12 months. Frise's feature earned an official title, *Life's Little Comedies,* a few months later, along with a cast of characters that was inspired by his experiences growing up on a farm in Scugog, just north of Toronto. By the early 1920s, the feature had evolved from one panel to a more traditional strip format and had its title changed to *Birdseye Center.* This version of the strip, which featured a large likable cast of folksy characters, bore striking similarities to *Toonerville Trolley,* a popular U.S. strip by Fontaine Fox. One of Frise's most popular characters, Pigskin Peters, wore a derby hat and a sleeveless red–and–white striped t–shirt—an almost identical outfit to that worn by Mickey McGuire, a *Toonerville* regular.

Beyond these visual similarities, *Birdseye Center* is probably best described as a light–hearted, more eccentric version of Frank King's *Gasoline Alley*[15] that was populated by quirky characters who inhabited a fictional town that Frise summed up as "any Canadian village with a hotel, gasoline station, barber shop and a town pump."

By 1930, Frise was among the best–known cartoonists in the country, with an enviable reputation as a gentle, nature–loving soul. His colleague, Greg Clark, summarized Frise's appeal in his introduction to a 1965 collection of *Birdseye Center* strips: "Jimmy was an original, unbendable, bemused, rapt, lovable guy in love with the gentleness and decency of life amid all the storm and rage." But he was also a habitual gambler and major–league procrastinator who never met a deadline he couldn't dodge. His aversion to getting his strip done on time was so chronic that on a number of occasions the publisher of the *Star* was forced to stop the presses while his staff scoured the town's gambling dens looking for the AWOL cartoonist. Fortunately for Frise, this serious allergy to deadlines had scant effect on his popularity. *Birdseye Center* was a bona fide sensation

thanks to its art and its concern with the foibles of small town life, which gave uprooted rural Canadians a welcome weekly dose of the simple life back home. The title's iconic status was certified during the Depression, as Frise's gentle–humoured strips came as welcome relief in a paper packed end–to–end with stories about the impact of the socio–economic crisis.

In 1947, after nearly four decades, Frise severed his relationship with the *Star* to join his friend Clark at the *Montreal Standard.*[16] Since the *Star* owned the copyright to *Birdseye Center,* Frise was forced to change the name of his strip to *Juniper Junction,* but he continued to chronicle the adventures of his large cast of characters such as Archie Weaver, layabout Eli Doolittle (the fattest man in town) and happy–go–lucky Pigskin Peters. Despite the name change, Frise's fans stood by the strip. In fact, the new full–colour *Juniper Junction* proved more popular than its original incarnation: it reached a record two million readers within the first few months, thanks in part to it being picked up by the *Philadelphia Bulletin* and the *Newark Evening News.*[17] Though his fortunes may have improved, Frise's fickle relationship with deadlines did not. He ignored his frustrated editors' requests to work ahead (the practice of producing an inventory of strips—from six weeks' to three months' worth—ahead of schedule) and would frequently end up nerve–wrackingly close to his deadlines. Dick Hersey recalled bringing Frise over from Toronto to Montreal by train and booking him into a hotel room with just his drawing board for company, in an attempt to keep him from his procrastinating ways.

Unfortunately, on June 13, 1948, Frise died of a heart attack[18] at the age of 57 somehow fittingly, in the middle of roughing out that week's strip.[19] Hersey and his fellow editors quickly realized that they were in a jam. With less than a week before the next *Juniper Junction* was scheduled to go to print, all they had in their hands was a partially pencilled page. Luckily for Wright they promptly devised a plan with him in mind.

[16] Years after Frise's departure, the *Star* debuted a new strip called *Rural Route* drawn by cartoonist Walter Ball. Though lesser known, Ball's strip about life on a small farm was a hit and ran in the pages of the *Star Weekly* and a handful of farm bulletins until 1968. Though almost entirely forgotten, Ball (who started and ended his career at the *Star* as a staff illustrator, was a surprisingly gifted cartoonist whose work has been unfairly overlooked.

[17] Thanks to this, Frise also earned the prestige of being the first Canadian cartoonist to be syndicated in the U.S.

[18] Known as a healthy outdoorsman, Frise's death came as a shock to his fans and friends. The *Star* ran a lengthy obit, and colleagues such as Clark and Gordon Sinclair lined up to offer heartfelt tributes. Frise's death even elicited an emotional (if belated) reaction from Ernest Hemingway. The author and cartoonist had met some 27 years before, when Hemingway started stringing for the *Toronto Star.* Clark recalled the 21–year–old reporter and aspiring author spending days in the small office he and Frise shared, sharing war stories and soliciting advice about journalism. Though Clark was wary of the young American, Frise immediately befriended Hemingway, bringing him along on his many skiing and fishing trips. The cartoonist certainly made an impression. In the winter of 1950, news of Frise's death reached Hemingway in Cuba, prompting him to write Clark with his condolences. "That word 'late,'" he said, referring to Frise, "is one that I could just about do without."

[19] Two conflicting accounts of Jimmy Frise's death exist. The obituary in the *Toronto Star* stated that Frise died in his home in west–end Toronto, while Wright repeatedly states in his correspondence that Frise died at his drawing board in Montreal. Given Wright's proximity to and familiarity with Frise's editors, and the *Star's* fractured relationship with Frise, Wright's is likely the more accurate version.

[14] The exact details of Frise's injury (and for that matter, his life) are hazy. The sources that do exist differ, saying that he lost either a few fingers on his left hand or part of his arm during the Battle of Vimy Ridge. In a 1981 biography of Greg Clark, author Jock Carroll writes that Jimmy lost a finger on his left hand, a fact which seems to align with biographical information supplied by Frise's family. Regardless, the injury limited Frise's usefulness on his family's farm, which likely played a role in his decision pursue cartooning after the war.

[15] Though its cultural significance has been largely overlooked by historians, *Birdseye Center* stands as Canada's first true comic strip sensation, spawning a mini–industry complete with jigsaw puzzles, product endorsements and a stage play.

JUNIPER JUNCTION by Doug Wright, May 19, 1962.

"I still remember a beautiful Sunday morning in Montreal," Wright said. "When Dick Hersey and Phil Surrey, who was then photo editor of the old *Montreal Standard,* called to take me down to the office to do the next *Juniper Junction,* which Jim had left half–finished and close to deadline. They told me that in the next few months I was also to get a daily version done, well ahead, which we would launch in 1949." The possibility of inheriting a daily strip with millions of built–in readers was no small carrot for a 30–year–old would–be cartoonist, and Wright quickly took on the challenge. Despite unfamiliarity with the strip's subject matter—"[My] knowledge about rural life you could put in your eye," he said—Wright proved a capable replacement for his predecessor, in both style and content. He also managed to bang out roughs of three months' worth of daily strips in a relatively short period, a feat that would have been sure to boil Frise's frogs.

Despite all his hard work, without its well–loved (and well–known) creator at the helm the *Standard* had difficulty marketing and maintaining interest in the new *Juniper Junction.* Later that fall Wright received the bad news: The strip had lost several client papers and had become too expensive to maintain. It would run its course in the new year. "I think that was one of the low moments of my life. Here was my opportunity to get into the real big comic strip field; I'd done everything they told me including months of roughs of dailies, and phllfft!" The next few months must have been demoralizing for Wright, as he worked on a strip that had already been cancelled and whose end was approaching quickly. Then, a few days before the last strip was scheduled to appear, Doug got a call from the editor of the *Family Herald,* a long–running weekly magazine that was popular in small towns and farming communities across Canada. Impelled by the death sentence given to "a great Canadian institution," its editor offered *Juniper Junction* a new home in his paper. Wright gladly accepted, on the condition that his pay ($30 a week) remain the same.

Thanks to the unexpected reprieve, Wright would continue Frise's flagship creation for the next two decades, making *Juniper Junction* one of the most durable strips in the history of Canadian cartooning. Despite this, Wright's residency on the strip (which almost exceeded that of his predecessor) is practically invisible. A share of the blame for this oversight can be placed on Wright himself, who, in apparent deference to Frise, chose to not sign the strips for more than five years.[20] Yet even with his signature, the strip had a loyal but small readership. Much like the population of rural Canada itself, the circulation of the *Family Herald* dwindled throughout the 1950s and 60s and Wright's audience decreased with it. Regardless of the reasons, the anonymity of this stage in Wright's career is a sincere shame. Not only is his *Junction* a joy to look at and to read (who knew that Wright had such a knack for dialogue and wordplay?) but it offers an unexpected glimpse into the cartoonist's enigmatic personality.

[20]Even when Wright changed his mind in March 1954 and began signing *Juniper Junction,* he settled on a strange half measure; "DAW" (his initials). It's possible that in doing so he was trying to distance himself—the man behind *Nipper*—from the strip, but in a 1960 letter to a *Juniper Junction* fan he offered up a simpler explanation. "I don't like to put [my] signature on *Juniper Junction* because it isn't really my cartoon—it was created by old Jimmy Frise. For a long time after he died it ran with no signature, but one day the *Family Herald* told me to sign it, so I put my initials...Sorry if it looks like KAW"

ABOVE: **cover,** FAMILY HERALD **March 14, 1957.**

ABOVE, RIGHT: **interior spread, November 28, 1957.**
BELOW: JUNIPER JUNCTION, **September 8, 1962.**

EGGHEAD strip, dated April 8, 1950. Why is it titled EGGHEAD when the identical strip appears in print as NIPPER? Upon closer examination, this work appears to be a redrawn version (slightly polished) with Wright's preferred title up front. Perhaps it is a sample piece he sent to the newspaper syndicates?

Unlike Frise, who used gentle humour to tease out the differences between rural and urban Canada, Wright adopted a more modern approach on the strip. Within months he shifted the focus of the strip from folksy characters like Archie Weaver (and his pet moose Foghorn) to Pigskin Peters, who worked as a mechanic at the town's garage run by Hank Hornblow.

The move was likely an attempt by Wright to appeal to the country's emerging car culture—of which he was an unabashed devotee—but what was more interesting was the transformation seen in Pigskin. Long a popular supporting character with a slacker mentality and an eye for the ladies,[21] Wright quickly re-imagined Peters; giving him a history as a Second World War veteran, with an abiding passion for vehicles that was a carry-over from his days as a RCAF mechanic. If the similarities weren't obvious enough, Wright made Pigskin trade in his trademark derby and striped shirt for a sweatshirt from "RCAF CNS No.1 Rivers, Manitoba"—the base where Wright spent most of his time during the war. Over time, Pigskin became an exercise in wishful thinking, perpetually stuck in his blissful bachelorhood as Wright was dwelling on the responsibilities of marriage and family. Further parallels between character and cartoonist will be explored in more depth in this book's accompanying volume.

ENTER 'EGGHEAD'

By 1949, barely a year after he left his staff job, Wright had steady business going as a freelancer. In addition to *Juniper Junction,* he received regular illustration work from the *Montreal Standard* (including several covers) and had branched out to other notable publications like *Maclean's*. On February 16, he dropped by the *Standard's* offices for his weekly meeting with Dick Hersey. While he was waiting for the art director, he spotted a comic strip from *Punch* magazine lying on Hersey's desk. The strip, by British cartoonist David Langdon, showed a London bobby attempting to dislodge a cast iron pot from a young boy's head. After several attempts the officer succeeded, only to turn around and see the pot back on the child's head again. The gag strip had a note attached to it from Hugh Shaw, the editor of the *Standard Magazine,* that said: "Why don't we have more strips about the contrariness of kids?"

A bachelor at the time, Wright had plans to follow in the footsteps of his comic strip forbears by creating an adventure strip, like Milton Caniff's *Terry and the Pirates,* or a crackpot comedy, like E.C. Segar's *Popeye*. But he also couldn't resist a challenge, not to mention a paycheque. When he got home that night, he described the strip—and his editor's query—to his mother. As it happened, she had just heard a similar story from an elderly neighbour who lived directly below a young family. "The kids were thumping and banging about," Wright said. "And she'd taken a broom and knocked on the ceiling, 'rat–a–tat–tat.' There was a dead silence. [Then] the kids went rat–a–tat–tat back. They were always doing things like that."

Caught in the moment, Wright sat down and drew up the anecdote, casting a tired looking middle–aged man in the role of the neighbour and a bucktoothed boy as his upstairs antagonist. Eager to get it done, he apparently didn't feel the need to bother with word balloons. A day or two later he dropped it off at the *Standard,* and explained how it came about. "We didn't think he could do it," said Hersey. "His previous portrayals of children had lacked sympathy. I think this annoyed him a little." Misgivings aside, Hersey bought the strip and ran it a couple of weeks later, on March 12, as filler in the back pages of the *Standard Magazine*. Based on its placement between a children's shoe ad and a recipe column (a far cry from the paper's popular comics section) Wright figured it was the last he'd ever see of the maniacal tot.

To everyone's surprise—especially Wright's—the nameless strip generated a couple of letters from mothers who recognized a little bit of their own children in the mischievous boy. Immediately Wright got called on to produce more. "The original intention was to run [it] as an occasional feature," Hersey recalled in a 1950 article he wrote for *Canadian Art*. "But when we noticed the composing room crew (the most blasé group on any paper) putting tear–sheets of the boy on the

wall, we changed our plans and ran him every other week." The only problem was Wright himself. Still smarting from the *Juniper Junction* ordeal a few months' before, he was reluctant to spend his time on a feature that he felt had a questionable future. Plus, he considered himself a lousy fit for a family strip.

"Nipper started by accident," he said. "I had no intention of doing more than one strip—if I had I would have picked a character I knew more about. I wasn't even married, let alone a Dad." A busy freelancer who lived with his mother and unmarried sister, Wright's opportunities to associate with real children were limited. And without even a niece or a nephew to serve as inspiration, his caution was understandable. Not only was it a bad fit, but it was potentially a creative death sentence.

Yet, after being goaded by Hersey he dashed off a couple of additional strips, one of which (described as "Baby Banging Baby" in his journals) ran two weeks later. This time, the reaction from readers was even more pronounced. "People were talking about [the boy]," Hersey said. "He was definitely stealing the limelight." When the order came to change to a weekly schedule, Wright was aghast. "Doug wasn't sure he could turn out a good gag every week 'without opening a vein,'" Hersey recalled. "But, at length, he consented to try."

Within the month, the anarchic, and entirely accidental, strip found a home in the *Standard Magazine*. In response to reader reaction, the publisher took out a full–page ad to promote the strip's new weekly schedule. Somehow, after years of assiduously shopping around his own ideas, Wright had suddenly struck gold with an improvised strip based on a flimsy second–hand anecdote. In a way, Wright's out–of–the–gate success owed as much to good timing as it does to talent.

At the time, the late 1940s, the effects of the post–war baby boom were exerting themselves on North American society and culture. Between 1948 and 1949 the population in Canada jumped by more than 600,000,[22] as sure a sign as any that the Baby Boom had arrived.

Wright, with his no–nonsense strip about life with a hell–raising toddler, was perfectly poised to capitalize on this social revolution. In effect, he had unwittingly tapped into one of the biggest cultural juggernauts of the 20th century. Any objections expressed were surely worn away by the sheer utility of his strip. His arms–length depictions of children as both amoral and adorable—wailing on drums, mauling cats, and attacking each other with abandon—provided young parents with a laugh and so much more. What he was providing was a form of comic strip commiseration: proof that someone out there understood the joys and frustrations of parenthood. (The fact that Wright actually knew very little about their experiences was beside the point.)

ABOVE: Film box for Brian White's British "Nipper."

While he was by no means the only cartoonist to capitalize on this demographic, he was among the first. *Peanuts,* Charles Schulz's arch take on modern childhood, wouldn't debut for another year–and–a–half, and *Dennis The Menace,* created by Hank Ketcham, was still two years away.[23]

[22]According to Statistics Canada, in 1948 there were more than 12.8 million people living in Canada; a year later there were nearly 13.5 million.

[23]In fact, Ketcham's first *Dennis* strip (which was inspired by his four–year–old son of the same name) debuted on March, 12 1951; two years to the day after Wright's strip was published. Some 15 years later the two cartoonists' paths would cross when Wright wrote to Ketcham looking for advice and work. The two corresponded for several months, but nothing solid ever came of it—luckily for fans of Wright and Canadian comics as a whole.

[21]According to Jocko Thomas, a veteran *Toronto Star* sports writer, in the 1940s and 50s fans of the strip would dress up as Pigskin Peters (complete with his striped shirt and derby hat) during CFL games.

SKITTLES and KITTLES. What appear to be two sample gag panels for syndicate submission. Wright is clearly fishing about with his kid feature. Perhaps here he is emulating the highly succesful DENNIS THE MENACE single–panel format. Circa early 1950s.

Another variation—this time Wright has dusted off his wartime name OZZIE and given it to his tot. You'll also notice that OZZIE can speak. Wright most likely felt that the pantomime quality of the NIPPER strip might prove a real restriction for an ongoing comic. Ironically, the lack of dialogue probably helped Wright avoid the cloying cuteness that characterizes features like THE FAMILY CIRCUS and other such kiddie strips. The above strip hints at the path NIPPER might have taken had the characters used dialogue.

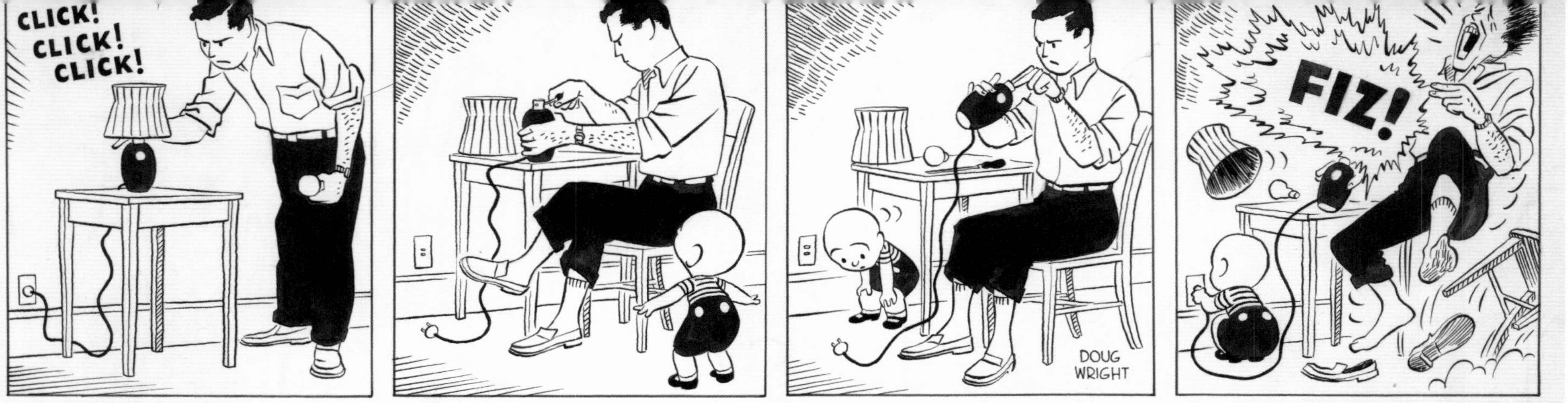
CLICK!
CLICK!
CLICK!
DOUG
WRIGHT
FIZ!

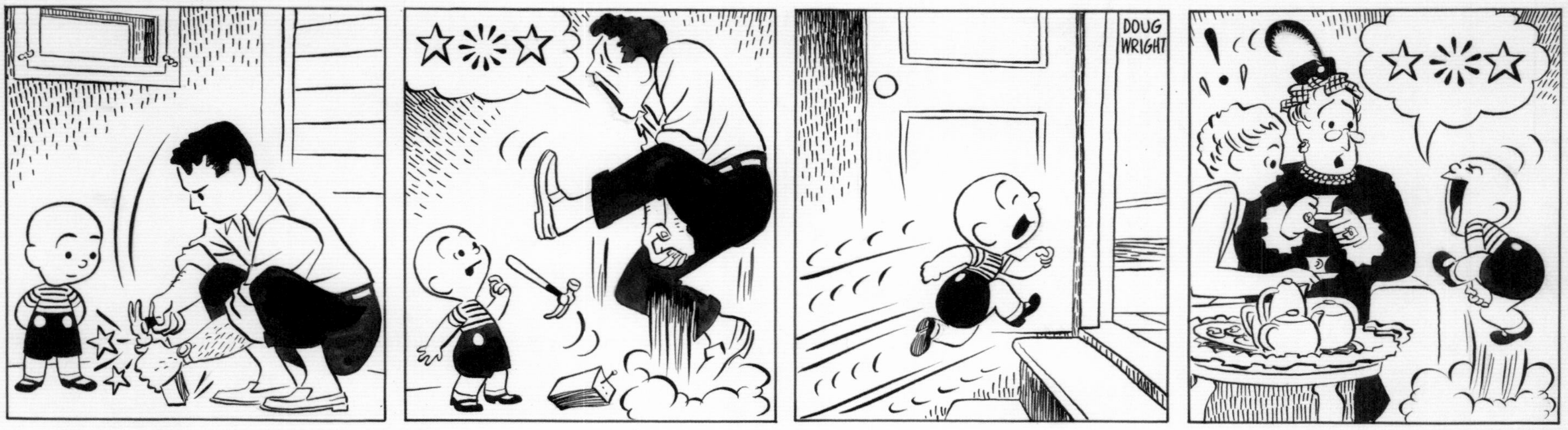
DOUG
WRIGHT
!

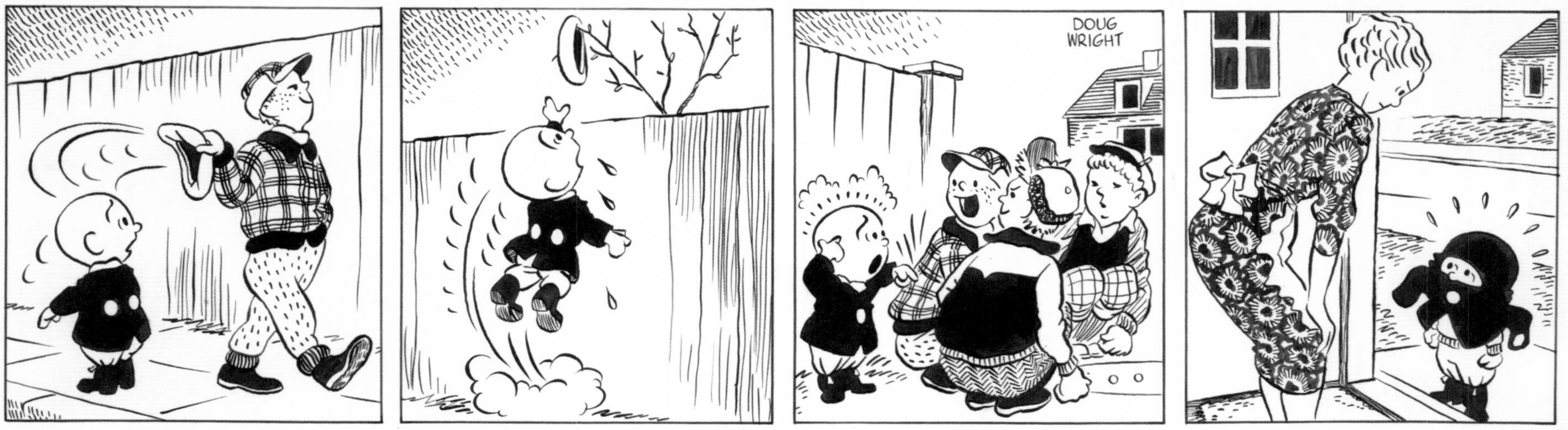
DOUG
WRIGHT

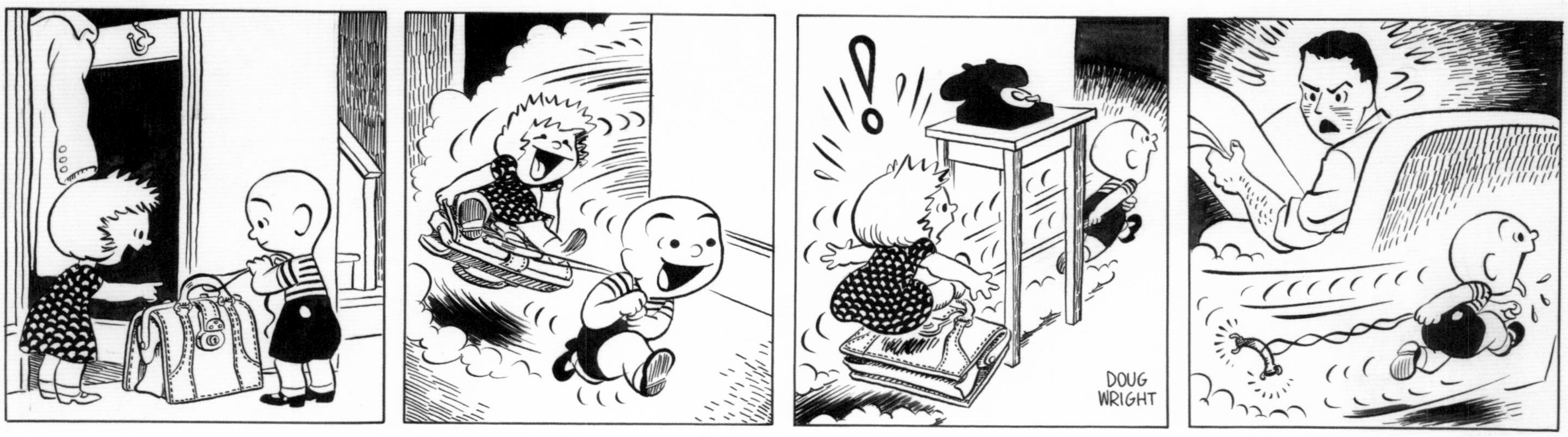
!
DOUG
WRIGHT

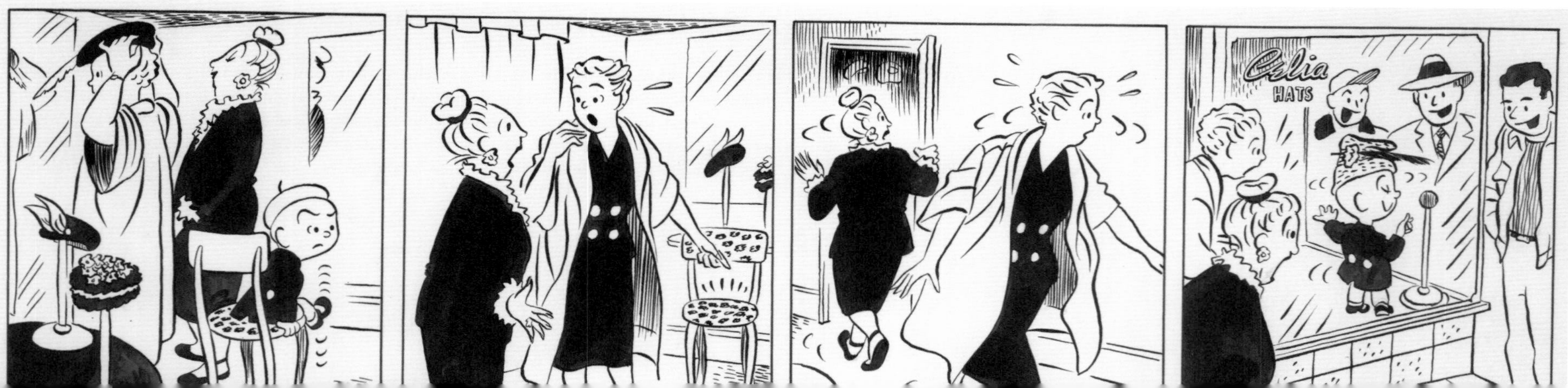
Celia
HATS

ABOVE: A typed list of accident claims from Wright's days at the Sun Life Insurance Co. It reads like a guidebook for the early slapstick era of the NIPPER strip.
LEFT, FACING PAGE: More redrawn strips, probably part of a syndication strip submission, circa 1951.
RIGHT: An abandoned NIPPER comic. Why Wright gave up on it is a mystery —especially as it is such an atypically joyous conclusion to Nipper's antics, circa 1951–55.

Meanwhile, in the spring of 1949, it became apparent to both Wright and his editors that the increasingly popular strip needed a name. Doug preferred "Egghead" (a nickname he had picked up from the guys in the *Standard's* art department) but the paper's publisher had a more populist solution in mind: a reader contest. Announced in May, the heavily hyped contest elicited entries from across the country, ranging from Vancouver, Toronto and Montreal to Charlottetown, P.E.I., Glace Bay, Nova Scotia, not to mention England, where Wright's strip had become a fixture in the popular *London Sunday Pictorial*.[24] Suggestions ranged from the insipid (Kiddles, Bawdly, Buttons) to the absurd, including Doomsie, Rackety, Sabu, Soupcon, Skittles, Ogpu, Little Murgatroyd and— inexplicably—Pervy. After sifting through the entries Wright's editors agreed on "Nipper," a common nickname for young children at the time (as well as the name of a popular canine mascot for the British Gramophone Company).

Unfortunately, in their haste to choose a name, none of them bothered to run it by Wright before it went to press. Like many cartoonists before—and since—[25] Doug did not respond well to having a title forced on his strip. "[Nipper] was a name for a little dog, not for a kid," he recalled. "But they said don't make waves, we already printed the paper this week and that's it."

But Wright's discontent was rooted in more than just his personal dislike of the new name. To him, the new title bore too much of a resemblance to a strip he remembered reading as a boy called *The Nipper*, which also featured a young boy in the lead. A year later his fears were confirmed. "We got registered letters from a man called Brian White in England saying that, though his strip no longer appeared, he still owned the British Empire copyright.[26] So [the editors], who were scared stiff of getting sued, decided to send him $150 a year for the first Canadian rights to the name," Wright said in the 1960s. "I screamed, but to no avail."

[24] Wright's strip was published in the popular weekly newspaper—circulation seven million—shortly after it first appeared in Canada, thanks to its inclusion in a package of syndicated material which the *Standard* distributed internationally (as a tax loss, according to Wright). The paper's editors took the liberty of naming it *Charlie Boy* after Prince Charles, who was about three months old at the time. Initially a sensation in Wright's country of birth, the paper stopped carrying it in the early 1950s, in large part because of its Canadian references, which were lost on their audience.

[25] Wright's displeasure put him in the company of many other cartoonists who chafed at the names their strips were given, the most notorious being Charles Schulz, who right up until his death in 2000 publicly maligned the editors who insisted his strip be called *Peanuts*. (He preferred *Li'l Folks*, the name he had given to a similarly–themed early strip.)

[26] White's *The Nipper*, which ran in the *Daily Mail* for some 17 years, was a more traditional humour comic and had little in common with Wright's work. After it ended its run in 1950, White produced a series of filmstrips based on his character that proved to be as popular, if not more, as the strip itself.

THE ENGAGED COUPLE **on the stoop of their brand new home in Lachine, a Montreal suburb.** BOTTOM: **Wedding announcement.** TOP RIGHT: **Wedding day, September 4, 1952.**

His instincts were right. By paying White off the paper had tacitly legitimized his claim, which put Wright in an excruciating spot. He was now forced to share any revenue he earned from his popular creation—which included a series of ads for Kellogg's "Pep Flakes" that he had begun work on—to an ex–cartoonist an ocean away. The situation angered Wright so much that he resolved to turn down any future advertising opportunities in order to avoid paying a dime to White. (He described his decision in an uncharacteristically terse letter to the British cartoonist.)

Though unfortunate for Wright, the predicament goes a long way toward explaining one of the lingering mysteries of his career: the scarcity of any *Nipper* merchandise.[27] Aside from of a pair of colouring books and an oversized souvenir book made for the opening of Montreal's Place–Ville–Marie in 1963, no *Nipper* tie–ins or products—from *Nipper* action figures to "Hot Rod" replicas—ever graced store shelves. In addition to missing out on a potential windfall, Wright also lost out on the opportunity to permanently brand *Nipper* onto the hearts and minds of several generations of Canadian kids.

Though he continued to do ad work throughout his life, lending his art and name to a number of popular campaigns (he even created a number of new characters, such as Dow Ale's "Li'l Bar" mascot), his most famous, and potentially most lucrative, character was never destined to fulfill its mass media potential.[28]

By 1950, as Wright began to settle into *Nipper's* universe, he fleshed it out with an identifiable mother and father, and a playmate/nemesis named Ingrid.

MISS PHYLLIS GRACE LEAH SANFORD, daughter of Mr. and Mrs. William D. Sanford, of the Town of Mount Royal, and MR. DOUGLAS AUSTIN WRIGHT, son of the late Capt. Alan Austin Wright and of Mrs. Wright, of Dixie, Que., whose marriage has been arranged to take place on Thursday, September 4 at half-past three o'clock, in Mount Royal United Church.

[27]Like Schulz's characters, *Nipper* appealed to both the young and old making him a natural fit for a wide range of possible tie–ins from toys and dolls to board games and pyjamas. In a way, *Nipper* became something of a funhouse mirror version of *Peanuts*, which over time came to be defined as much by its ever–present swag as by the genius of its creator. Interestingly, years later Wright maintained that his decision was made out of a fear that he would fracture his reader's perception of the strip as being based on actual people.

[28]Looking back on the critical drubbing that Schulz's *Peanuts* took over his mass (and crass) commercialization, in the end perhaps *Nipper* is better off for it.

With no kids of his own, Doug quickly learned to cadge story ideas whenever and wherever possible, whether it meant eavesdropping on conversations on the streetcar or lending a sympathetic ear when a bedraggled Sun Life employee needed to vent. By the early 1950s, the strip—which was now easily recognizable by its vertically–stacked layout—had settled into a reliable and predictable rhythm. Wright's story formula is nicely summed up by some notes he scrawled in the margins of an original from this period: "Egghead shoots arrow over fence. Runs to get it. It hits father. Egghead comes sauntering back. Sees father. Runs like hell."

Though by no means lacking charm, Wright's work during *Nipper's* first few years is primitive compared to the confident modernism of the strip's heyday of the late 1950s and early 1960s. It's almost as if Wright was approaching *Nipper* as little more than a gag strip. And, as his fruitless trip to New York a few years before had proven, he was by no measure a gag man. As a result, in his early years Nipper behaves more like a cartoon demon in short pants than the honest–to–goodness brat that most Canadians remember. Indeed, *Nipper* 1.0 is far too one–dimensional, a mere *Nipper* Lite compared to his later incarnation. And he might have stayed that way if life, and love, didn't conspire against Wright.

PHYLLIS AND DOUG

In the spring of 1948, shortly after Wright had taken over *Juniper Junction,* Phyllis Sanford started her new job at an advertising firm in the Sun Life building. A pretty teenager raised in Montreal's Town of Mount Royal neighbourhood, she recalls being especially nervous on her first day. "We were just this little Montreal office of this big Toronto agency. There was only one girl—I was going to be the second. Then the other girl, Mary Gaffney, said to me 'You know who works across the hall? Doug Wright'. "I said: 'Who's he?'" Even after a formal introduction, she was unimpressed with Wright's standing as the building's resident cartoonist. "He was working in this little inside studio. It was just a cubby hole, with no window," she recalled. "Besides, I didn't even know who the man was. I never read the comics."

SEPT 4
1952

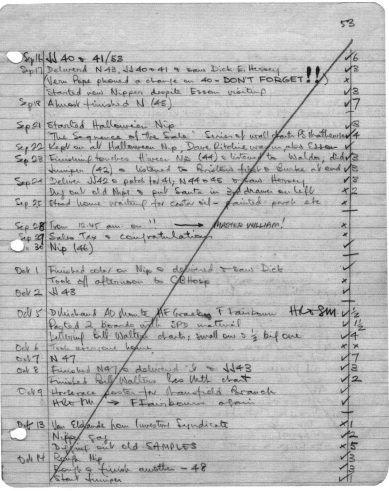

Over the following weeks and months the two got to know each other over countless cups of coffee and soon began dating steadily. Despite their significant age difference (Phyllis was 19 when they met; Doug was 31) the couple quickly hit it off. In the fall of 1951, with *Nipper* riding its first wave of success, Wright suggested the two take a weekend drive to Lachine, a then–burgeoning suburb of Montreal. "Doug had bought a house there and since it was still being built we went out there to look at it," Phyllis recalls. "And then he just said 'Would you like to live in this house?'"

His plainspoken proposal was accepted on the spot and the pair were married on September 4, 1952.[29] After honeymooning in Maine, the newlyweds settled in to their new home in Lachine that fall.[30] It didn't take long for his new life to spill over onto the page. Now comfortably ensconced in the suburban lifestyle, Wright's work began to exhibit the influences of an entirely different aesthetic.

Prior to this, his characters had occupied a threadbare comic strip world with only the most basic of real–world qualities.

[29] Wright marked the day in his journals with an over–sized—and fittingly automotive–themed—"CRASH!"

[30] Wright's mother, Rita, used the occasion to move out of Montreal (where she and Doug had shared an apartment for years) to Long Island, New York where Wright's sister Marge had moved a couple of years earlier after getting married to an American. Rita lived with the couple for a short while before moving into her own apartment in nearby Hempstead. She spent the balance of the decade there, visiting Montreal on the holidays and during the summer. Then in 1959, Rita—a heavy smoker like her son and daughter—died of a stroke at her home.

LEFT: **Wright was a methodical journeyman cartoonist. He kept a detailed logbook of his studio activities. An exception to his usual dry entries is the one for Sept. 28, 1953: "From 12:45 a.m. on → MASTER WILLIAM!"**

BELOW: **The new father and son, Christmas 1953.**

DEC. 1954   DEC. 1954   DEC. '54

FEB. 1954   FEB. 1954   MAY-JUNE 1954

JUNE '55   JUNE 1955   JUNE 1955

X-MAS '55   X-MAS '55   X-MAS '55

AUG. 1955   AUG. 1955

APRIL 1956   APRIL 1956

APRIL '56   APRIL 1956

SKETCHBOOK DRAWING, Montreal, 1948.

SKETCHBOOK DRAWING, Lachine, August 29, 1948.

From 1949 to 1952 (Wright's pre–marriage years) the *Nipper* cast acts on a bare, minimalist stage, often with nothing more than a chair or a sofa as set pieces, a style common to many mid– century strips. Yet in the months after his move to Lachine (summed up as "the airy haven for the small fry" by Wright's editor) Wright's fictional universe becomes visibly grounded in the real world. Nipper now skips and saunters through a more fully realized world made up of hundreds of moving parts, from driveways and doormats to street lamps and sprinklers.

Around the same time, *Nipper's* print home—the *Montreal Standard*—was facing some changes of its own. With its circulation still lagging behind the rival *Star Weekly,* in 1951 the paper's new owner decided to replace the expansive weekly with a smaller, streamlined magazine called *Weekend.* Inspired by a popular U.S. newspaper magazine supplement called *This Week,* the new publication saw many of the *Standard's* reliable sections—such as condensed novels, photo–news and colour comics—dropped in favour of a dedicated focus on "light entertainment."

Luckily, *Nipper,* which was never a part of the *Standard's* comic section, survived unscathed when *Weekend* launched that September as a supplement to eight papers. The new easy–to–read magazine, with its bright look and frothy features, was a hit with readers: it started with a circulation of around 900,000, and within five years was reaching nearly 1.5 million Canadians, far outstripping the *Star Weekly.*[31] As *Weekend* grew, so did *Nipper's* popularity, with its readership growing in both size (a jump of more than 50%) and scope as it reached in increasingly wider audience across the country.

One of these new readers was Greg Clark, the author and good friend of the late Jimmy Frise. After reading *Nipper,* Clark wrote to Wright to congratulate him for having "given birth to a boy which is a member of every family in the country." The two exchanged letters in the ensuing years, with Clark providing the occasional storyline for *Nipper* and *Juniper Junction.*

Meanwhile, as 1953 rolled around, both Wright's life and art matured further. With Phyllis expecting their first child, Wright's fictional first–born continued to evolve in unexpected ways. *Nipper* strips circa this period begin to exude an unprecedented dimensional strength, as Wright experimented with complex compositions and elaborate staging. Unlike the meat–and–potatoes compositions of his earlier work, Wright now positioned his characters in increasingly daring ways—with their backs to the reader for example—and the centre of attention is often asymmetrical, with the action taking place near the fringes of the panels. The result is a far more visually engaging, and rewarding, strip. A concrete example of the strip's new kineticism is the "Hot Rod," Nipper's pedal–powered car that Wright introduced on Aug. 29, 1953.

Not only was the plucky little car a terrific plot device, giving the boy opportunity to act out

numerous adult fantasies, it introduced a visual velocity to the strip as it barrelled down suburban sidewalks, its wheels defying gravity, with its diminutive pilot at the wheel. The debut of the Hot Rod likely also played a more practical role, as it provided Wright a regular opportunity to indulge in his passion for drawing automobiles; especially ones in motion. (His love of cars was such an abiding preoccupation that in the late 1960s, *Weekend* sent him to cover the Indy 500.)

In September 1953, almost exactly a year after they were married, Doug and Phyllis welcomed their first child, William Alan Wright, into their lives. While artists typically (and understandably) fret over the impact that new parenthood will have on their creativity, for Wright the exact opposite proved true. Rather than impinge on his output, his infant son actually spurred him to new heights. In this way, Bill was more than just Wright's first–born; he was his own pint–sized muse.

As Bill aged so did Nipper and Wright's real–life experiences with parenting began to reveal themselves in his strip.[32] Always a keen observer of human nature, Wright began to depict the two poles of family life—parent and child—with eagle–eye precision.

By mid–decade, *Nipper* had hit a new stride, with the bald boy doling out all manner of havoc on his poor parents. This was childhood at its best and worst with the violent and selfish nature of childhood merrily coexisting with the sweetness and light. The influence of the real world is also seen on Wright's paternal stand–in, who started to express himself in increasingly creative ways. To better illustrate his character's full range of technicolor rage, Wright let loose with an explosion of imagery; flames, smoke, steam, sweat and even eye–daggers are deployed to brilliant (and hilarious) effect. Words, in this case, would have been less effective. But Wright's imaginative use of symbols proved too much for some; on at least one occasion an editor told him to replace the knives bursting from Nipper's Dad's eyes (which were targeted at Nipper) with a more compassionate dotted line.

Indeed, Wright's beleaguered father figure regularly seems to be one frayed nerve away from completely losing it. From the mid–50s onwards, he often reacts to even the slightest provocation from his offspring with scowling, screaming and/or spanking. Though readers today may find this excessive—maybe even abusive—it's important to note that the behaviour in Wright's strips is emblematic of his era, and are not necessarily indicative of the cartoonist's own approach to parenting.

Wright's reinvention of his strip during this period extended to his technique, eventually affecting the way he used colour. During the first five years of *Nipper's* lifespan, colour appears in a fairly pedestrian way; with alternating coronas of green, red, yellow and blue used as frames for the crisp

[31]*Weekend's* success can be credited in part to its innovative means of distribution. The relatively new business model of the free supplement gave papers not only a cost–efficient way of adding value for their readers (*Weekend* originally paid the papers to carry the magazine), but it also offered them a share of their advertising revenues. As circulation grew, advertising rates rose, providing a win–win situation for both publisher and papers. As *Weekend* cornered the new free supplement market, the *Star Weekly* suffered at the newsstand. The Toronto–based periodical would revive its fortunes years later, after it followed suit and became a free magazine supplement as well.

[32]Even *Weekend* was wise to the change underway in Wright's work. In an editor's note published in the winter of 1953, Hugh Shaw notes the effect that young Bill had wrought on Wright: "Nipper's doings at first were recorded with none of the parental emotion that goes with a real father's description of the latest achievements of his little monster." Over the years, Wright would come to rely on his growing family as a source of material for his fictional one. He even organized what he called "bull sessions" with his sons, which involved the three of them sitting around brainstorming ideas for that week's strip. In a 1977 letter Wright confirmed their role, when he observed wryly "They're not much use to me now, but for a long time they earned their keep by keeping me in ideas."

[33]The exception being his Christmas (and occasionally Easter) strips when he did beautiful full–page painted strips.

SKETCHBOOK DRAWING, Côte–des–Neiges, 1948.

SKETCHBOOK DRAWING, Montreal, date unknown, probably early 1950s.

black–and–white art. By mid–1952, Wright abandoned this and integrated colour into the art it-self. But rather than dive head–on into full colour, he chose just one—red.[33] His use of spot red (which he had experimented with in his illustration work) was deliberate, bringing not only a rec-ognizable visual panache to *Nipper* but giving him a way to delicately draw the reader's eye to key elements in the story; a kind of secret narrative weapon.[34] In the years to come, red would play an increasingly significant—if largely unheralded—role in *Nipper,* subtly stepping in where words couldn't to push the story forward.

In 1954, not long after he moved his suburban studio, Wright was given a chance to develop a new feature for the *Montreal Star,* a local sister publication to *Weekend.* The fat matron of the city's powerful English–speaking minority, the *Star* regularly outsold the city's other English–language daily, the Montreal *Gazette.* Impressed by his success with *Nipper,* the paper tapped Wright as the man to helm a new weekly editorial cartoon that would address the concerns of its readership. Wright hit the largely white, middle–class nail on the head with a series of cartoons that took aim at everything from Montreal's sordid political scene to the city's infamously uncivilized drivers. A mélange of comic strips and traditional political cartooning, these intricate one–panel cartoons share little in common with *Juniper Junction* and *Nipper* (outside of the complex layouts) and instead appear to have been inspired by the work of the phenomenally popular British cartoonist Giles.

Giles, aka Carl Giles, was known for a long–running cartoon feature published in London's *Daily Express.* Drawing from high cartooning culture (ie. editorial) and low (gag cartoons), his de-tailed one–panel cartoons relied on a recurring cast of archetypal British characters to pass com-ment on current events. Born a year before Wright, Giles rose to fame as a correspondent in the Second World War, where he earned a huge fan base that was reputed to include members of the Royal Family (in 1959, Giles was knighted). Perhaps the best measure of his fame was the series of best–selling annual paperbacks that collected his previous year's work; at 60 volumes they out-lasted even him, and continued for years after he died in 1995. Like most Britons and many Cana-dians, Wright was a huge fan of Giles and his influence is drawn all over his work for the *Montreal Star.* Like Giles, Wright's cartoons are a visual cornucopia for the eyes with tiny details competing for the reader's attention. They also tended to pit everyman characters, like traffic cops, toll booth collectors, and taxi drivers, against the humorous and occasionally harsh realities of modern life. Wright's frequent backdrops included freeways and street corners, both of which gave him a chance to sound off on a litany of urban ills including gridlock, stuck up city folk and unhelpful civil servants. Though seen by few outside Montreal, these cartoons gave Wright a rare opportu-nity to air his personal, political and moral views. "I think this is just about my favourite outlet,"

he said to a fan in 1960. "Because every one is different, it gives you a fine feeling of freedom after so long on something like *Nipper* or *Juniper Junction,* where you feel you ought to go through all your old files to see if you've used a particular scene before."[35]

With three weekly features now under his belt, Wright was making a respectable living as a car-toonist by the mid–1950s. And with the help of *Weekend's* promotional department he'd soon have the fame to match. In the spring of 1956, a photographer from the magazine spent a day in Lachine chronicling the life of the people behind *Nipper.* The photos, which ran in a *Weekend* fea-ture over the course of a few weeks, follow Doug, Phyllis and Bill as they are trotted through a se-ries of everyday events from grocery shopping and washing the car to attending a doctor's appointment. Luckily, the innate charms of the young family managed to shine through the more stagy elements of the photos.

With Wright now officially identified as the man behind *Nipper,* the media began to flock to his door. Pretty soon he was a regular guest on *Weekday,* a local TV talk show, and started sitting in on a popular radio show where he fielded callers' questions about comics, kids, and the life of a profes-sional cartoonist. Spurred by the media exposure, Wright began reaping some of the benefits of his new–found celebrity including an endorsement (his first) for Colibri lighters. Perhaps the truest measure of his fame, was the emergence of the first *Nipper* parody. In the winter of 1956, a McGill

A RARE EXAMPLE of personal celebrity for Mr. Wright.

[34]This was made abundantly clear during a three–day research expedition Seth, Chris Oliveros and I made to the Na-tional Archives in Gatineau, Quebec in 2005. While combing through the more than 4,000 pieces of art donated by Wright's family, we came across a couple of *Nipper/Doug Wright's Family* strips that made no sense at all. After several attempts at deciphering them, we put them aside, assuming that collective fatigue had set in. Hours later we came across two orphaned overlays that Wright had used to add in the red without damaging the art itself. Without them the entire point of the strips was lost on the reader.

[35]A selection of Wright's *Montreal Star* cartoons was published in 1965, and is worth tracking down.

University campus humour magazine called *The Fig Leaf*, published "Tippler," a send–up drawn by "Dug Rite." The strip depicted a bald young boy who, after being left home alone, ingests the contents of his parent's liquor cabinet and demolishes the family home with the assistance of his pint–sized pals. The strip concludes with the boy's Dad returning to his debauched home and breaking out in an oblivious chuckle.

Wright's emerging status as "Canada's Best Known Cartoonist"[36] was sealed a few years later when he was asked to represent Canada at an international cartoonist summit in Amsterdam. Organized by KLM Airlines, the swank affair[37] gave Wright a rare opportunity to rub shoulders with the world's cartooning elite, his favourite being Zack Mosley, creator of the American adventure strip *Smilin' Jack*. During their trip Wright quizzed Mosley about the U.S. market, which continued to hold sway over him, as it did with most ambitious Canadian cartoonists. This was especially true during Wright's time, when the work of Canadian cartoonists did not translate well south of the 49th parallel.

As a result, those who yearned to make it big in America had to—almost without exception—leave Canada behind. The examples are legion: Quebec native Palmer Cox, who created the early media phenomena known as *The Brownies;* Richard Taylor, who found fame in the 1920s in the pages of the *New Yorker*; *Prince Valiant's* Hal Foster, a native of Nova Scotia; and George Feyer, who left Toronto for the States in the 1950s—only to later take his own life in a Hollywood apartment.

Sensing Wright's unrest, Mosley told him that the U.S. cartooning scene was a "young man's game" and advised him, "that if I was making a half–decent living where I am, I should stay there," Wright recounted. "For the hundred or so men whose characters are household words in North America," he recalled Mosley saying, "there are thousands who took to drink, couldn't stand the pace, or otherwise didn't measure up. And I'm afraid he's right."[38] Then in his early 40s and responsible for a young family, Wright followed Mosley's advice.

The fall of 1956 saw Doug and Phyllis welcoming their second child, James Douglas Wright, into their busy home. More than just another mouth to feed, Jim would help pave the way for the strip's golden period.

A few years later, *Weekend* was undergoing a major expansion of its own. With its circulation rising across Canada, in 1959 it introduced a French–language sister publication called *Perspectives* as part of a concerted push into the Quebec market. Thanks to its pantomime format, *Nipper*

made for a smooth transition to the new magazine under a new name, *Fiston*.[39] The French version proved popular with its new readership, making it one of a small handful of Canadian strips to successfully overcome the country's cultural divide.

Over the years, Wright occasionally had to "translate" certain sound effects, symbols and the odd word for his Francophone readers, but during most weeks *Nipper* and *Fiston* differed in name only.[40] Thanks in part to its successful foray into Quebec, *Weekend* began to outperform even the industry's highest expectations. According to historian J.L. Granatstein, by the early 1960s, *Weekend* was being carried in 41 newspapers across Canada and had achieved a circulation of more than two million—a record at the time (and perhaps to this day). The huge success of *Weekend* meant that *Nipper* was the most read Canadian strip at the time, outpacing other popular features of the day like James Simpkins' *Jasper* and Walter Ball's *Rural Route*.

Meanwhile, in January 1960, Wright was busy spreading the good news: Phyllis was expecting their third child. After offering his congratulations, an editor asked "When are you going to get around to giving Nipper a little brother of his own?" With a three–year–old and a six–year–old scurrying around his house, the thought had already crossed Wright's mind. But he had resisted following through out of a fear of upsetting the strip's chemistry; perhaps *Nipper*, like *Dennis the Menace* and *Henry*, was better off with just one kid. But, his editor argued, with the average nuclear family touting three (or more) children wasn't it high time for *Nipper* to catch up with the rest of the nation?

Wright agreed. On March 19, 1960, Nipper's mom appeared for the first time with a visible bulge in her belly, launching one of Wright's rare forays into sustained storytelling. Over the next three months the Nipper household busies itself with preparations for the bundle of joy; a happy Mom and Dad get the nursery in shape, while Nipper's previously unseen grandmother turns up to help around the house and care for her increasingly antsy grandson. After twelve uninterrupted years of having everyone at his beck and call, Nipper was not overjoyed with the prospect of a little brother. Many of the strips in this run are given over to the four–year–old's various machinations to obstruct the newborn's arrival. At one point, he's shown fantasizing about meeting the stork and giving him wrong directions to his house.

Then in June, a month after his own son Ken was born, Wright unveiled the new baby in the Nipper household.[41] The impact of "Nipper Jr." (for lack of a better name[42]) can be seen on the fabric of the strip almost immediately. Long–time supporting characters, like Ingrid, get relegated to minor roles and Nipper, who had been three or four years old for about a decade, begins to age in real time. Pretty soon, Nipper abdicates his reign as a troublesome toddler to his younger brother, while he gracefully matures into an unruly seven–year–old. The strip's new era also saw Wright temporarily depart from one of its trademark conceits: bald boys. For months, Nipper Jr.

---

[36]This title was being used to describe Wright in newspaper profiles during the late 1950s, though Wright himself wasn't quick to condone it. When questioned about it, Wright usually deferred to other cartoonists, like Peter Whalley, Duncan MacPherson or Len Norris, as more deserving of the title.

[37]I must admit that I have no substantive proof that this event was, in fact, a swinging affair; it could have easily taken place at a non–descript convention centre. But the notion of an international gathering of 1950s–era cartoonists summons mental images of a lavishly catered, booze–fueled bash. I sincerely hope that the reader will indulge this small liberty on my part.

[38]Mosley certainly wasn't wrong. By the 1950s, the American cartooning market was lucrative, highly competitive and extremely demanding. As a result, it had its share of notorious alcoholics, cranks and depressives including Jack Cole, Wally Wood and Ham Fisher, who all took their own lives.

[39]"Fiston" being French vernacular for "young son."

[40]Despite its popularity in Quebec, *Fiston* would eventually prove problematic for Wright. In the 1960s, in an apparent concession to the growing nationalist sentiment in the province, the editors at *Perspectives* began omitting Wright's unmistakably Anglophone name from the strip. The move infuriated Wright and contributed to his simmering discontent with the social and political changes that were mounting across Quebec.

[41]After weeks of scheming, Nipper welcomed his little brother with trademark overreaction; to the horror of his parents he invited every kid in the neighbourhood over to the house for an impromptu show–and–tell.

actually appears with hair on his little head; wispy, wavy locks that would likely bewilder anyone familiar with the strip in its later years. By drawing his cartoon boys with clean–shaven heads (a practice common in the 1950s and 60s) Wright was continuing a bizarre tradition of bald cartoon boys that stretched back to the creation of the Yellow Kid at the end of the 19th century. In the century since, the clean–shaven style had been sported by such famous baldies as Henry, Barnaby, Sluggo and, more recently, good ol' Charlie Brown. Fortunately, Wright's follicular footnote only lasted a couple of years. As Nipper Jr. grew a little older, he started to get bean shaves just like his big brother. (Though, in an effort to give the boys distinct appearances, Wright gives "Junior" a jaunty cap.)

Despite his initial apprehensions, Wright quickly became accustomed to the feature's new cast member. "It makes life a little easier having four characters instead of just three," he explained in a letter to a friend shortly after the switch. "It gives me an extra element to play with in any situation." It also helped open the door to more naturalistic storytelling. Wright was now free to portray the kind of commonplace low–level childhood violence that occurs in most families (especially those with two or more boys). The pair wasted little time with niceties, as they mercilessly kick, punch, slap, bite and choke[43] each other in a recurring display of fraternal brinksmanship. Wright also surprises his unsuspecting audience with some genuinely sweet moments. One memorable Mother's Day strip shows Nipper's scruffy, dishevelled Dad sneak his boys out of the house to grab breakfast at a diner. In the last panel, the boys' mom is shown asleep in bed, with a single flower and a Mother's Day card on the bedside table.

By 1962, the Wright household was full to bursting with three boys, ranging from two to eight years old, which Wright encountered as he worked in his studio. Always observant, he began to draw ready inspiration from his own life. Countless family antics and anecdotes made their way to the page in this period, and even the tiniest of details got baked right into the strip. Keen–eyed readers will notice the dad's car sweater (which was based on one Phyllis knitted for Doug) and the aluminium "W" on the cartoon family's screen door. Luckily, Wright's commitment to infusing the strip with a sense of the real extended into his subject matter. He was careful never to let his strip lapse into the kind of sentimental paeans to domesticity that populated so many of the comics pages of the day.

In an era of *Family Circus*–style homilies, *Nipper*—with its boys perennially laughing as their parents dealt with the wreckage from their latest mishap—served as a long–overdue dose of rambunctious childhood. Over the years, Wright would regularly receive letters complaining about the bad example he was setting with his strip, but he held little stock in this brand of moralizing, preferring to reflect his own real experiences back to his readers. The result was pure pop culture magic. His realistically rendered, and unerringly honest, depictions of family life were embraced by millions of readers. A popularity buoyed by the fact that the strip was wordless, which meant that it could be enjoyed by anyone regardless of age—parents and kids—or language.

[42]Thanks to the strip's wordless format, few of the characters in *Nipper* were ever given official names. Even the mother and father are only ever referred to as "Mum" or "Dad" on the occasional birthday or valentine card. Nipper himself and Ingrid are the rare exceptions to this rule.

[43]Although, considering the red–faced, eye–bulging looks on their faces this might be more accurately characterized as "strangling."

He couldn't have pulled it off better if he had planned it that way. From the get–go, Wright had an uneasy relationship with his most famous creation, agonizing over each weekly instalment while secretly yearning to draw an adventure strip like Milton Caniff's rousing *Terry and the Pirates*. By the time he finally got around to having kids of his own, *Nipper* was already a certified hit. By then, the ironic detachment that he had accidentally cultivated on *Nipper* allowed him to accomplish an unprecedented feat: re–inventing the moribund family strip for a modern audience.

As a result, by the early 1960s Nipper had become not only a tart paean to parents and children, but the first masterpiece of post–war Canadian comics.

THIS PAGE AND OPPOSITE:
Magazine illustrations, circa late 1950s/early 60s.

TOP LEFT: Cover of one of Wright's many scrapbooks.
LOWER LEFT: Interior of studio log book (1960–1980).
ABOVE: Interior of scrapbook.
BELOW: The Doug Wright Award for excellence in Canadian cartooning.

A FEW WORDS FROM THE DESIGNER

This book (and its eventual companion volume) is the culmination of about twenty years of collecting and studying Doug Wright. Even though I read his work in childhood I have to admit I pretty much forgot all about him in my late teens and early twenties. It wasn't until sometime around the end of the 1980s when I chanced upon a couple of battered issues of the *Canadian* magazine in a junk shop and saw again the old familiar bald heads of his characters that my interest in his work was rekindled. It was at that point that I recalled how much I had enjoyed *Doug Wright's Family* as a boy and I determined to find more examples of his comic strip.

My mother had always liked the strip as well—but she had referred to it as *Nipper*, which struck me as odd since there was never any indication that either of the boys had a name—let alone the name *Nipper*. It was only later, after I began digging backward that I discovered the earlier incarnation of the strip and the source of this name. And this journey was not an easy one. Although it took little effort to discover that the strip had appeared in *Weekend* magazine before *Canadian* (both were newspaper insert magazines) I really had no idea just when it had begun and exactly when it had changed publications. Unlike American comic strips, which have been somewhat documented over the last few decades, there weren't any standard reference works to turn to for help on these matters. Canadian cartooning was a subject that had been almost entirely ignored or forgotten. Some interest had been shown in the comic book artists who worked in Canada during WWII but practically nothing had been written on the newspaper and magazine cartoonists. I knew it would come down to collecting. I would simply have to find as many copies of these old magazines as possible and track down the history of Wright's work. And that is primarily what I did for the next 15 years or so. This meant a great deal of scrounging about. It was all hit and miss. Sometimes I would find a box of old *Weekend* magazines at a paper show or sometimes a great pile in the back of a Goodwill or Salvation Army. Once, Book Brothers of London, Ontario opened a back room up to me where I found hundreds of issues. These were the rare finds, though. Mostly it was a matter of coming across them one or two at a time. In retrospect, I'm amazed that I was able to find so many of the strips. I amassed hundreds of issues and slowly got a grounding in Wright's work. Now, had this been an American comic strip this could have been a much simpler task. At the same time a good friend of mine, Joe Matt, decided to collect the entire run of Frank King's brilliant *Gasoline Alley* strip. He was able to tap into an American collectors' market for clipped newspaper strips and in a span of a few years (and thousands of dollars) was able to assemble an almost complete run of King's forty years of publication. This was impossible with Wright. By the time I started looking for his work his name was already falling into obscurity and even the handful of old paper dealers working here in Canada had little knowledge of him. This seemed a sad state of affairs—I felt that Wright was an important Canadian artist and I began to suspect that I was the only person interested in him. I worried that if someone didn't collect his work it would be lost forever. Even then, I knew that someday a book would have to be published and I would need to have the strips on hand for that book.

Little did I realize that while I was desperately searching out these old faded magazines, a virtually complete record of his work was sitting in the National Archives in Ottawa (and later, Gatineau, Quebec) waiting to be catalogued. It would be a long time until I found out about that, though—just a few years ago, actually. In a way, it's a good thing I didn't know about them because the long journey to find those strips gave me a deeper understanding of his work. Coming across them one by one I studied them carefully, beginning to understand just how his work had evolved and changed. I can recall how surprised I was when I continued to find strips going back, past the sixties, and into the 1950s. I had no idea the strip was that old. Again, how amazed I was at finding a *Nipper* strip from 1949!! Just how far back did it go? (1949, it turned out).

Somewhere along the way I discovered other strips he'd worked on: 30 years of *Juniper Junction... Wheels, Cynthia, Tickytacky Township*. I also unearthed stunning example after stunning example of magazine illustrations from a long career as a commercial artist. These turned out to be just the tip of an iceberg. He did a tremendous amount of commercial work. In the end, I discovered that Wright had had a long and very prolific career as a cartoonist. So much work and shockingly—so little of it recalled today.

During these years I'd also been studying and collecting other Canadian cartoonists as well. James Simpkins, Jimmie Frise, Walter Ball, Peter Whalley, George Feyer and others. They all had two things in common with Wright:

1.) They had produced a fascinating body of work.
2.) They were largely forgotten.

It seemed obvious to me that these artists, along with Doug Wright (and Quebec cartoonist Albert Chartier) would make a marvelous book. Something that would open the eyes of the Canadian public to the overlooked pop culture history of their own country. I knew that I was capable of hunting out old papers and I figured I could put such a book together but I also understood that rooting out the stories of these artists—actually talking to people—was not my strong point. I would need some help there. That's when I invited Brad Mackay into the project. I'd only briefly met Brad, but I knew he was a journalist and that he was good with people and I knew he loved comics. I invited him over to talk about the project and as I shared the work of these artists with him I could see his forgotton connection to Wright resurfacing just as it had with me. Without Brad this book would be a much poorer volume—it would lack the insight into an artist's work that comes only from a detailed study of their life. Brad went out there and found the facts and made the connections. Without Brad's forthright journalist's moxie I doubt whether I could have gained the Wright family's trust and unflagging assistance. And thank goodness we did get their help. For in coming in contact with Doug's widow, Phyllis, and his three sons, Bill, Jim, and Ken, we discovered both the amazing storehouse of works donated to the National Archives and the personal treasure trove of Wright's art and records which the family still retains. I was more than happy to set aside my comparatively meager Wright archive when this cornucopia presented itself. This windfall allowed us to make this book the one that he deserved.

By a miracle it turned out that Doug kept scrupulous records of his work—decades worth of scrapbooks filled with clipped and glued strips and illustrations. Logbooks of his daily activities in the studio and literally stacks of his original art. A staggering El Dorado of paper to a collector like myself. The biggest problem in assembling this book (and the next) is what to leave out.

That earlier book I mentioned about Wright and the other cartoonists (to be titled *The Gang of Seven*) was put on the backburner. Not simply because the Wright book became a priortiy but also because it turned out that Canadian book publishers were a lot less eager to publish such a project than I figured. After a few rejections I realized that not everyone saw these cartoonists as such obviously important cultural figures as I did. Fortunately, at this point Chris Oliveros entered the story. Chris had been my own publisher for more than a decade—I'd introduced him to Wright's work years earlier and he had become a genuine enthusiast about it. If anyone said, let's do a book about Doug Wright, it was Chris. At every step of the way in the creation of these books Chris has been the person making it happen. He never balked at the cost or the effort required to assemble them. He's remained steadfast in his support and editorial assistance.

The most important aspect, I suppose, of any artist's work is the personal vision that is revealed in it. Doug Wright's record of his world, his thoughts and feelings are here for you to see. Perhaps though, not in the clear way that a diarist or a novelist or a fine artist's work might communicate. The cartoonists of Wright's era worked in commercial forms and their vision was usually subsumed by the restraints of the marketplace. A lot of commercial cartoonists said very little about themselves in their work. I don't believe this is the case with Doug Wright. I think his life's work is an excellent record of the man and the times he lived in. But much like his strip, it is a quiet record. It grows in sophistication also. *Nipper,* over the course of this first volume, transforms from a rather typical precocious–tot strip into the beginnings of something much subtler. It is in the next volume that we really see the full flowering of Wright's approach to the family. Much of these early strips are still "gags." However, by the end of this book you can see his focus turning from the joke to the small incident. This unsentimental focus on the tiny events of daily life are what make *Doug Wright's Family* (the eventual title of the strip) one of the most unique comic strips in cartooning history.

And there is one last windmill I must tilt at. Wright, and those other Canadian cartoonists mentioned earlier, deserve credit for their role in the shaping of our modern Canadian identity. It is an almost entirely neglected fact that these artists, who worked mostly in the middle of the 20th century, had an instrumental role in taking the moldy old 19th century images of Canada and making them modern. They recast all those Mounties and trappers and habitants into contemporary (for that era), streamlined icons. It's the kind of thing, done in plain sight, that no one thinks to notice. The Canadian pop culture images that we know so well today were largely reshaped in those times. Images which had once served a wilderness culture were recontextualized with humour and machine–age drawing styles for a Canada that was turning largely urban and suburban. You can almost chart Canada's transformation from the rural to the urban in a flow chart from Jimmie Frise to Doug Wright to Peter Whalley. Admittedly, the modernizing of these popular images wasn't the work of these artists alone—but they did have a very vital and sadly unrecognized role in it. Something that should be of real interest to Canadians. The other important aspect of Wright and his contemporaries was that they showed Canadians to themselves at a time when the American media was playing a greater and greater role here. Even today it is refreshing, almost startling, to look at Wright's work and see how CANADIAN everything is. It has a ring of familiarity we are not used to seeing in cartoons.

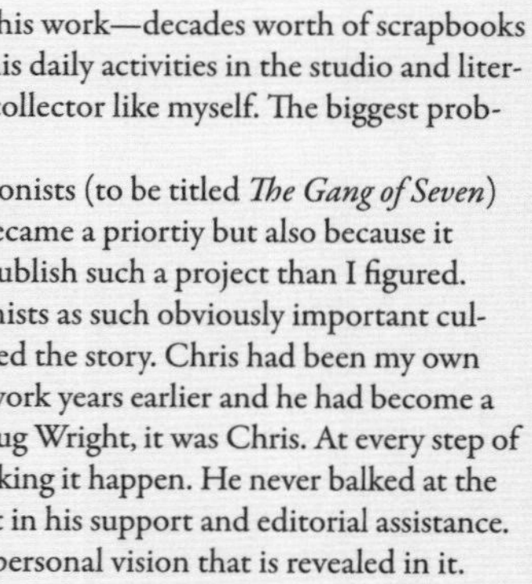

I mention these things because I'd like to see Wright get his due. It's wonderful work and it honestly doesn't need anyone to speak for it. But I can't help myself. I have derived a great deal of pleasure looking at Wright's art—one cartoonist to another—and I am humbled to be allowed to put it out into the world again.
SETH, 2009

Portfolio

How's Your Cold?...Page Nine

What Lies Ahead?...Page 6

Has Justice The Right To Kill?..Page 3

A Break In Prices?...Page 3

Covers from the MONTREAL STANDARD magazine.

The Standard Magazine

MONTREAL, SATURDAY, AUGUST 13, 1949

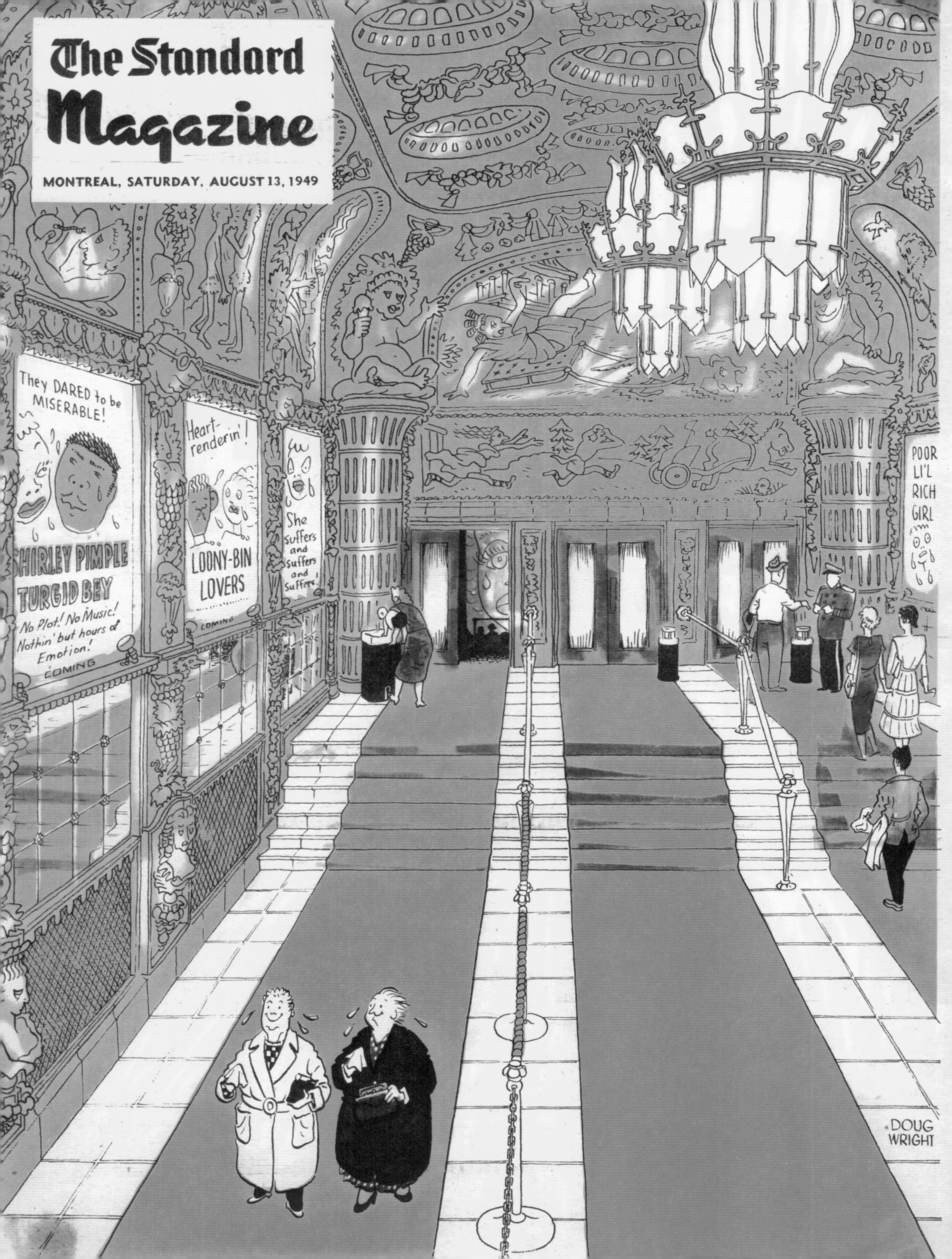

They DARED to be MISERABLE!
SHIRLEY PIMPLE
TURGID BEY
No Plot! No Music! Nothin' but hours of Emotion!
COMING
Heart-renderin'!
LOONY-BIN LOVERS
COMING
She suffers and suffers and suffers!
POOR LI'L RICH GIRL
DOUG WRIGHT

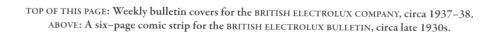

TOP OF THIS PAGE: Weekly bulletin covers for the BRITISH ELECTROLUX COMPANY, circa 1937–38.
ABOVE: A six–page comic strip for the BRITISH ELECTROLUX BULLETIN, circa late 1930s.

Original cover art for the MONTREAL STANDARD magazine, July 2, 1949.

Magazine illustration? Possibly from the STANDARD or WEEKEND magazine, circa mid–to–late 1950s.

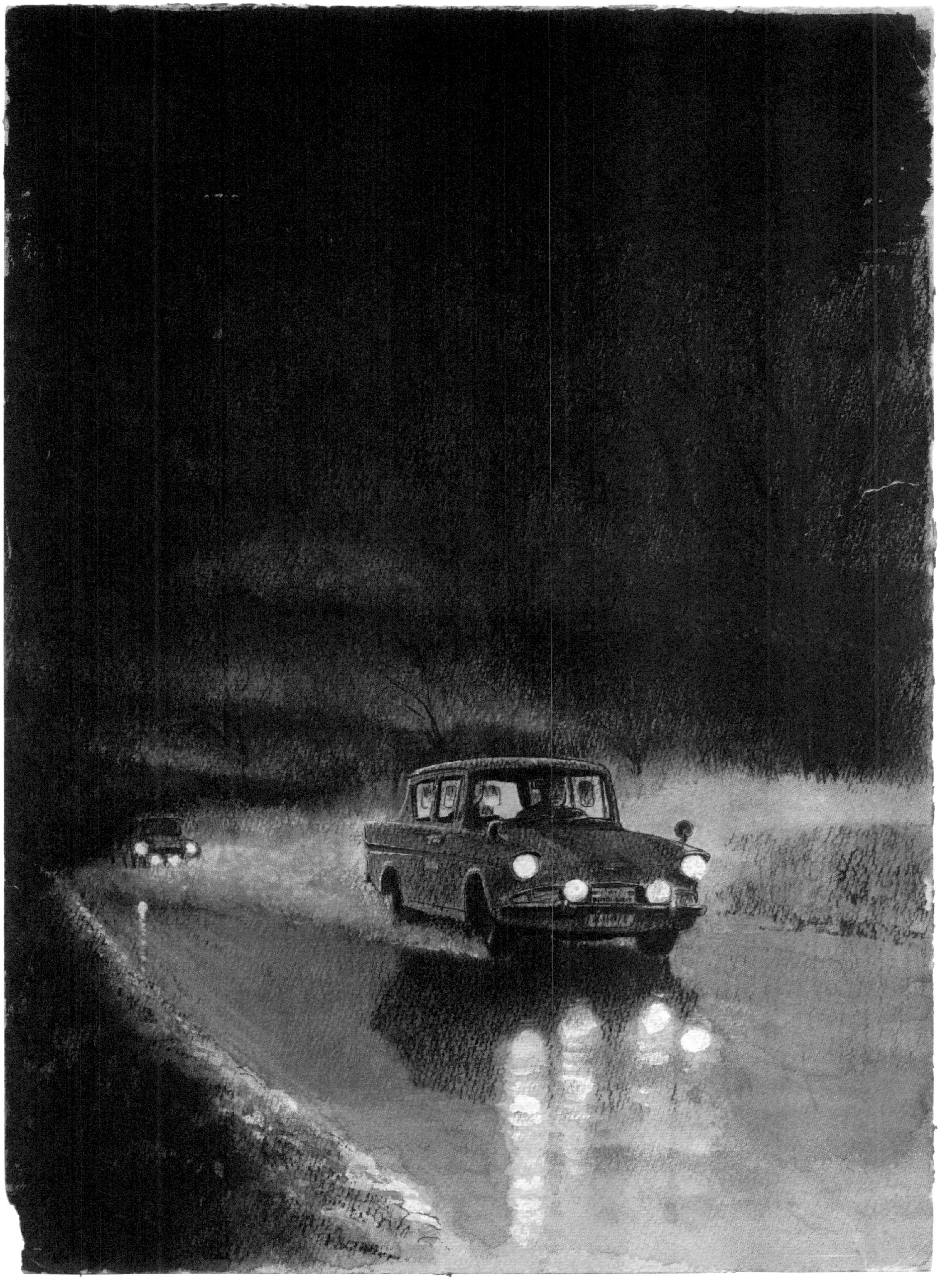

The companion drawing.

SUBURBIA

by DOUG WRIGHT

1   You can't find out much about a house while it's being built.

4   Weekends: lots of visitors and lots of advice — "Throw in a few shrubs here, throw in a driveway there . . . ."

2   Moving-in day: the painter's not finished, the water is not turned on, the electrician doesn't show up, it's pouring rain.

5   Don't buy any garden chairs if you want any assistance.

6   As a rest from landscaping, you can make some screen windows. In fact, your wife will probably insist on it.

3   Once in, you face the problem of getting out—every morning.

7   Once the city paves the street, the kids are off your hands.

8 That will be a lovely shade tree, twenty years from now, when the house falls down.

9 The neighbors aren't going to like it if you get too far ahead of them.

10 They will also feel bad if you get too far behind.

11 The best thing to do is to stay absolutely level with them.

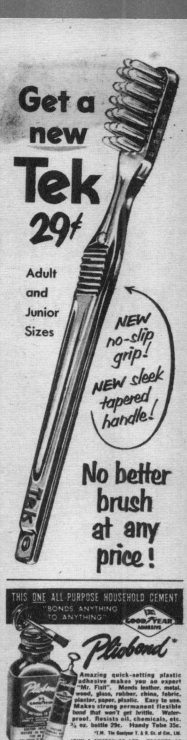

ABOVE: Original cover art for the MONTREAL STANDARD magazine, May 14, 1949.
OPPOSITE: Original cover art for the MONTREAL STANDARD magazine, February 12, 1949.

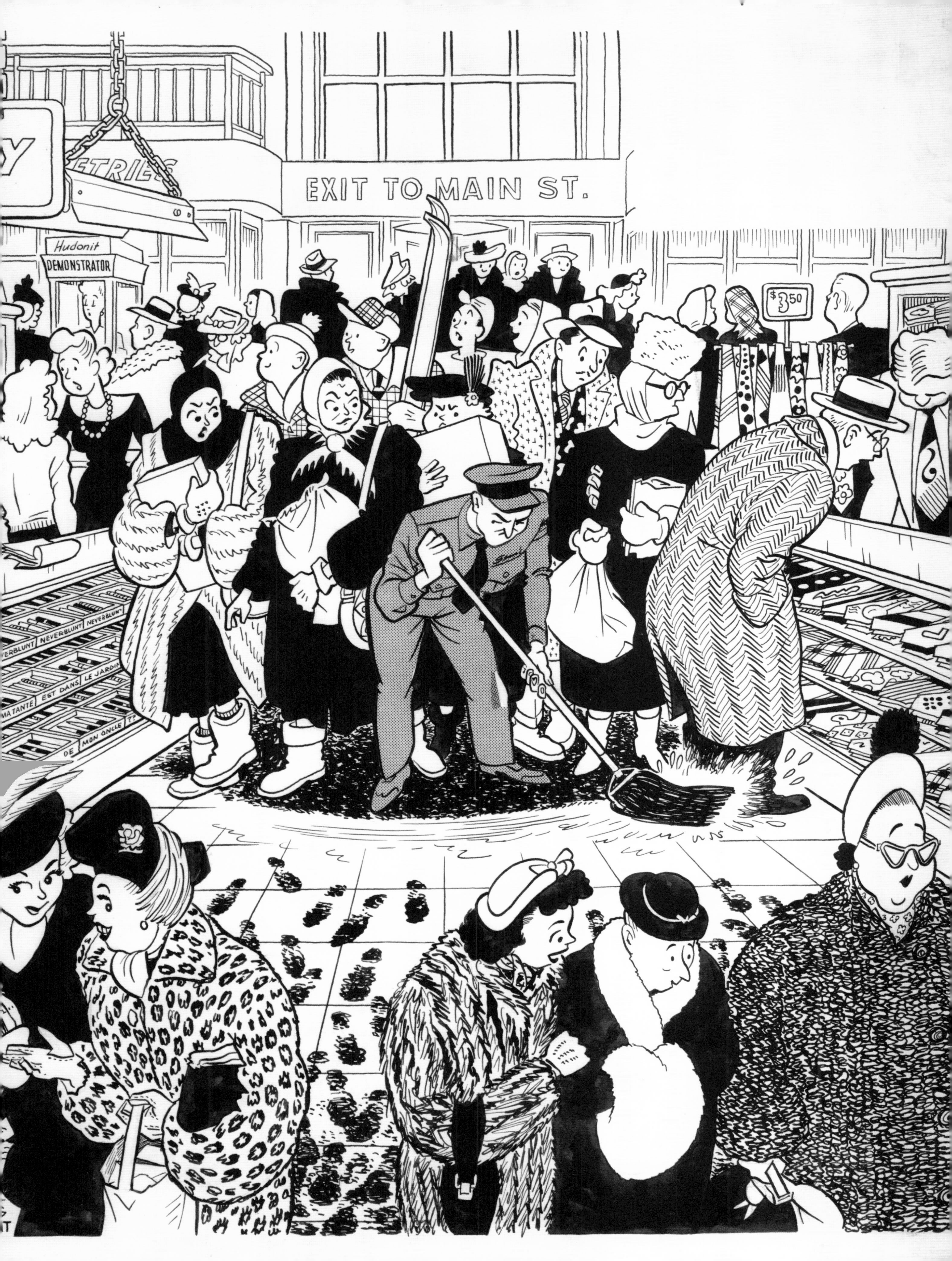

EXIT TO MAIN ST.
Hudonit
DEMONSTRATOR
$3.50
NEVERBLUNT
NEVERBLUNT
MA TANTE
EST DANS
LE JARDIN
DE
MON ONCLE
??

Why Husbands Leave Home

Wifey shouldn't bring home too much bacon.

New baby gets lion's share of affection

Pets can be provoking.

Smart girl picks homely little Joe — no competition

There's no home-wrecker like Mother-in-Law

The housekeeping can be too good.

DOUG WRIGHT

Husbands must be considered as overgrown children

WEEKEND

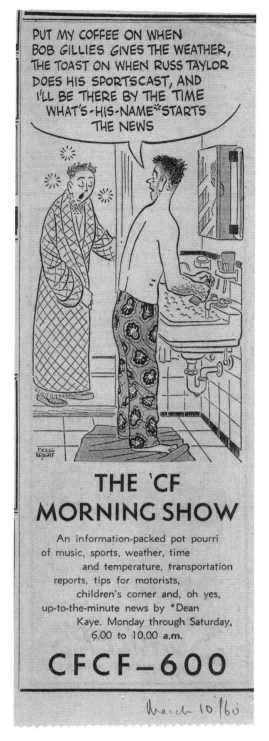

PUT MY COFFEE ON WHEN BOB GILLIES GIVES THE WEATHER, THE TOAST ON WHEN RUSS TAYLOR DOES HIS SPORTSCAST, AND I'LL BE THERE BY THE TIME WHAT'S-HIS-NAME* STARTS THE NEWS

THE 'CF MORNING SHOW

An information-packed pot pourri of music, sports, weather, time and temperature, transportation reports, tips for motorists, children's corner and, oh yes, up-to-the-minute news by *Dean Kaye. Monday through Saturday, 6.00 to 10.00 a.m.

CFCF–600

ALL WE DID WAS ASK PAT MARINI TO ANNOUNCE ON CFCF THAT WE'D HAVE SOMETHING TO INTEREST EVERY MOTHER AT OUR MEETING TONIGHT!!

SPECIALLY FOR THE LADIES

Breakfast Club with Don McNeill — 10:05 to 11:00 a.m.
Easy Street with Hal Gibson and Pat Marini — 12:45 to 1:00 p.m.
My True Story, women's drama from ABC network — 3:00 to 4:00 p.m.
. . . and a generous portion of good music.

DAILY ON CFCF–600

LEFT: Illustration spread for WEEKEND magazine, September 22, 1951.
ABOVE: Various newpaper ads for Montreal radio station CFCF–600, circa 1960.

ON THESE PAGES, EXAMPLES OF WRIGHT'S GREAT PASSION FOR THE MOTOR VEHICLE—
AND HIS REMARKABLE SKILL IN CARTOONING THEM.

ABOVE: **Illustration for the article, "Why I Hate Men Drivers."** WEEKEND magazine, September 18, 1954.
OPPOSITE: WEEKEND **magazine illustrations, circa 1962.**

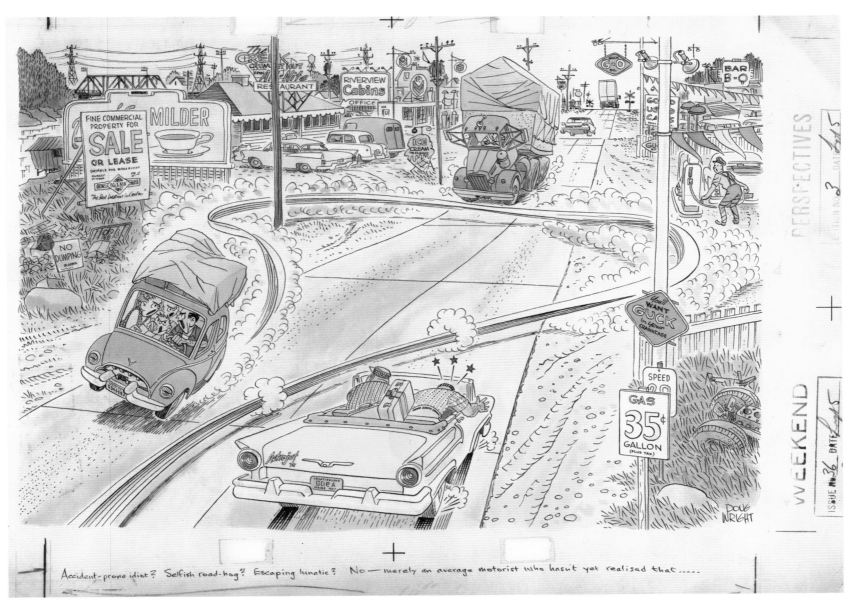

Accident-prone idiot? Selfish road-hog? Escaping lunatic? No — merely an average motorist who hasn't yet realised that.....

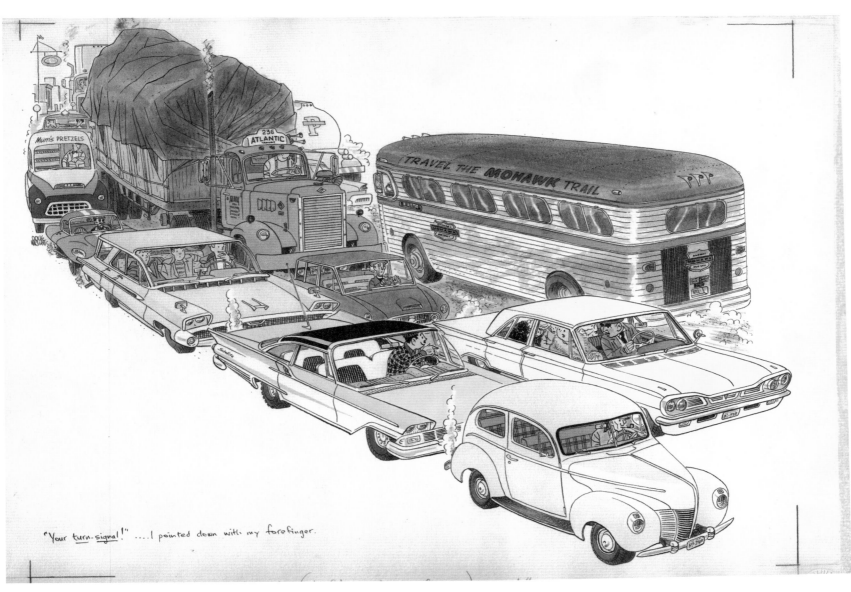

"Your turn-signal!" ....I pointed down with my forefinger.

Facing the TV Viewers — Alone

ABOVE: **Cover for the** MONTREAL STAR **magazine (Saturday supplement), May 5, 1962.**
OPPOSITE TOP: **Original cover art for the** MONTREAL STAR **magazine, December 2, 1961.**
OPPOSITE BOTTOM, LEFT: **A charming spot drawing. Publication information unknown.**
OPPOSITE BOTTOM, RIGHT: **Editorial illustration,** WEEKEND **magazine, October 22, 1960.**
(NOTE: **Detroit Red Wings changed to Chicago Blackhawks in final printed article.**)

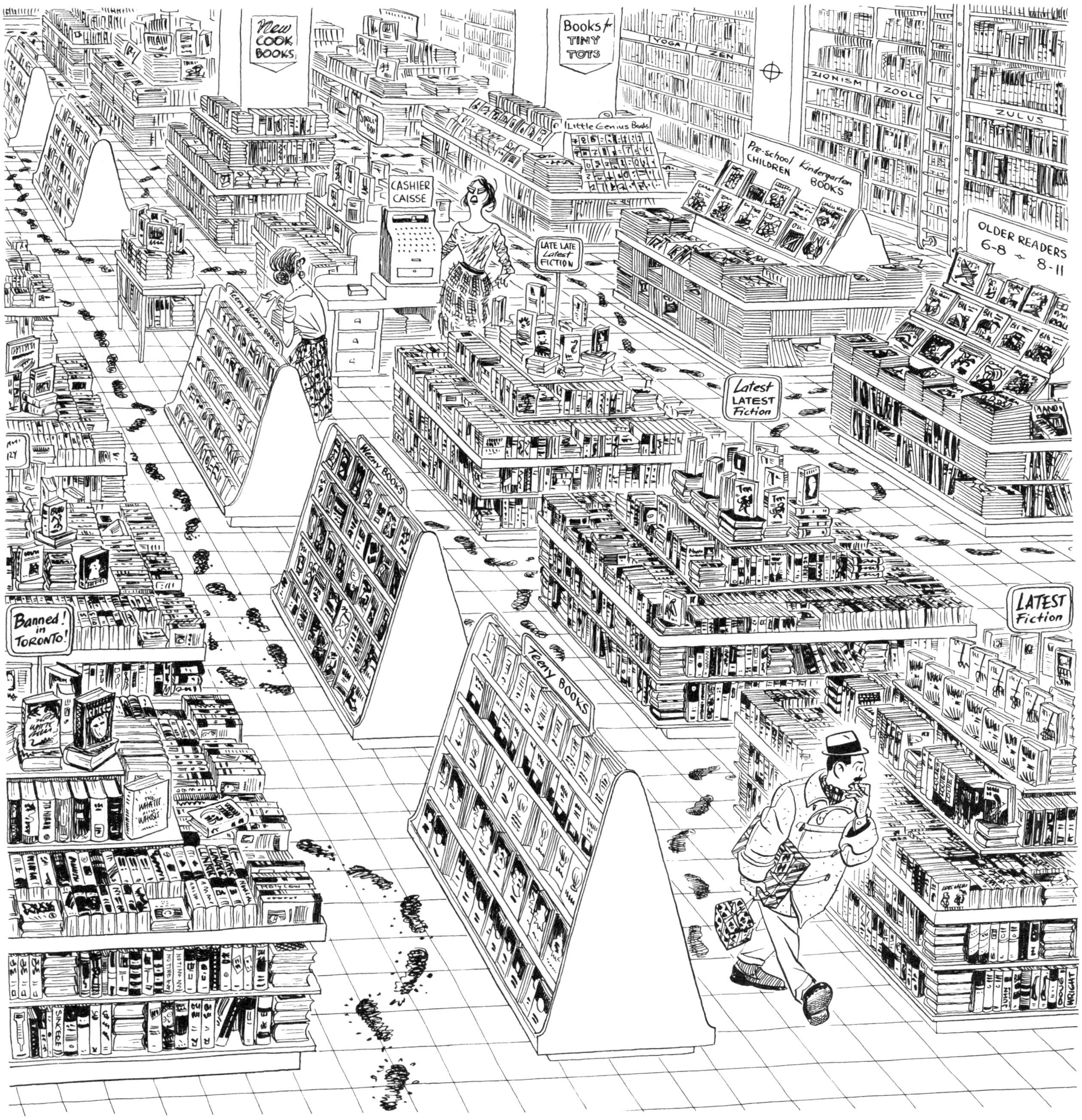
New COOK BOOKS
Books for TINY TOTS
YOGA
ZEN
ZIONISM
ZOOLOGY
ZULUS
Little Genius Books
Pre-school Kindergarten CHILDREN BOOKS
CASHIER CAISSE
OLDER READERS 6-8 + 8-11
LATE LATE Latest FICTION
Latest LATEST Fiction
Weeny BOOKS
Teeny BOOKS
Banned! in TORONTO!
LATEST Fiction

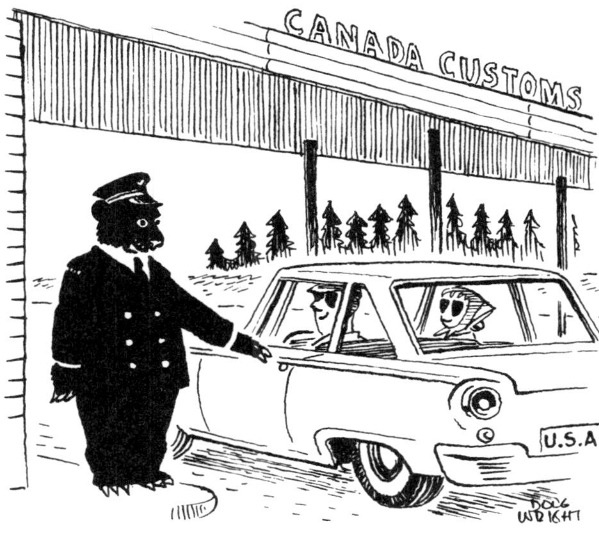
CANADA CUSTOMS
U.S.A
DOUG WRIGHT

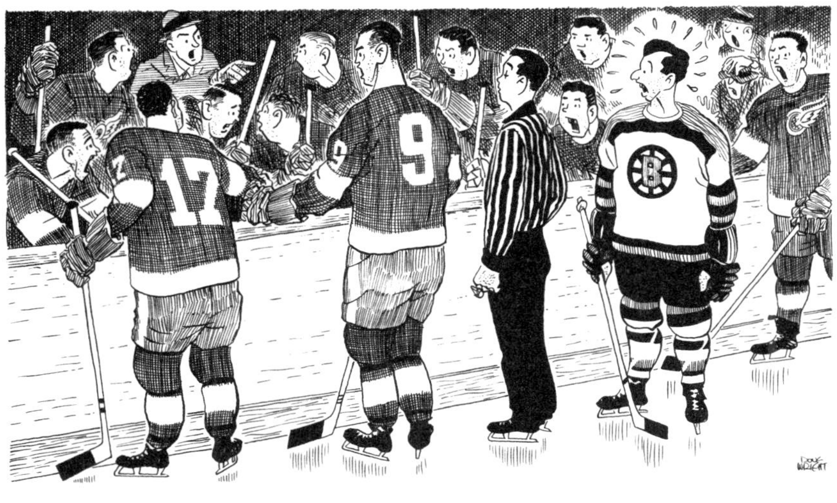
17
9

Seen on these two pages are elements of a major advertising campaign that Wright handled in the late 1950s. I have seen at least ten separate Wright ads for SIMONIZ *wax starring this cute red–headed* NIPPER *clone* —SETH.

ABOVE, LEFT: Concept sketch, circa 1959.
ABOVE, MIDDLE: Rough pencils, circa 1959.
ABOVE, RIGHT: Final full page ad, circa 1959.

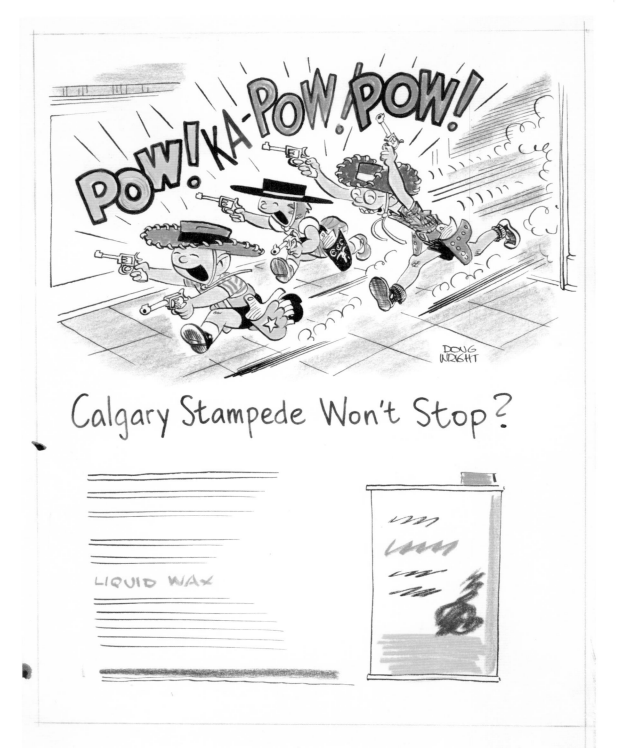

LEFT: Layout comp. Note: NIPPER appears in this sketch. Does this indicate an earlier concept for the campaign, starring NIPPER rather than the red–headed boy? Or was it a later ad that failed to materialize?

ABOVE: Another ad from 1959. This one is a charming bit of Canadiana.

OPPOSITE: Yet another example, also from 1959.

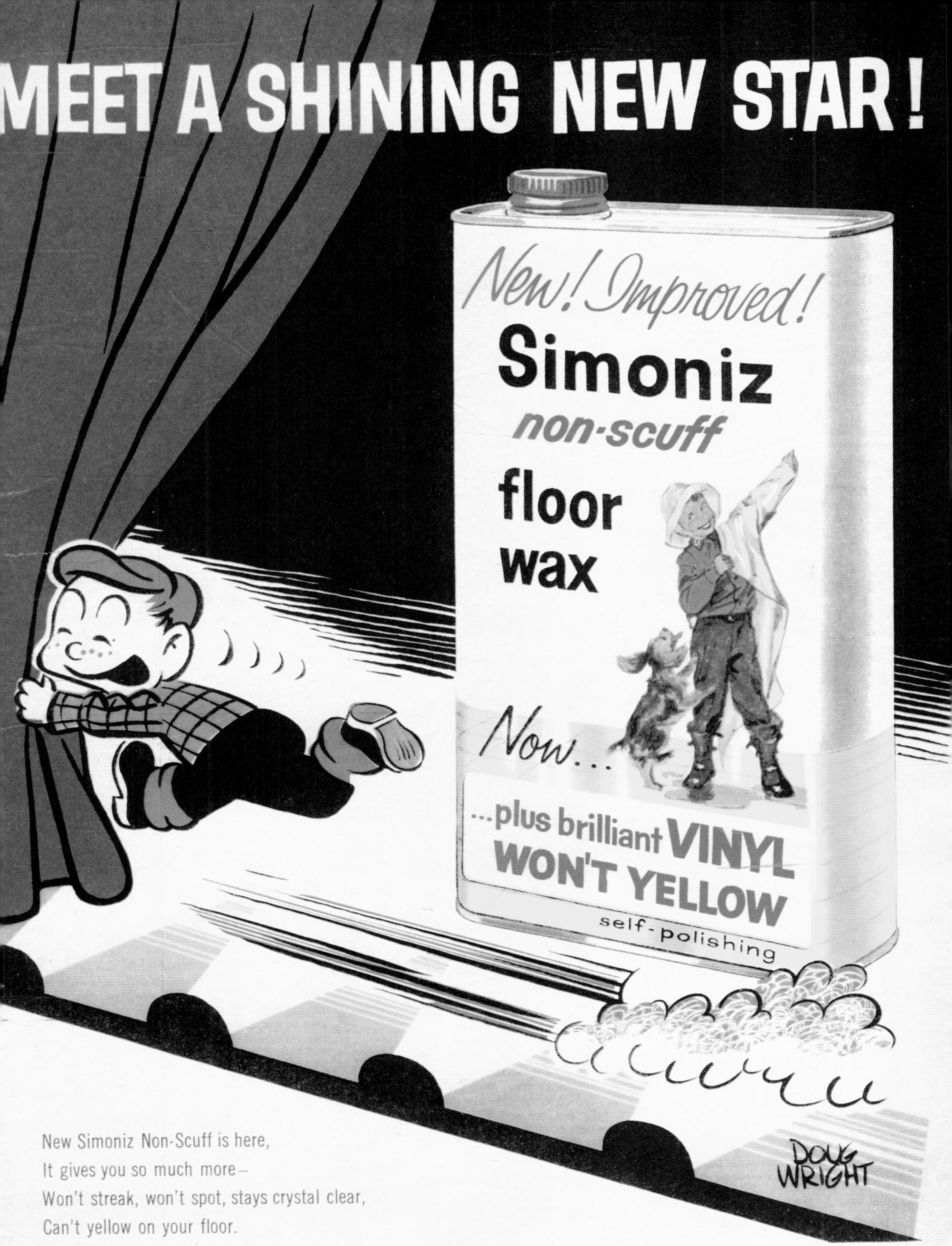

New Simoniz Non-Scuff is here,
It gives you so much more–
Won't streak, won't spot, stays crystal clear,
Can't yellow on your floor.

10"

① # 51
p. 18

2 sets of Negg
an film
2 pos.

ABOVE: Christmas–related editorial illustrations, WEEKEND magazine, circa 1950s.
OPPOSITE: Illustration for "The Christmas Ties That Bind." WEEKEND magazine, December 24, 1960.

ENTERTAINMENTS
theatres · books · art · music · tv · radio

ABOVE: **Cover for the** MONTREAL STAR **magazine (Saturday supplement),**
December 22, 1962.

ABOVE: An assortment of Doug Wright's personal Christmas cards, circa 1950 to 1965.

ABOVE: **Cover for the** MONTREAL STAR **magazine (Saturday supplement),**
September 29, 1962.

Stratford Draws All Kinds Of Shakespeareans

ABOVE: **Cover for the** MONTREAL STAR **magazine (Saturday supplement),**
June 16, 1962.

Wright did a great deal of work for the MONTREAL STANDARD, *the* WEEKEND *magazine, and the* MONTREAL STAR *throughout the 1950s and 60s. Alas, most of that work is very hard to find today—hidden away wherever great piles of yesterday's newsprint goes to hide. Even Wright's personal files only provide a scattershot collection of tearsheets—many of them torn or stained with aging glue. I can only dream that someday a complete collection of them can be amassed.* —SETH

Nipper

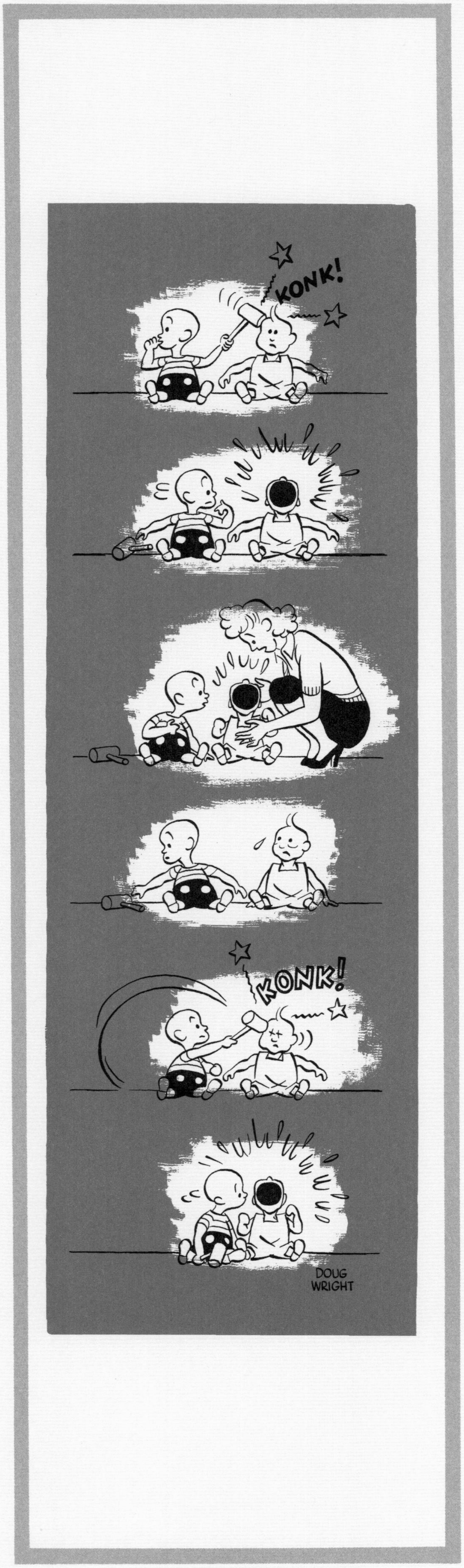
KONK!
KONK!
DOUG WRIGHT
January 8, 1949

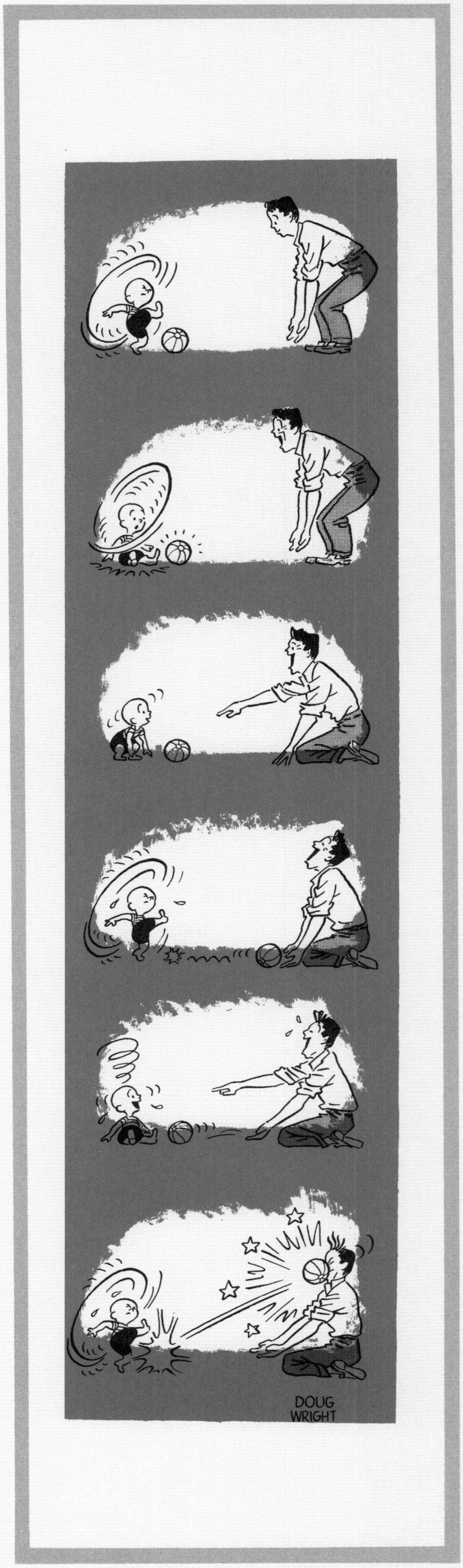
DOUG WRIGHT
October 8, 1949

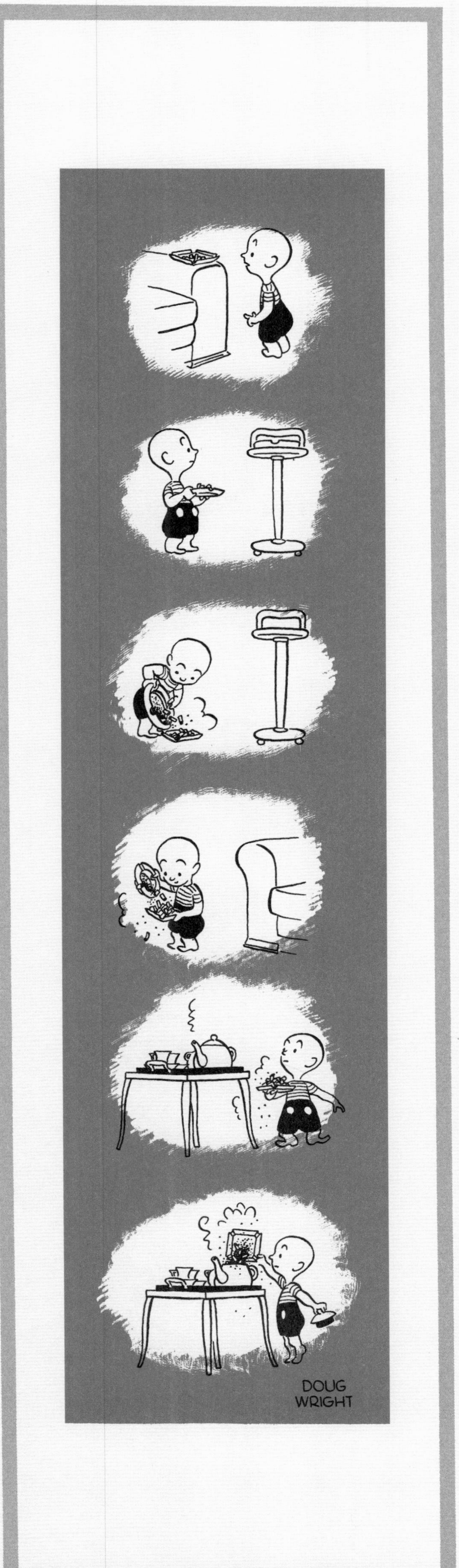
DOUG
WRIGHT

October 15, 1949

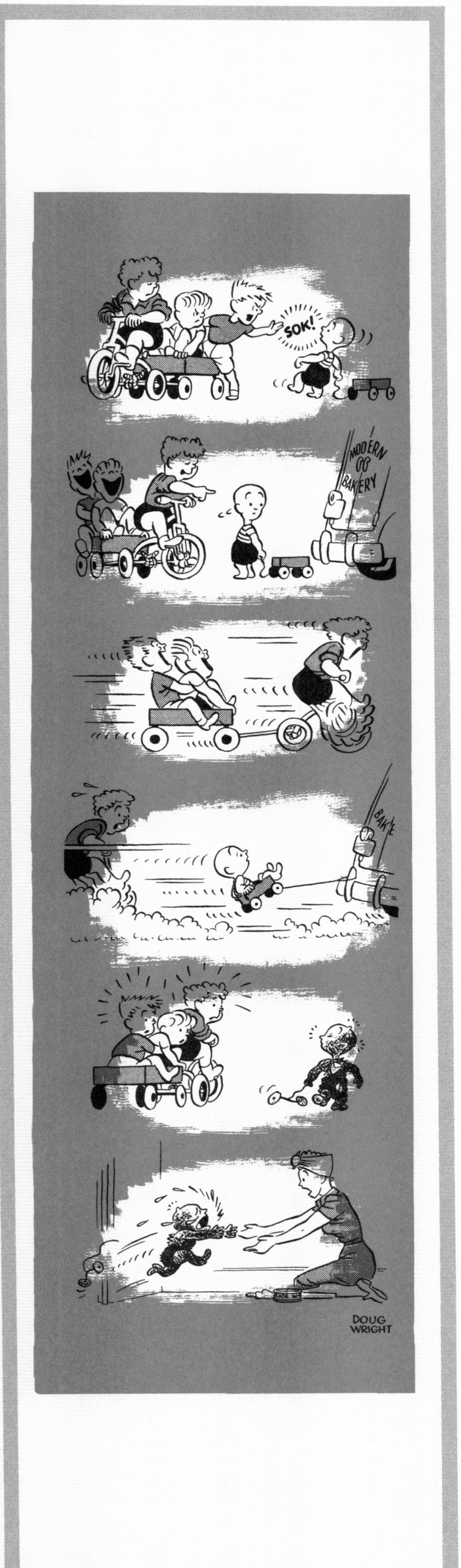
SOK!
MODERN
BAKERY
BAKE
DOUG
WRIGHT

Date unknown, 1949

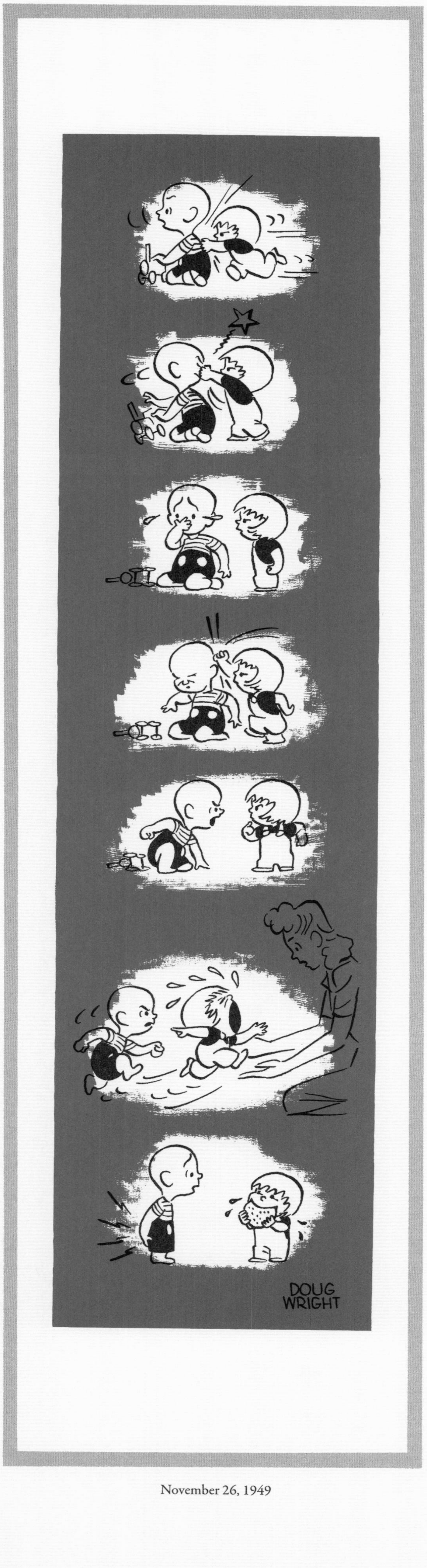
DOUG
WRIGHT

November 26, 1949

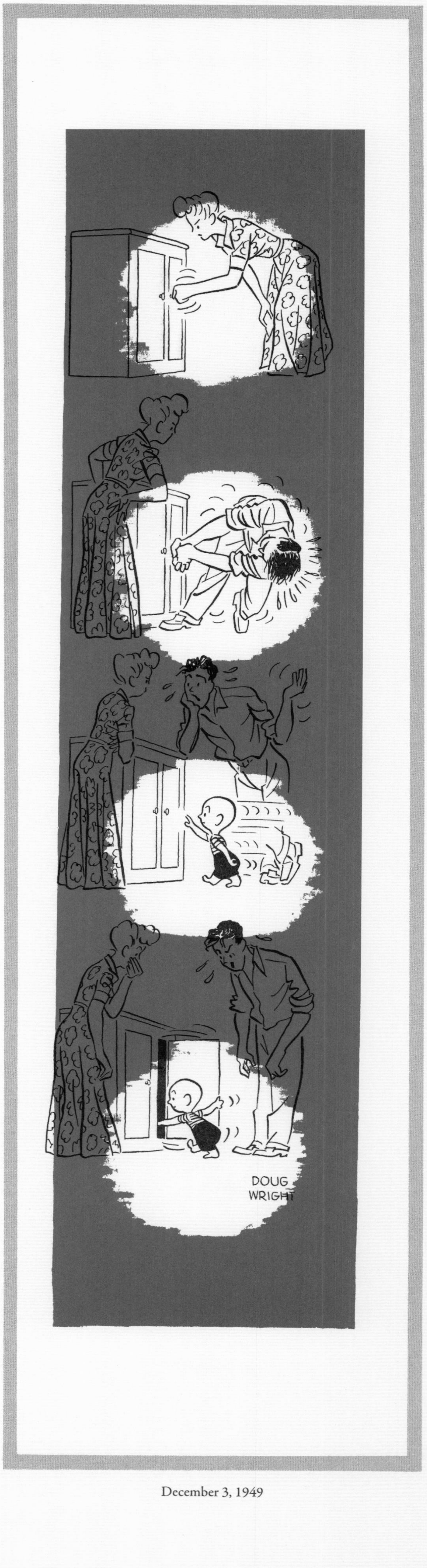
DOUG
WRIGHT

December 3, 1949

Note the name of the boat. Doug and Phyllis were married two years later on September 4th, 1952.

Date unknown, 1949

January 7, 1950

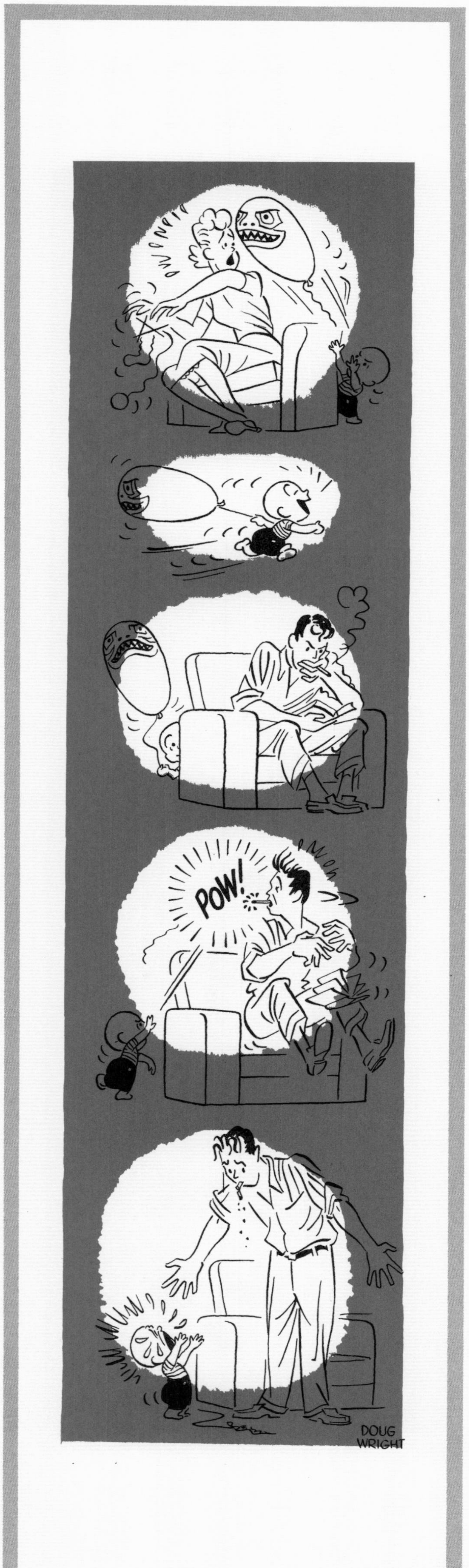
POW!
DOUG WRIGHT

January 14, 1950

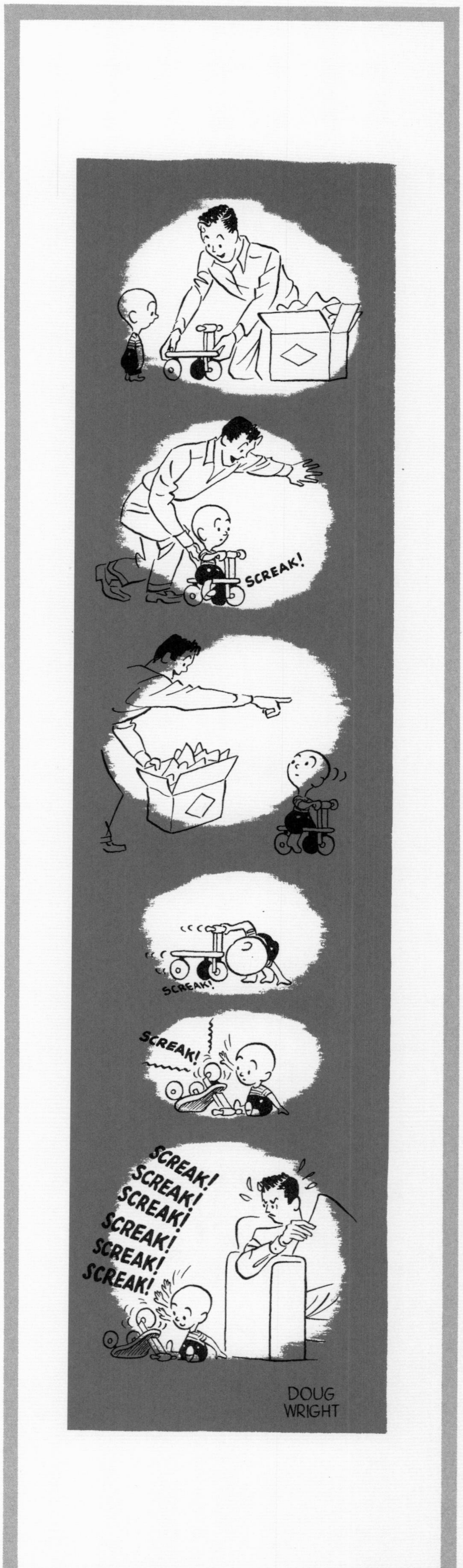
SCREAK!
SCREAK!
SCREAK!
SCREAK!
SCREAK!
SCREAK!
SCREAK!
SCREAK!
SCREAK!
DOUG WRIGHT

January 28, 1950

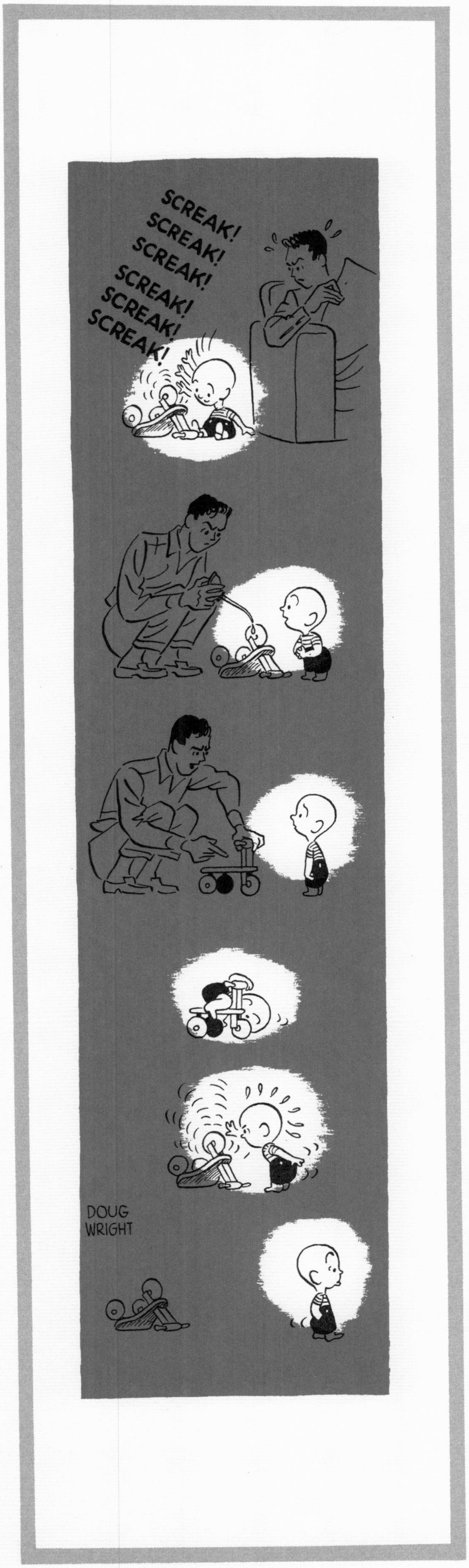
SCREAK!
SCREAK!
SCREAK!
SCREAK!
SCREAK!
SCREAK!
DOUG
WRIGHT

February 4, 1950

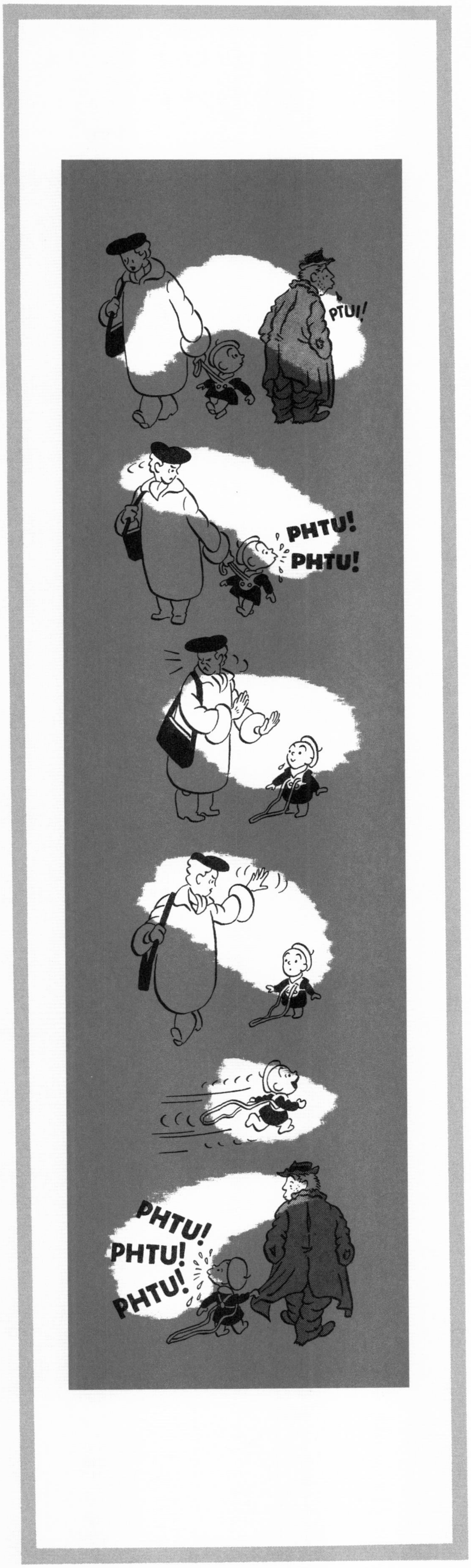
PTUI!
PHTU!
PHTU!
PHTU!
PHTU!
PHTU!

April 15, 1950

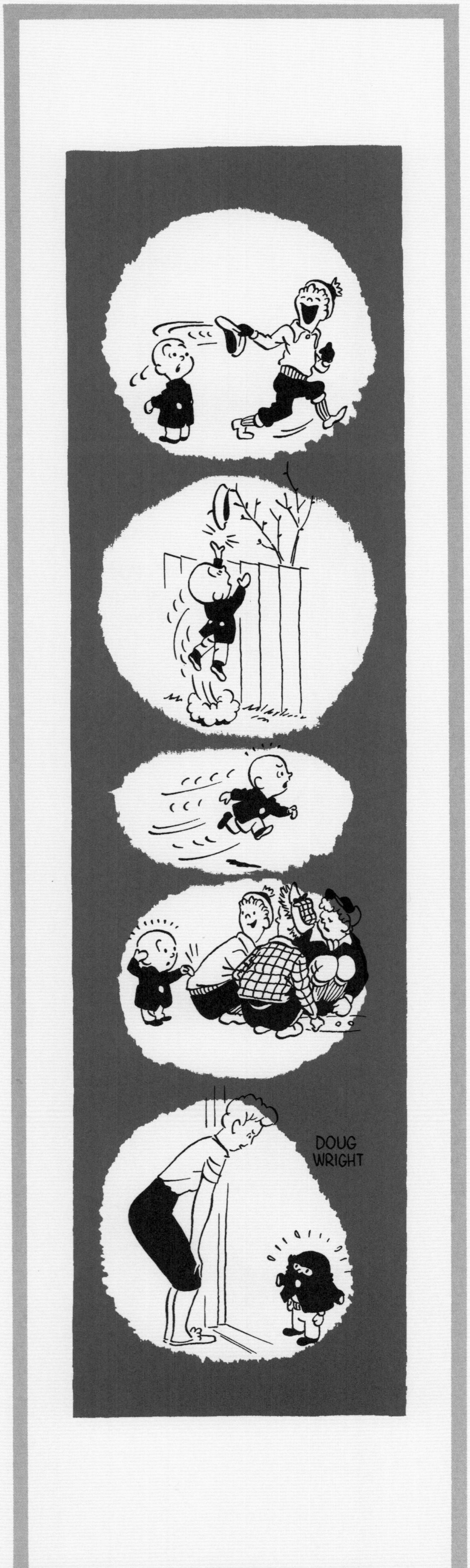
DOUG
WRIGHT

April 28, 1950

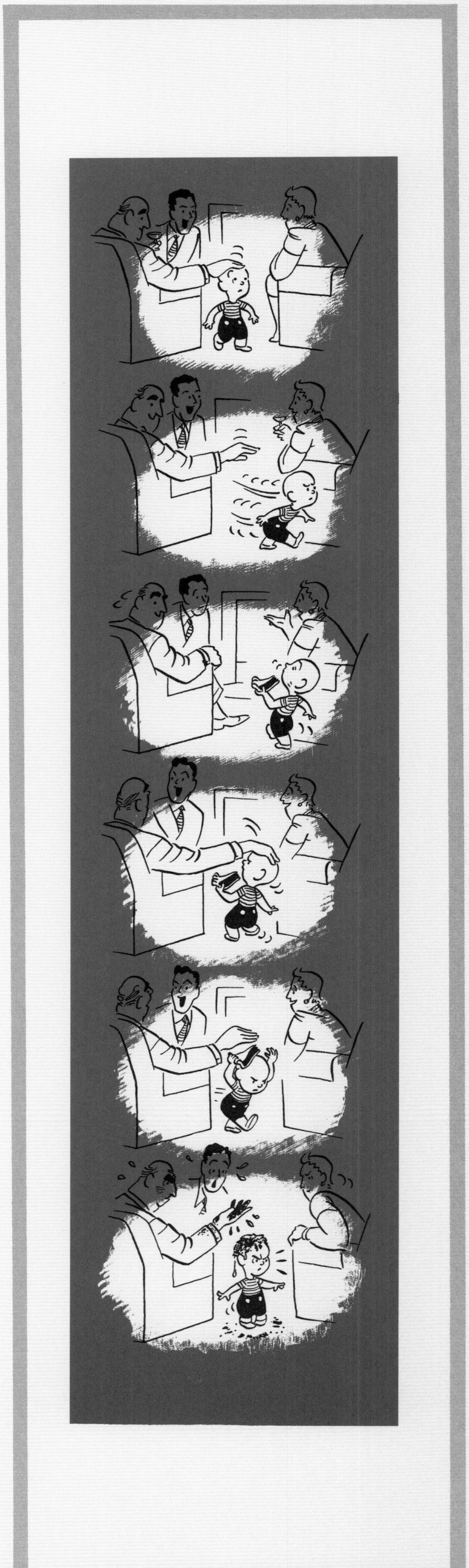

May 15, 1950

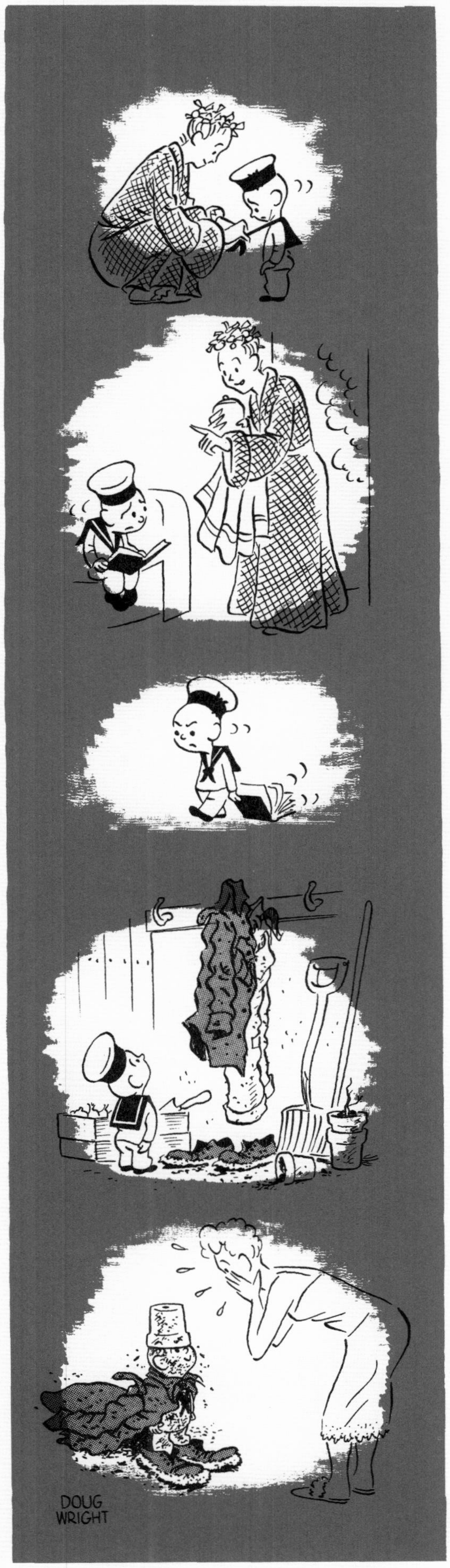
DOUG WRIGHT

June 1, 1950

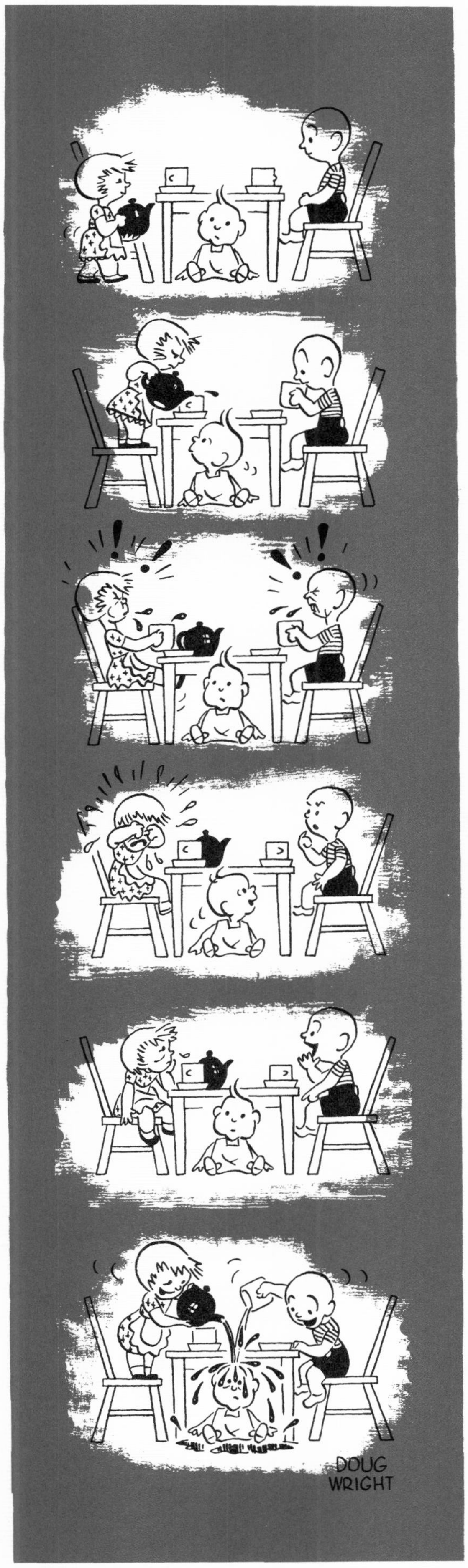
DOUG WRIGHT

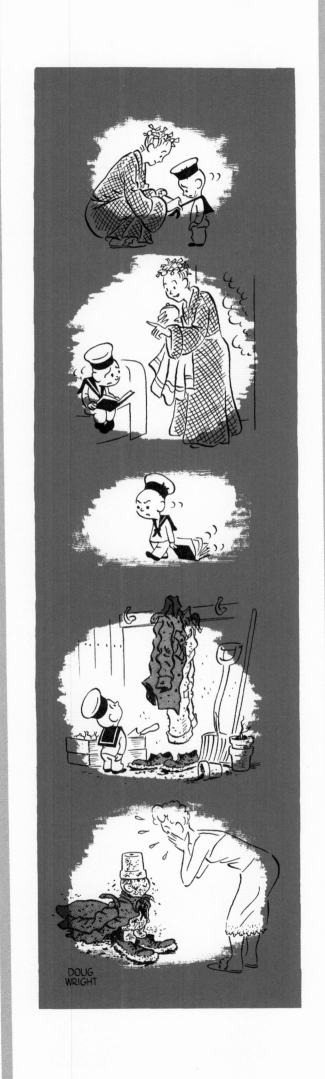

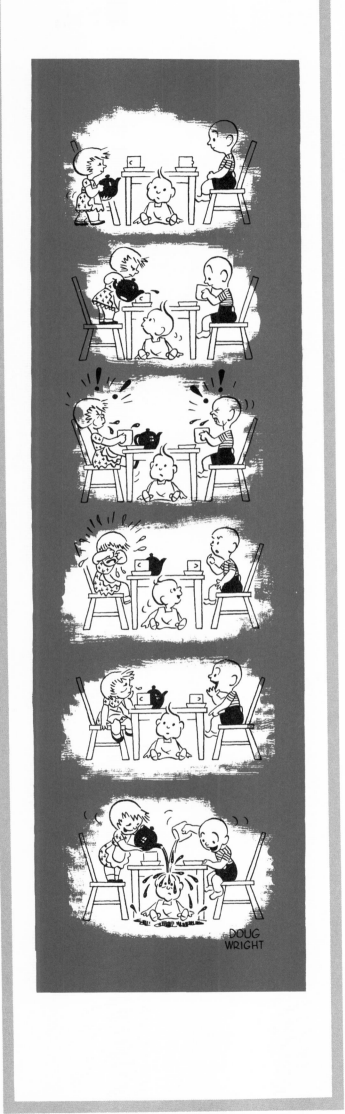

July 22, 1950

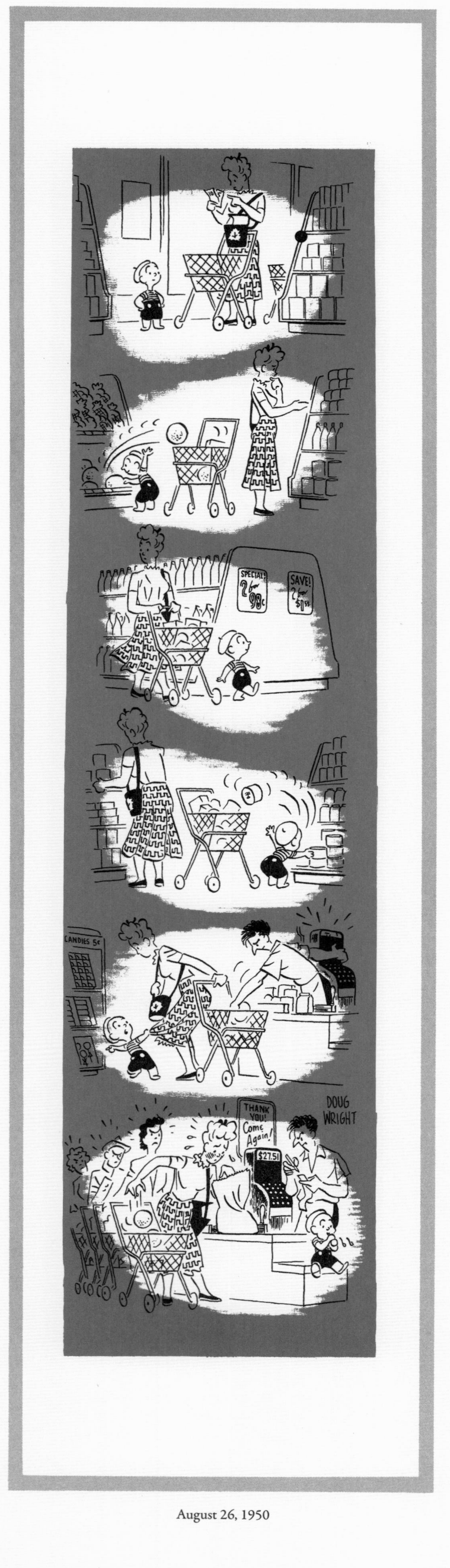
SPECIAL! 2 for 98¢
SAVE! 2 for $1.55
CANDIES 5¢
DOUG WRIGHT
THANK YOU! Come Again!
$27.51

August 26, 1950

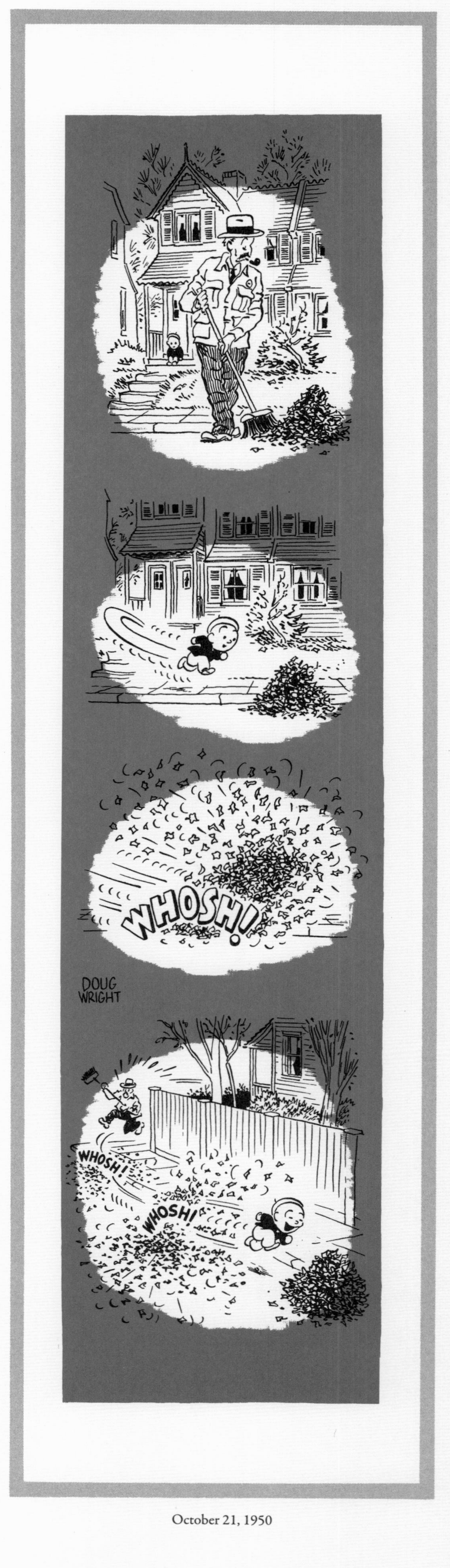
WHOSH!
DOUG WRIGHT
WHOSH!
WHOSH!

October 21, 1950

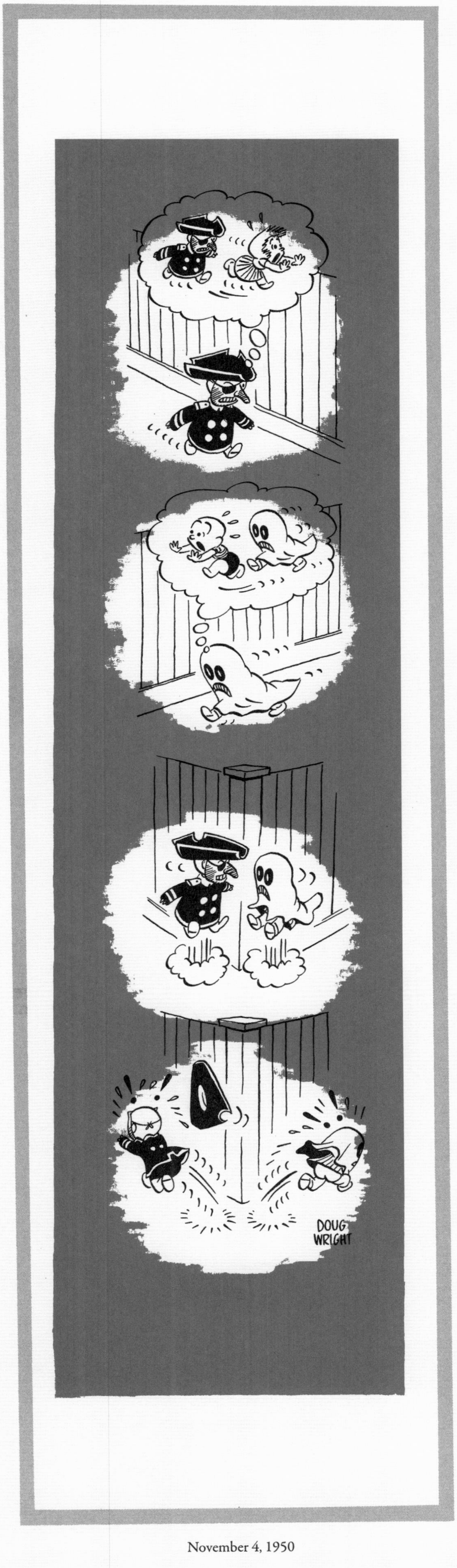
DOUG
WRIGHT

November 4, 1950

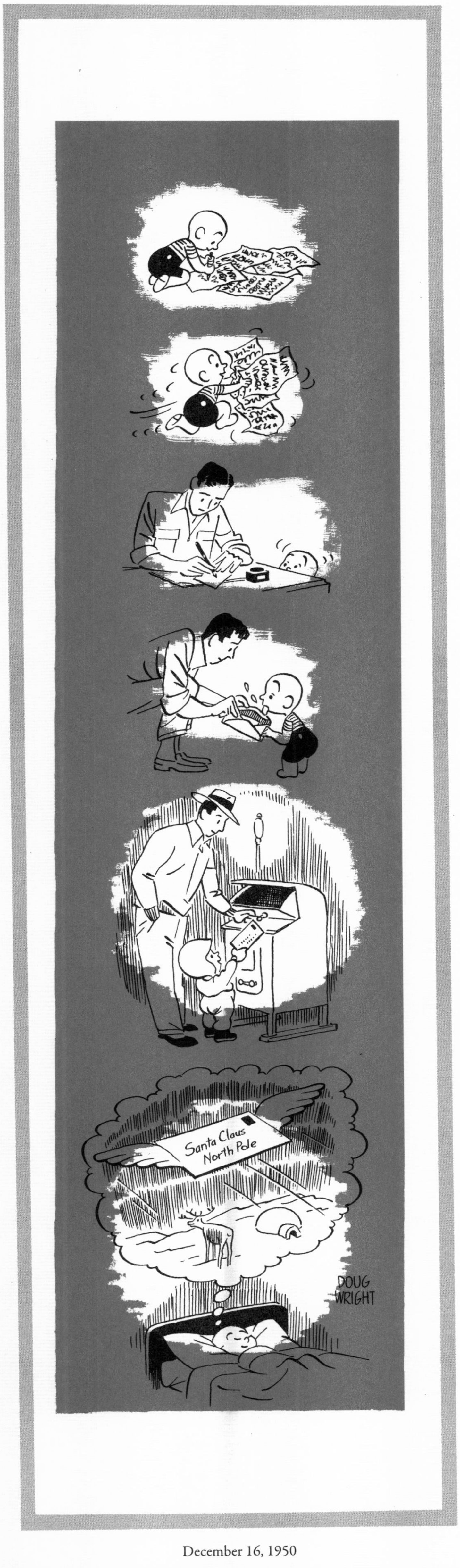
Santa Claus
North Pole
DOUG
WRIGHT

December 16, 1950

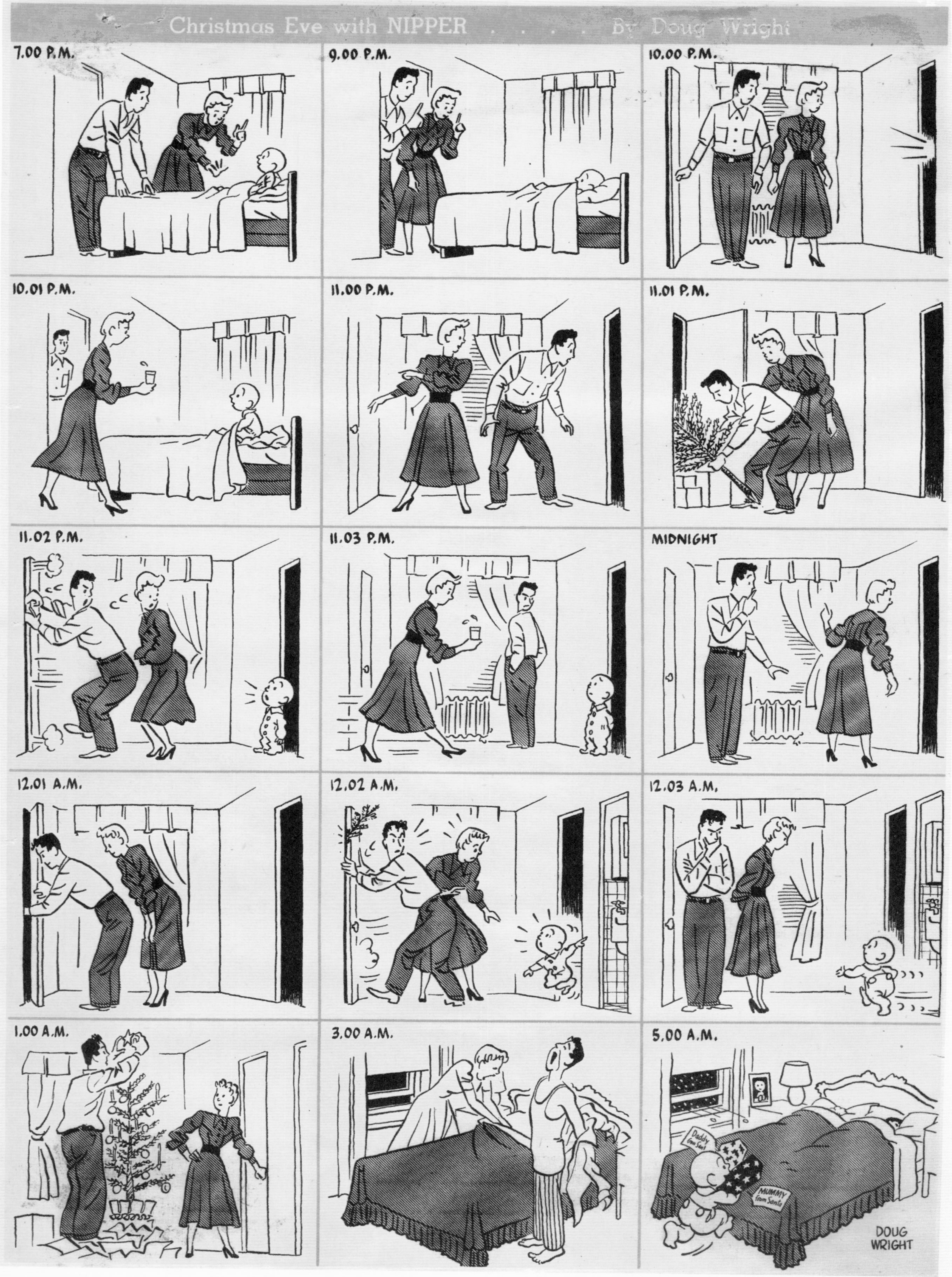
Christmas Eve with NIPPER . . . . By Doug Wright
7.00 P.M.
9.00 P.M.
10.00 P.M.
10.01 P.M.
11.00 P.M.
11.01 P.M.
11.02 P.M.
11.03 P.M.
MIDNIGHT
12.01 A.M.
12.02 A.M.
12.03 A.M.
1.00 A.M.
3.00 A.M.
5.00 A.M.
DOUG WRIGHT

This is the first of Wright's annual full page Christmas strips.

December 23, 1950

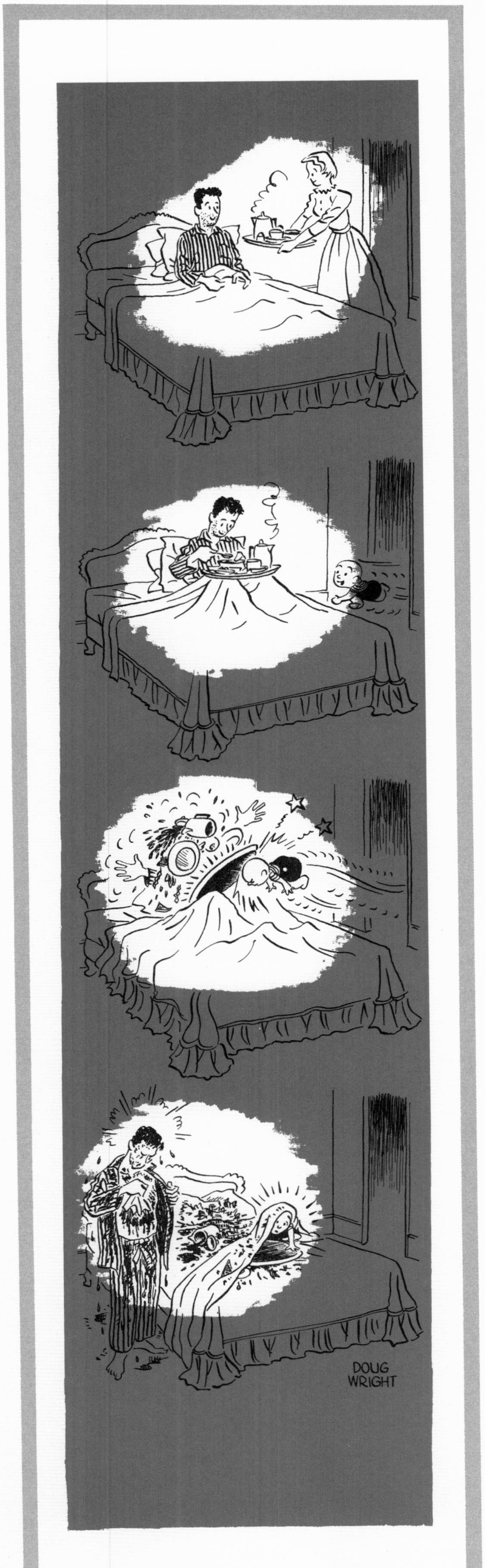
DOUG
WRIGHT

January 6, 1951

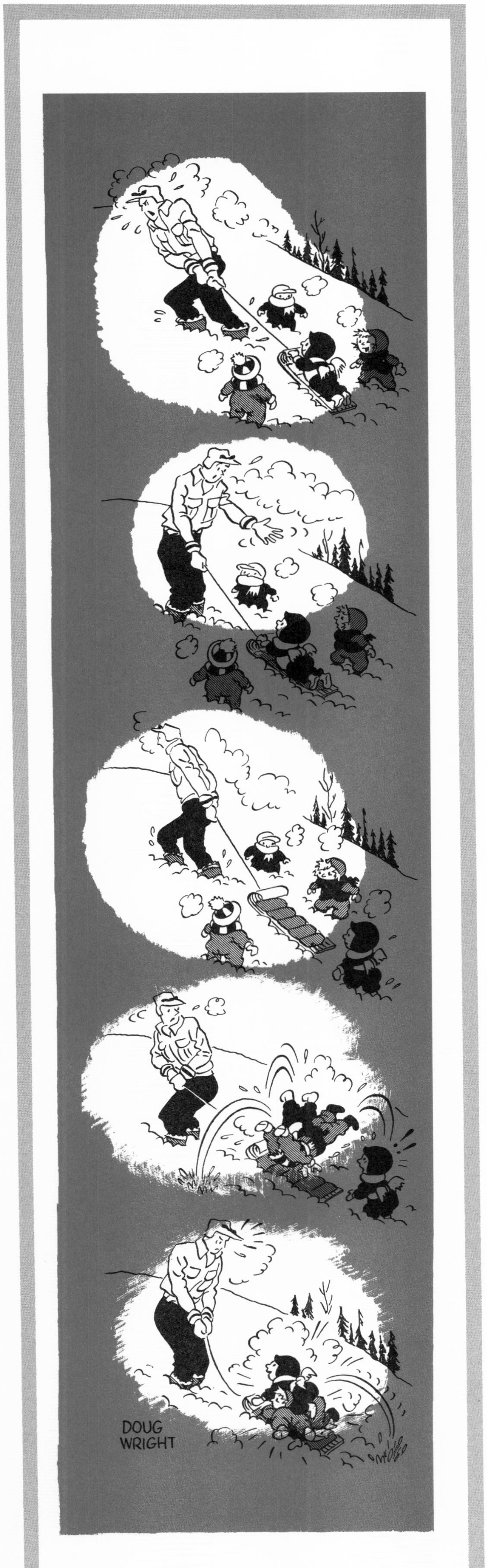
DOUG
WRIGHT

January 13, 1951

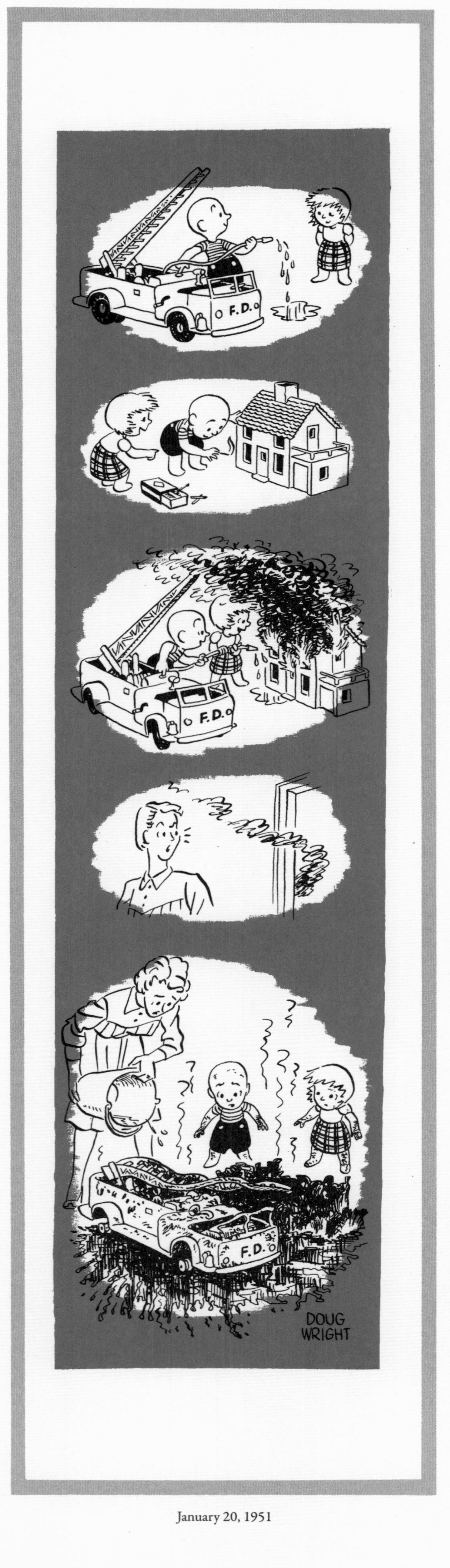
F.D.
F.D.
F.D.
DOUG WRIGHT

January 20, 1951

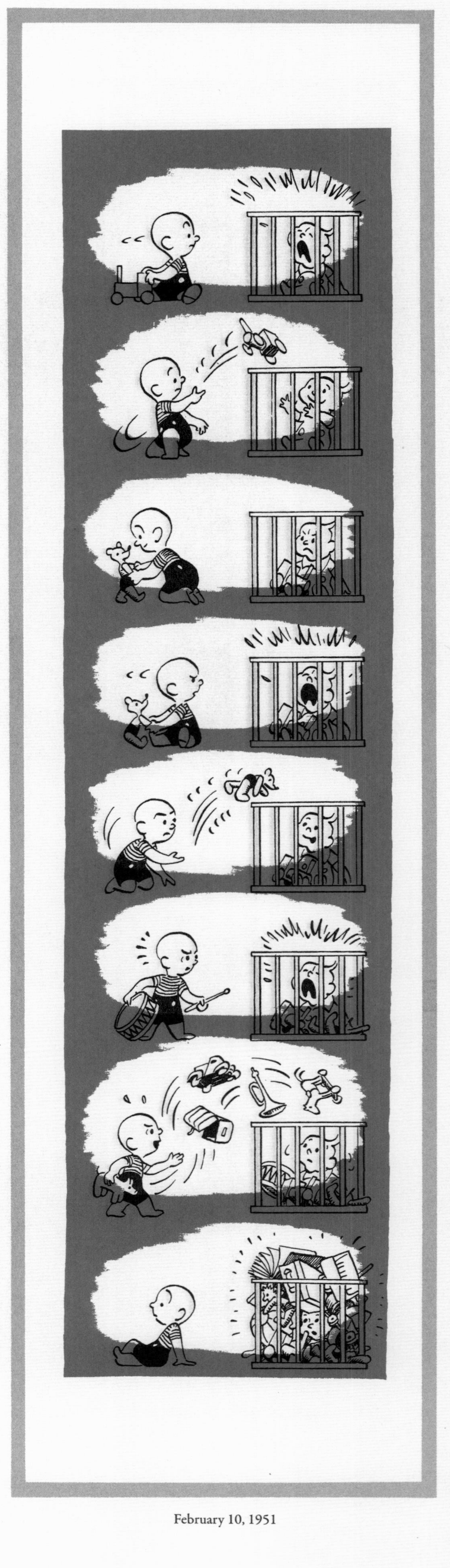

February 10, 1951

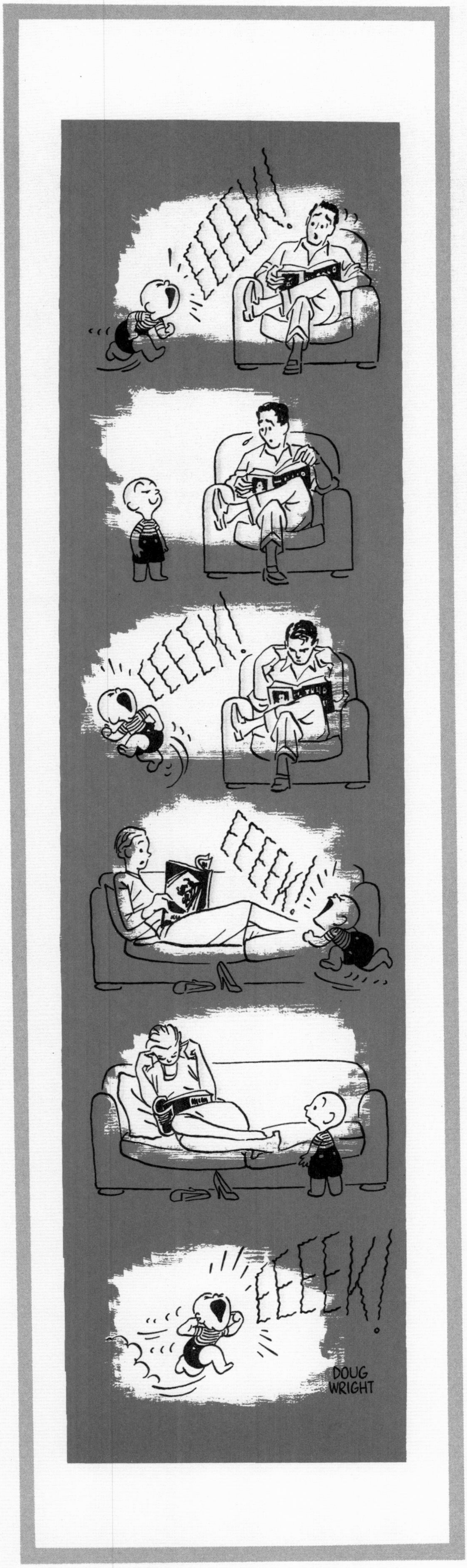
EEEEEK!
EEEEK!
EEEEK!
EEEEK!
DOUG WRIGHT

April 28, 1951

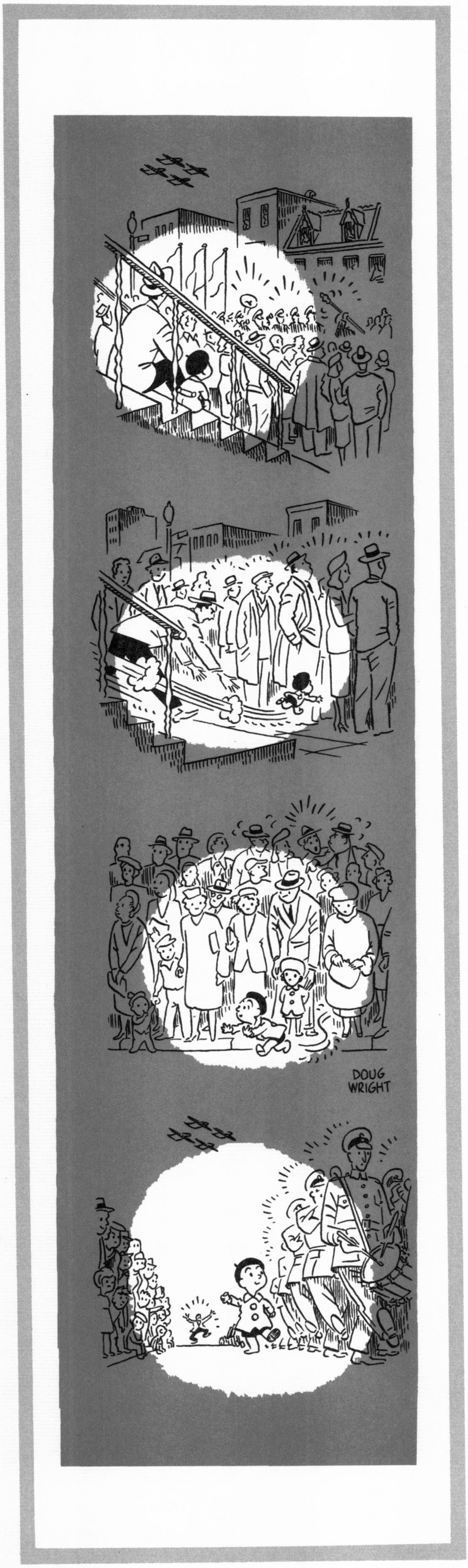
DOUG WRIGHT

May 26, 1951

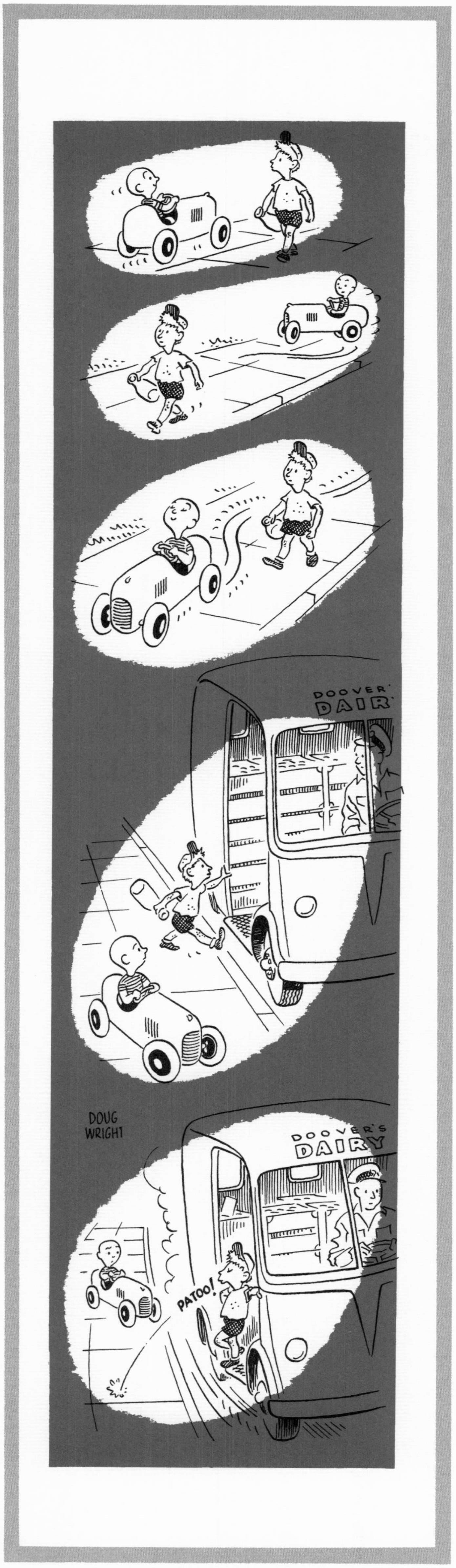
DOOVER'S
DAIRY
DOUG
WRIGHT
DOOVER'S
DAIRY
PATOO!

July 21, 1951

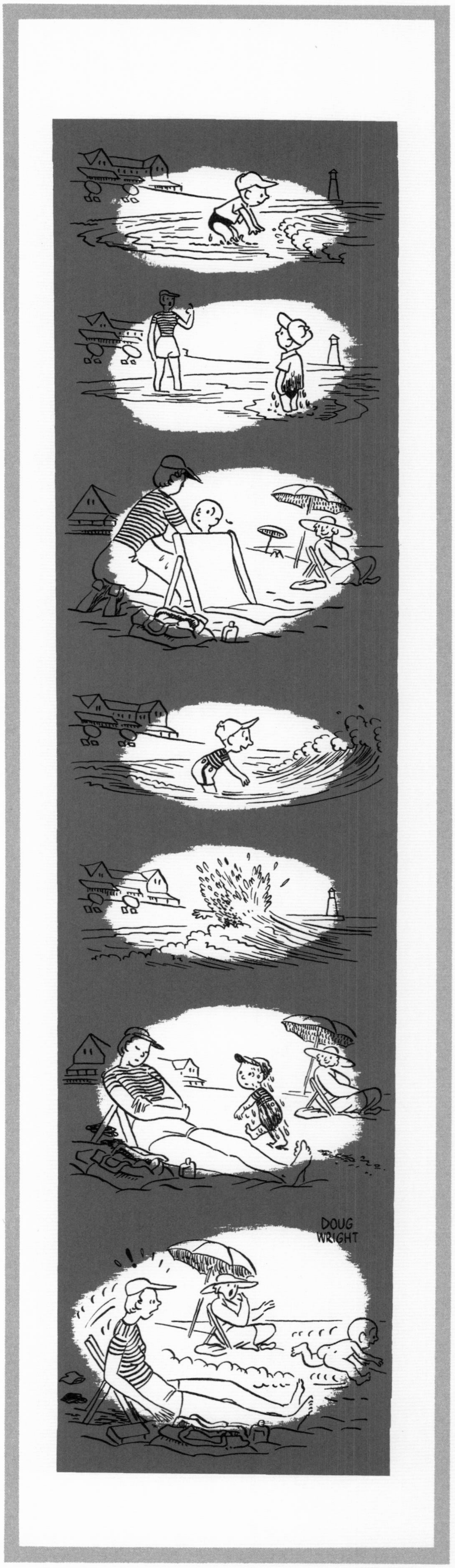
DOUG
WRIGHT

August 4, 1951

DOUG WRIGHT

August 11, 1951

DOUG WRIGHT

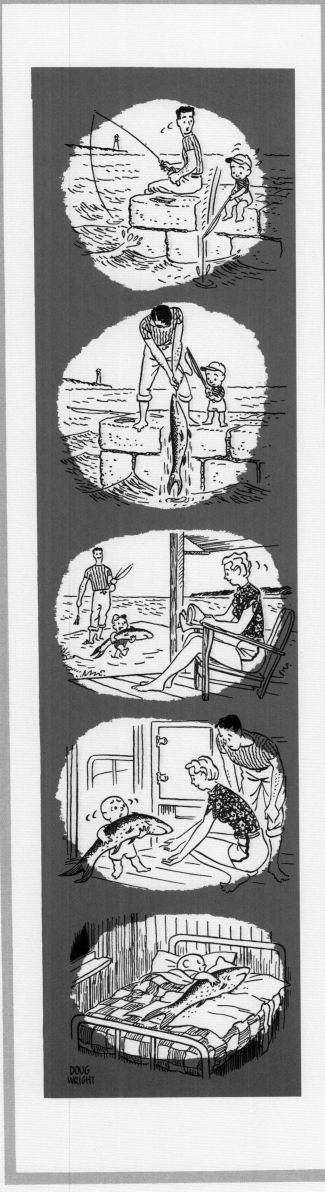

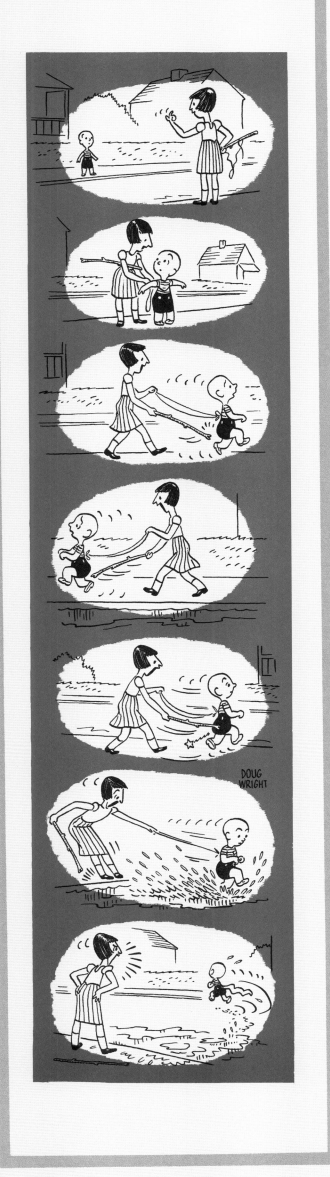

August 18, 1951

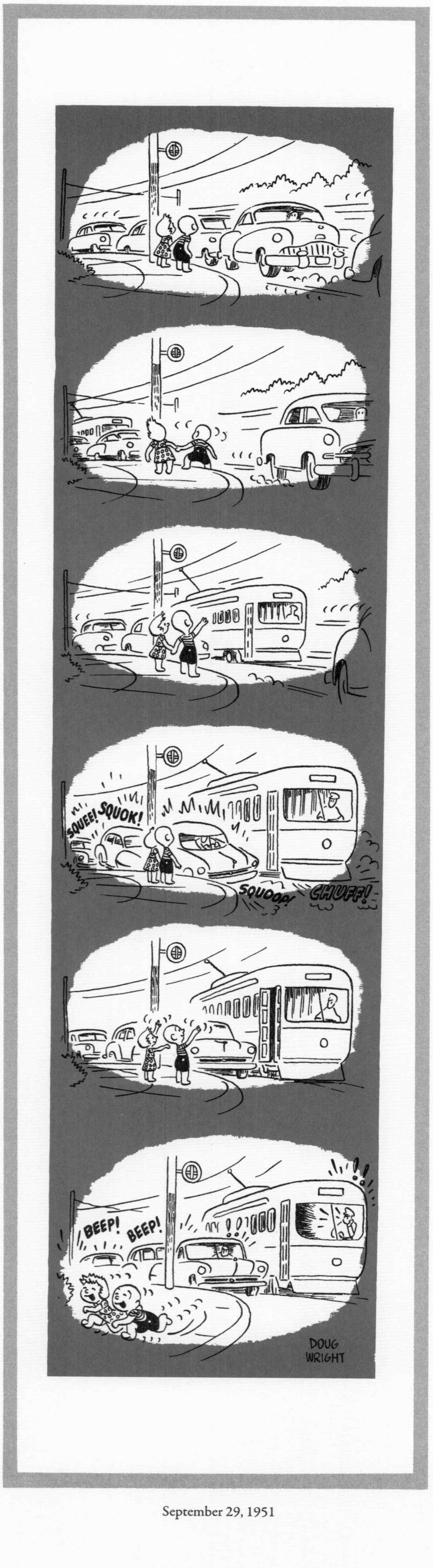
SQUEE! SQUOK!
SQUOOP!
CHUFF!
BEEP!
BEEP!
DOUG WRIGHT

September 29, 1951

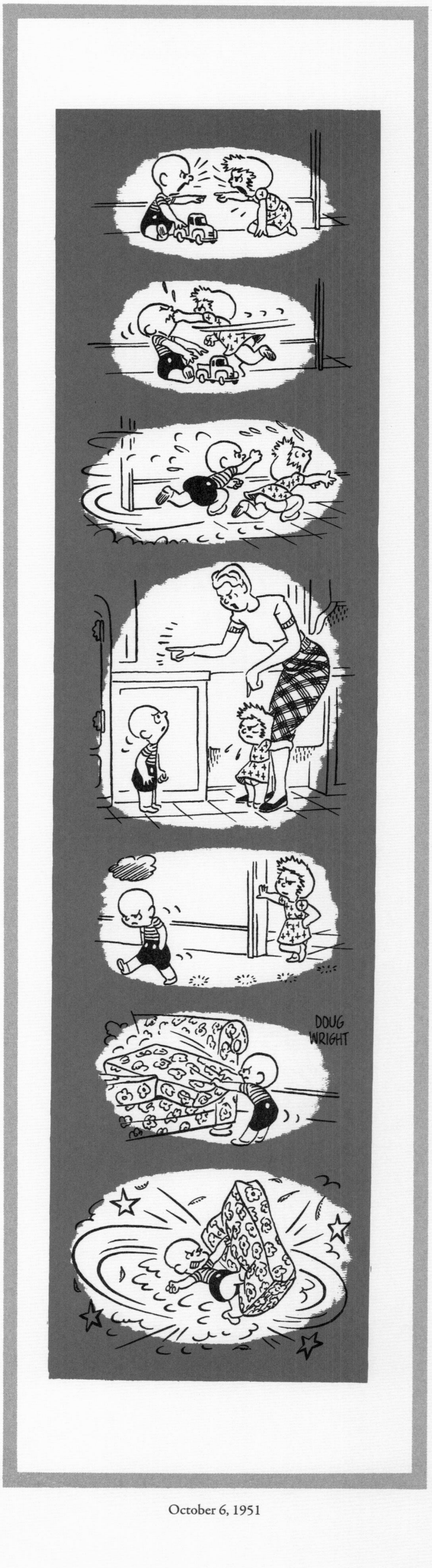
DOUG WRIGHT

October 6, 1951

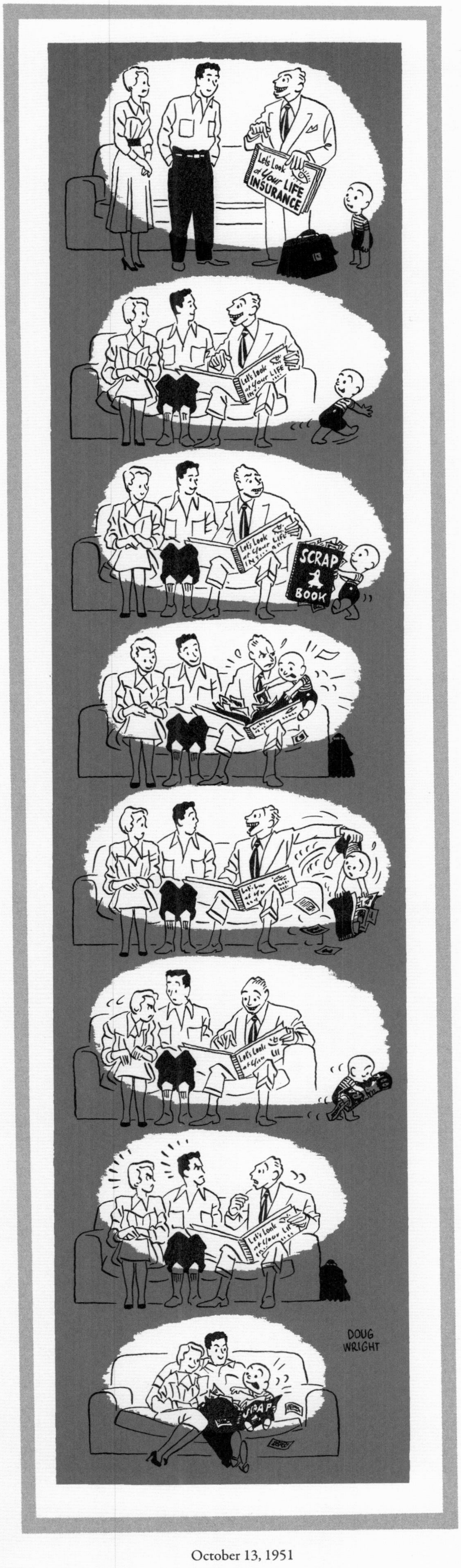
Let's Look at Your LIFE INSURANCE
SCRAP BOOK
DOUG WRIGHT

October 13, 1951

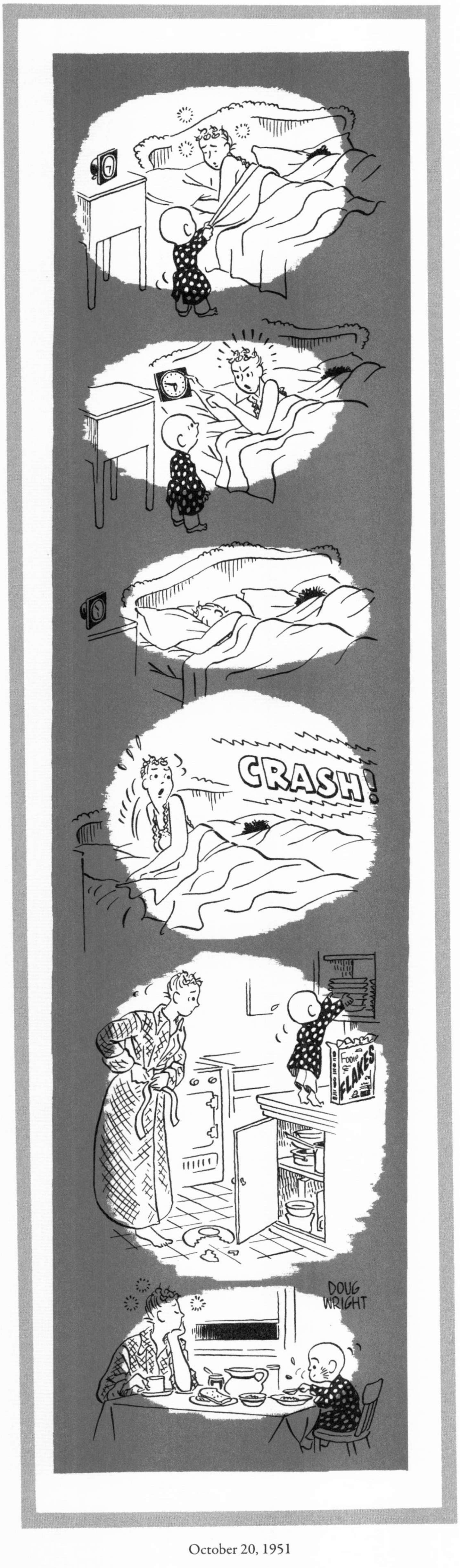
CRASH!
FOOF FLAKES
DOUG WRIGHT

October 20, 1951

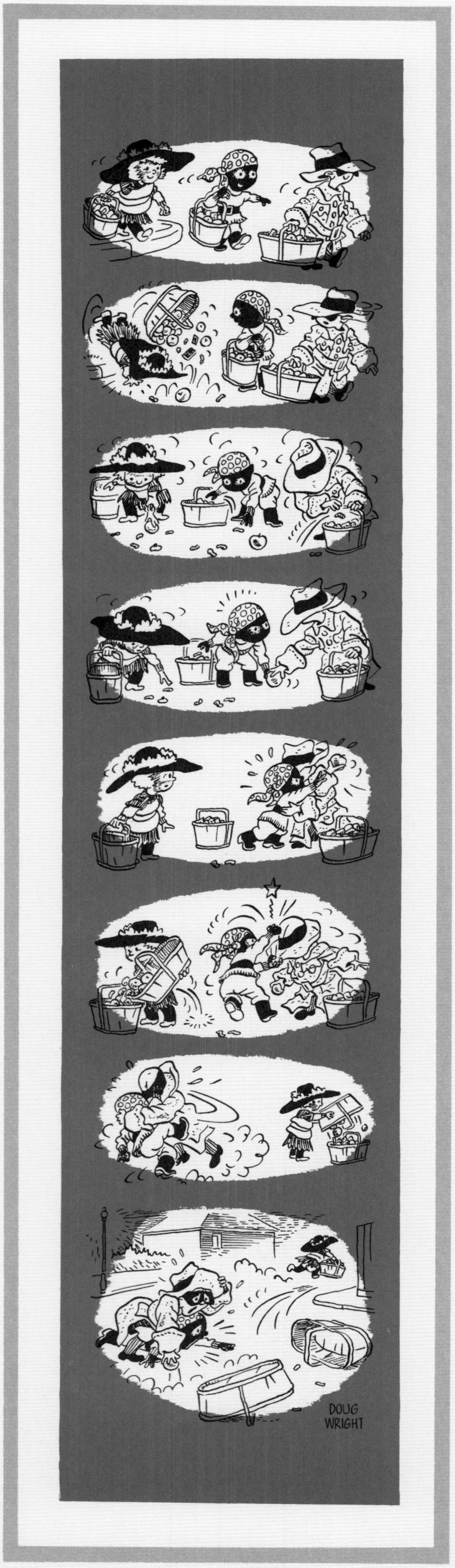
DOUG
WRIGHT

October 27, 1951

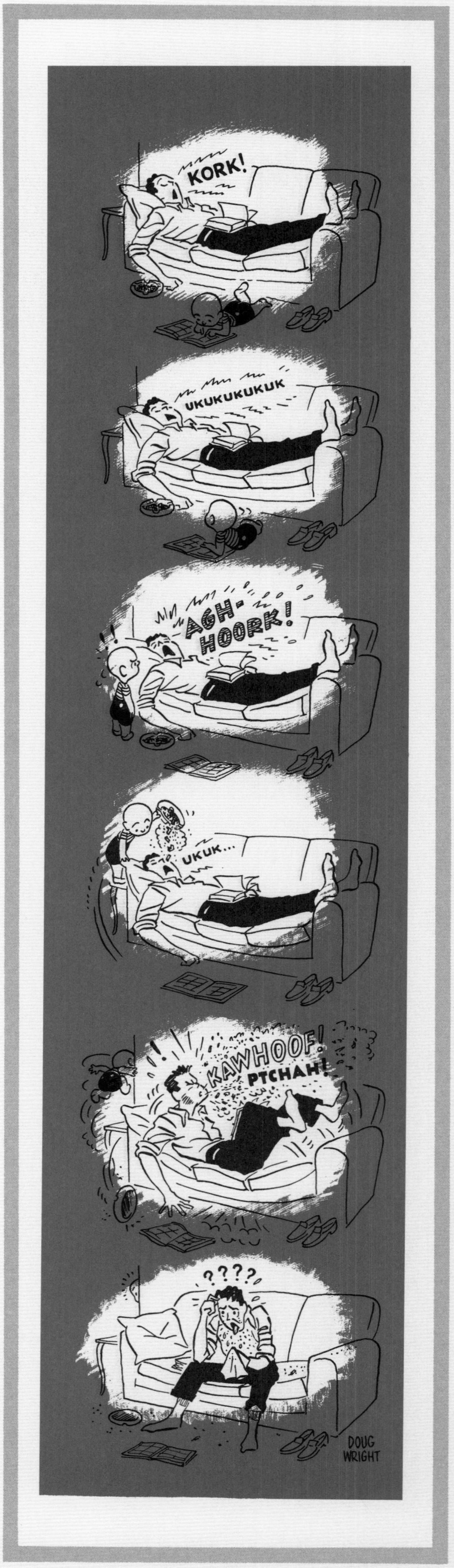
KORK!
UKUKUKUKUK
AGH-
HOORK!
UKUK...
KAWHOOF!
PTCHAH!
????
DOUG
WRIGHT

November 3, 1951

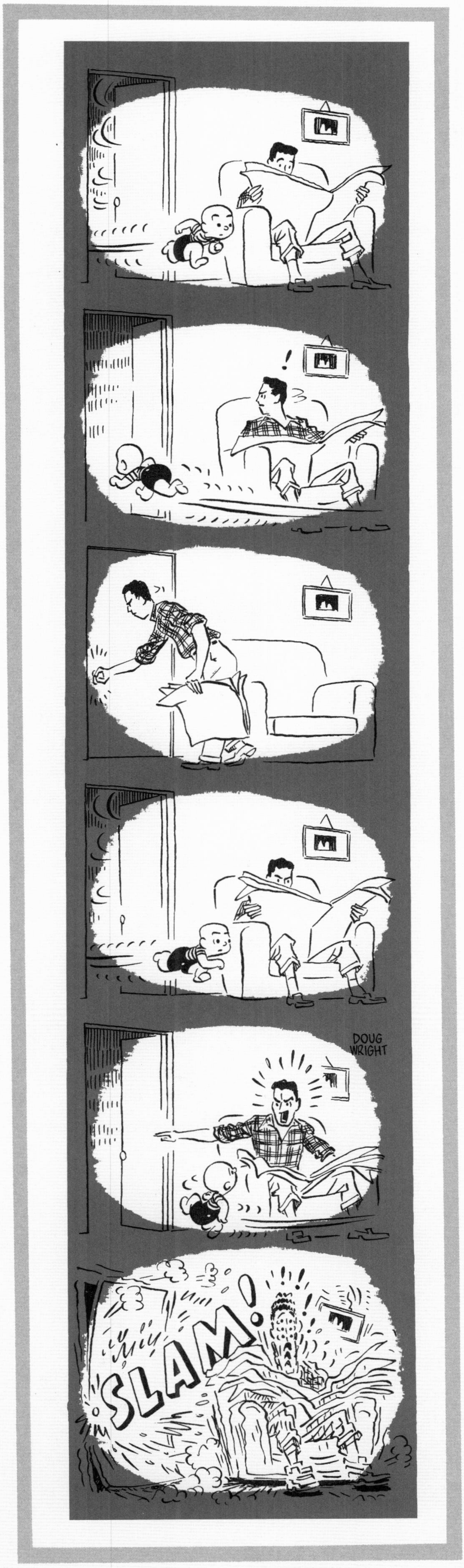
DOUG
WRIGHT
SLAM!

November 10, 1951

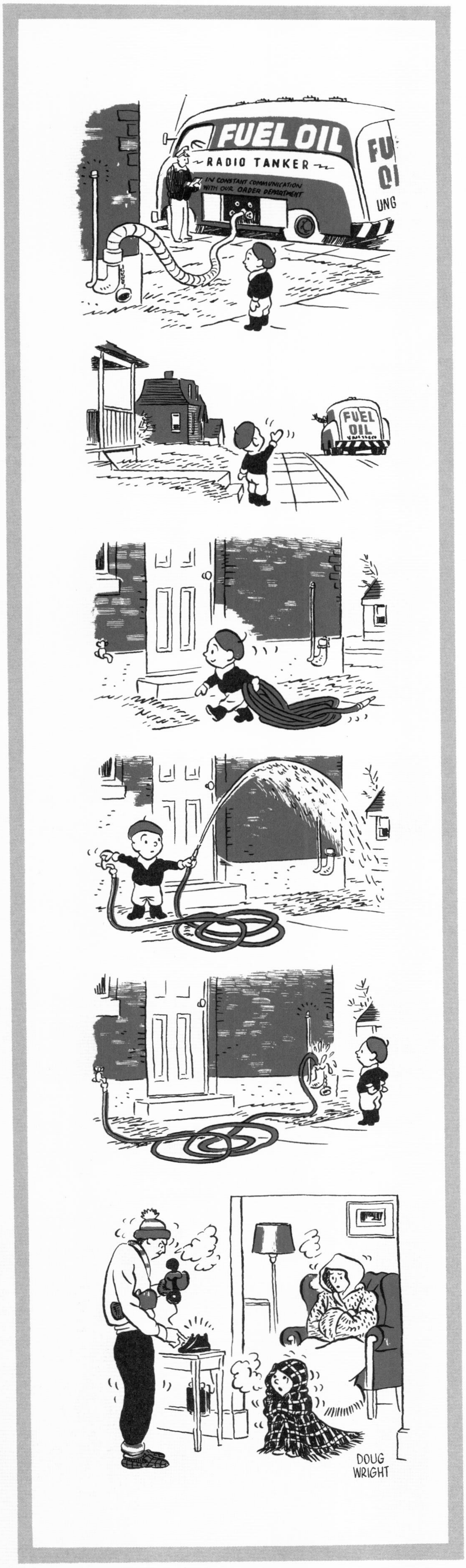
FUEL OIL
RADIO TANKER
IN CONSTANT COMMUNICATION WITH OUR ORDER DEPARTMENT
FUEL
OIL
DOUG
WRIGHT

November 24, 1951

Christmas Day with **NIPPER** by Doug Wright

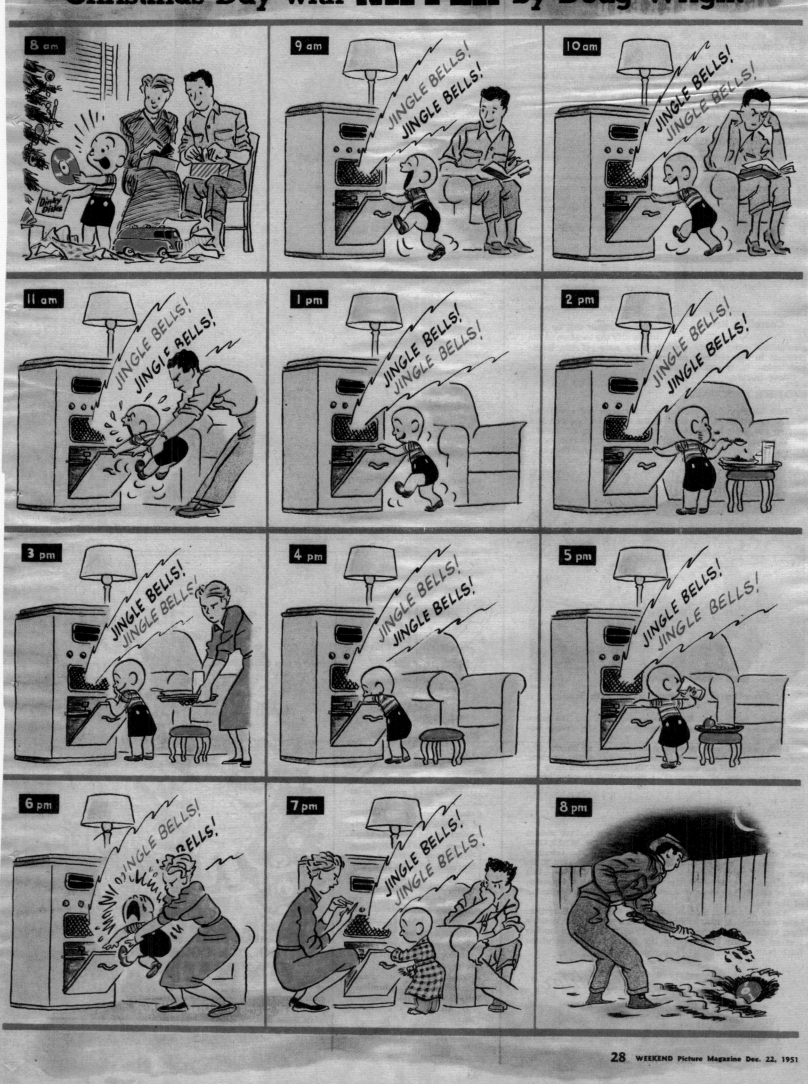

December 22, 1951

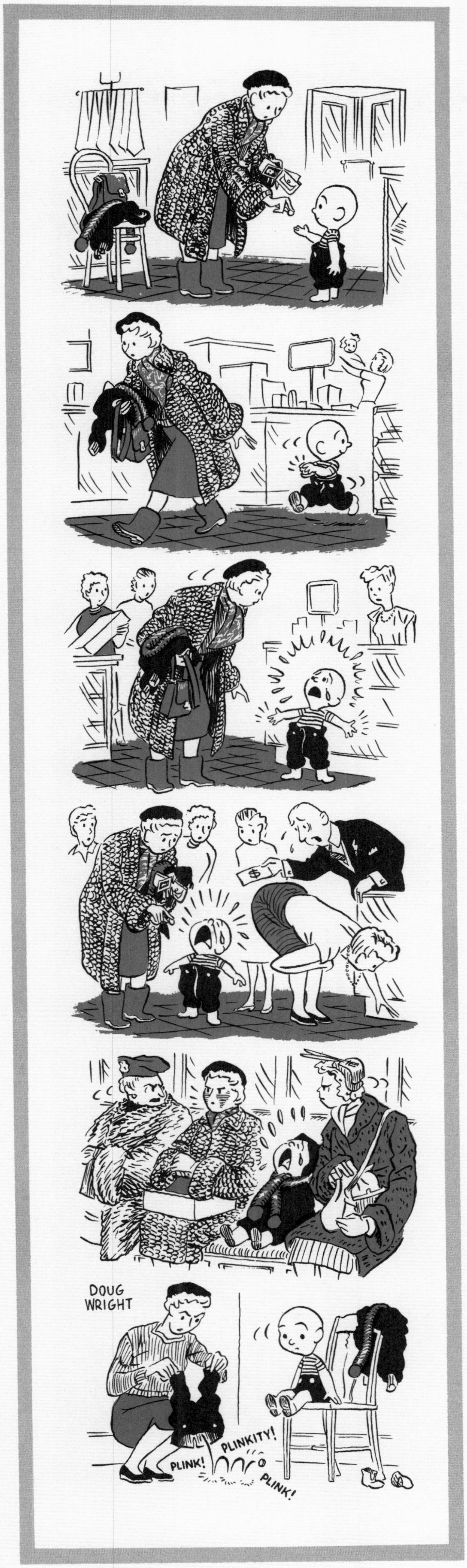
DOUG
WRIGHT
PLINKITY!
PLINK!
PLINK!

February 2, 1952

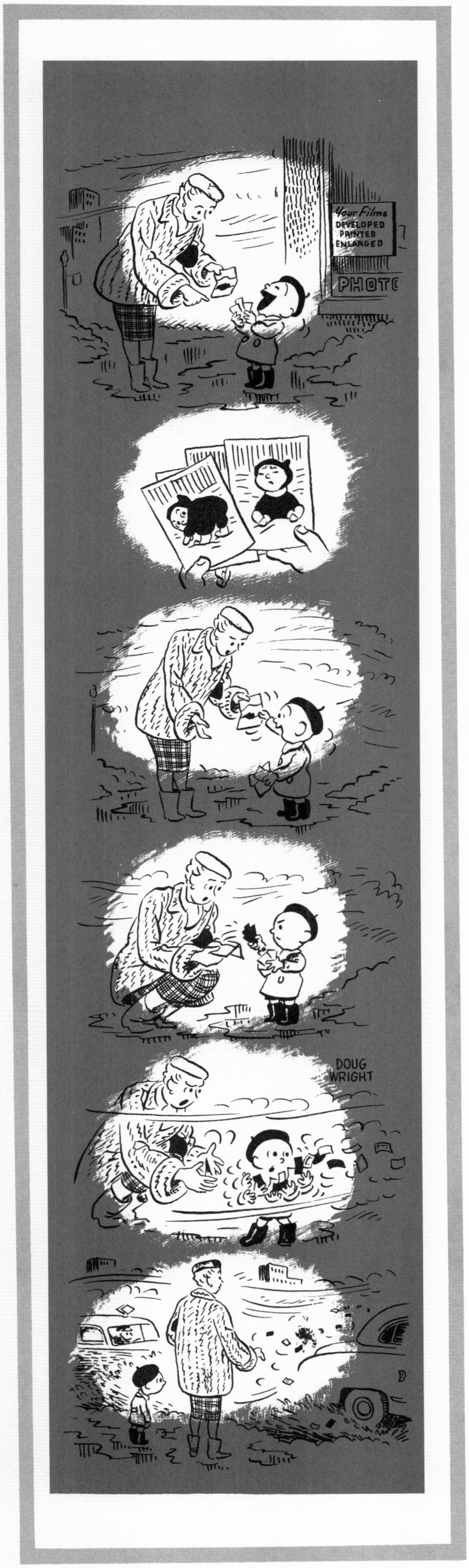
Your Films
DEVELOPED
PRINTED
ENLARGED
PHOTO
DOUG
WRIGHT

March 15, 1952

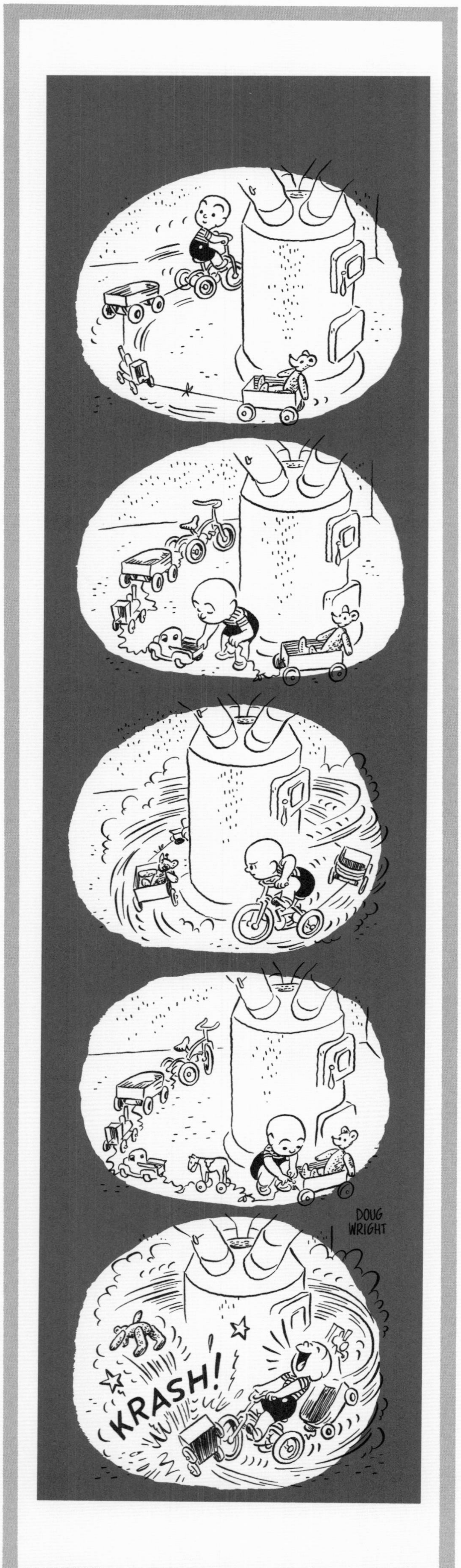
DOUG WRIGHT
KRASH!

March 22, 1952

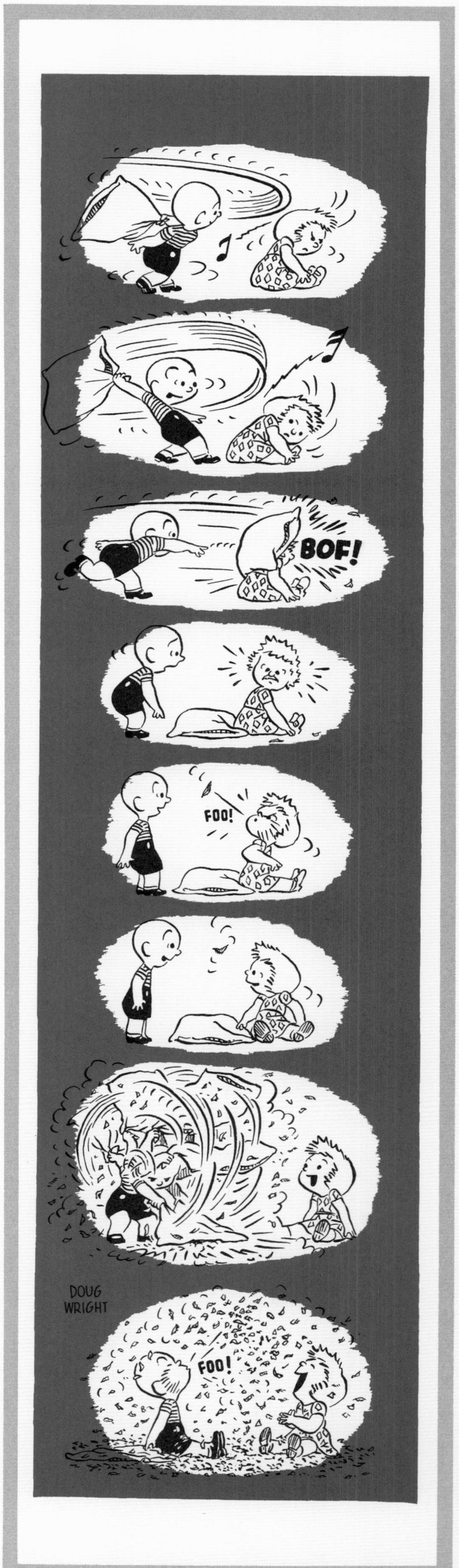
BOF!
FOO!
DOUG WRIGHT
FOO!

March 29, 1952

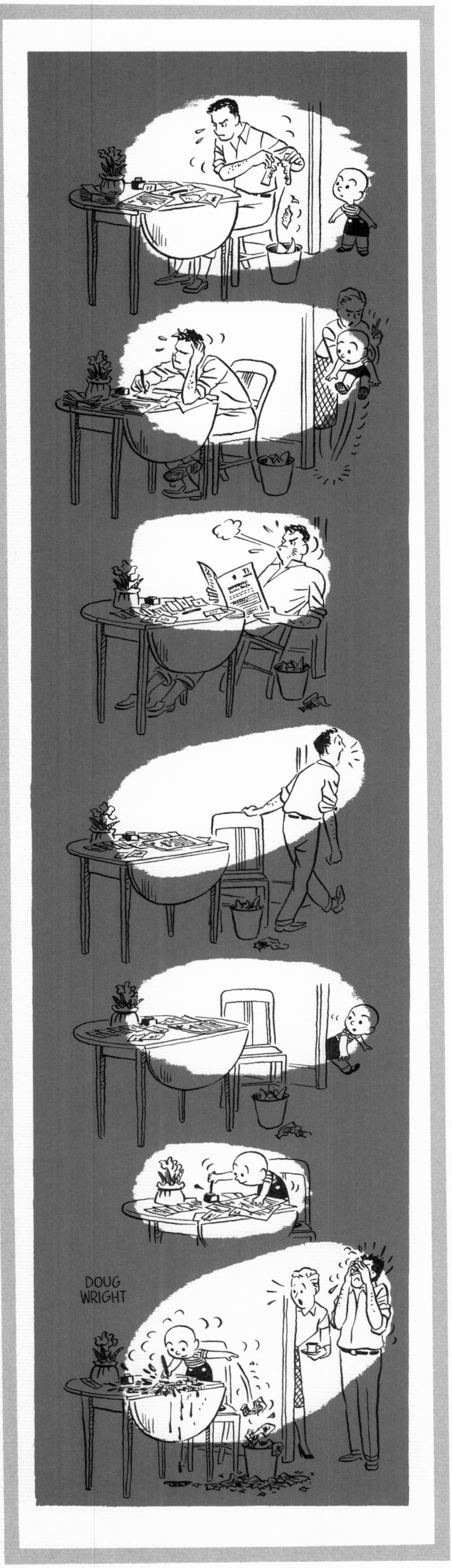
DOUG WRIGHT

April 26, 1952

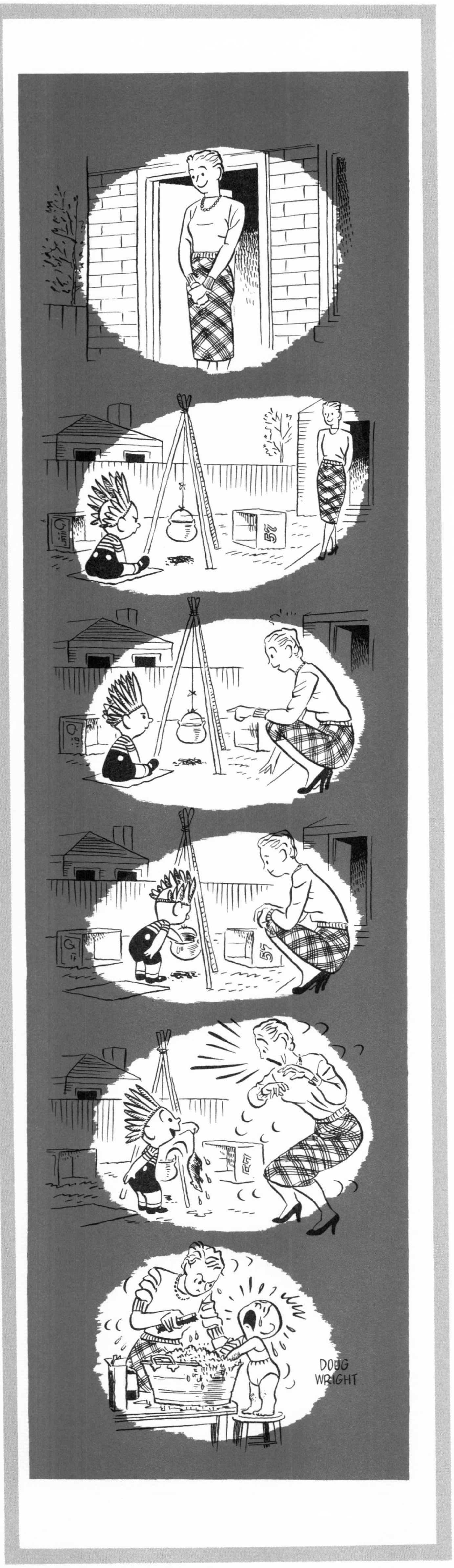
DOUG WRIGHT

May 10, 1952

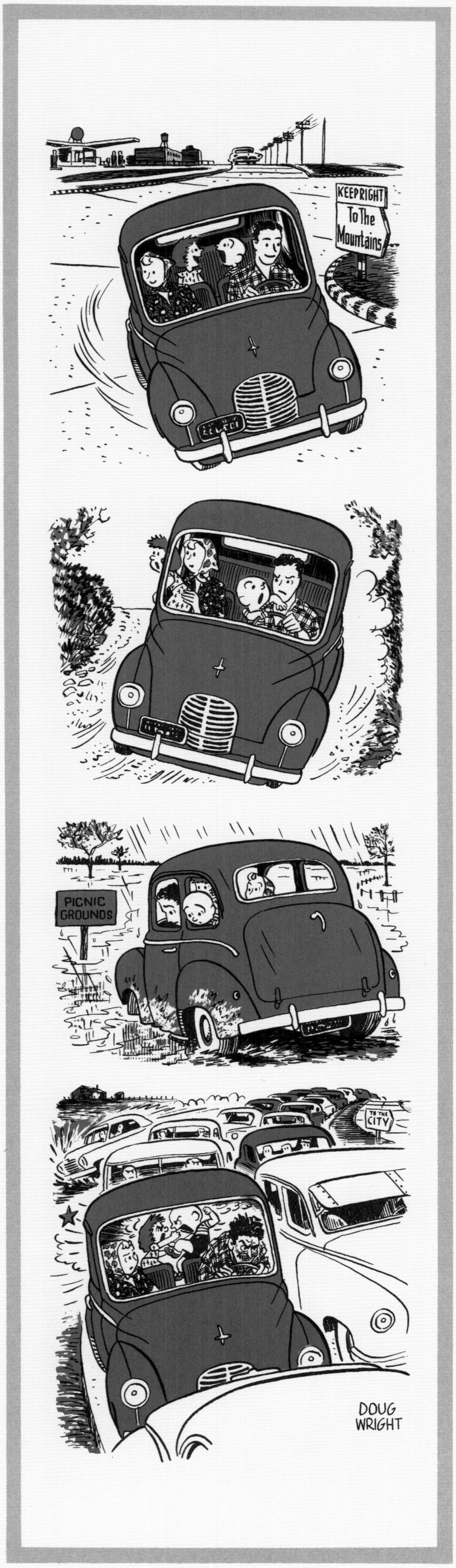
KEEP RIGHT
To The Mountains
PICNIC GROUNDS
TO THE CITY
DOUG WRIGHT

May 24, 1952

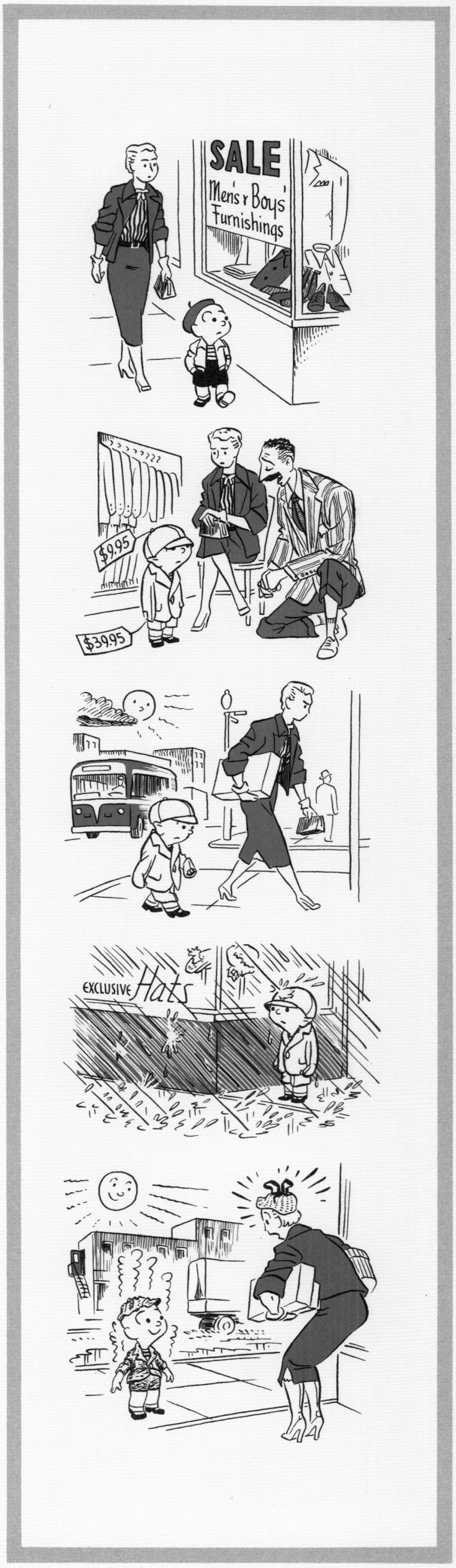
SALE
Men's 'r Boys' Furnishings
$9.95
$39.95
EXCLUSIVE Hats

May 31, 1952

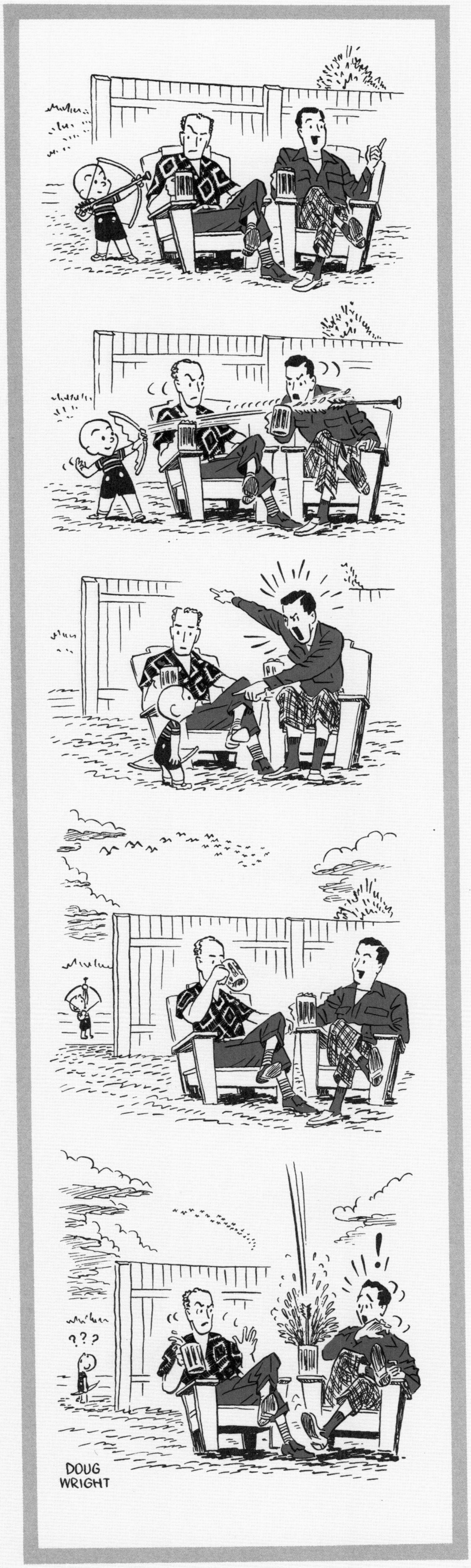
???
!
DOUG
WRIGHT

June 7, 1952

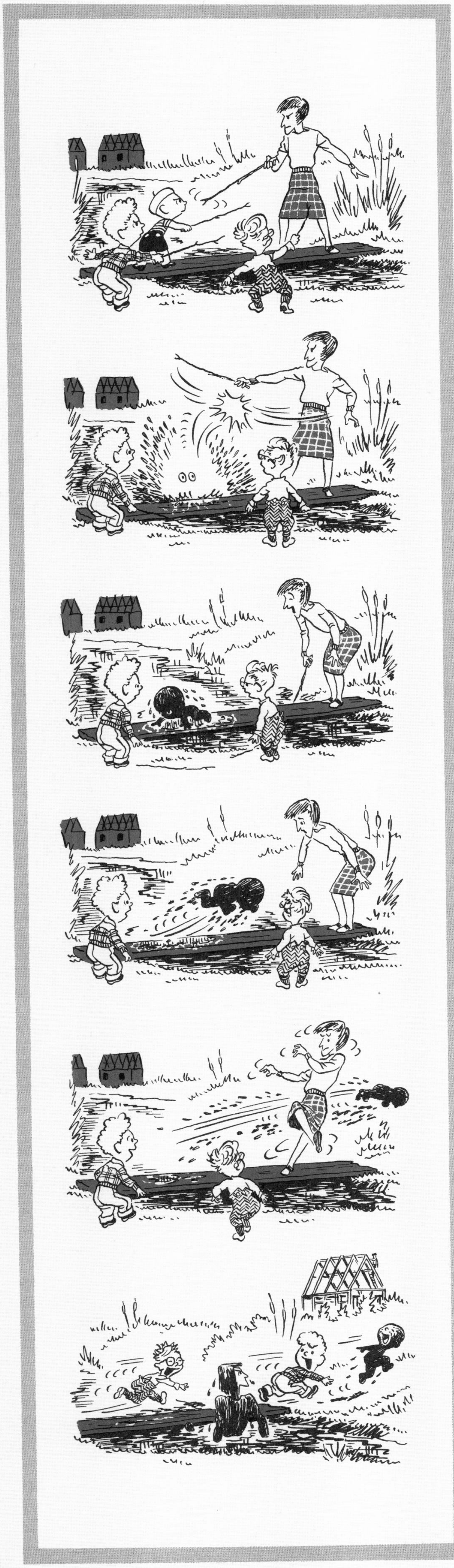

June 14, 1952

This strip never ran. The date was written on the original but another strip appeared that day. Apparently, a drunken babysitter and child didn't fly any better with an editor than it would today.

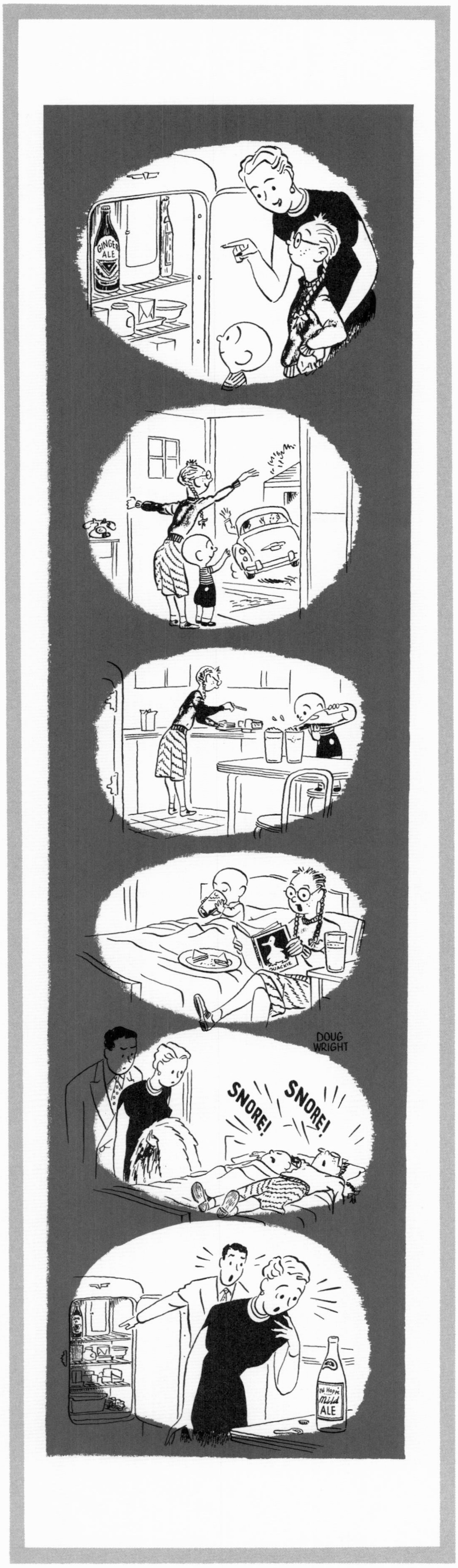
GINGER ALE
DOUG WRIGHT
SNORE!
SNORE!
ALE

July 12, 1952

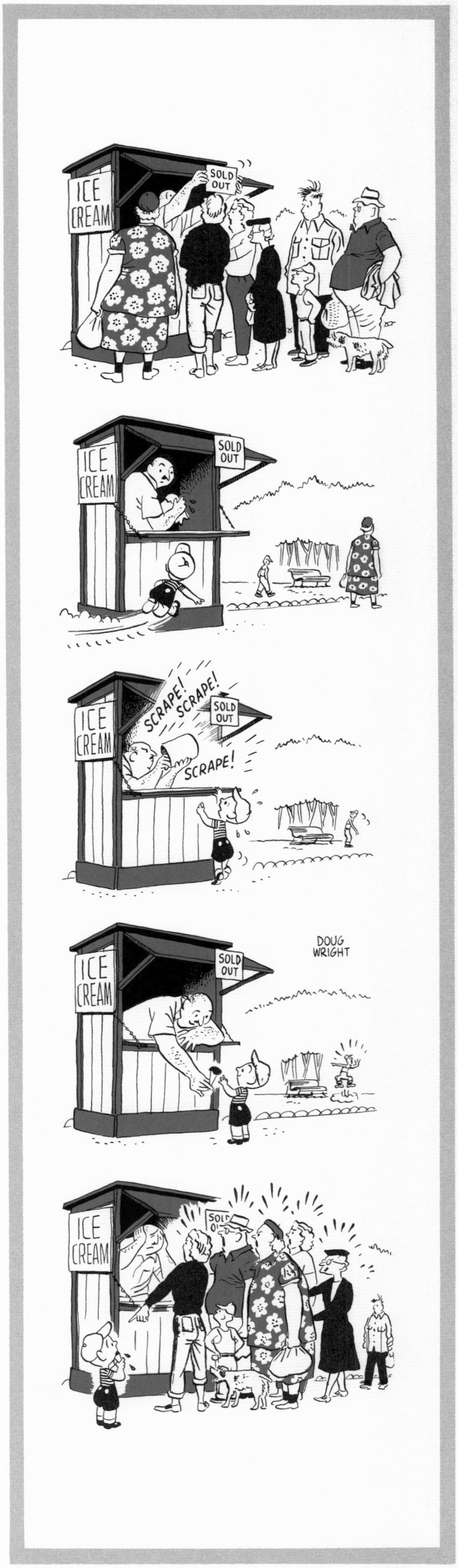
ICE CREAM
SOLD OUT
ICE CREAM
SOLD OUT
ICE CREAM
SCRAPE!
SCRAPE!
SOLD OUT
SCRAPE!
ICE CREAM
SOLD OUT
DOUG WRIGHT
ICE CREAM

July 19, 1952

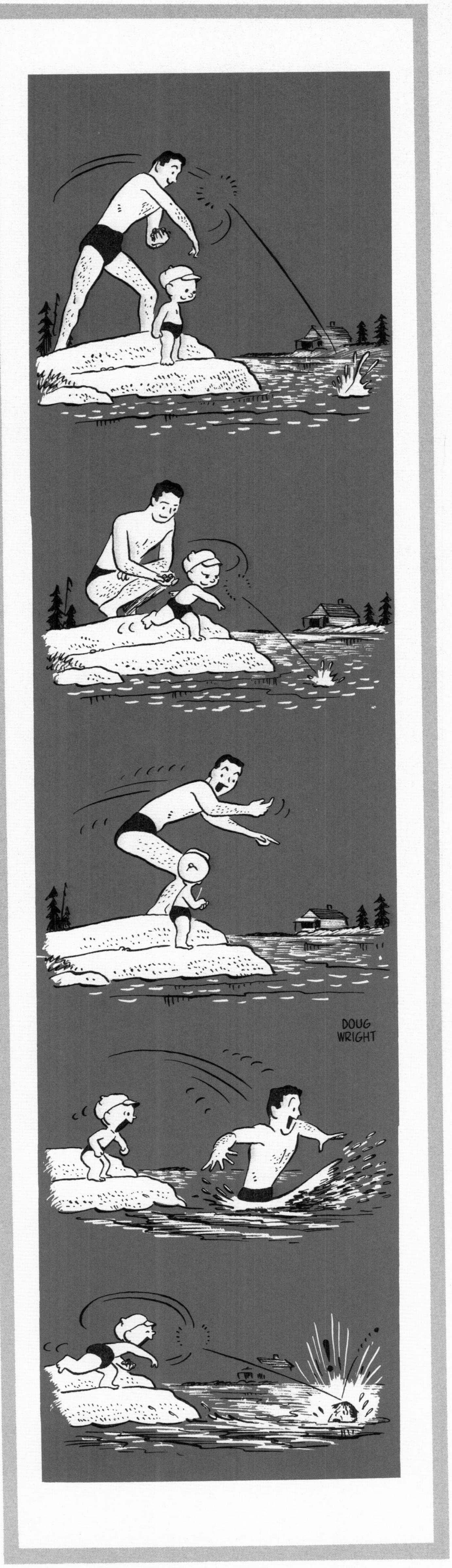
DOUG
WRIGHT

August 2, 1952

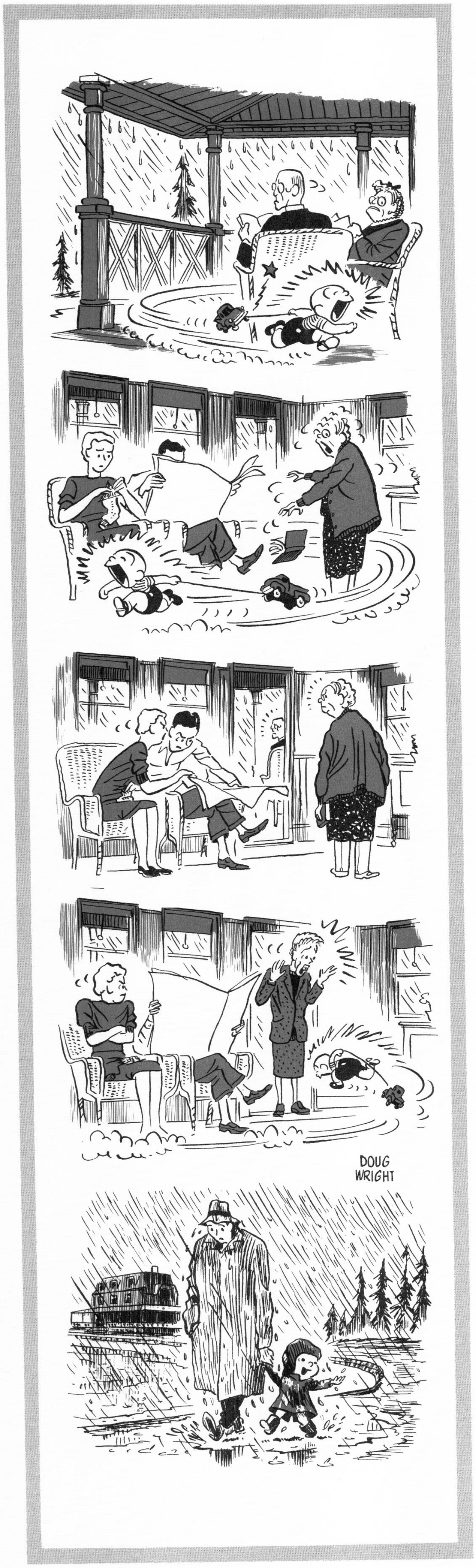
DOUG
WRIGHT

August 9, 1952

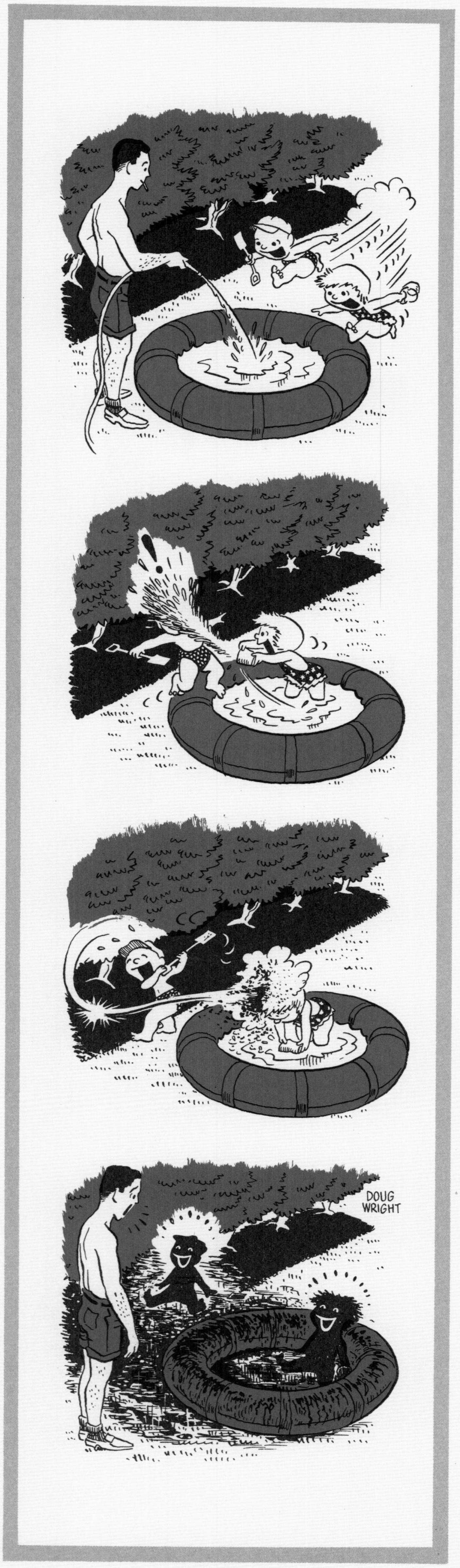
DOUG WRIGHT

August 16, 1952

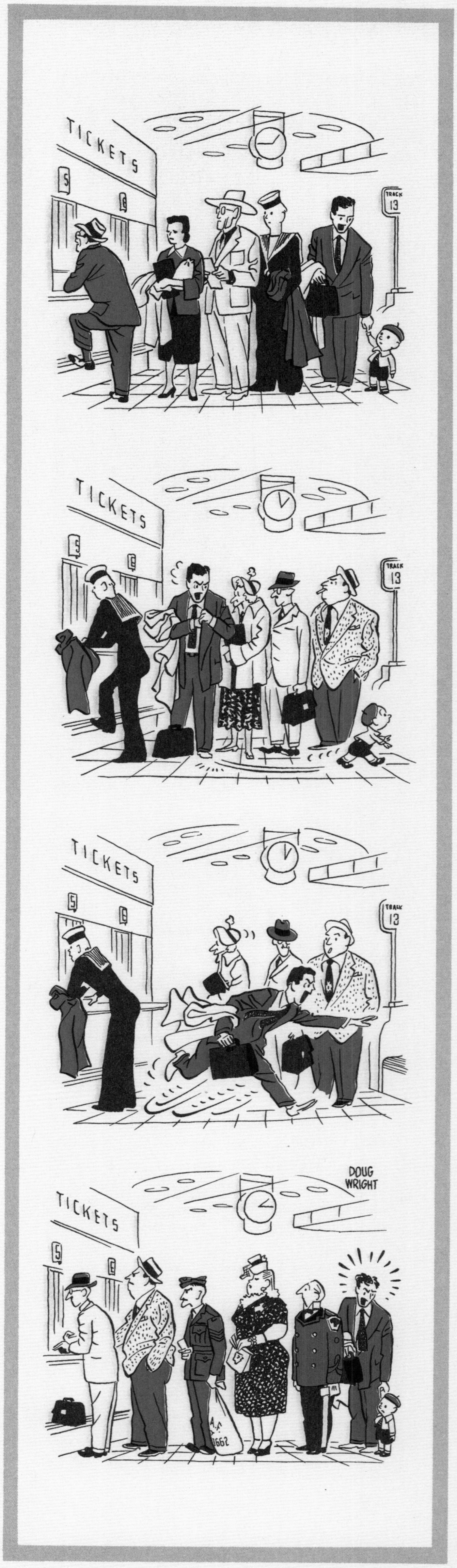
TICKETS
TRACK
13
DOUG WRIGHT

August 23, 1952

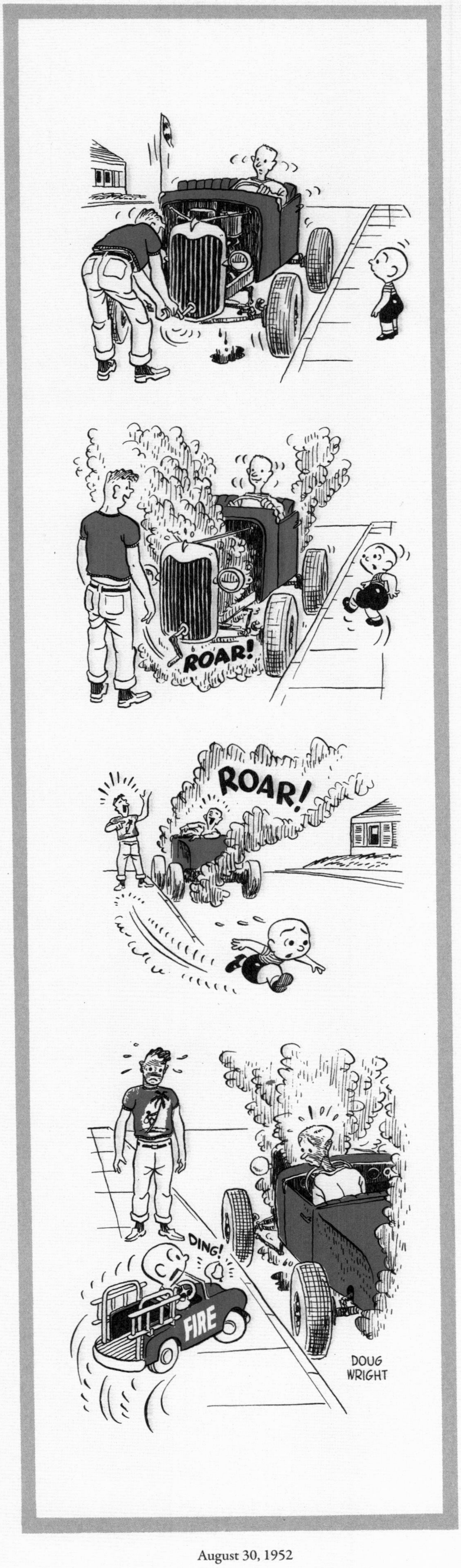
ROAR!
ROAR!
DING!
FIRE
DOUG WRIGHT

August 30, 1952

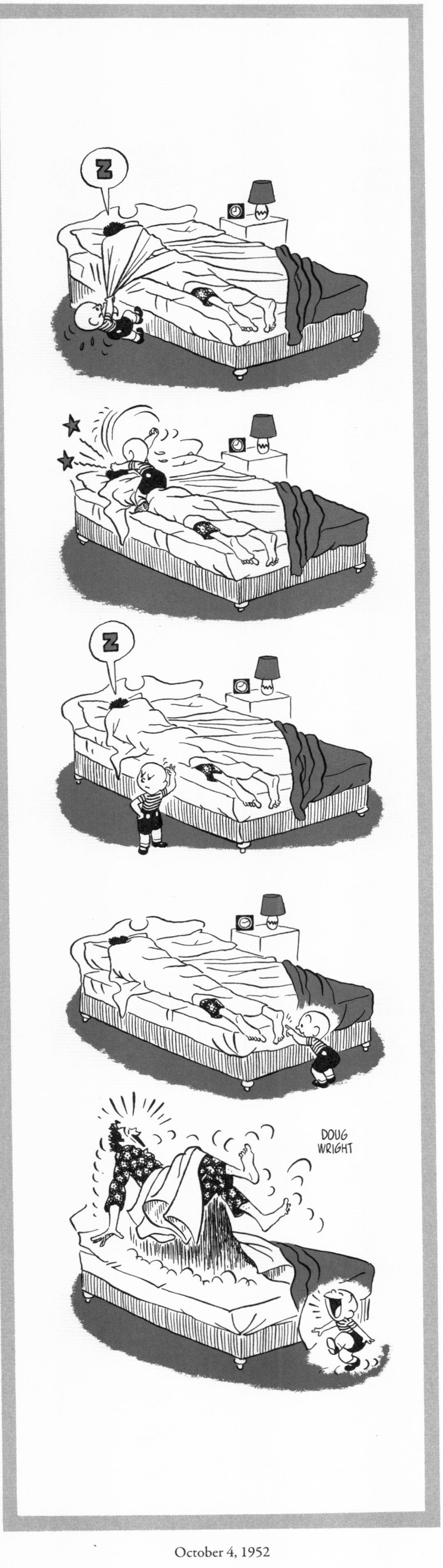
Z
Z
DOUG WRIGHT

October 4, 1952

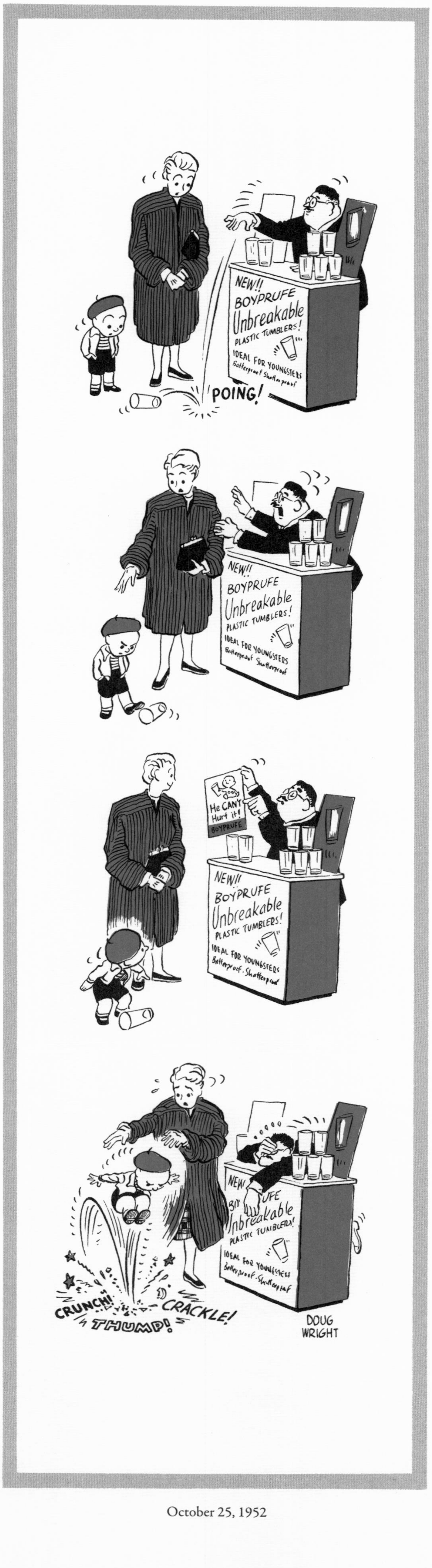

NEW!! BOYPRUFE Unbreakable PLASTIC TUMBLERS!
IDEAL FOR YOUNGSTERS
POING!
He CAN'T Hurt it! BOYPRUFE
CRUNCH! THUMP! CRACKLE!
DOUG WRIGHT

October 25, 1952

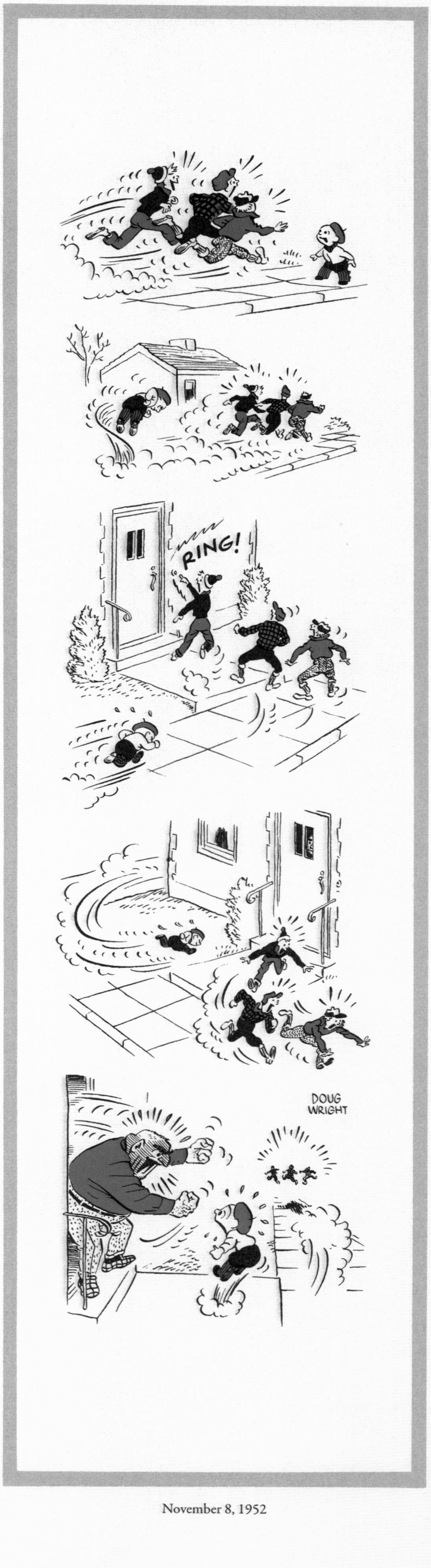

RING!
DOUG WRIGHT

November 8, 1952

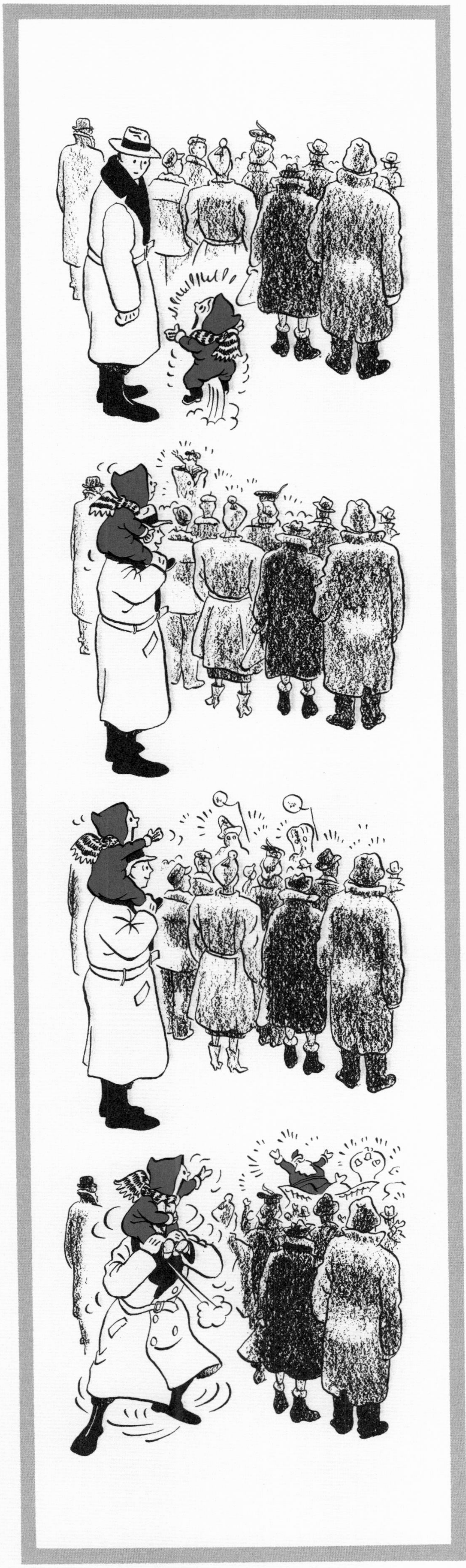

November 29, 1952

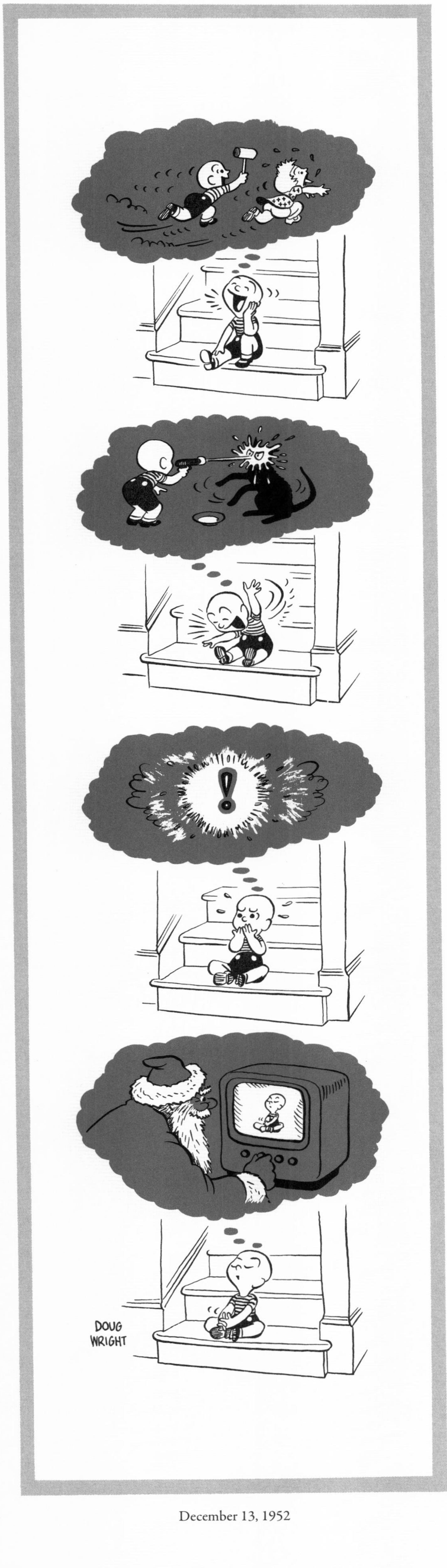
DOUG
WRIGHT

December 13, 1952

NIPPER (who knows how it feels to be a bad boy) GETS THE CHRISTMAS SPIRIT ...   by Doug Wright

December 20, 1952

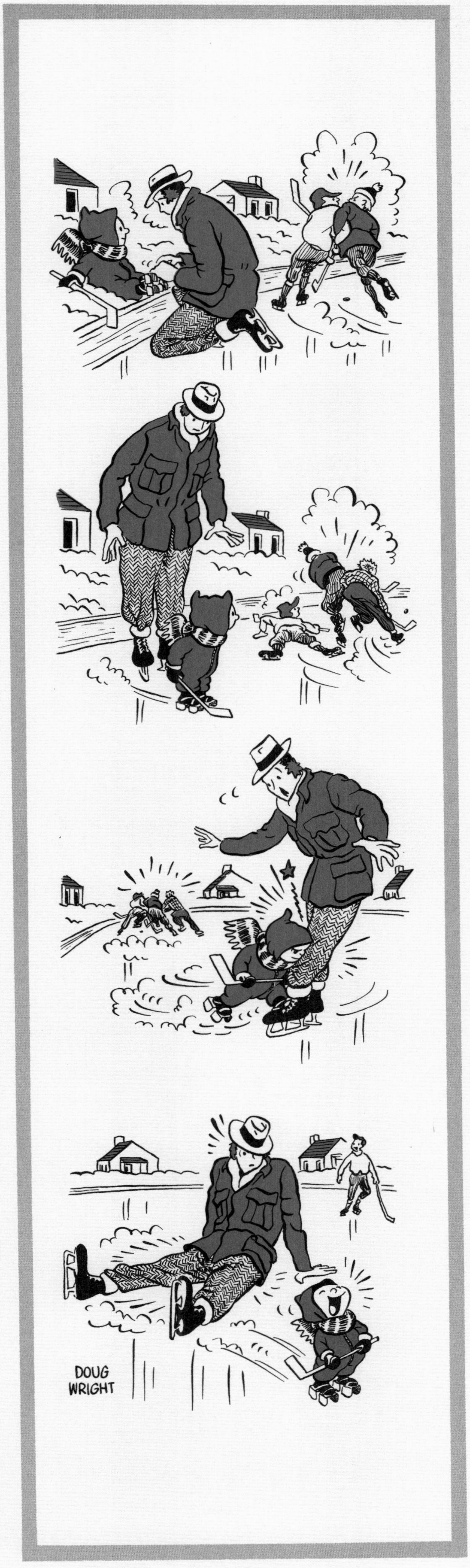
DOUG
WRIGHT

January 3, 1953

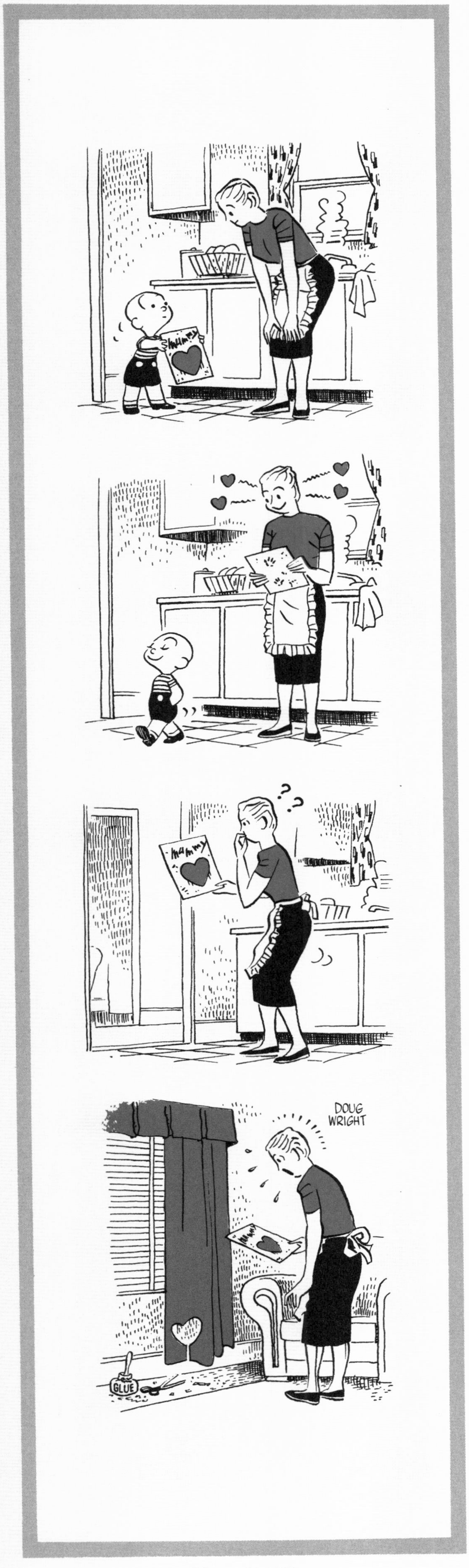
DOUG
WRIGHT
GLUE

February 21, 1953

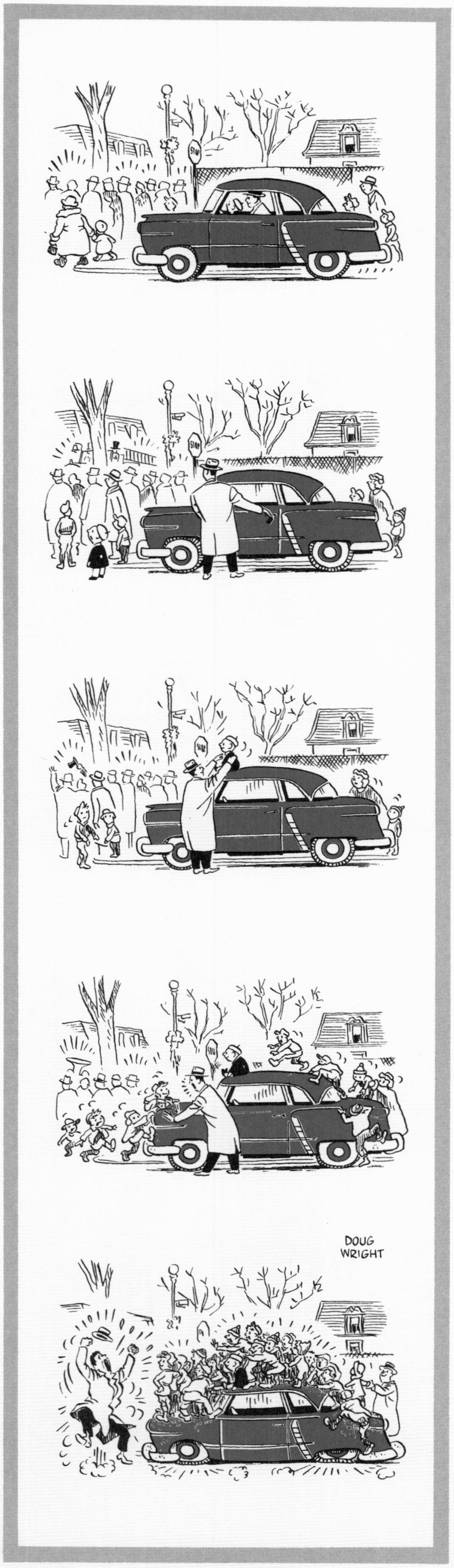
DOUG WRIGHT

March 14, 1953

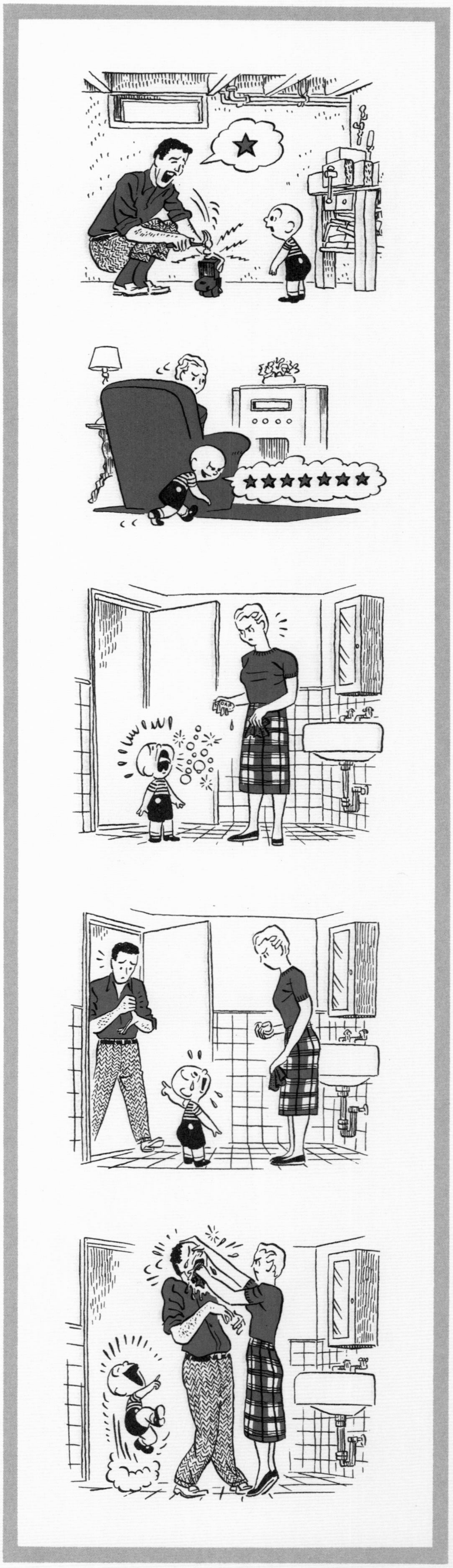

March 21, 1953

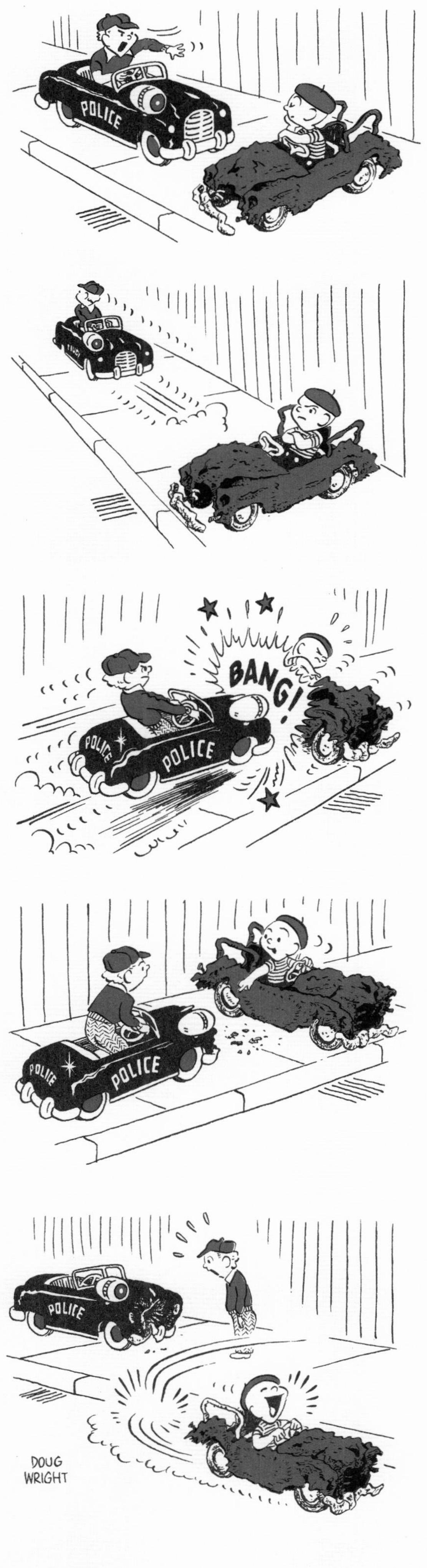
POLICE
BANG!
POLICE
POLICE
POLICE
POLICE
DOUG WRIGHT
April 25, 1953

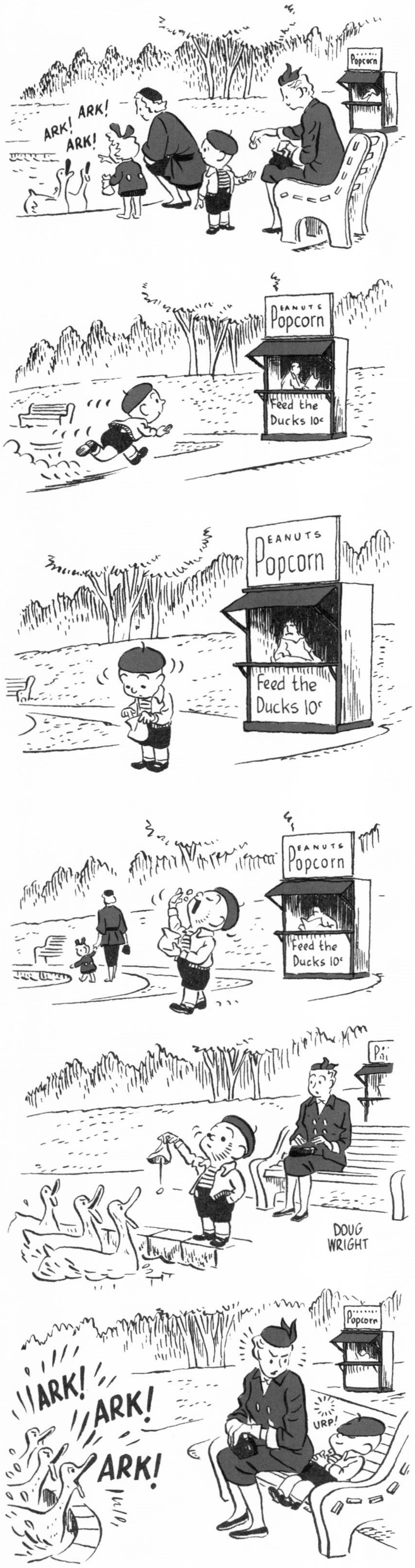
ARK! ARK!
ARK!
Popcorn
PEANUTS
Popcorn
Feed the
Ducks 10¢
PEANUTS
Popcorn
Feed the
Ducks 10¢
PEANUTS
Popcorn
Feed the
Ducks 10¢
DOUG WRIGHT
Popcorn
ARK!
ARK!
ARK!
URP!
May 2, 1953

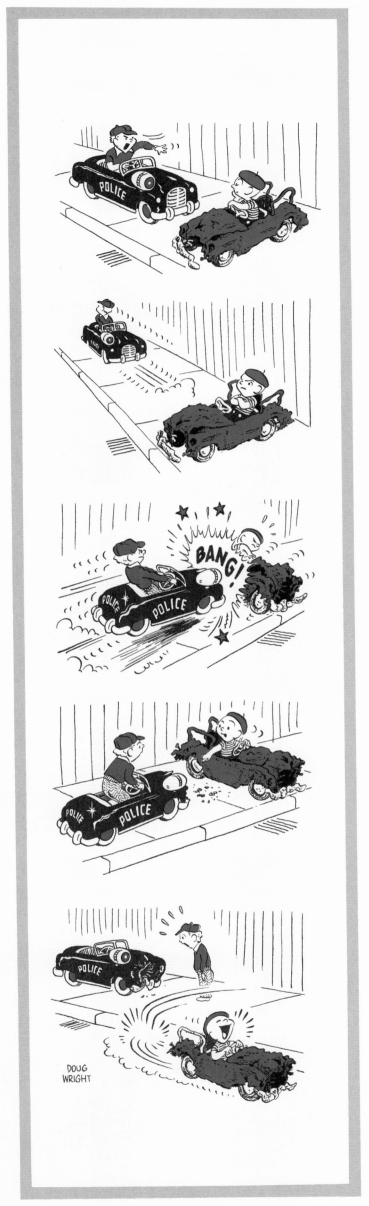

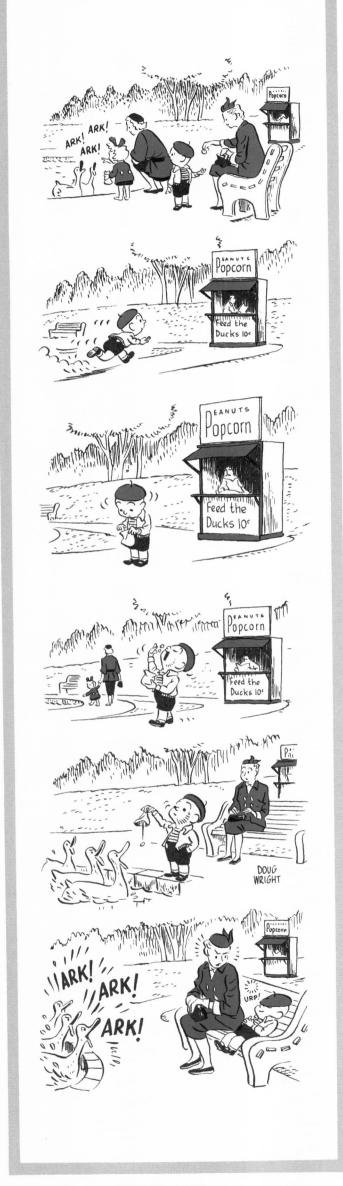

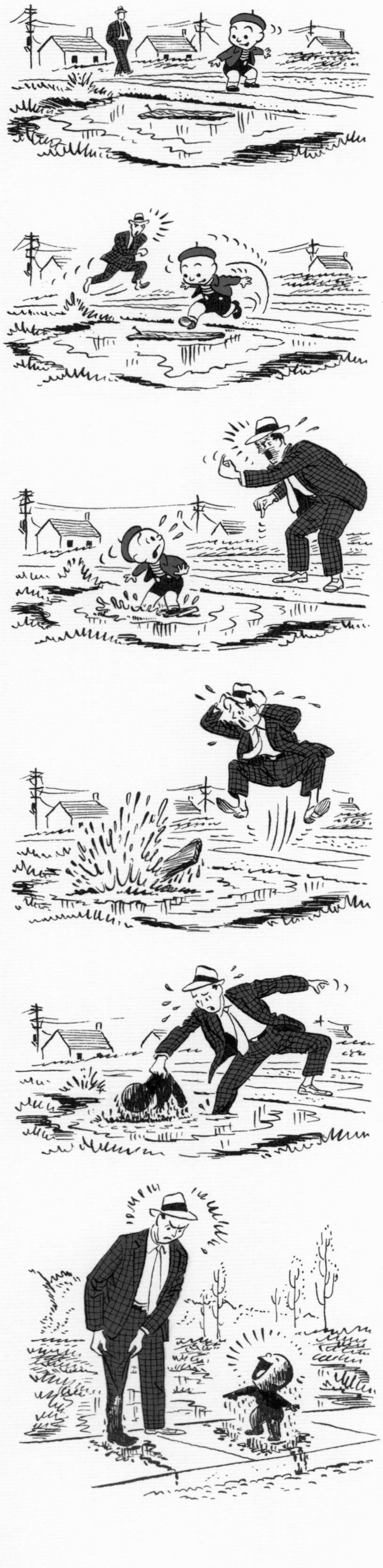

May 23, 1953

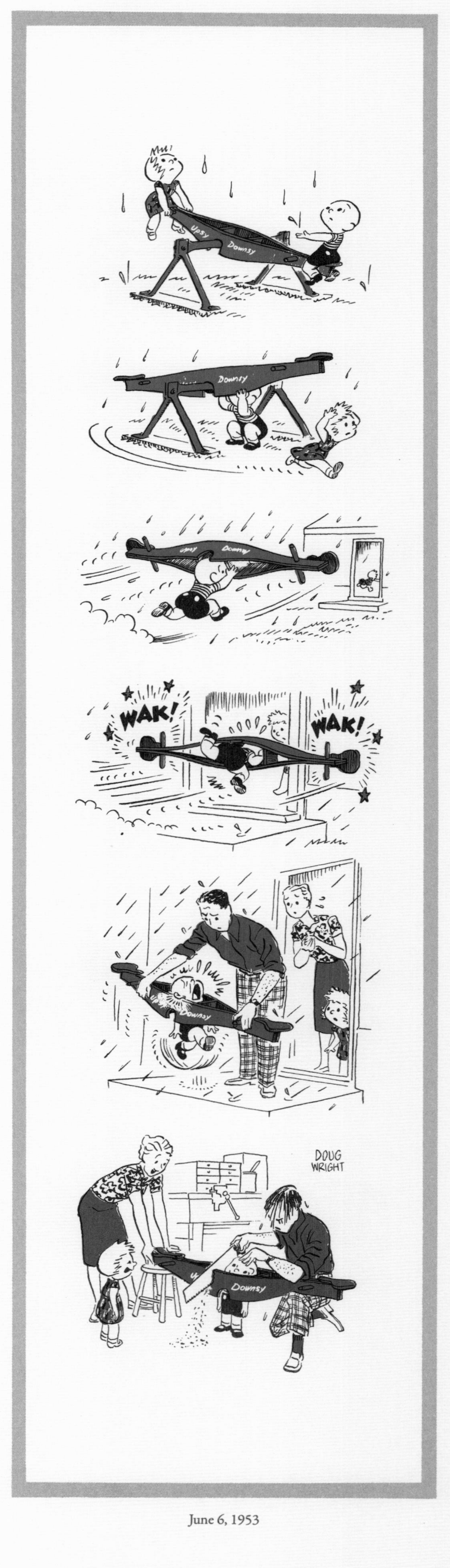
Upsy
Downsy
Downsy
Upsy
Downsy
WAK!
WAK!
Downsy
DOUG WRIGHT
Downsy

June 6, 1953

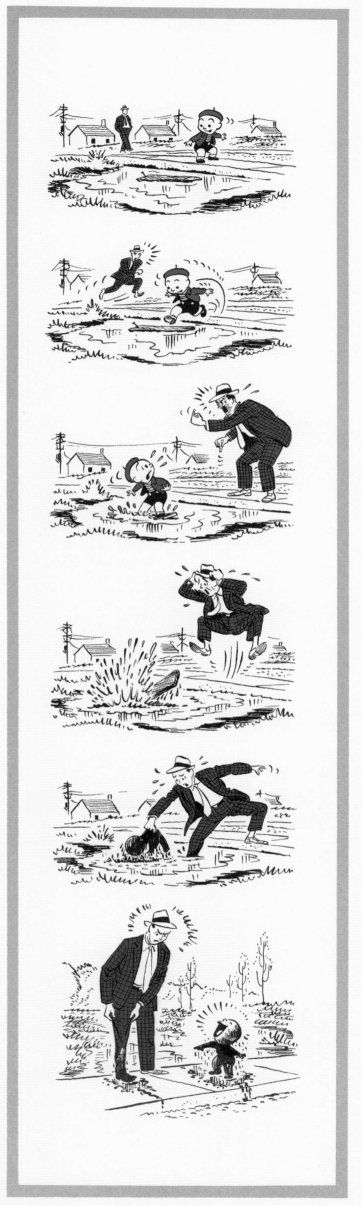

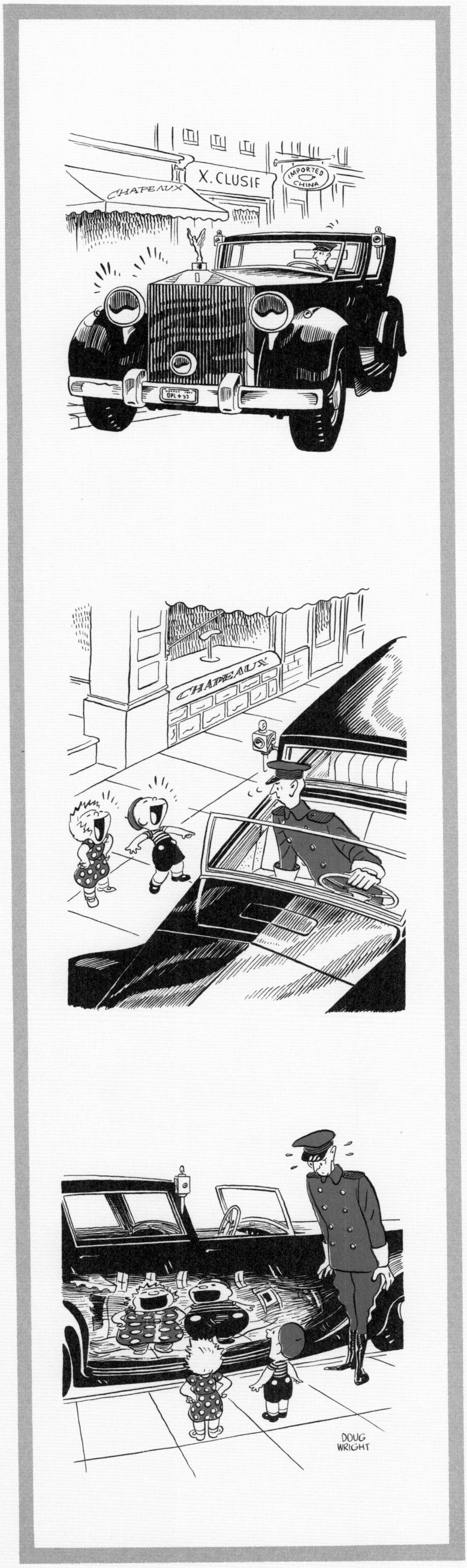
X. CLUSIF
IMPORTED CHINA
CHAPEAUX
CHAPEAUX
DOUG WRIGHT

July 18, 1953

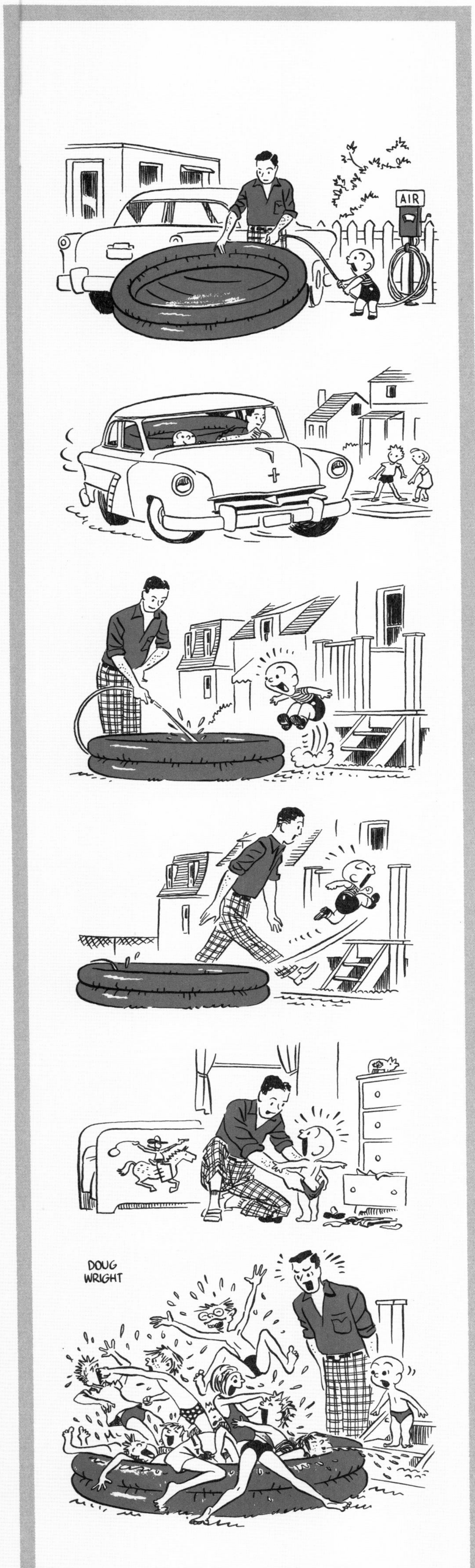
AIR
DOUG WRIGHT

July 25, 1953

August 8, 1953

August 29, 1953

The first appearance of the famous hot rod pedal-car.

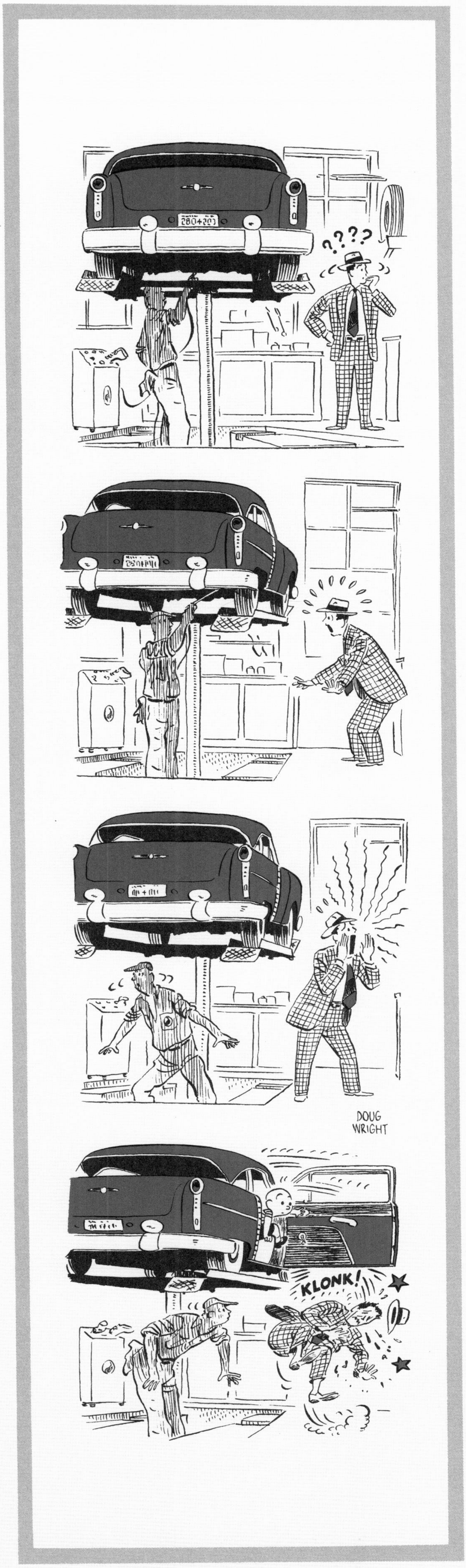
????
DOUG WRIGHT
KLONK!

September 19, 1953

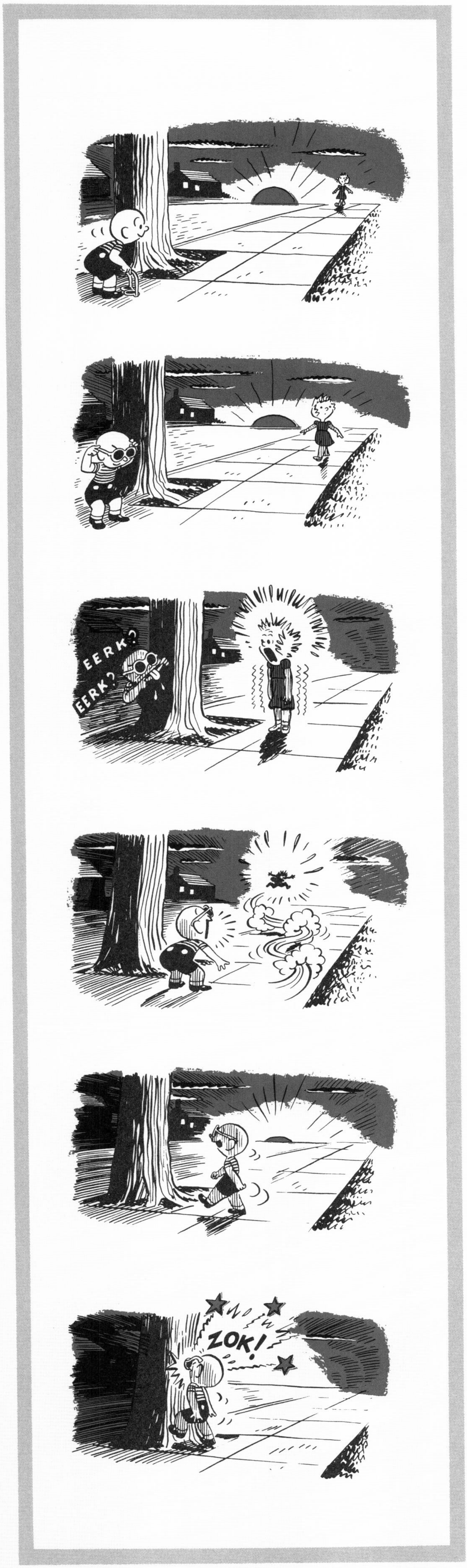
EERK?
EERK?
ZOK!

September 26, 1953

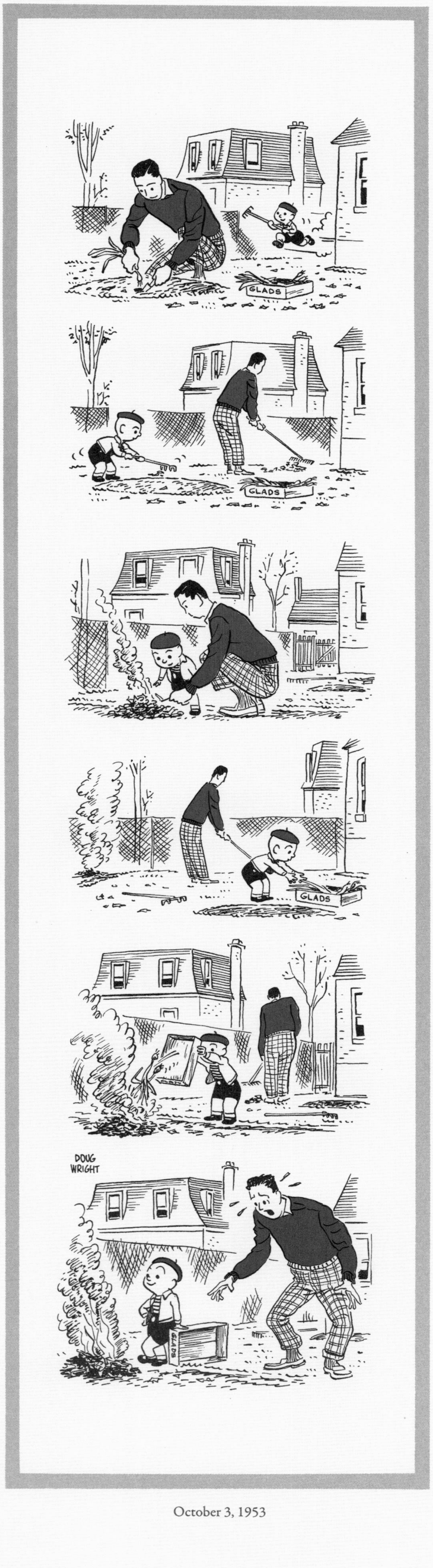
GLADS
GLADS
GLADS
DOUG WRIGHT
GLADS

October 3, 1953

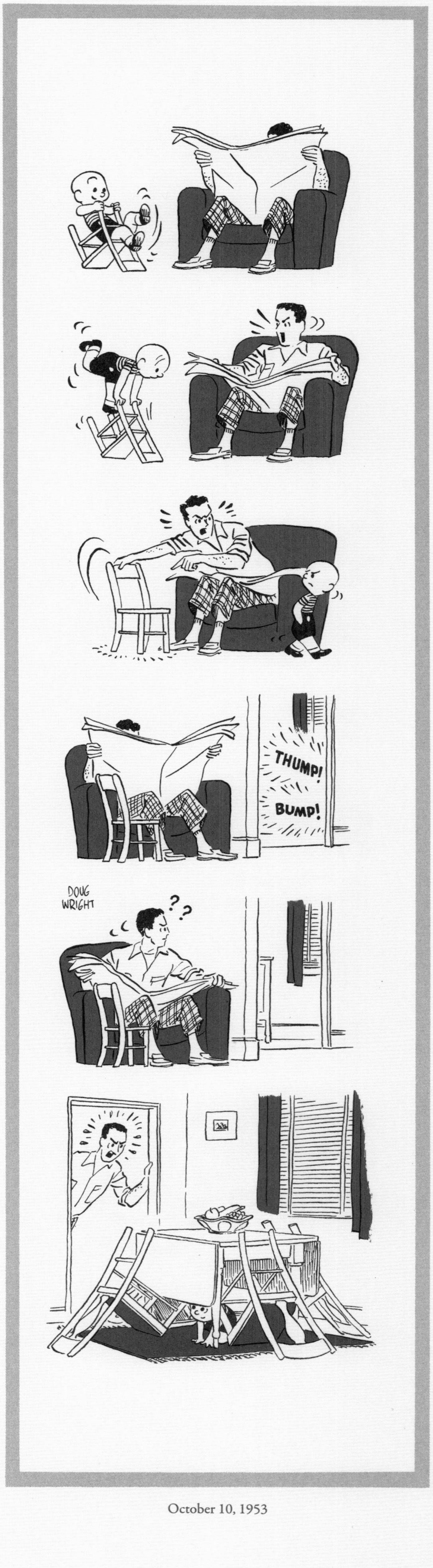
THUMP!
BUMP!
DOUG WRIGHT
??

October 10, 1953

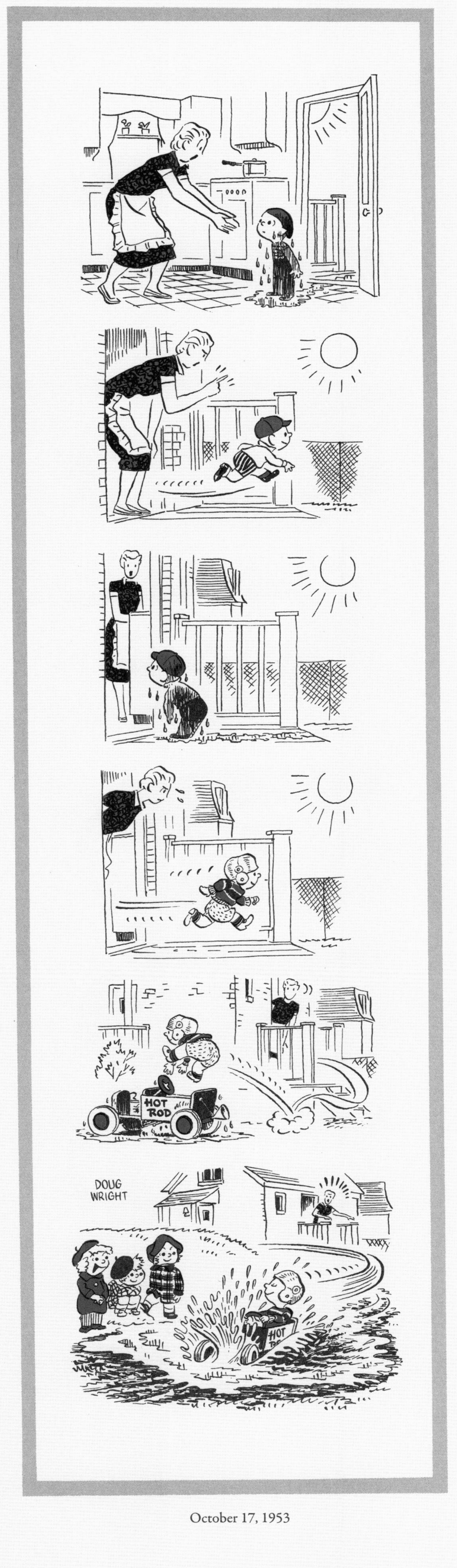
HOT
ROD
DOUG
WRIGHT
HOT

October 17, 1953

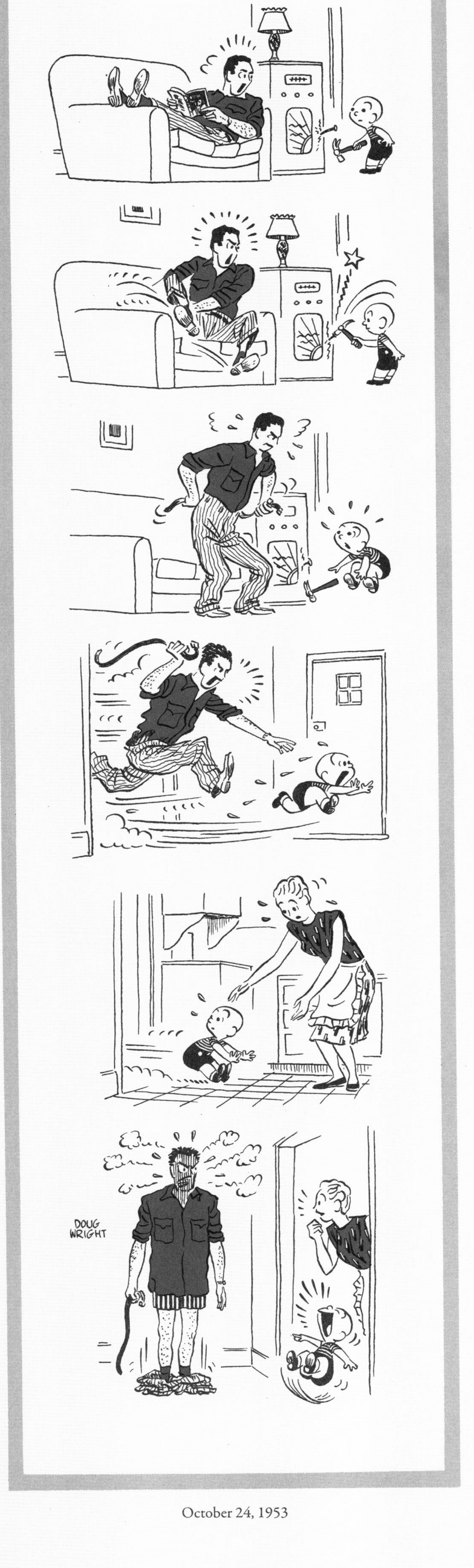
DOUG
WRIGHT

October 24, 1953

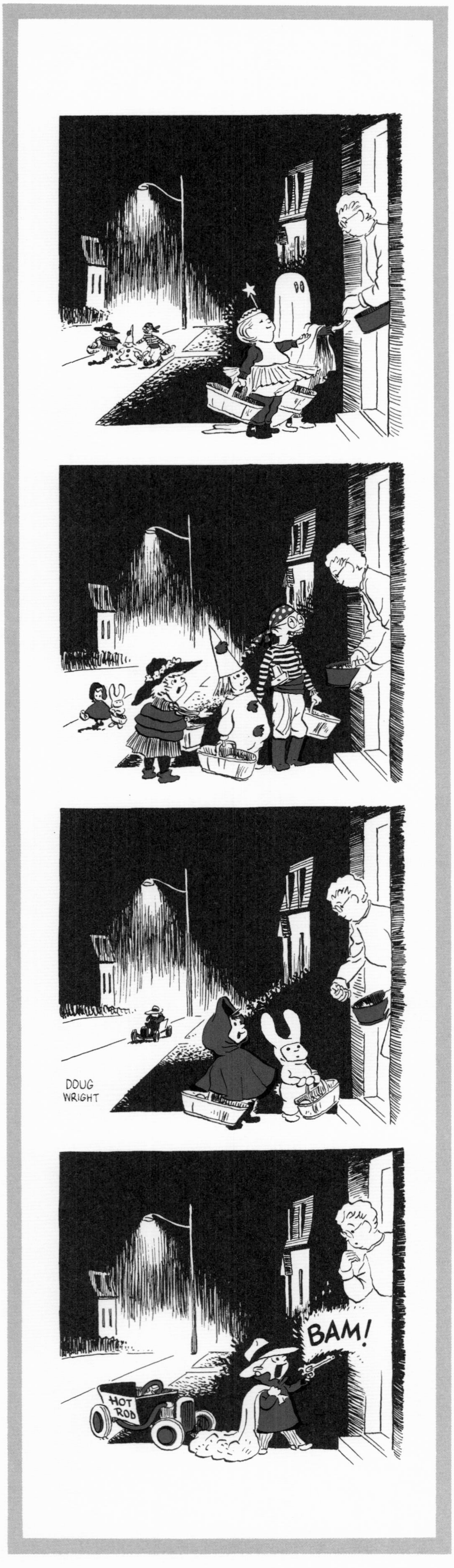
DOUG WRIGHT
BAM!
HOT ROD

October 31, 1953

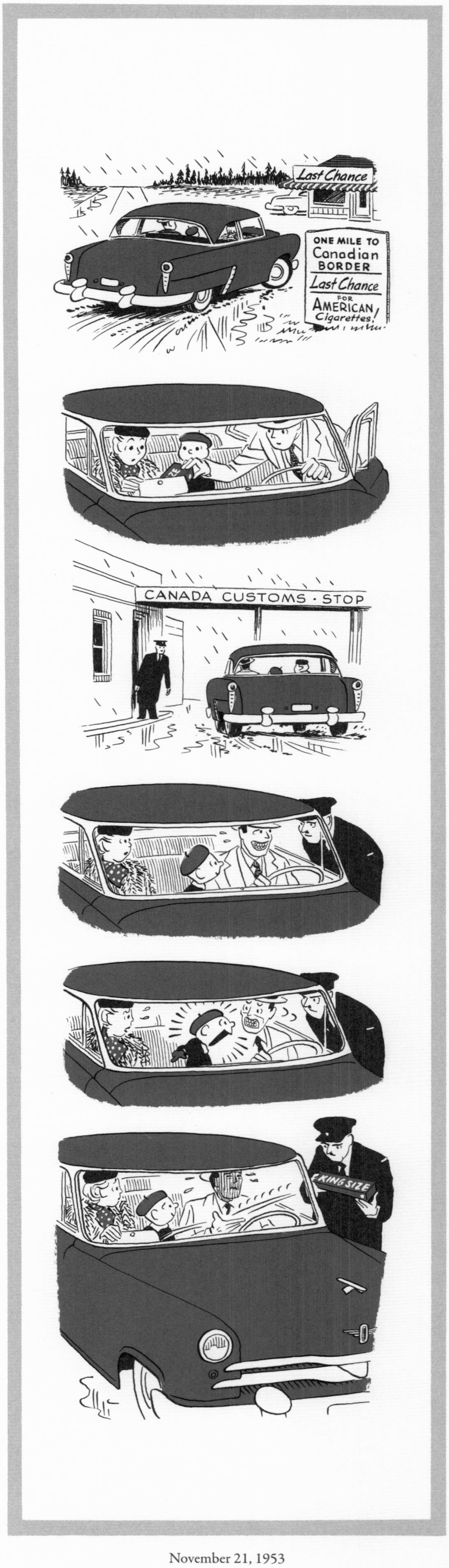
Last Chance
ONE MILE TO Canadian BORDER
Last Chance FOR AMERICAN Cigarettes!
CANADA CUSTOMS · STOP
KING SIZE

November 21, 1953

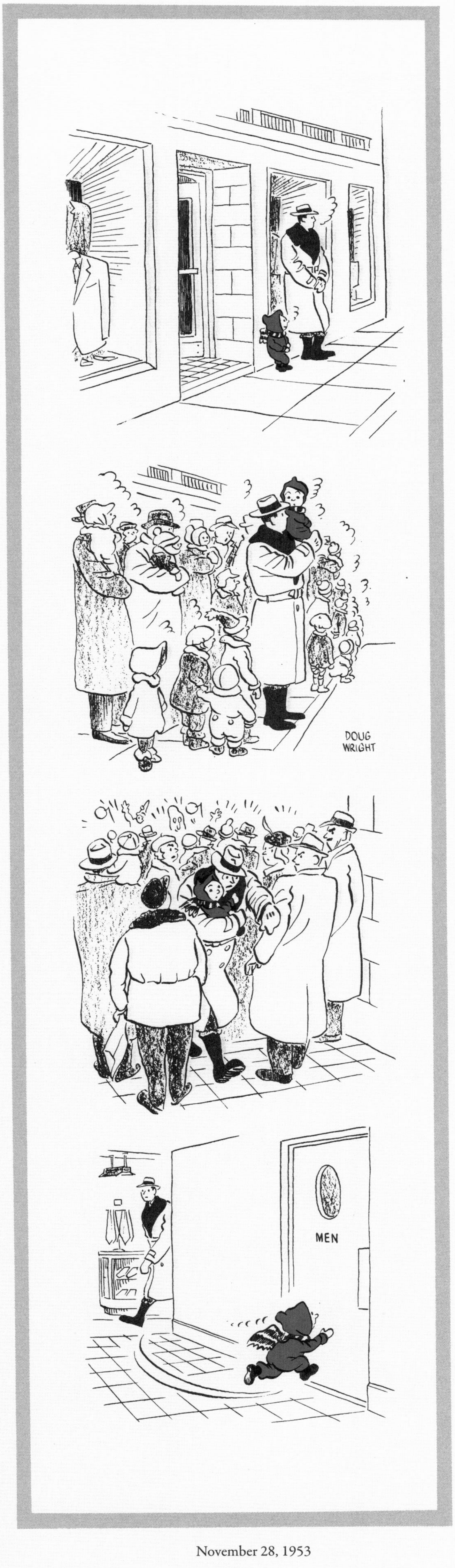
DOUG WRIGHT
MEN

November 28, 1953

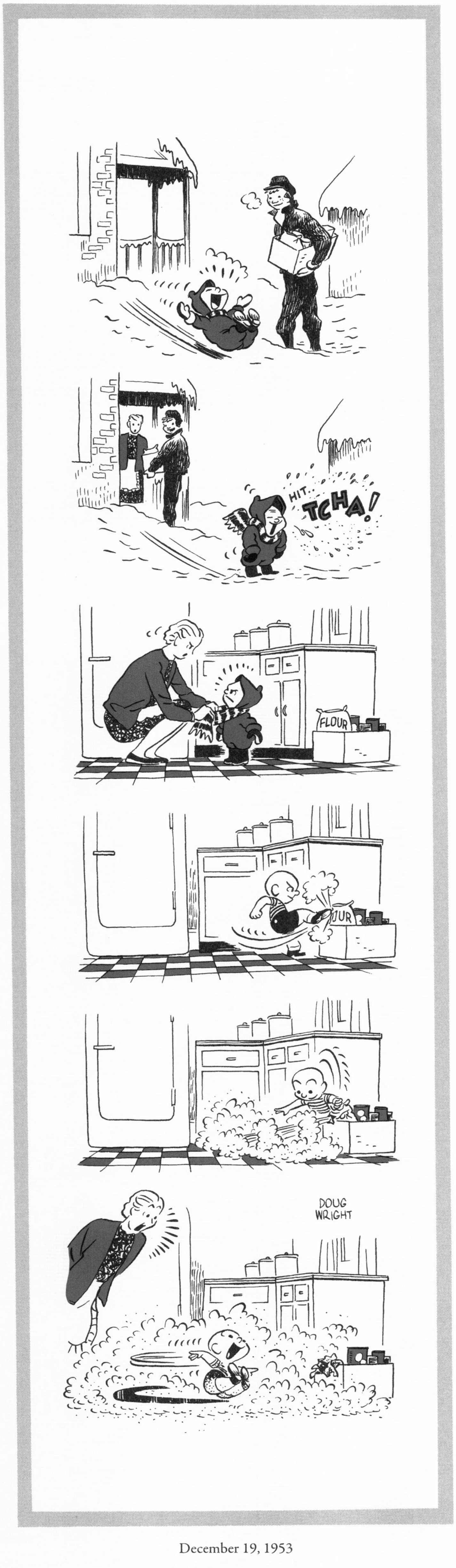
HIT.
TCHA!
FLOUR
DOUG WRIGHT

December 19, 1953

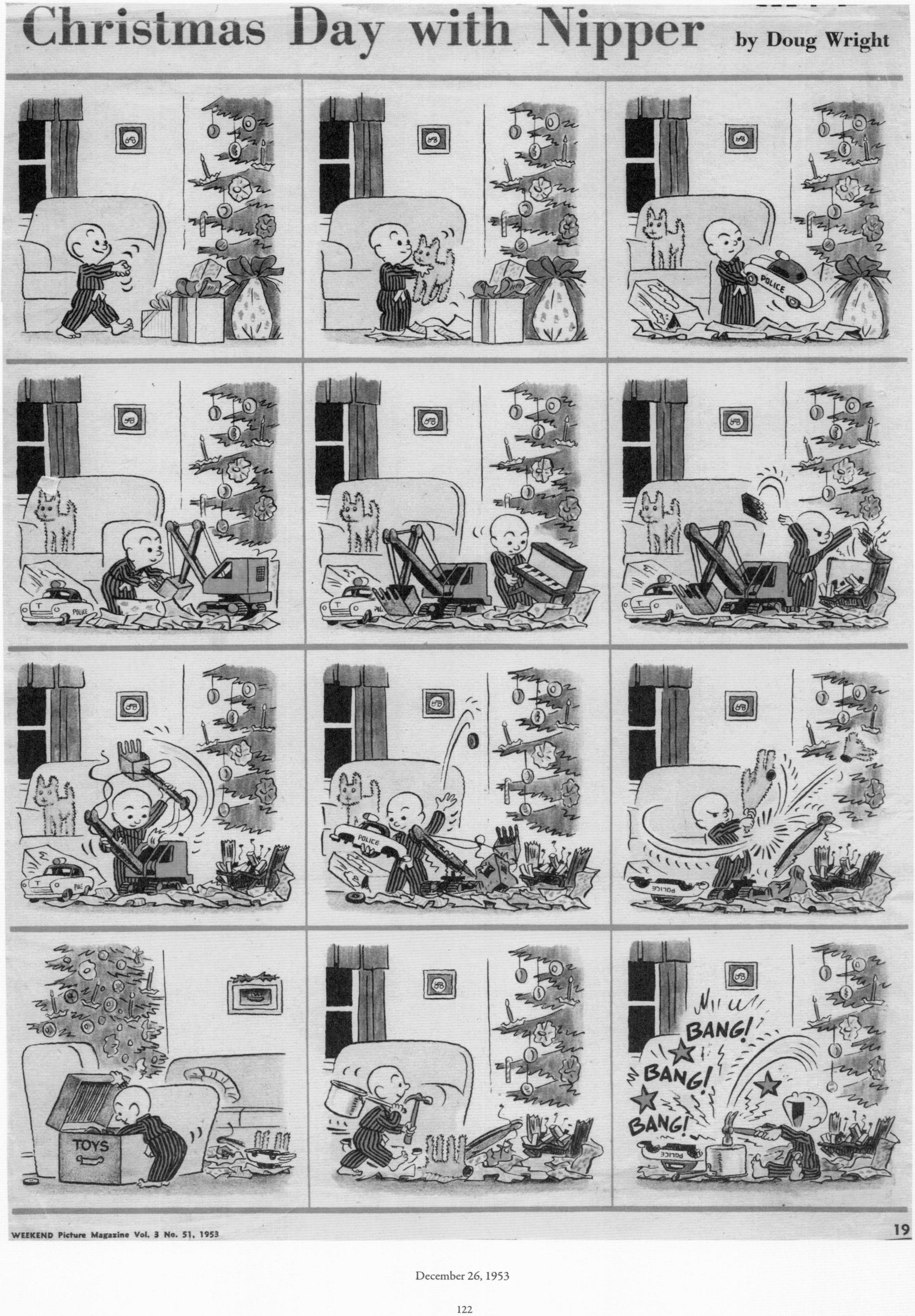

Christmas Day with Nipper
by Doug Wright
POLICE
TOYS
BANG!
BANG!
BANG!
WEEKEND Picture Magazine Vol. 3 No. 51, 1953
19

December 26, 1953

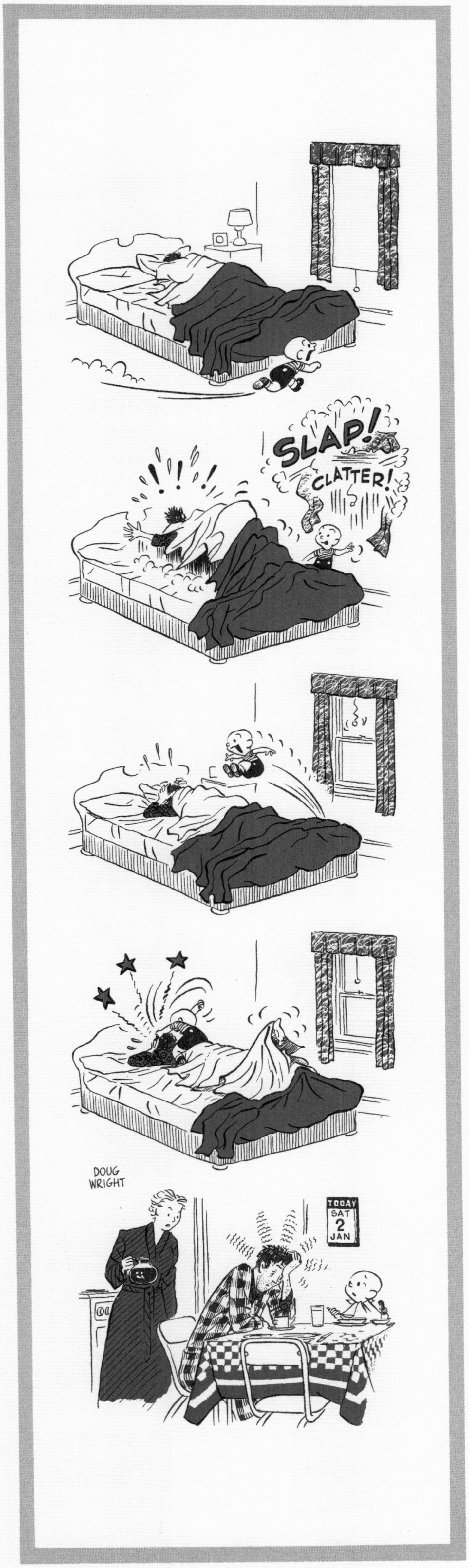
SLAP!
CLATTER!
DOUG WRIGHT
TODAY SAT 2 JAN

January 2, 1954

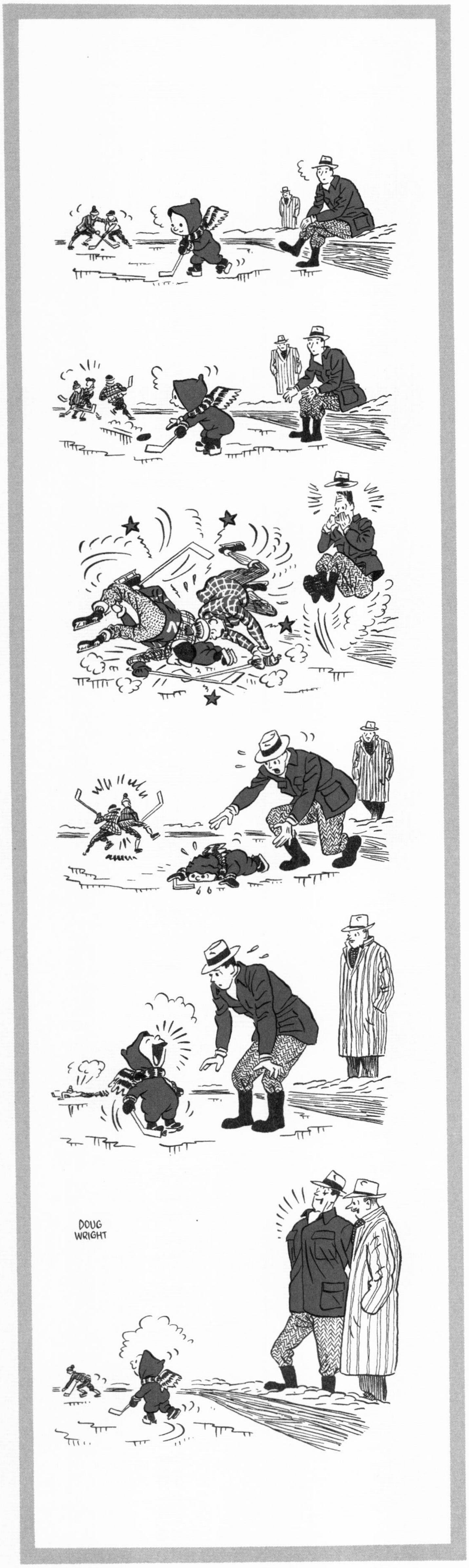
DOUG WRIGHT

January 16, 1954

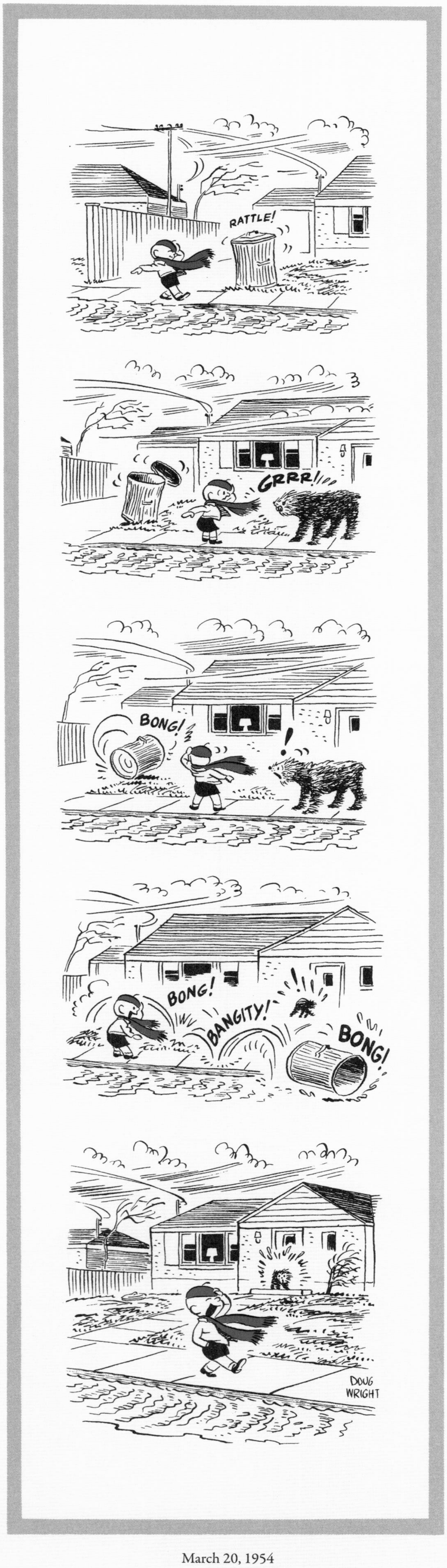
RATTLE!
GRRR!
BONG!
!
BONG!
BANGITY!
!
BONG!
DOUG
WRIGHT

March 20, 1954

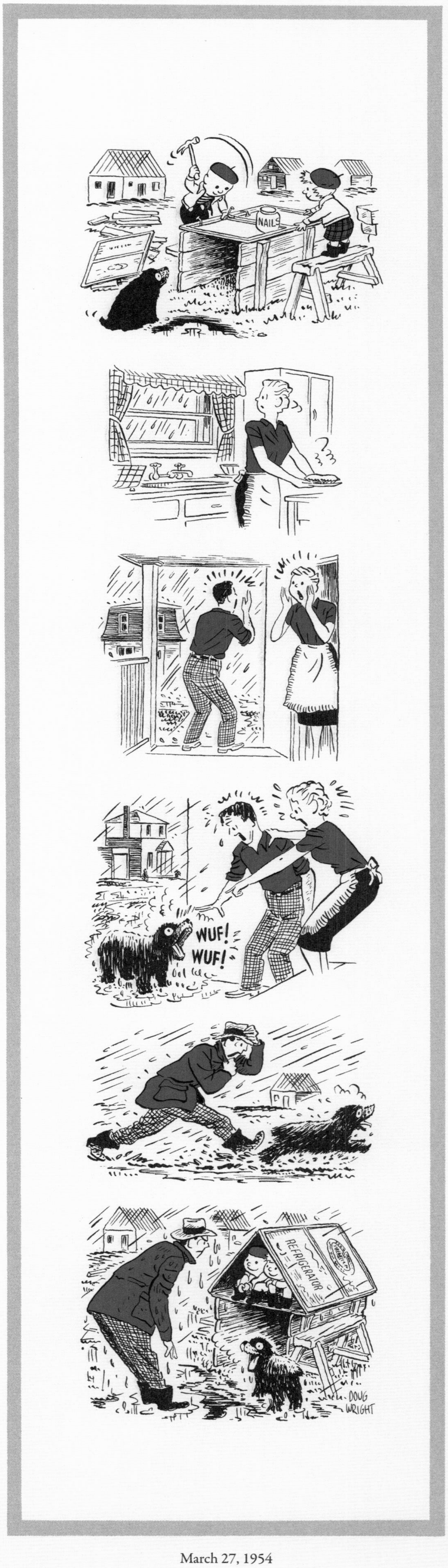
NAILS
WUF!
WUF!
REFRIGERATOR
DOUG
WRIGHT

March 27, 1954

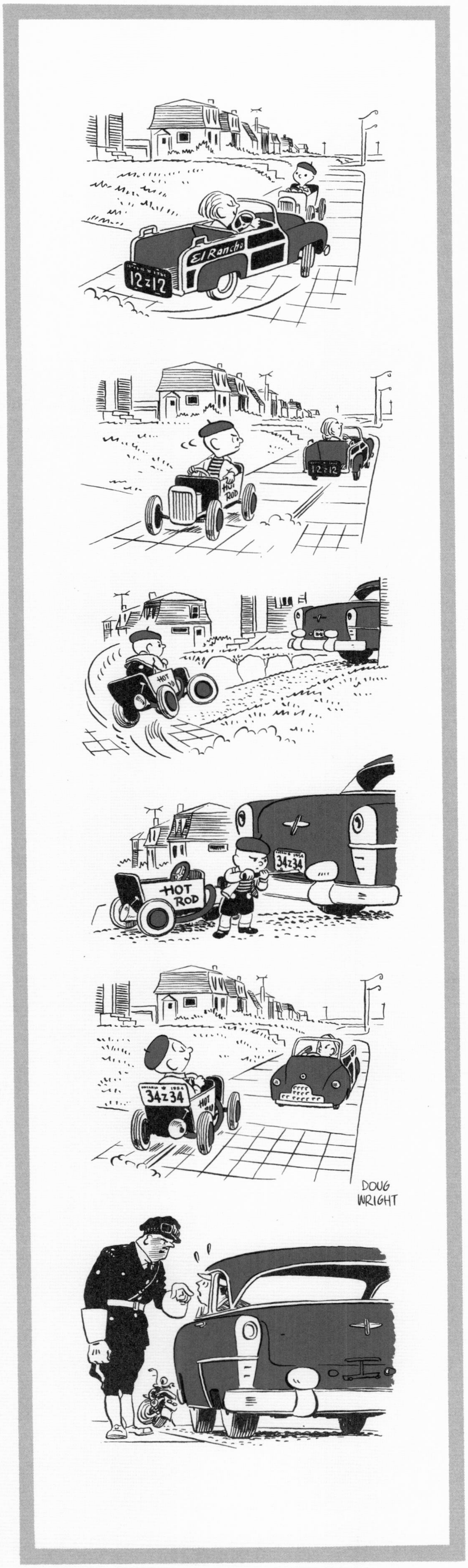
El Rancho
12z12
HOT ROD
12z12
HOT
HOT ROD
34z34
34z34
HOT ROD
DOUG WRIGHT

April 3, 1954

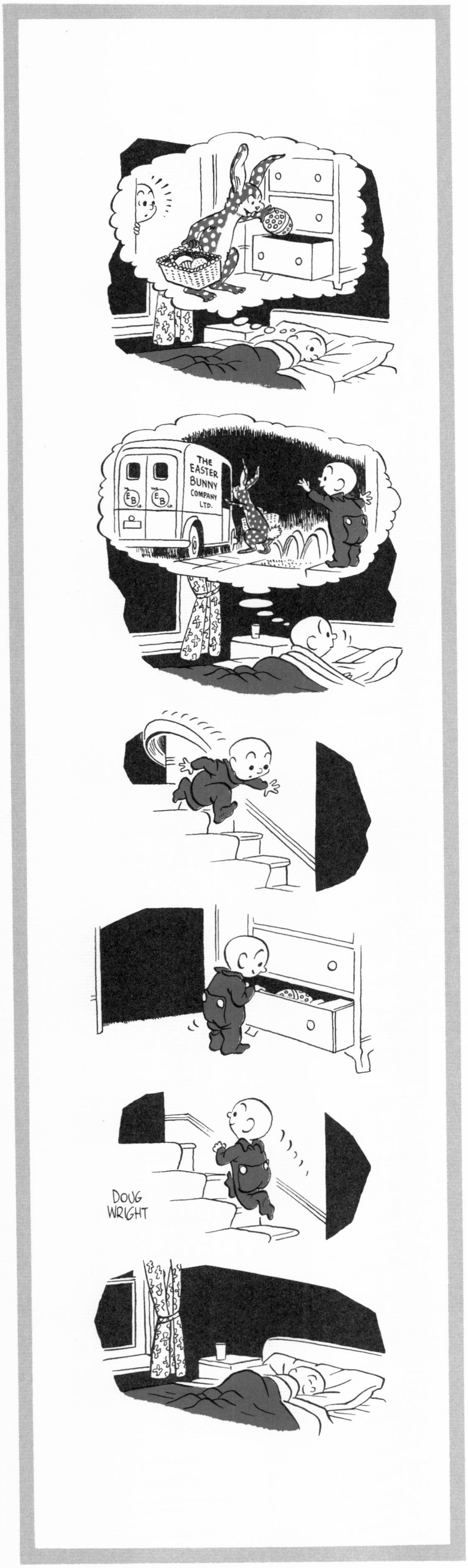
THE EASTER BUNNY COMPANY LTD.
EB
EB
DOUG WRIGHT

April 17, 1954

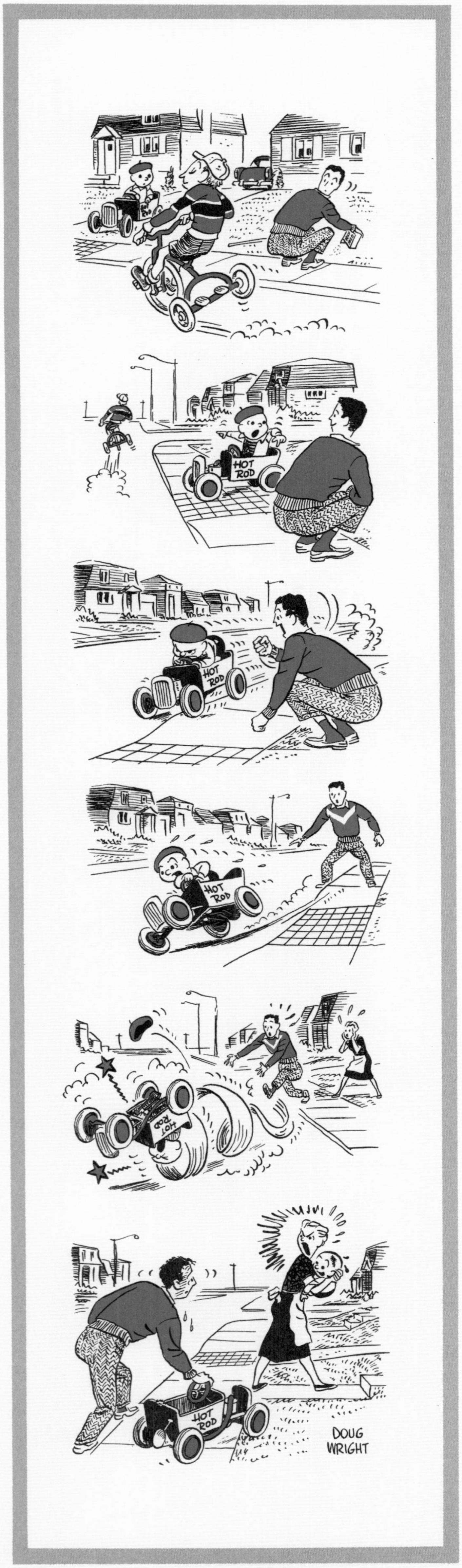

HOT ROD
HOT ROD
HOT ROD
HOT ROD
HOT ROD
DOUG WRIGHT

April 24, 1954

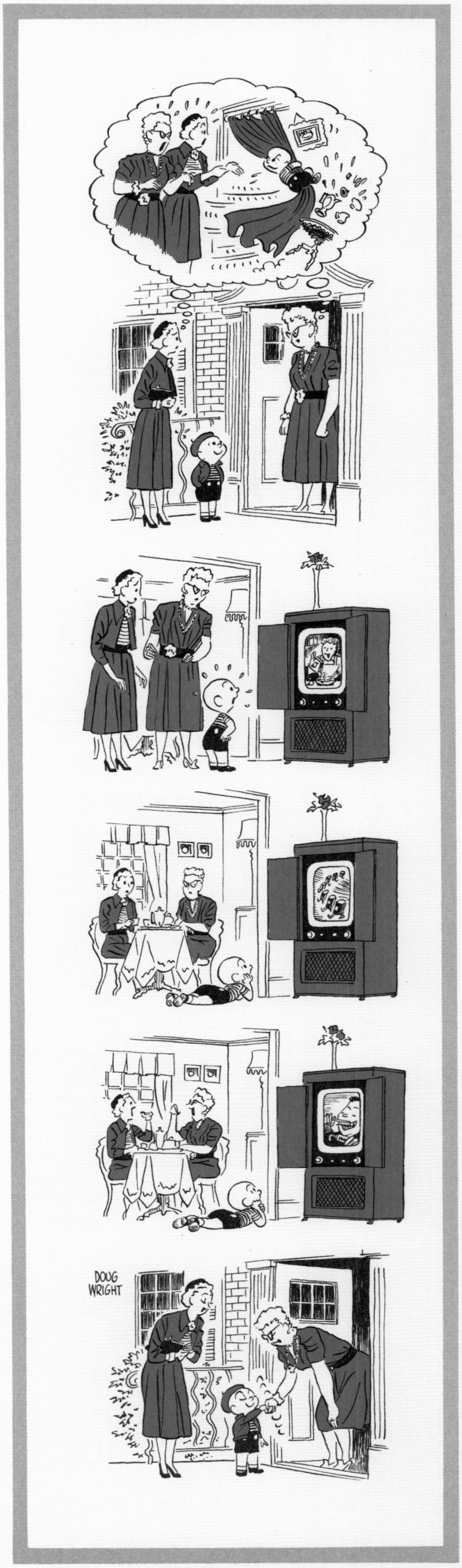

DOUG WRIGHT

May 1, 1954

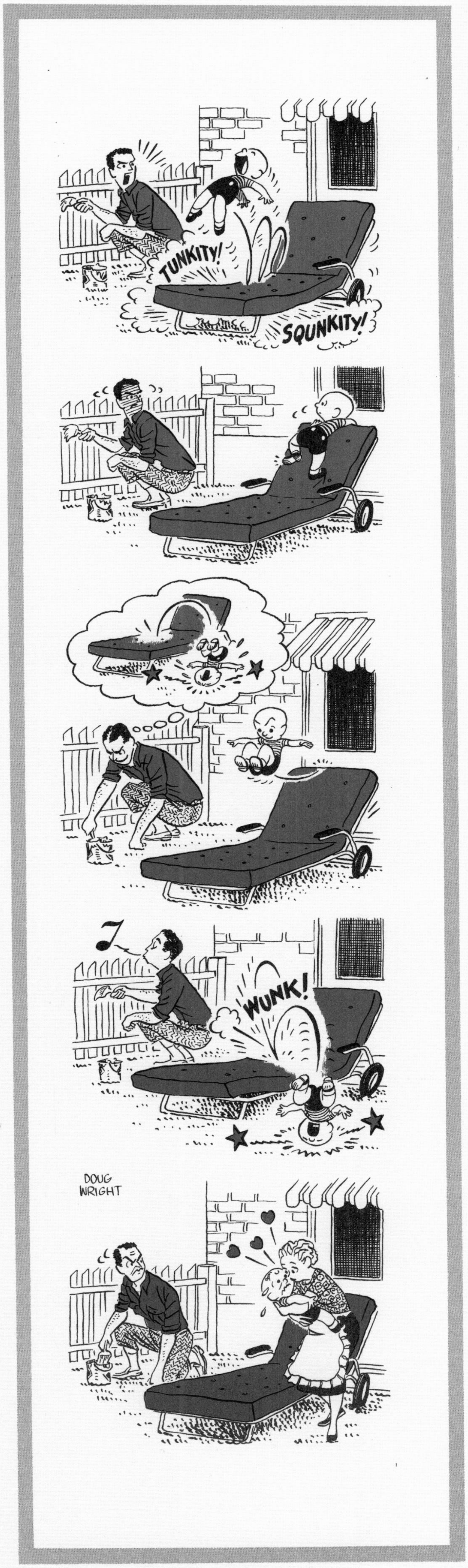
TUNKITY!
SQUNKITY!
WUNK!
DOUG WRIGHT

June 19, 1954

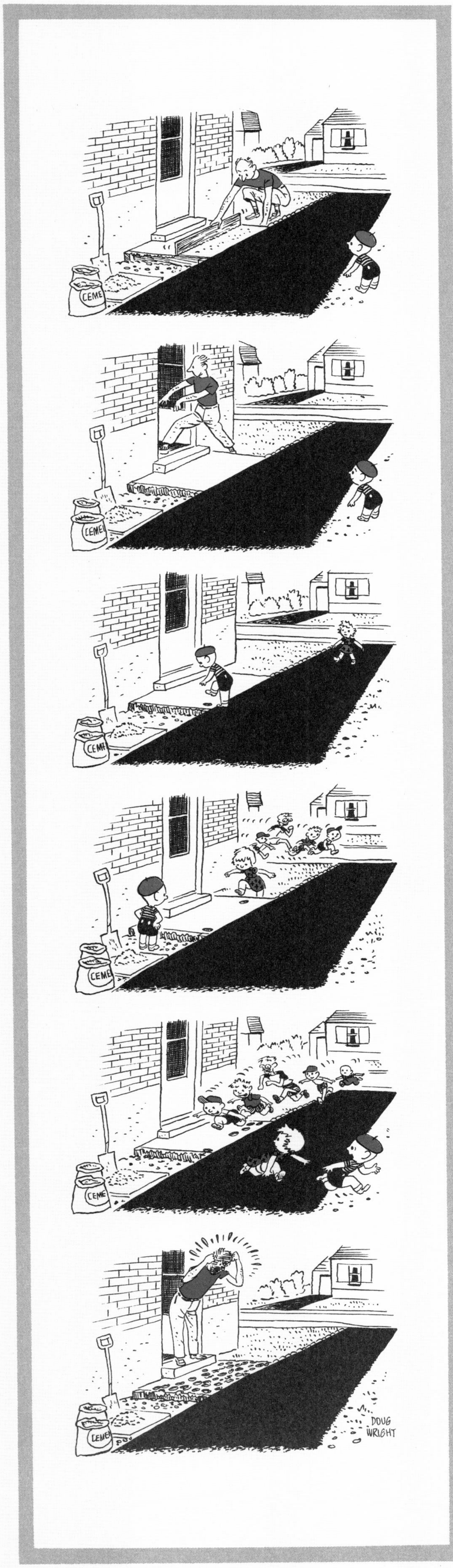
CEME
DOUG WRIGHT

July 3, 1954

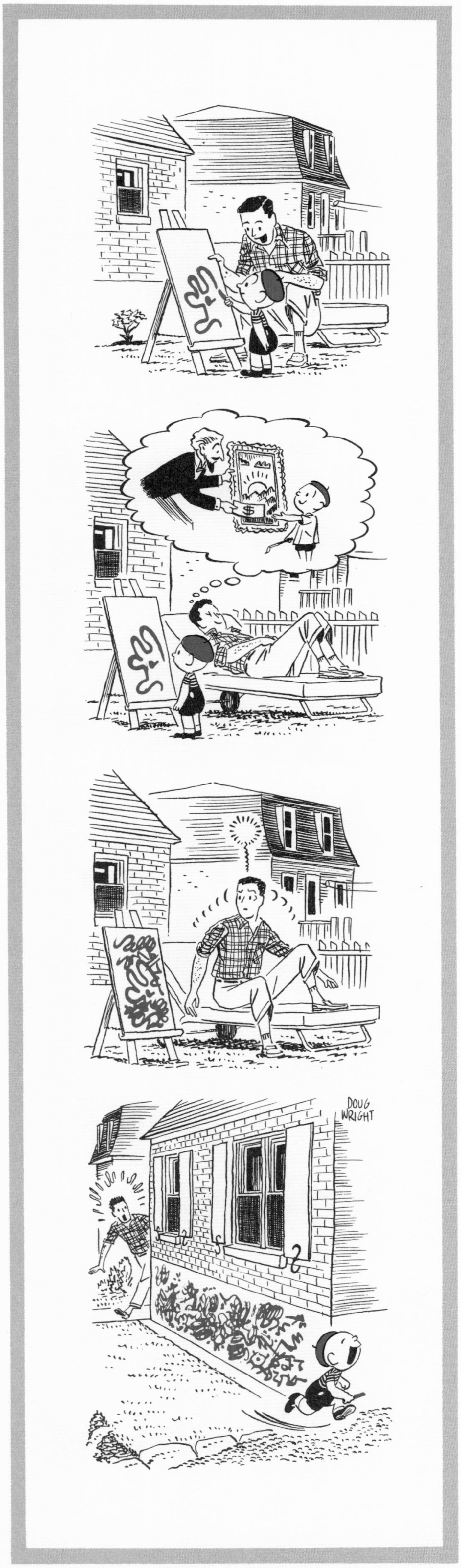
DOUG WRIGHT

July 10, 1954

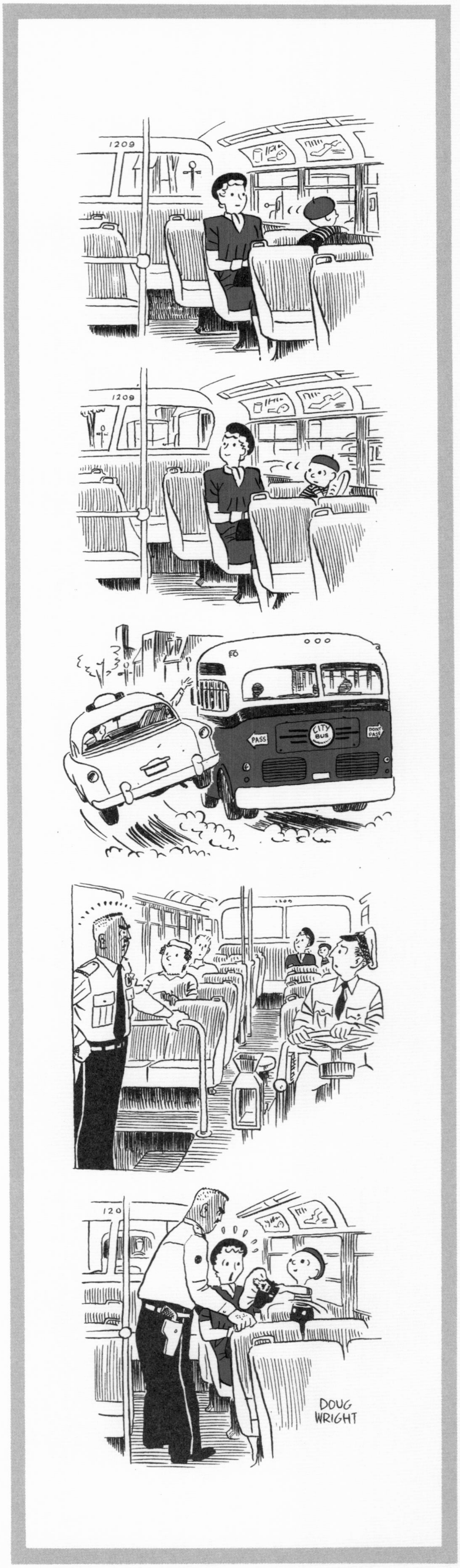
1209
PASS
CITY BUS
DOUG WRIGHT

July 24, 1954

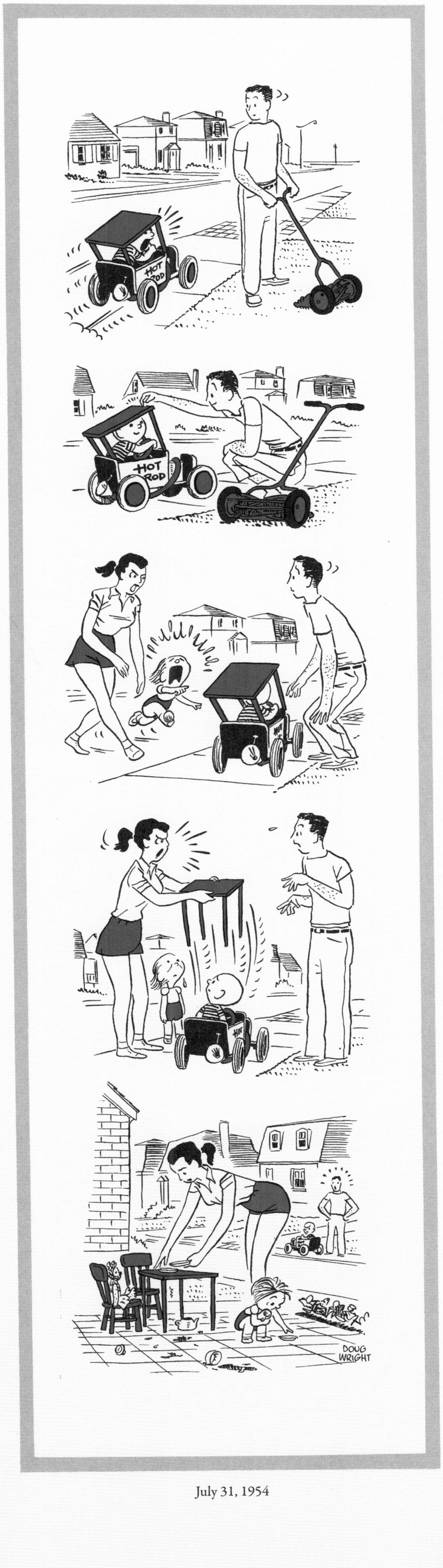
HOT ROD
HOT ROD
DOUG WRIGHT

July 31, 1954

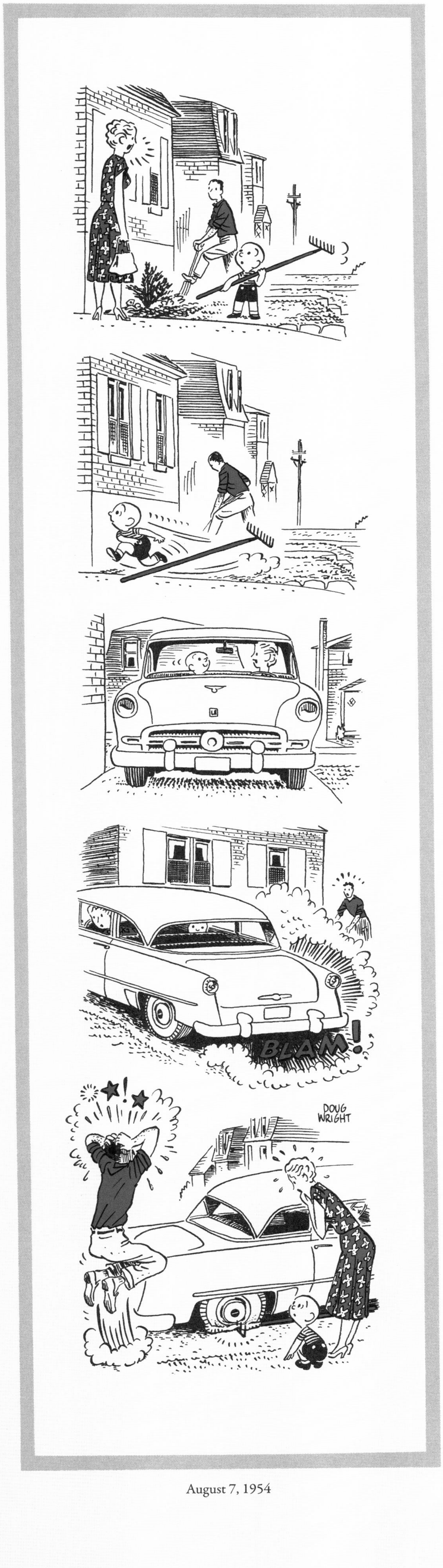
BLAM!
DOUG WRIGHT

August 7, 1954

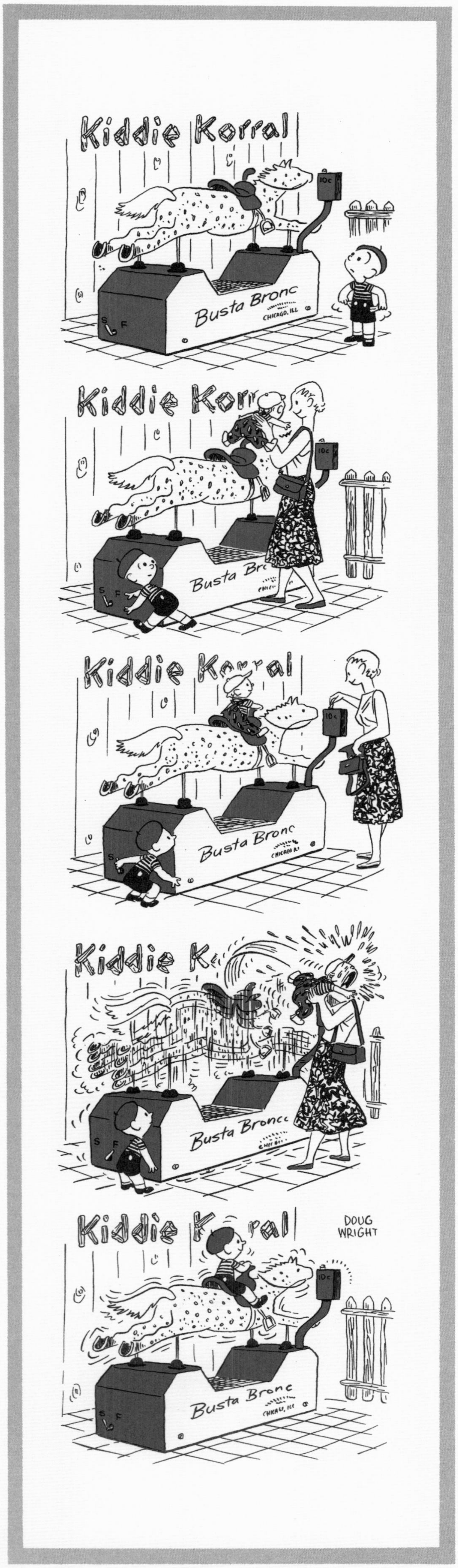
Kiddie Korral
Busta Bronc
Kiddie Korral
DOUG WRIGHT

August 28, 1954

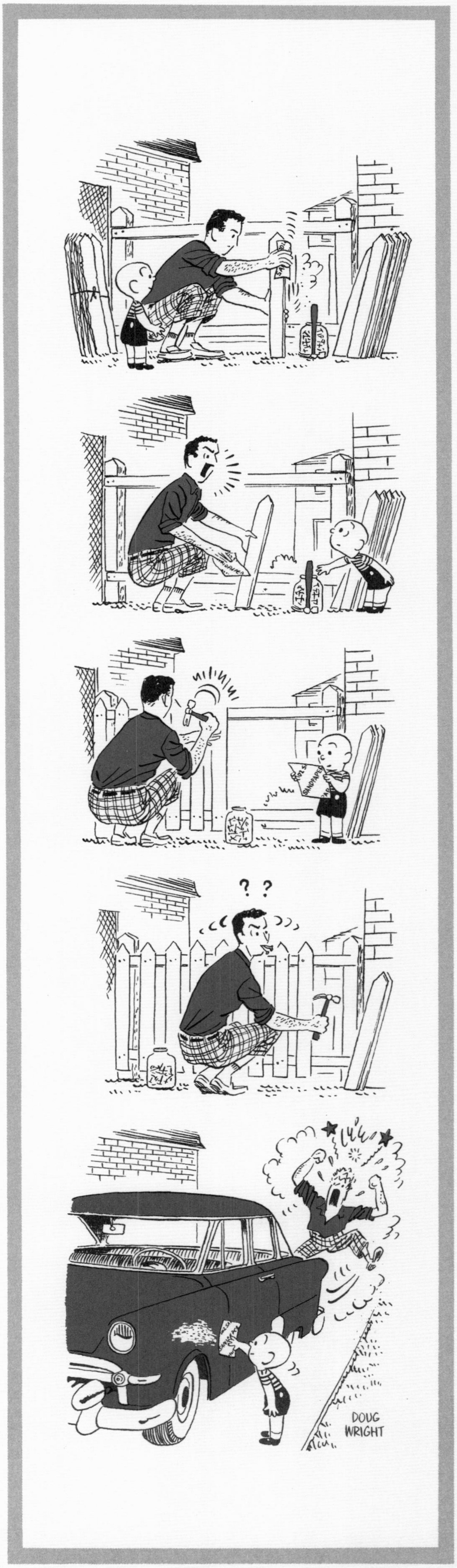
? ?
DOUG WRIGHT

September 4, 1954

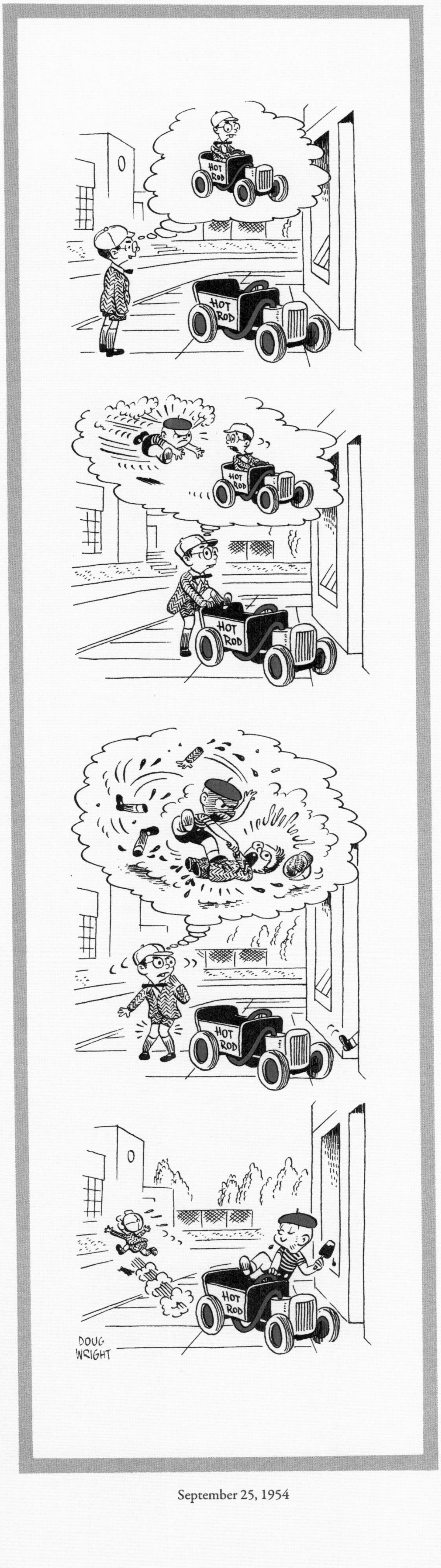
HOT ROD
HOT ROD
HOT ROD
HOT ROD
HOT ROD
HOT ROD
DOUG WRIGHT

A surprisingly gruesome episode.
It's hard to imagine this strip appearing
in a family magazine today.

September 25, 1954

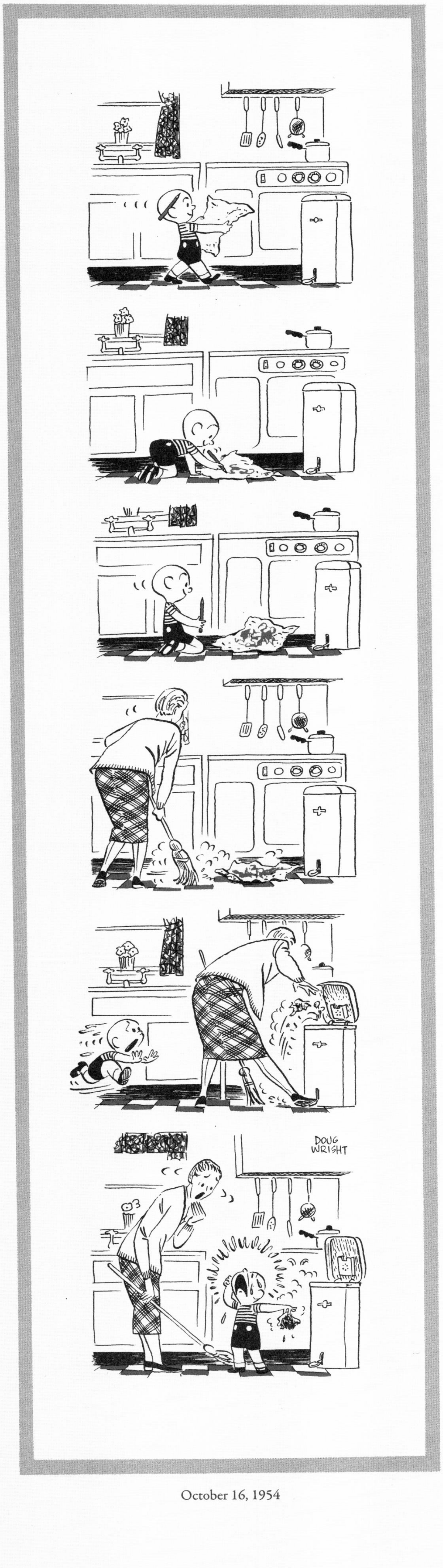
DOUG WRIGHT

October 16, 1954

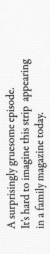

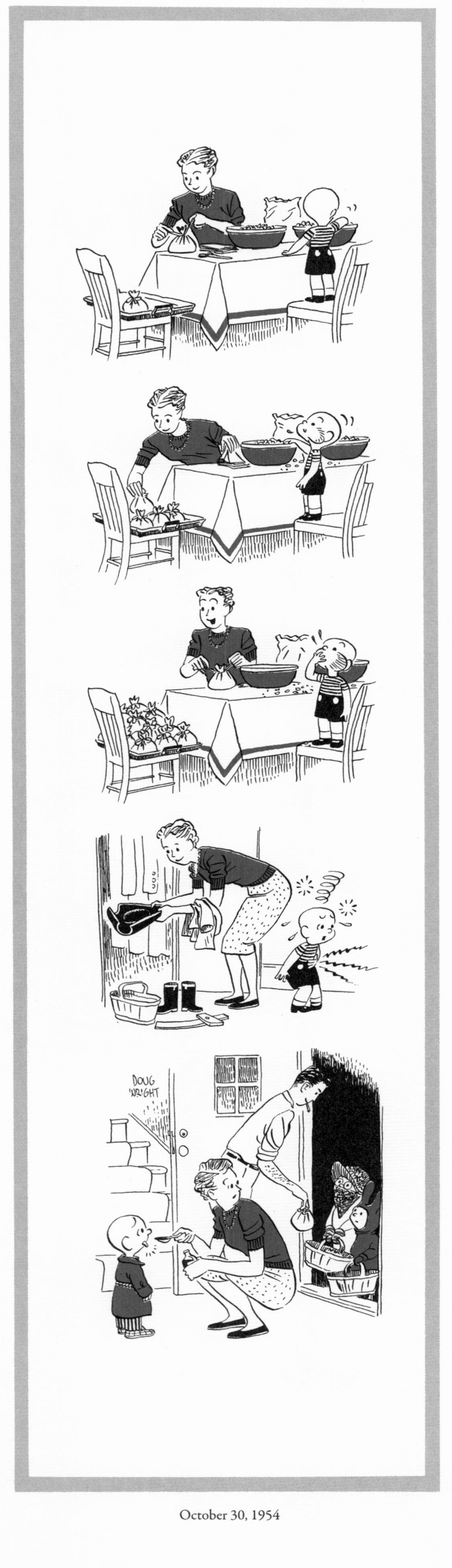
DOUG WRIGHT

October 30, 1954

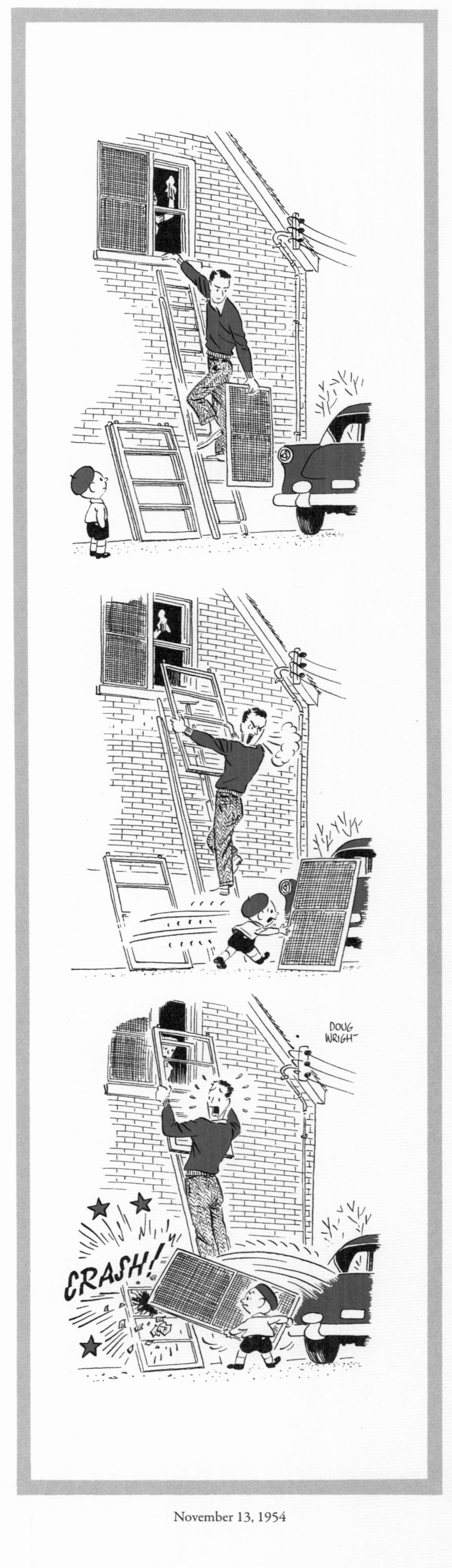
DOUG WRIGHT
CRASH!

November 13, 1954

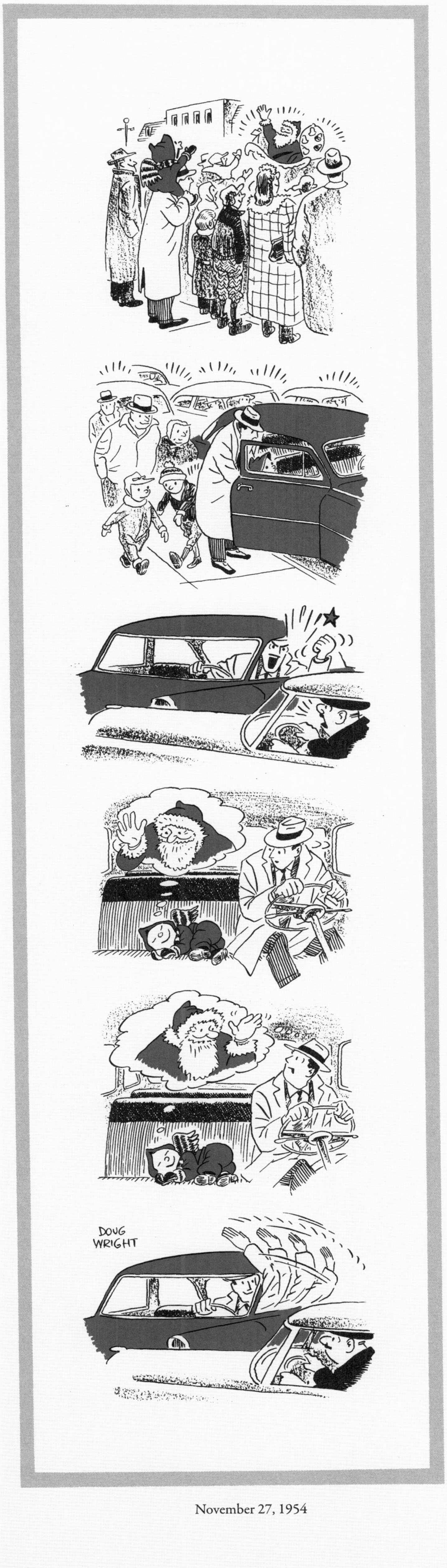
DOUG WRIGHT

November 27, 1954

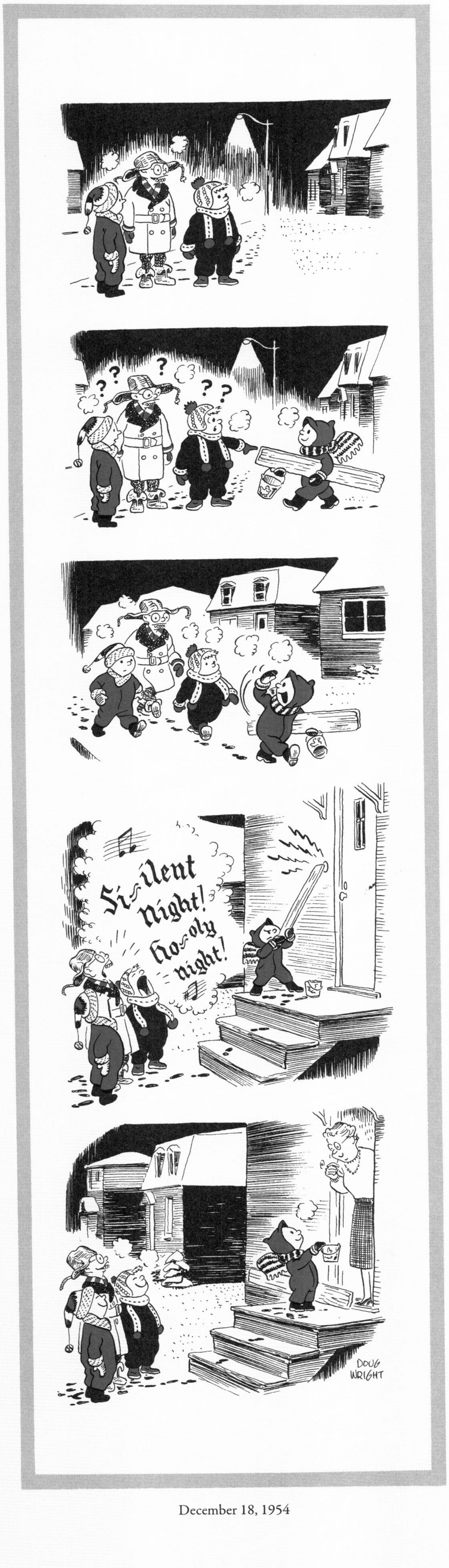
Si-ilent Night! Ho-oly night!
DOUG WRIGHT

December 18, 1954

Christmas Stuff ... with Nipper

WEEKEND Magazine Vol. 4 No. 52, 1954

December 25, 1954

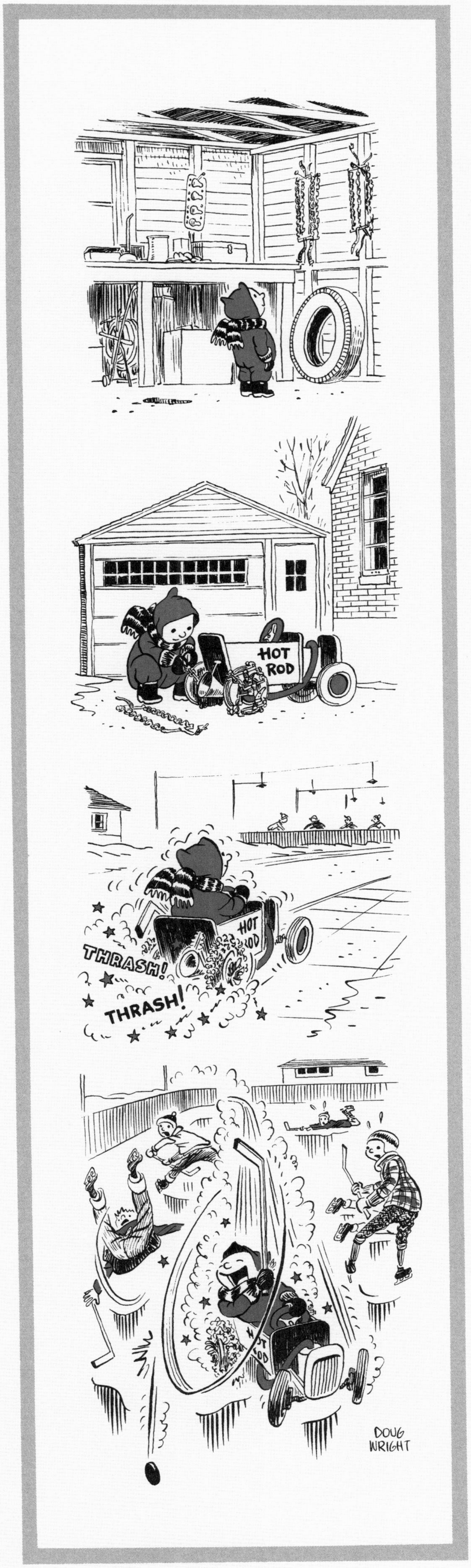
HOT ROD
THRASH!
THRASH!
DOUG WRIGHT

January 15, 1955

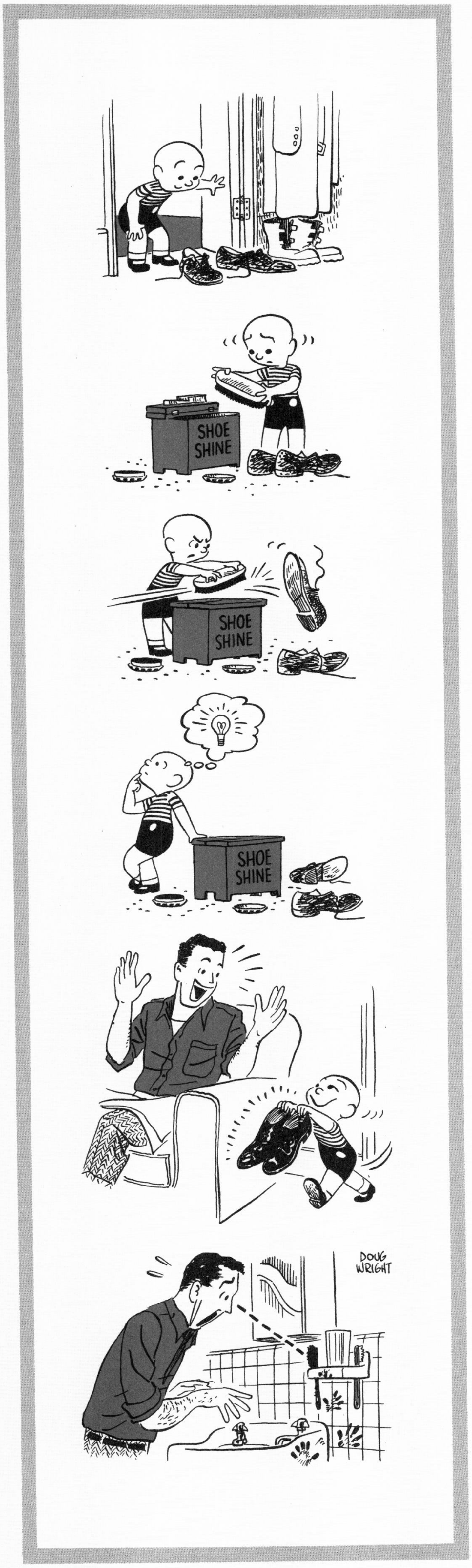
SHOE SHINE
DOUG WRIGHT

March 5, 1955

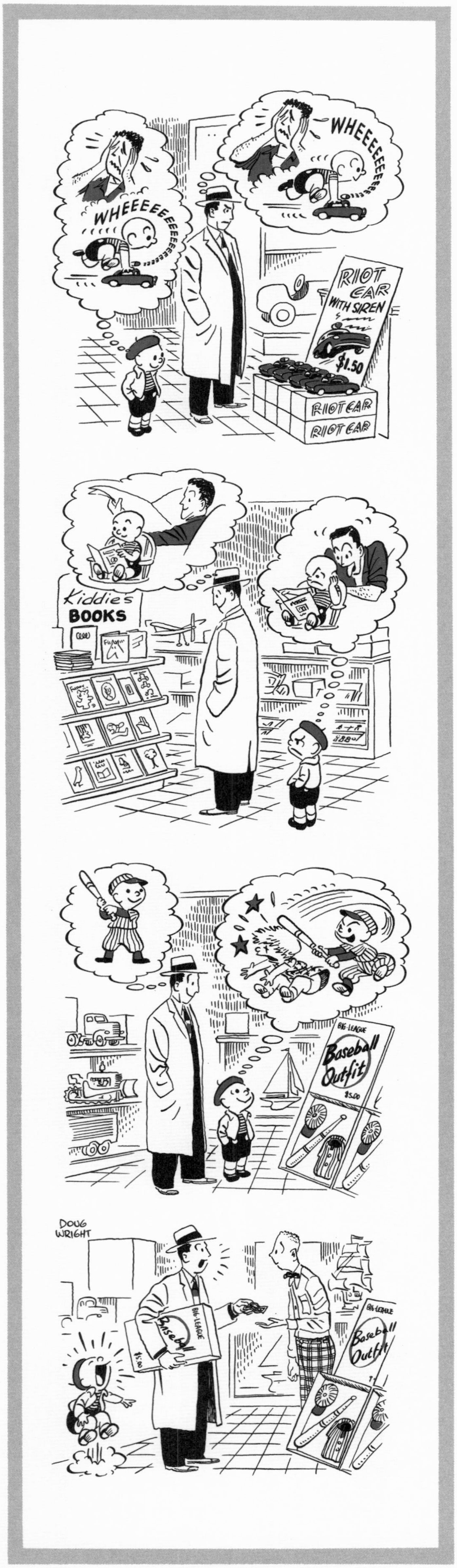
WHEEEEEEEEEEEEE
WHEEEEEEEEEEEEE
RIOT CAR WITH SIREN $1.50
RIOT CAR
RIOT CAR
Kiddies BOOKS
BIG LEAGUE Baseball Outfit $5.00
DOUG WRIGHT
BIG LEAGUE Baseball
BIG LEAGUE Baseball Outfit

March 26, 1955

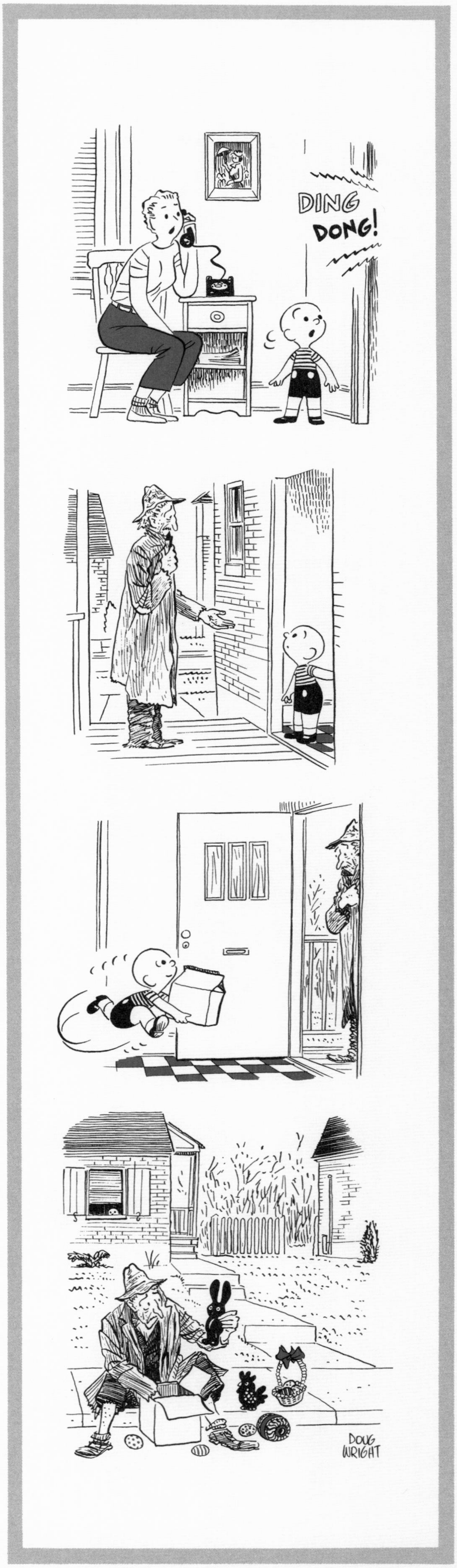
DING DONG!
DOUG WRIGHT

April 9, 1955

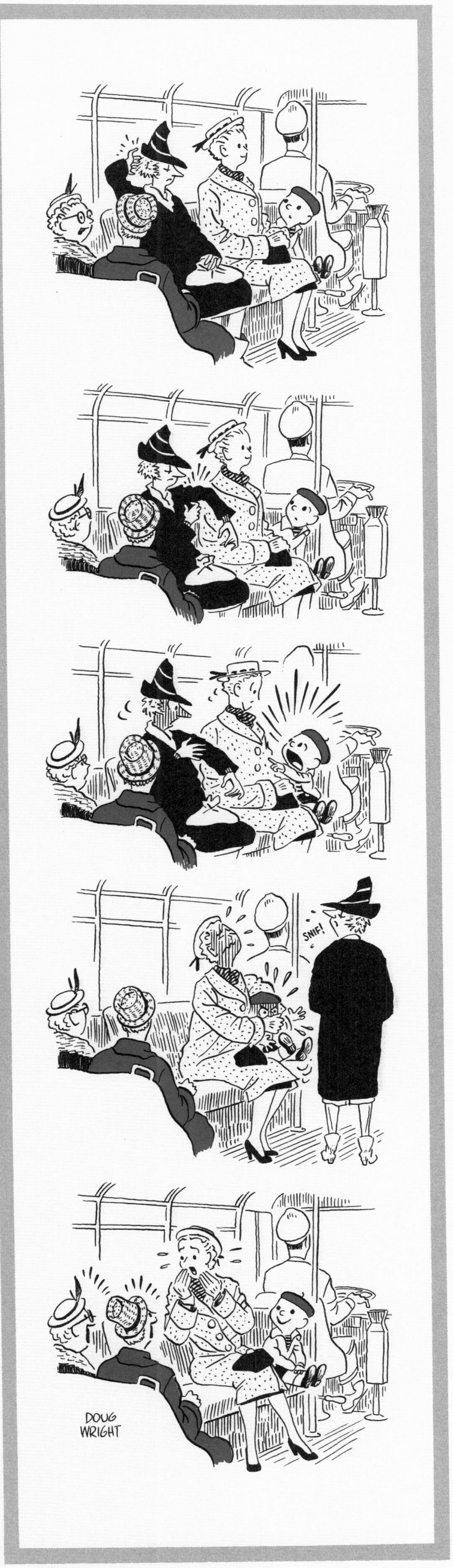
SNIF!
DOUG WRIGHT

April 16, 1955

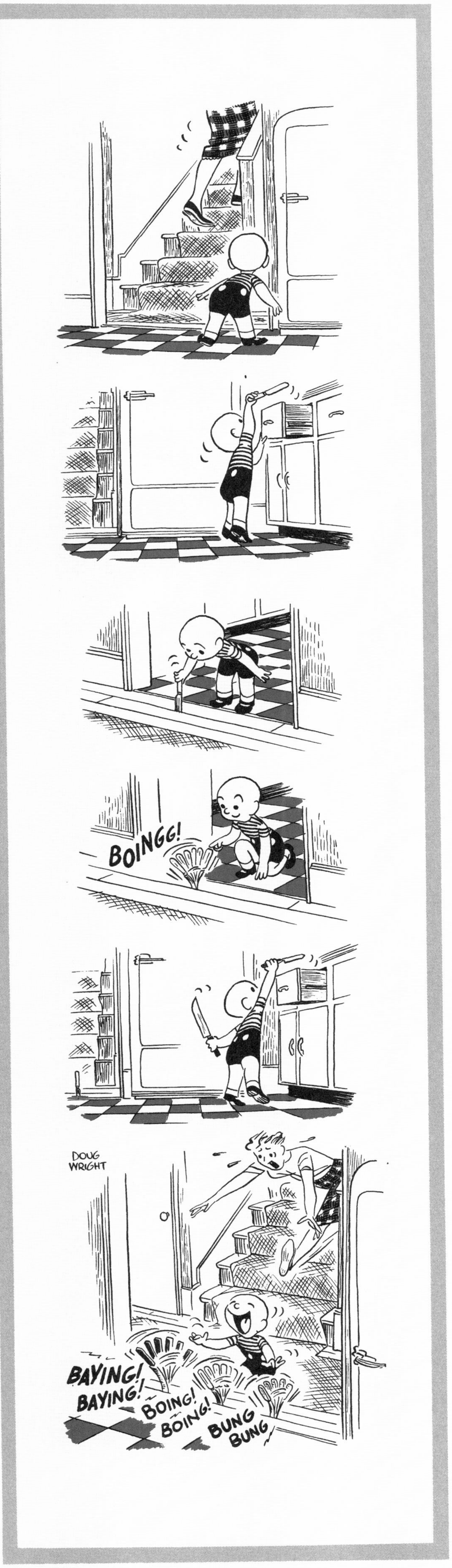
BOINGG!
DOUG WRIGHT
BAYING!
BAYING!
BOING!
BOING!
BUNG
BUNG

April 23, 1955

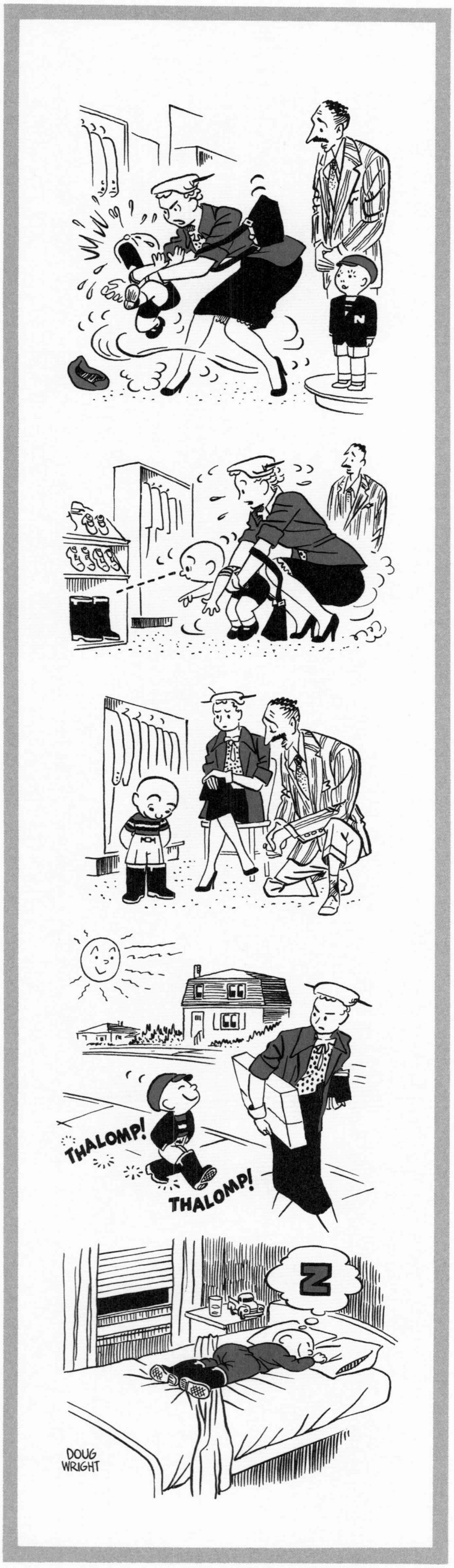
THALOMP!
THALOMP!
Z
DOUG WRIGHT

April 30, 1955

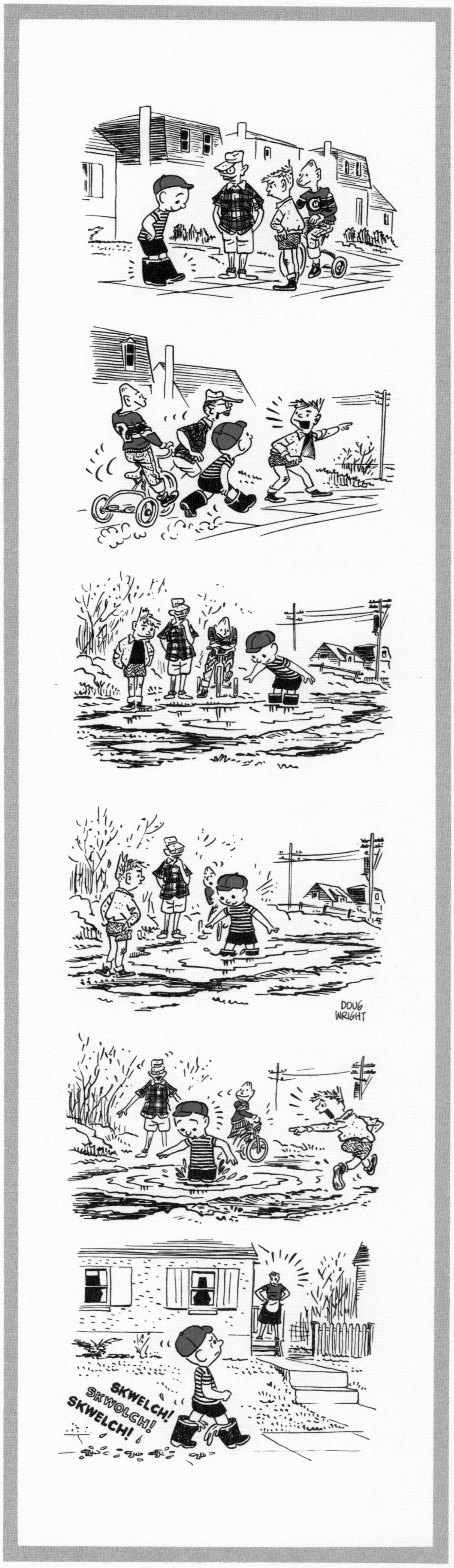
DOUG WRIGHT
SKWELCH!
SKWOLCH!
SKWELCH!

May 7, 1955

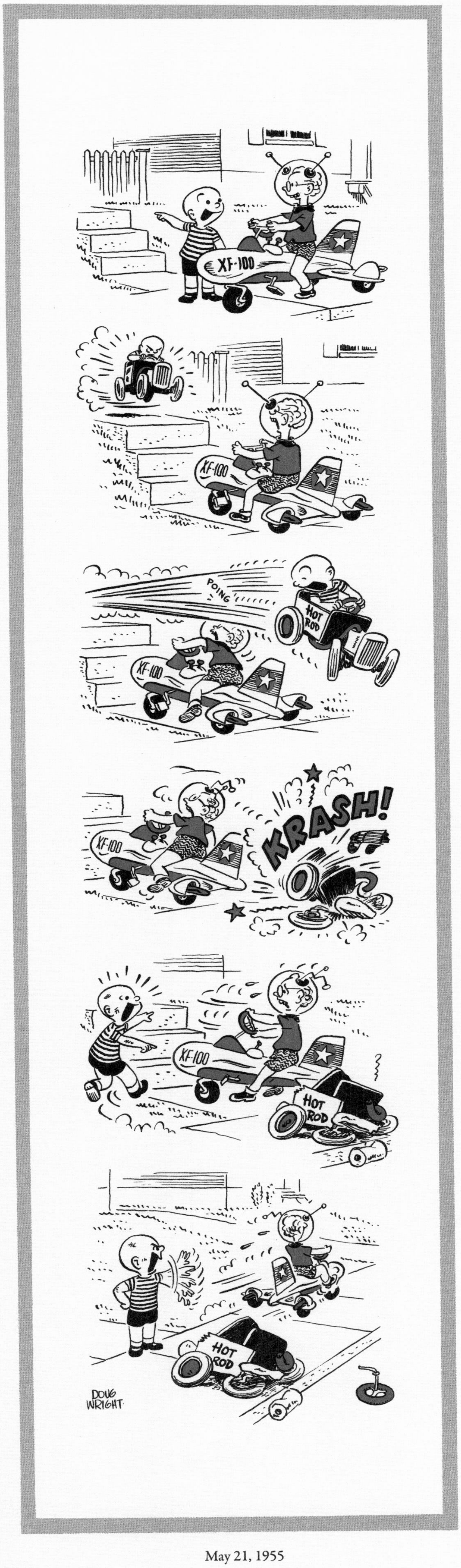
XF-100
POING
HOT ROD
KRASH!
DOUG WRIGHT

May 21, 1955

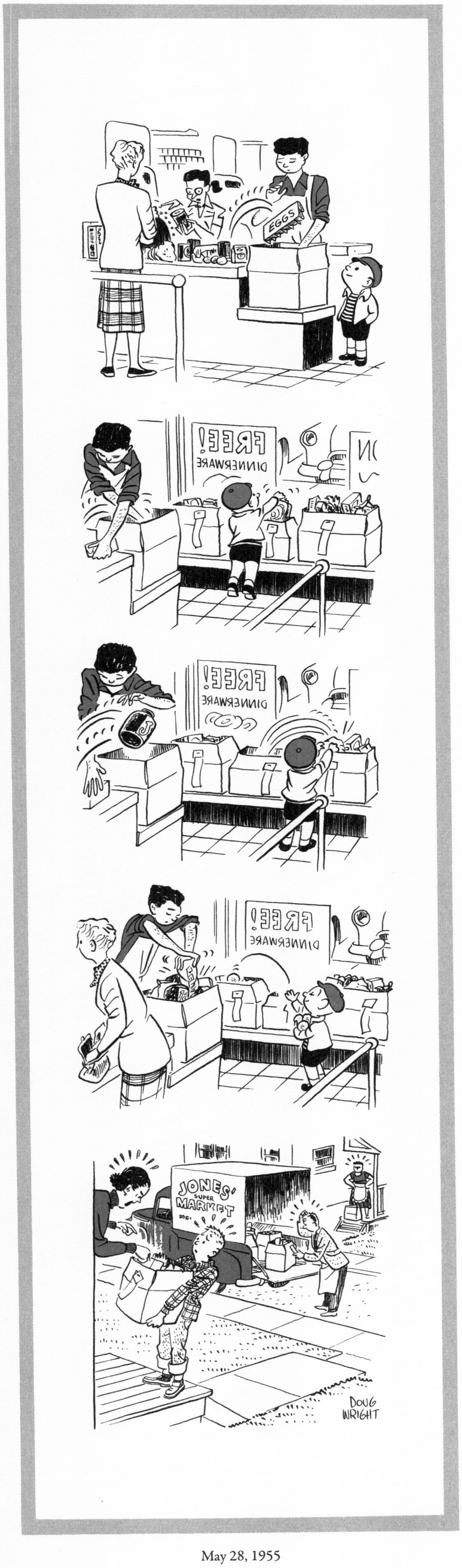
EGGS
FREE!
DINNERWARE
JONES' SUPER MARKET
DOUG WRIGHT

May 28, 1955

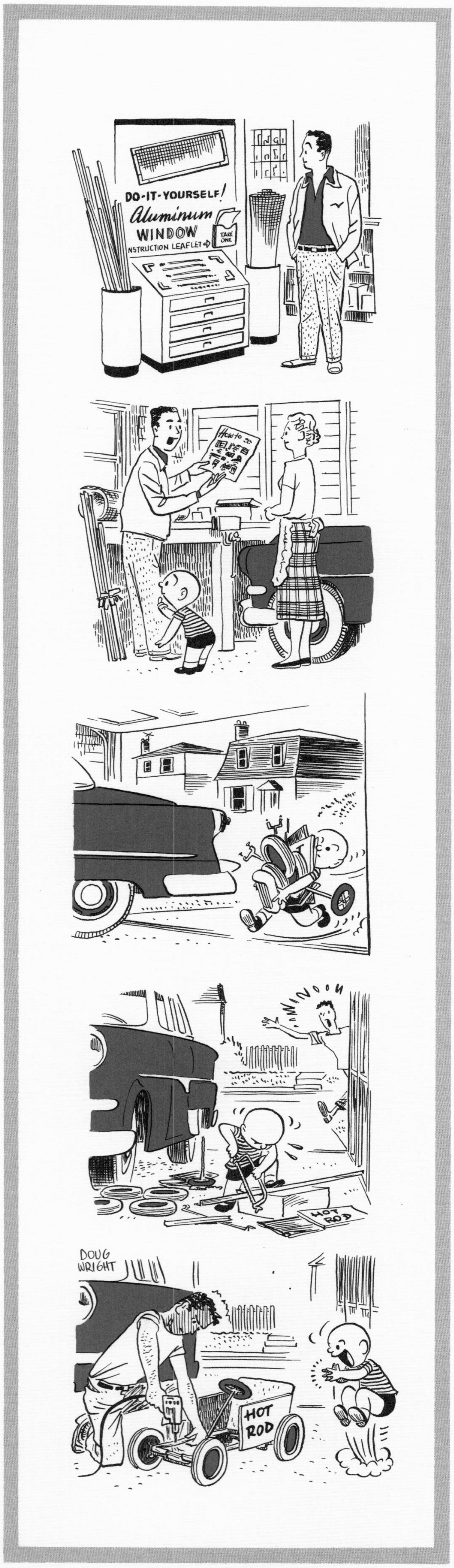
DO-IT-YOURSELF!
Aluminum
WINDOW
NSTRUCTION LEAFLET
TAKE ONE
How to
HOT ROD
DOUG WRIGHT
HOT ROD

June 4, 1955

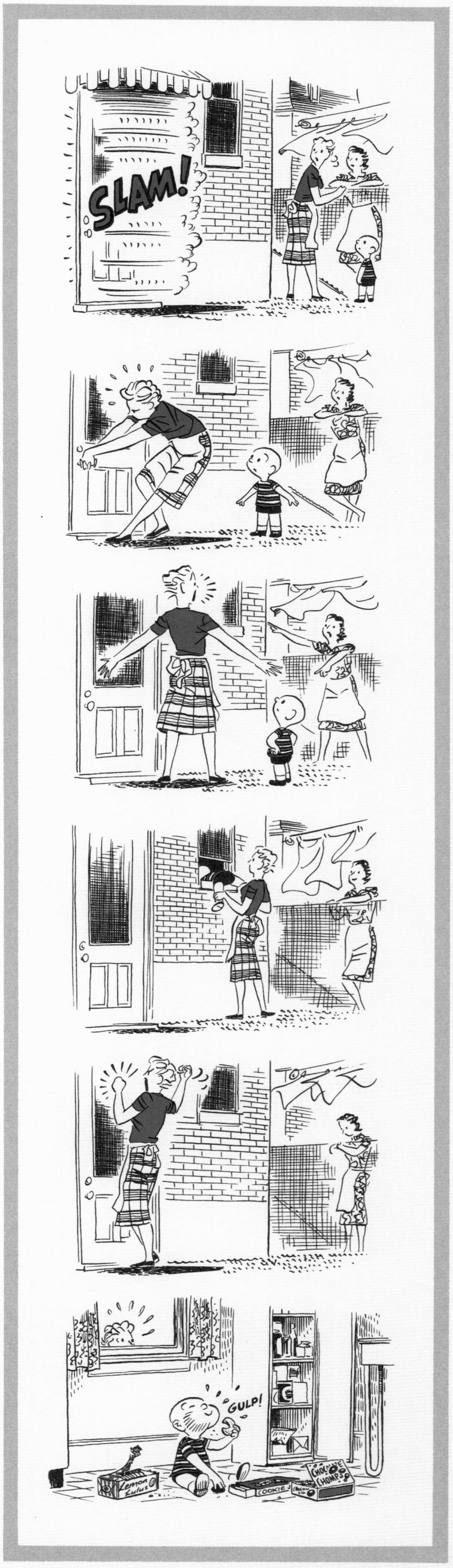
SLAM!
GULP!
Lemon Zulus
COOKIES
CHOC CHOMPS

June 11, 1955

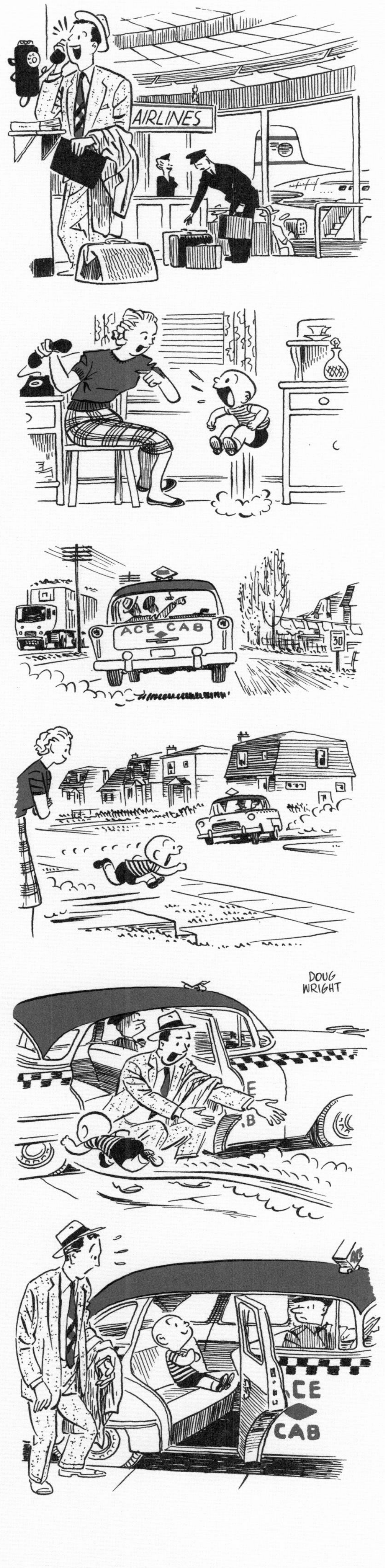
AIRLINES
ACE CAB
30
DOUG WRIGHT
CE
CAB

June 18, 1955

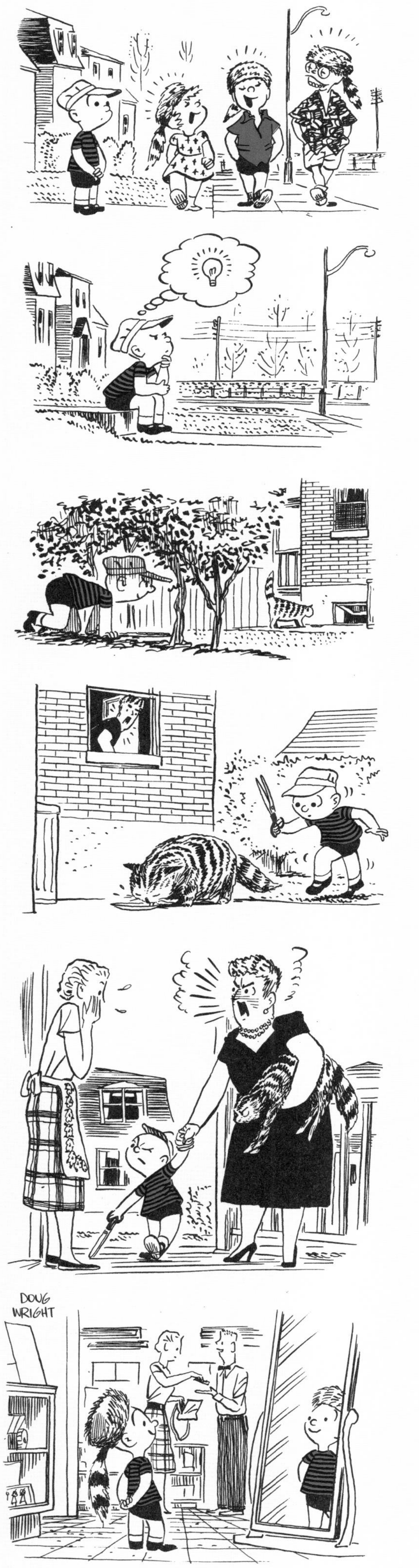
DOUG WRIGHT

June 25, 1955

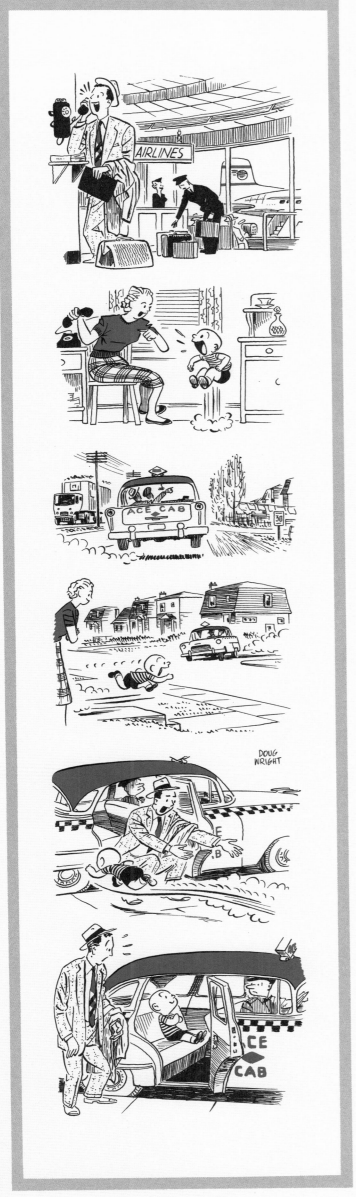

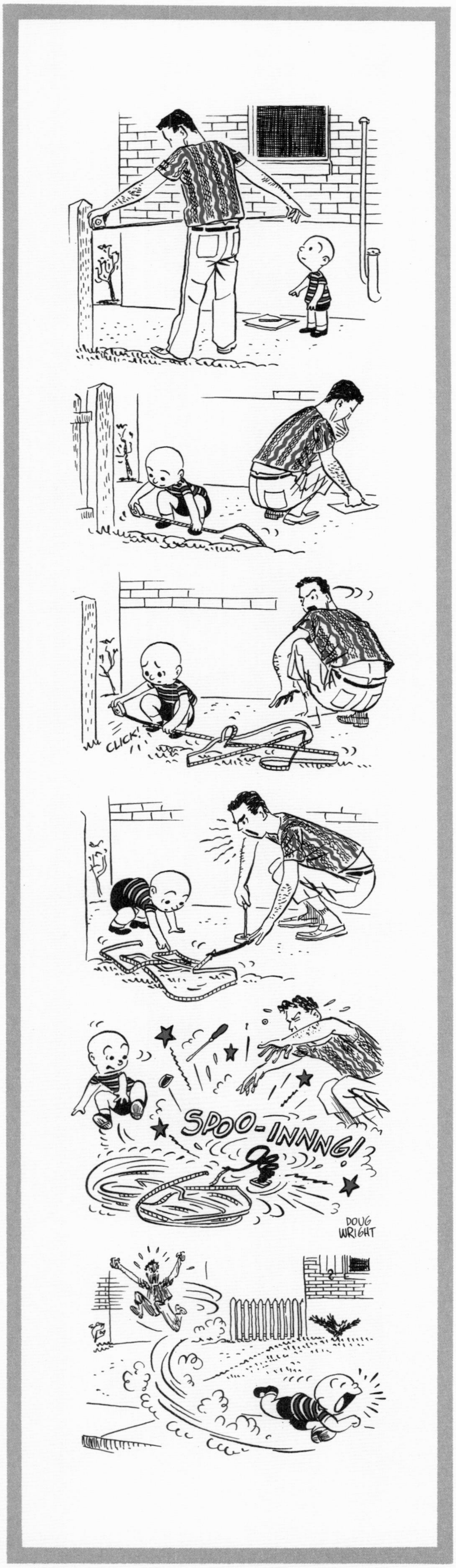
CLICK!
SPOO-INNNG!
DOUG WRIGHT

July 2, 1955

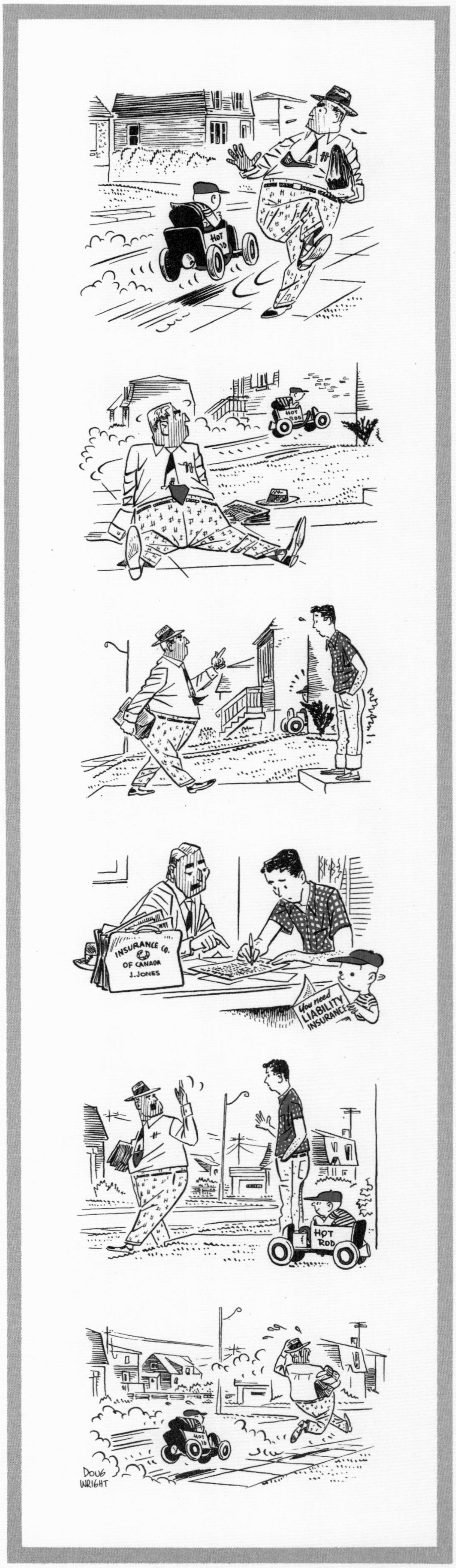
HOT ROD
INSURANCE CO. OF CANADA J. JONES
You need LIABILITY INSURANCE
HOT ROD
DOUG WRIGHT

August 6, 1955

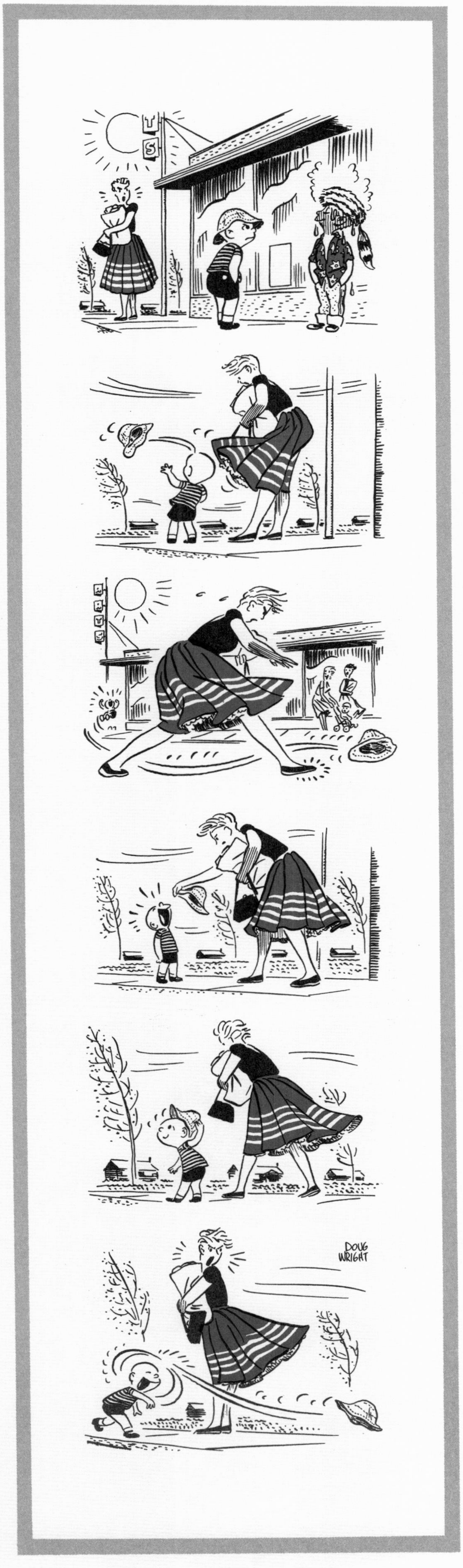
DOUG
WRIGHT

August 13, 1955

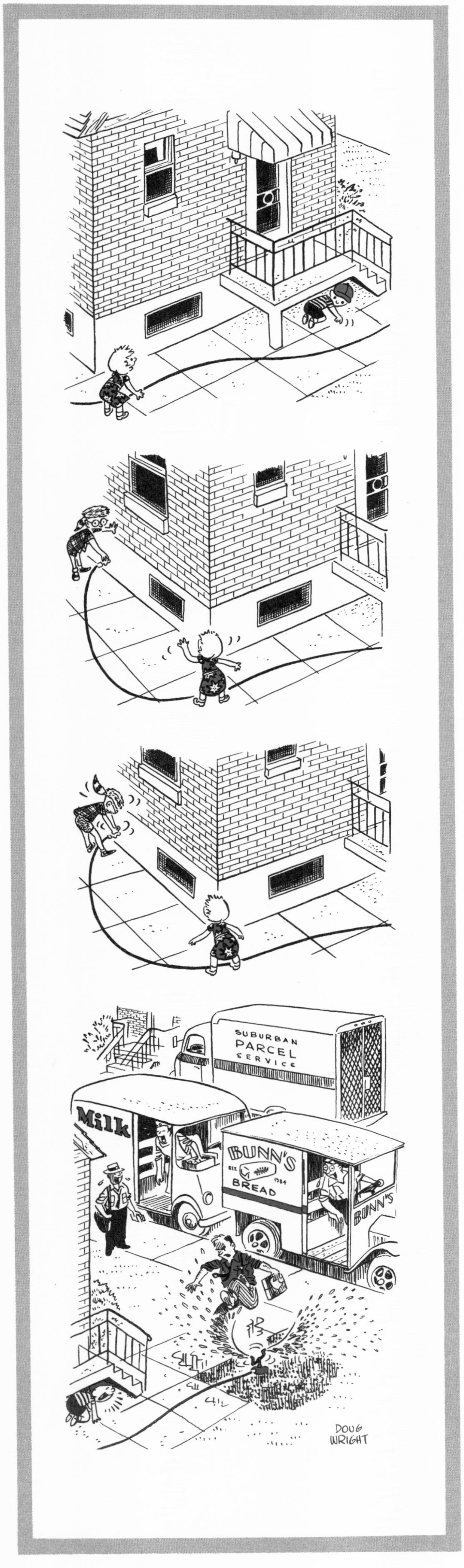
SUBURBAN
PARCEL
SERVICE
Milk
BUNN'S
BREAD
BUNN'S
DOUG
WRIGHT

August 27, 1955

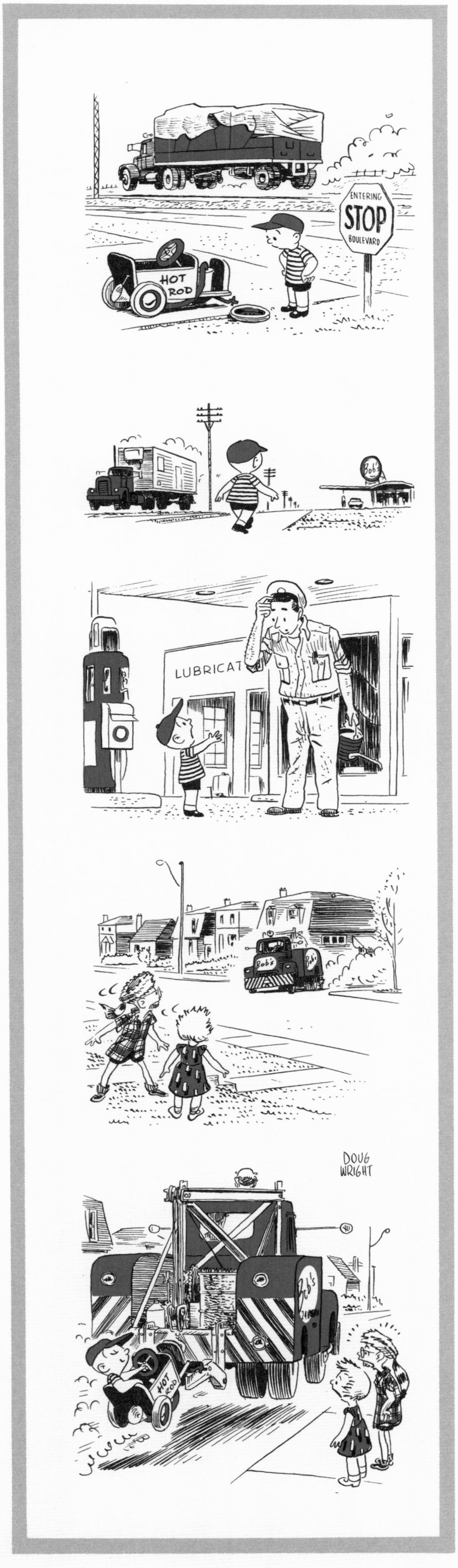
ENTERING
STOP
BOULEVARD
HOT ROD
Bob's
LUBRICAT
Bob's
DOUG WRIGHT
Bob's
HOT ROD

September 3, 1955

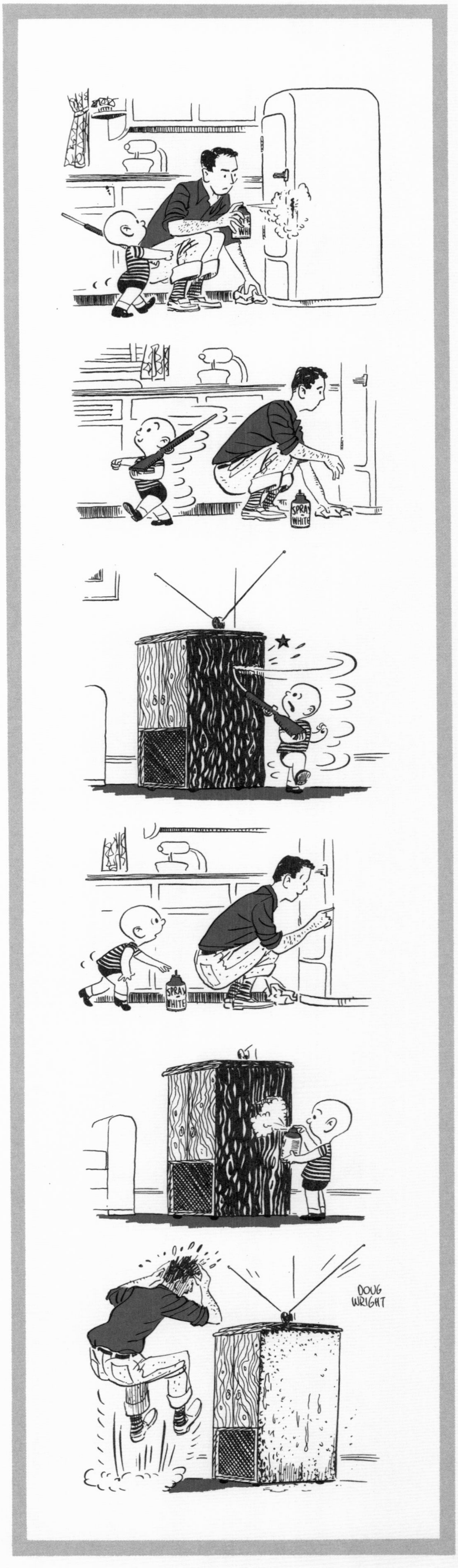
SPRAY WHITE
SPRAY WHITE
DOUG WRIGHT

September 10, 1955

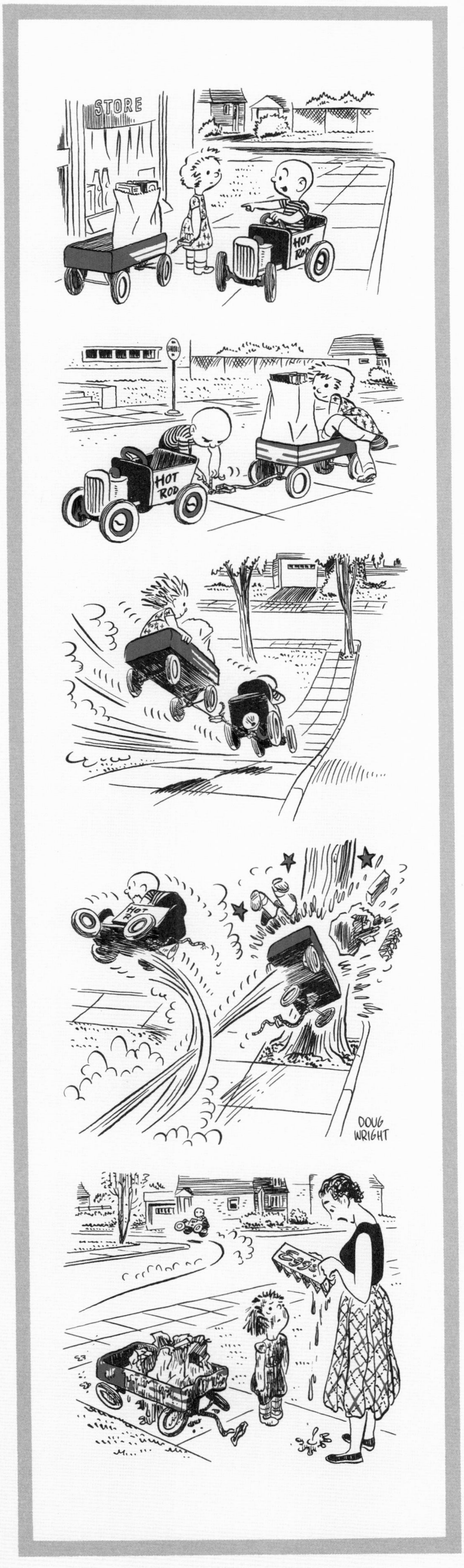
STORE
HOT ROD
HOT ROD
DOUG WRIGHT
September 24, 1955

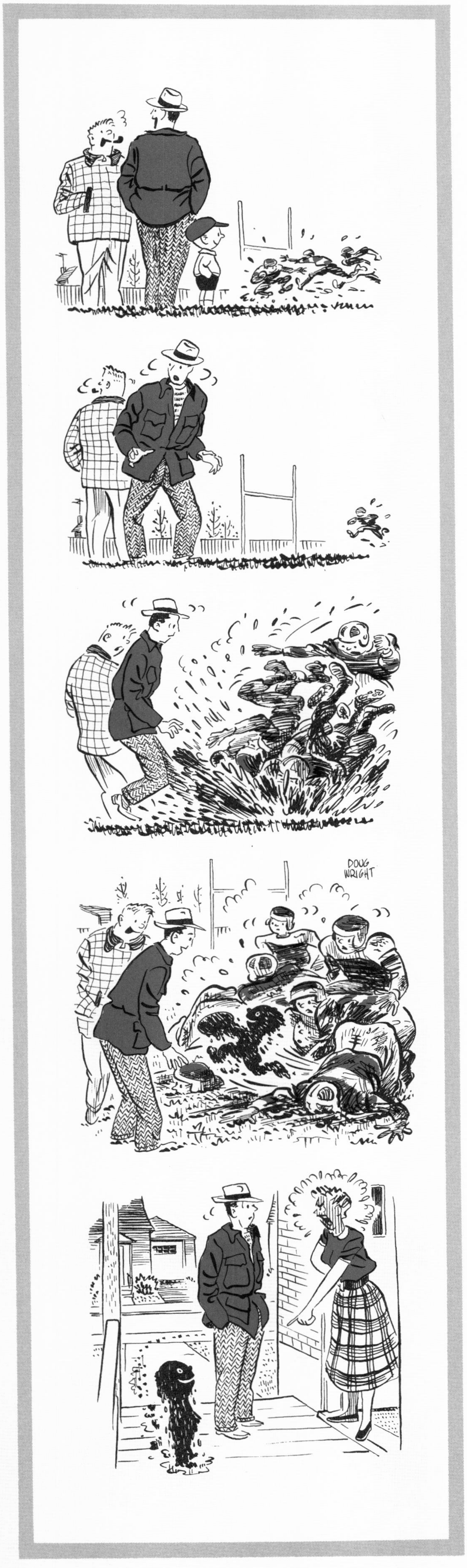
DOUG WRIGHT
October 8, 1955

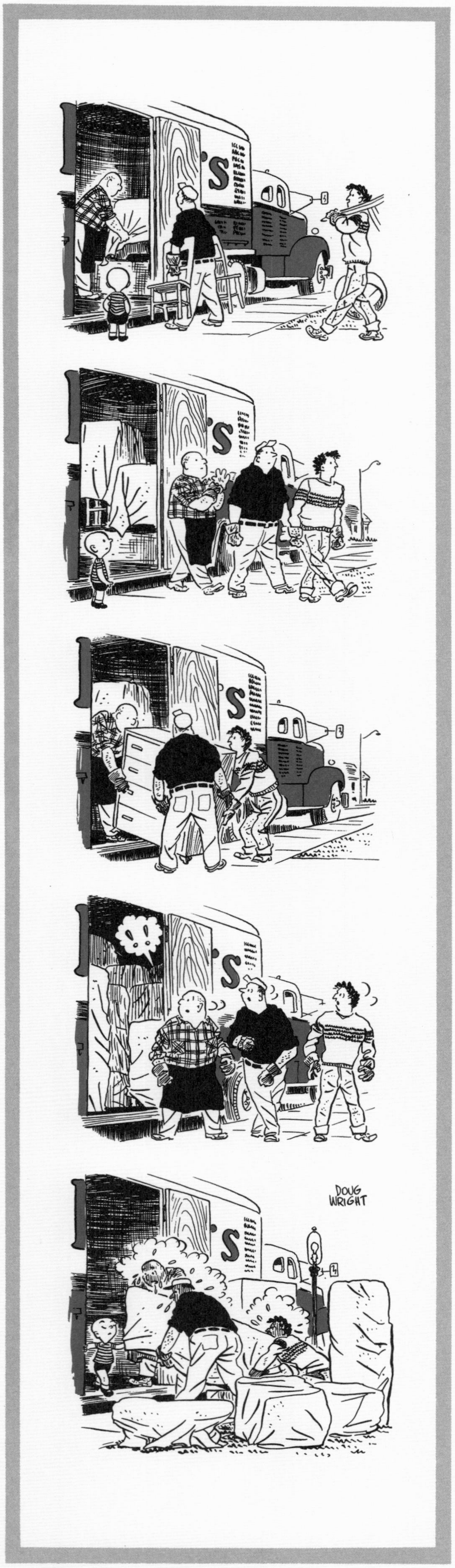
DOUG
WRIGHT

October 22, 1955

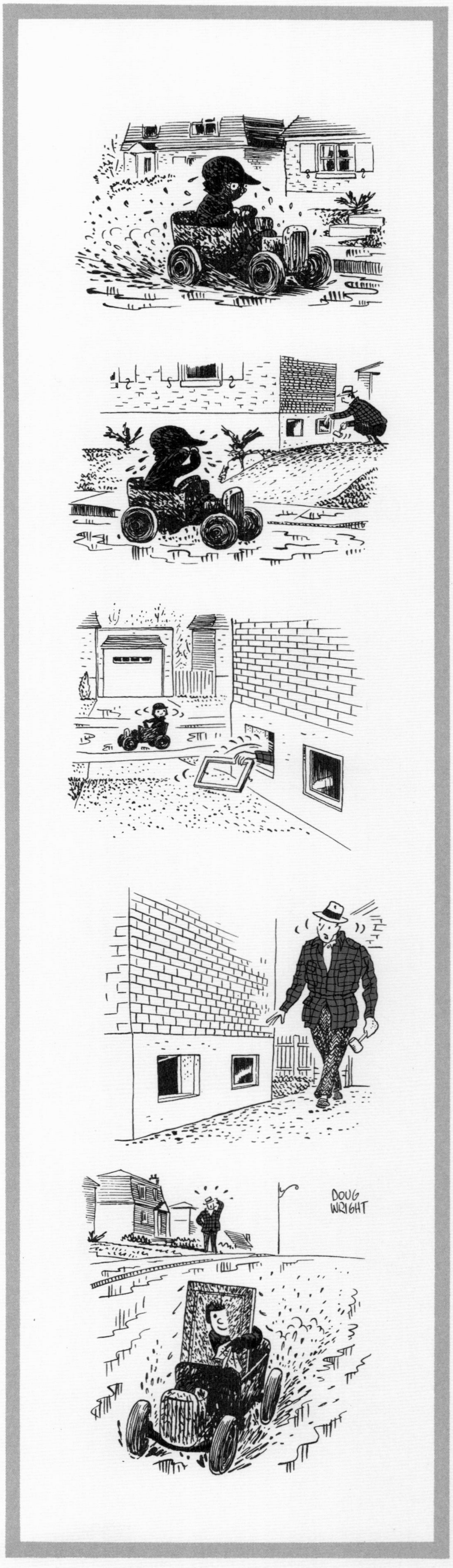
DOUG
WRIGHT

November 19, 1955

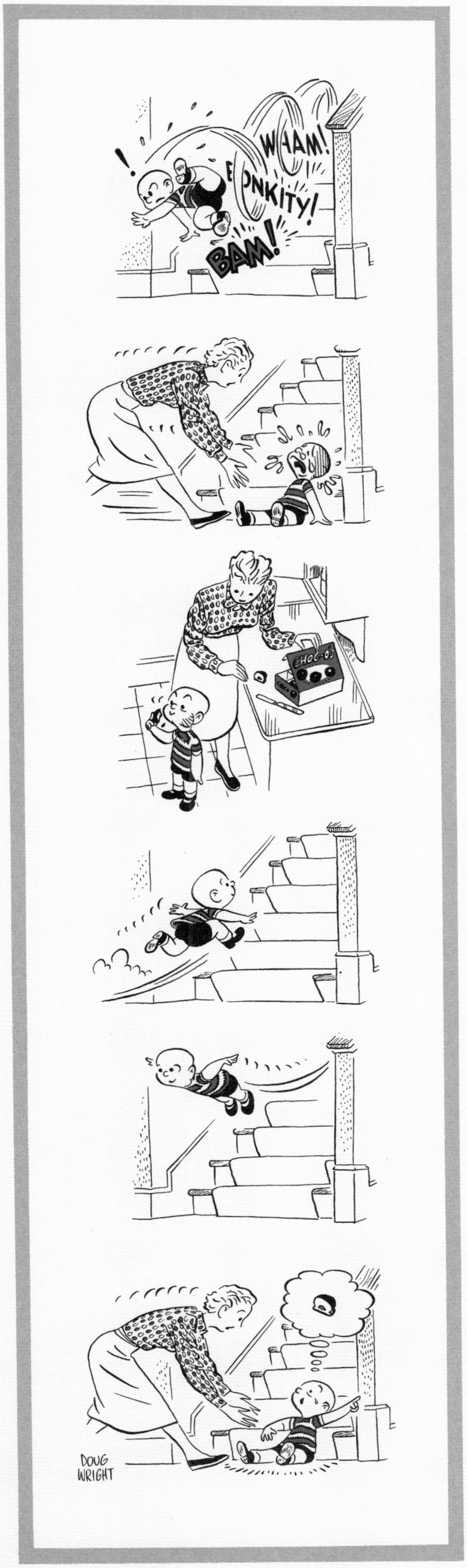
WHAM!
BONKITY!
BAM!
CHOC-OS
DOUG WRIGHT

December 10, 1955

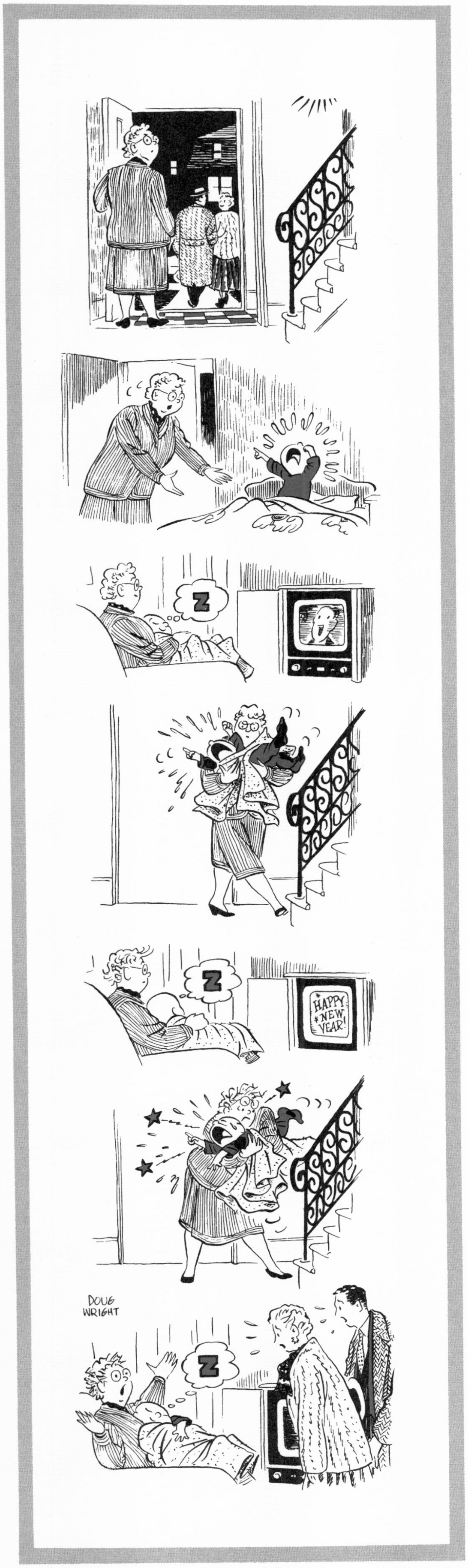
Z
Z
HAPPY NEW YEAR!
DOUG WRIGHT
Z

December 24, 1955

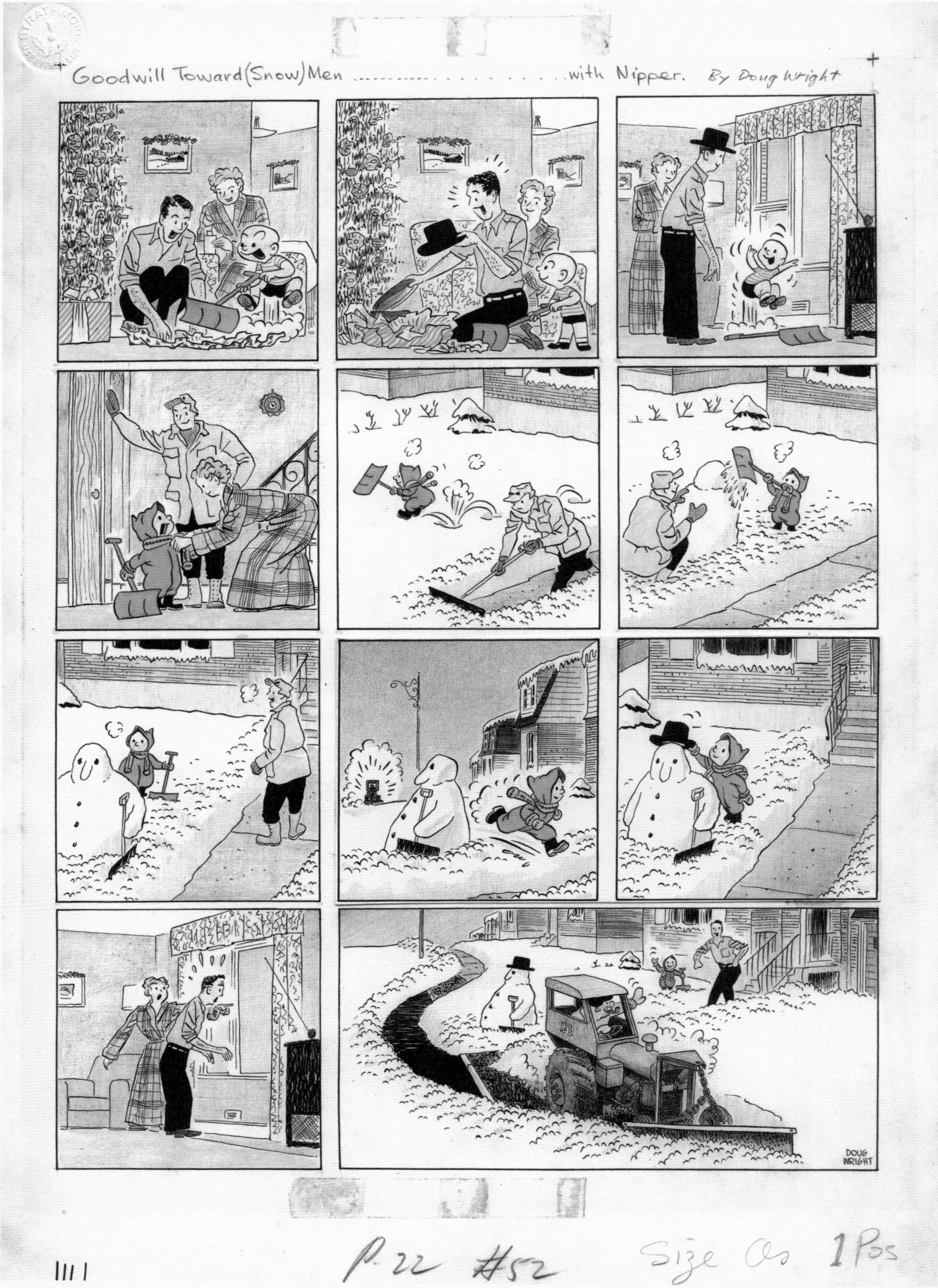

Goodwill Toward (Snow) Men .... with Nipper. By Doug Wright
21
DOUG WRIGHT
P. 22 #52
Size As 1 Pos

December 31, 1955

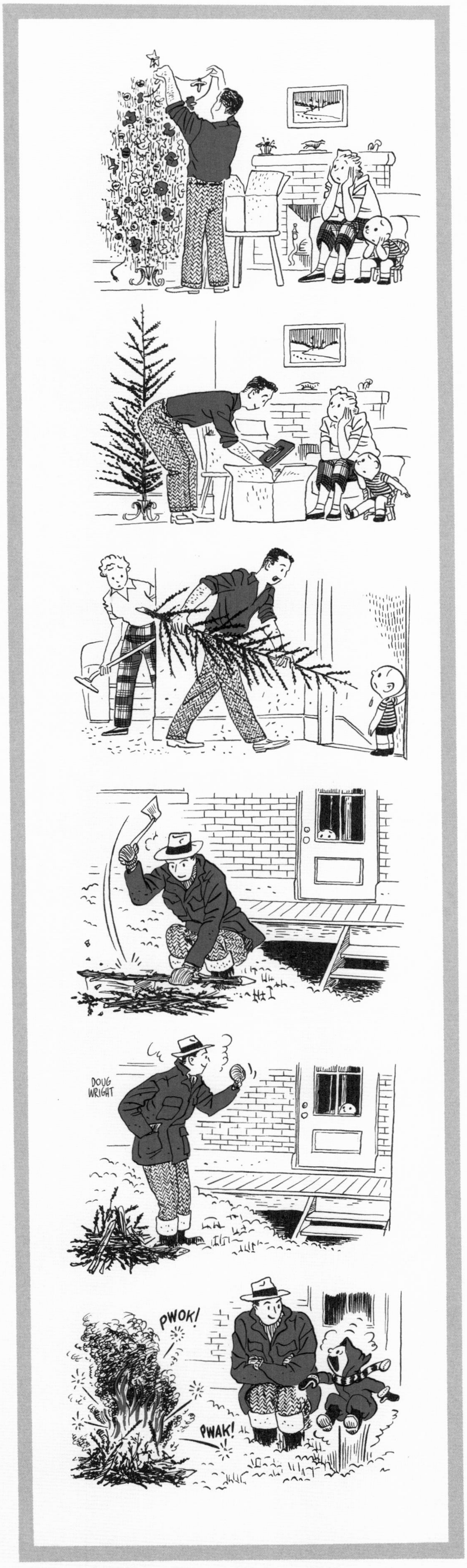
DOUG WRIGHT
PWOK!
PWAK!

January 6, 1956

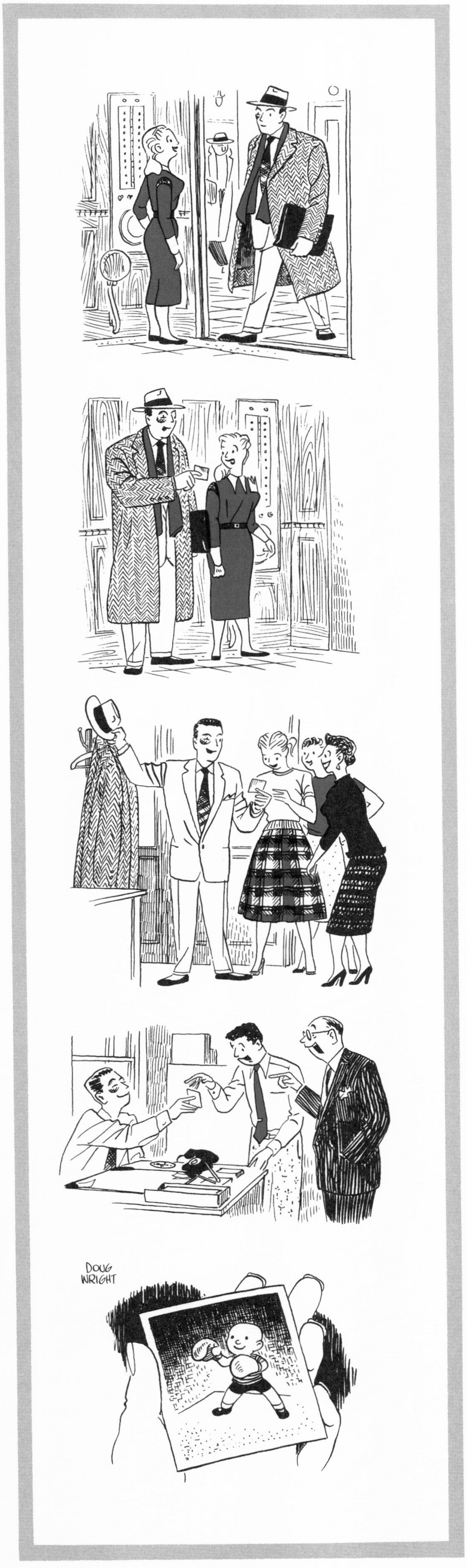
DOUG WRIGHT

January 14, 1956

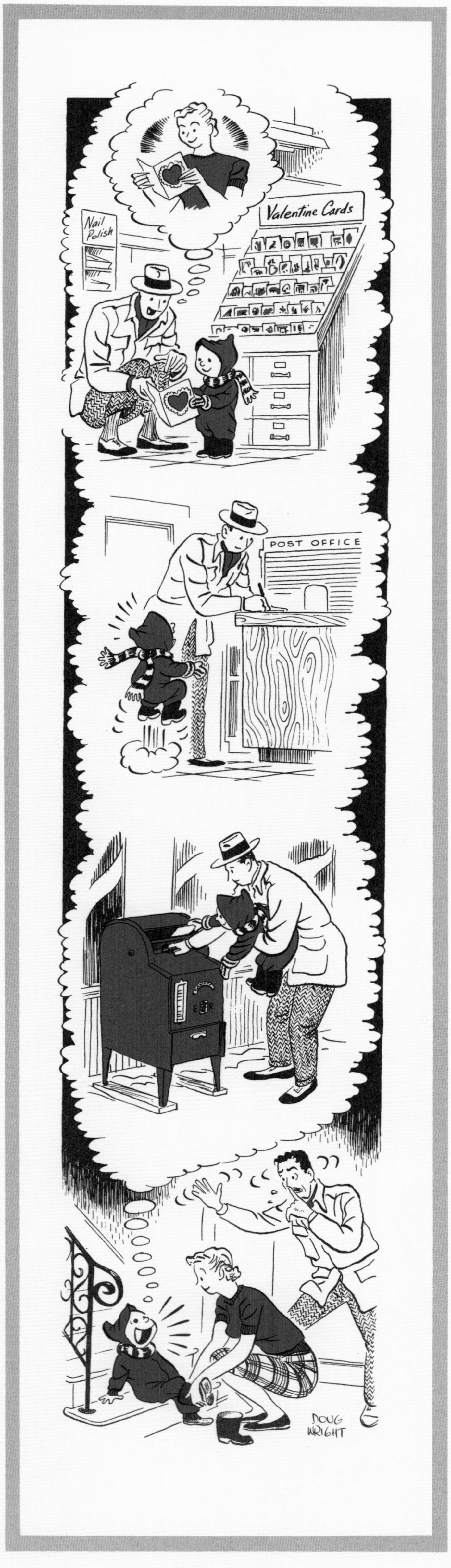
Valentine Cards
Nail Polish
POST OFFICE
DOUG WRIGHT

February 11, 1956

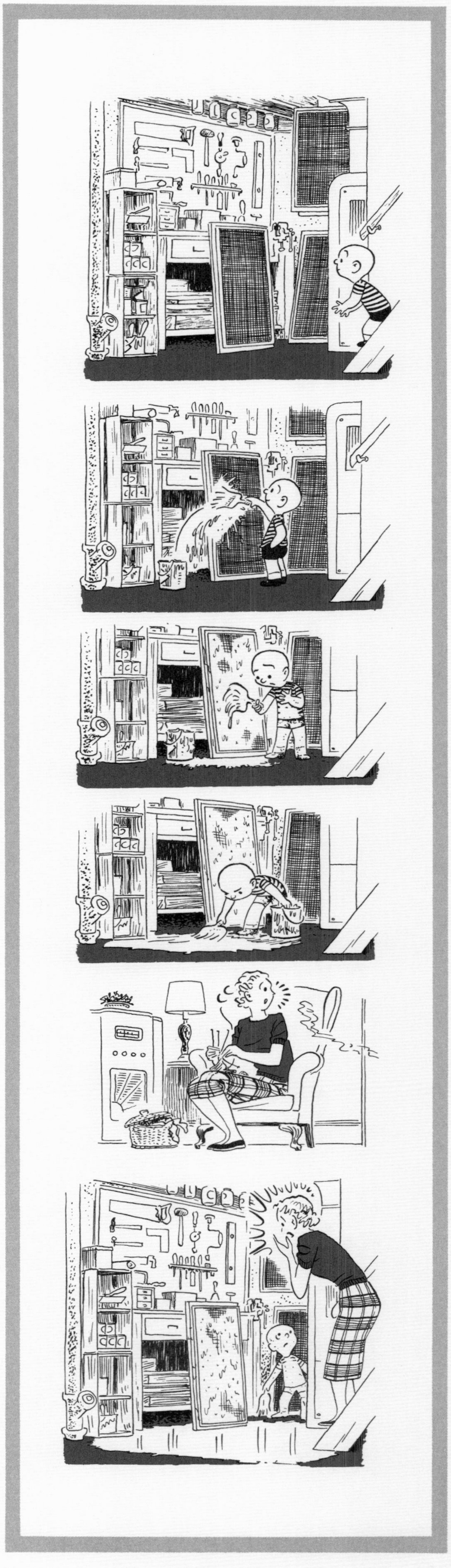

February 18, 1956

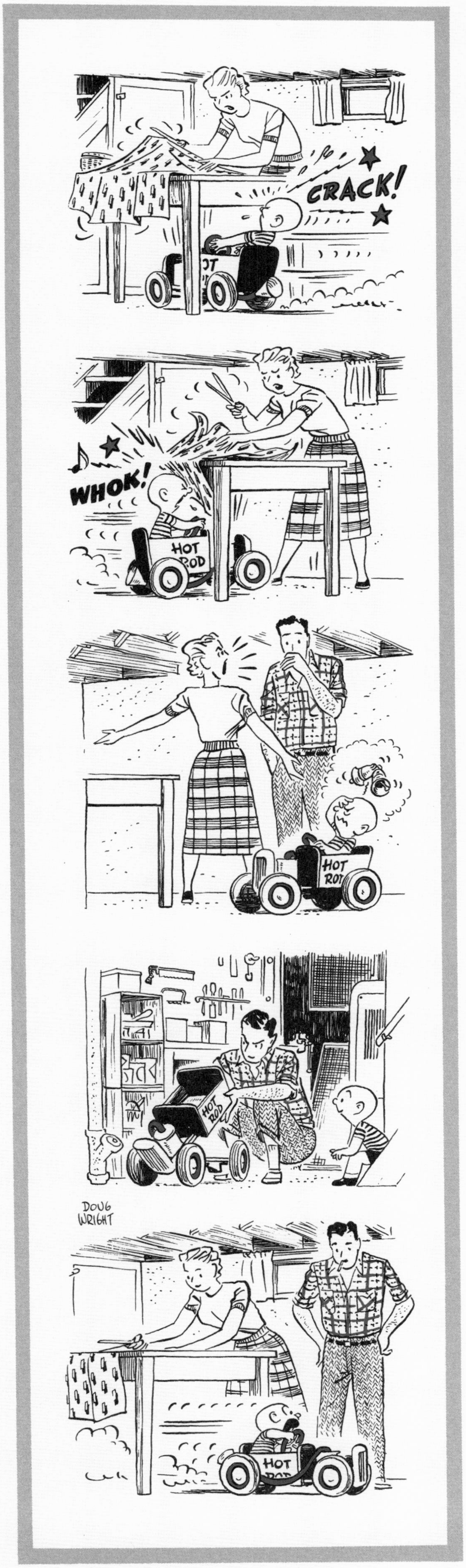
CRACK!
HOT
WHOK!
HOT ROD
HOT ROD
HOT ROD
DOUG WRIGHT
HOT ROD

February 25, 1956

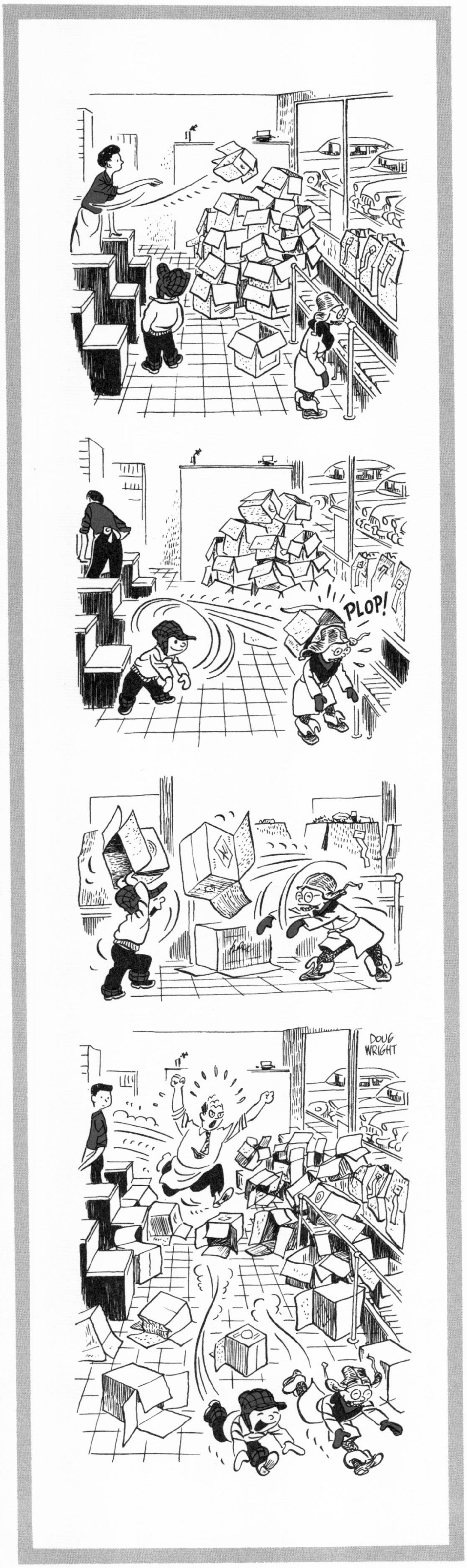
PLOP!
DOUG WRIGHT

March 10, 1956

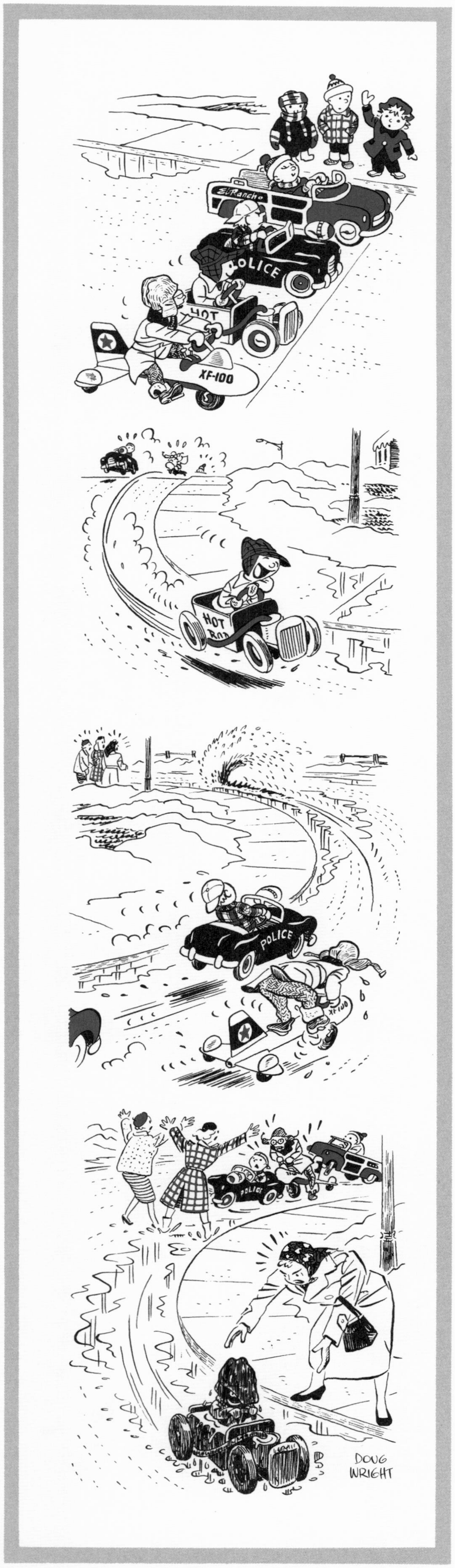
El Rancho
POLICE
HOT
XF-100
HOT ROD
POLICE
XF-100
POLICE
DOUG WRIGHT

March 24, 1956

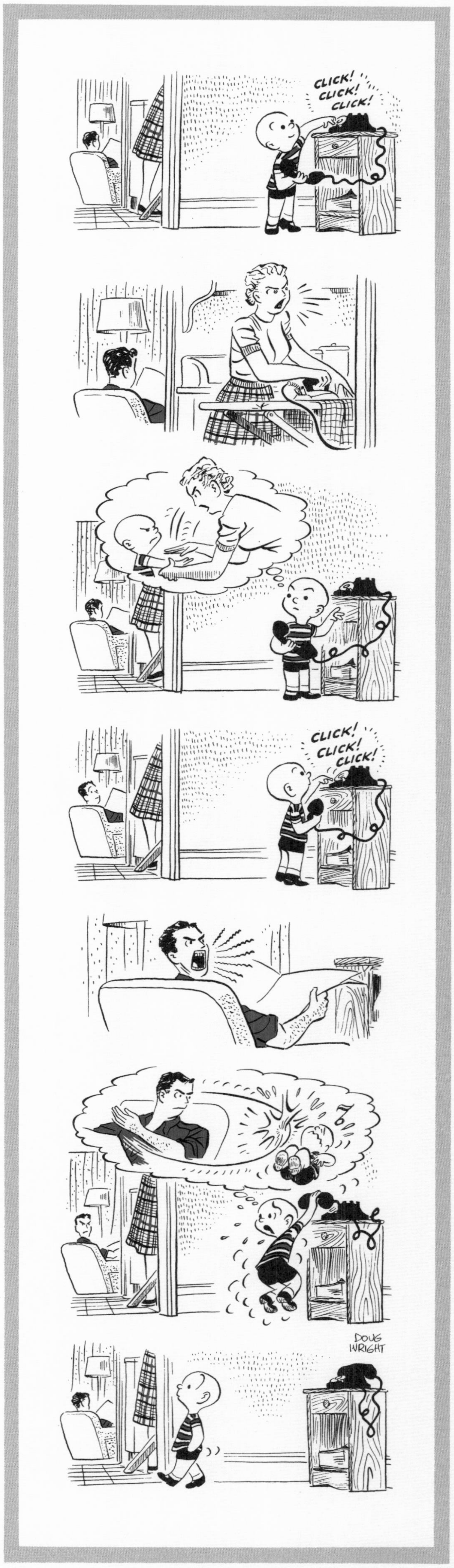
CLICK! CLICK! CLICK!
CLICK! CLICK! CLICK!
DOUG WRIGHT

April 14, 1956

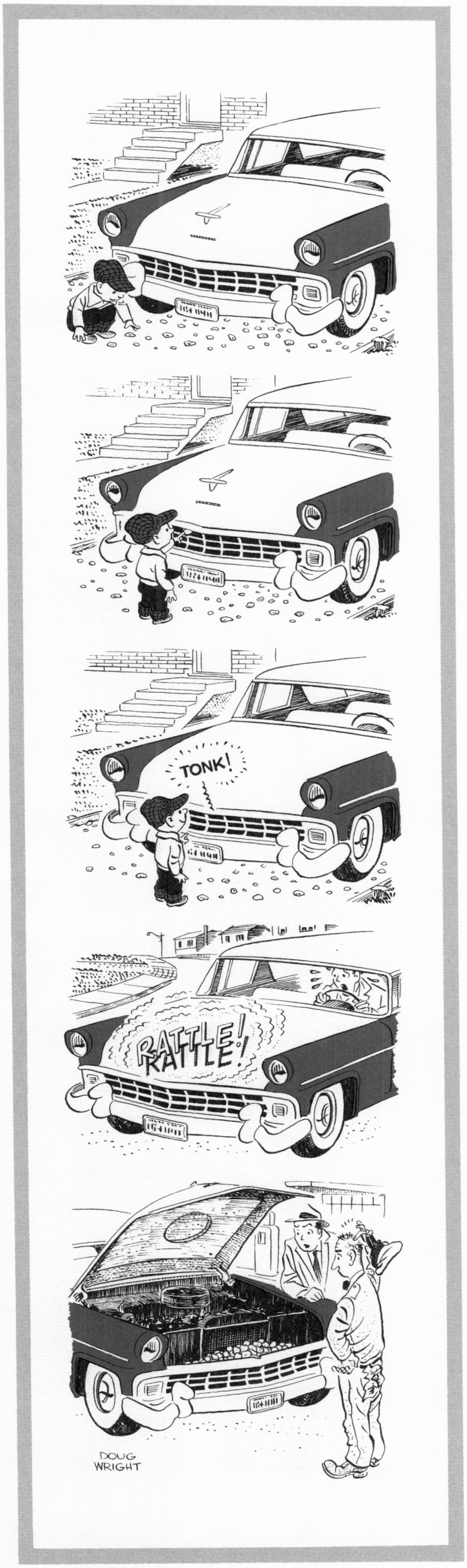
TONK!
RATTLE!
RATTLE!
DOUG WRIGHT

April 28, 1956

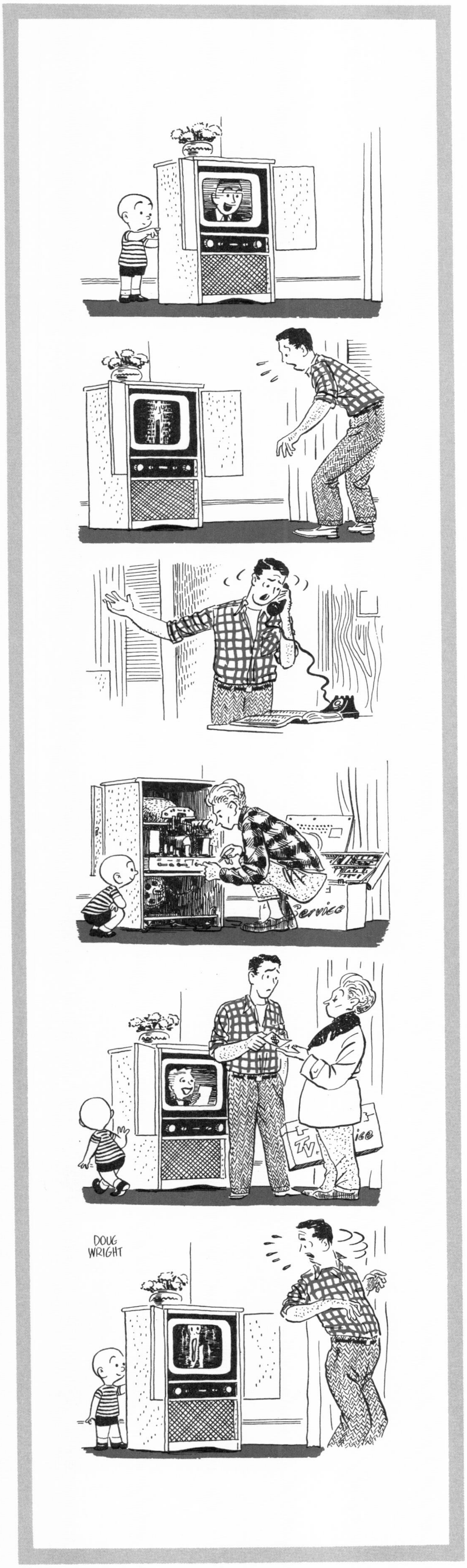
Service
DOUG WRIGHT

May 5, 1956

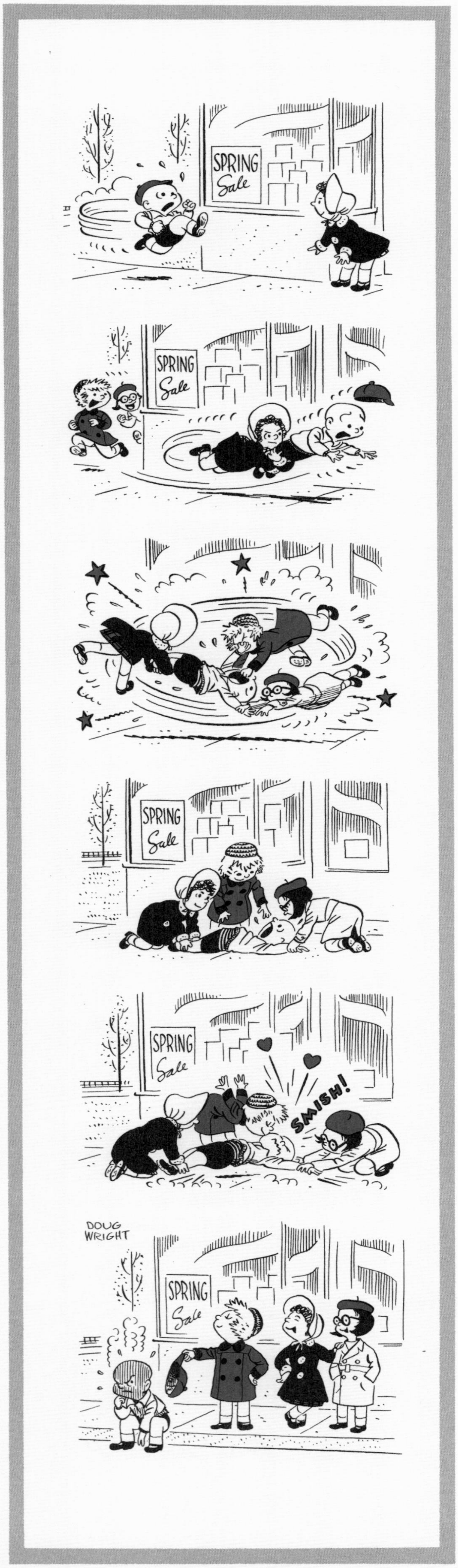
SPRING Sale
SMISH!
DOUG WRIGHT

May 12, 1956

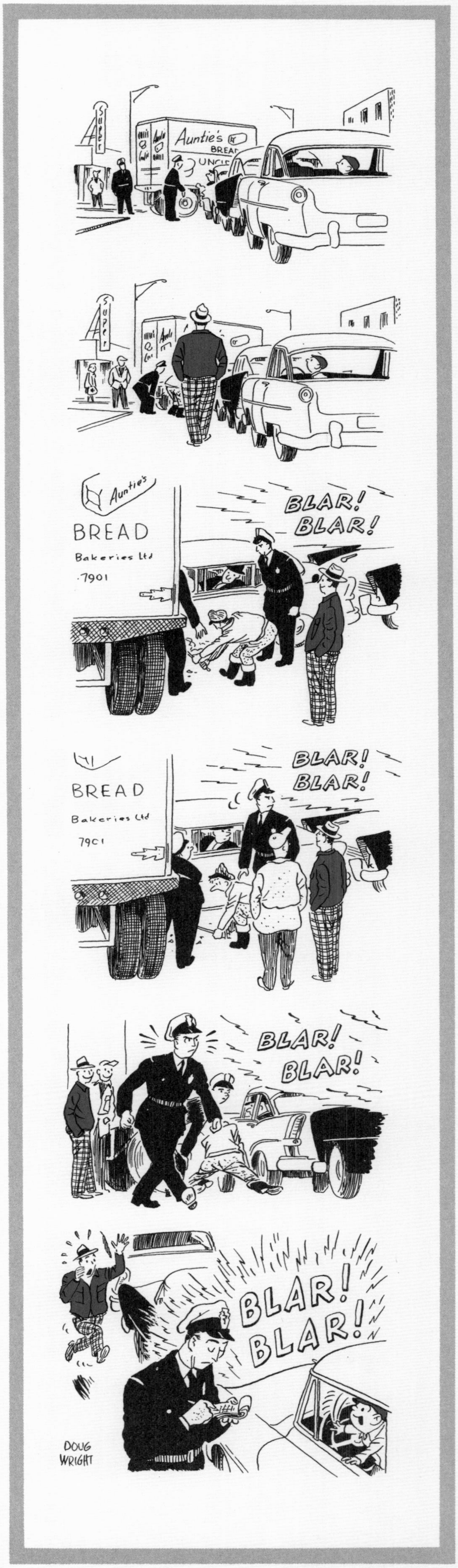
Auntie's BREAD
BREAD
Bakeries Ltd
BLAR! BLAR!
BLAR! BLAR!
BLAR! BLAR!
BLAR! BLAR!
DOUG WRIGHT

May 19, 1956

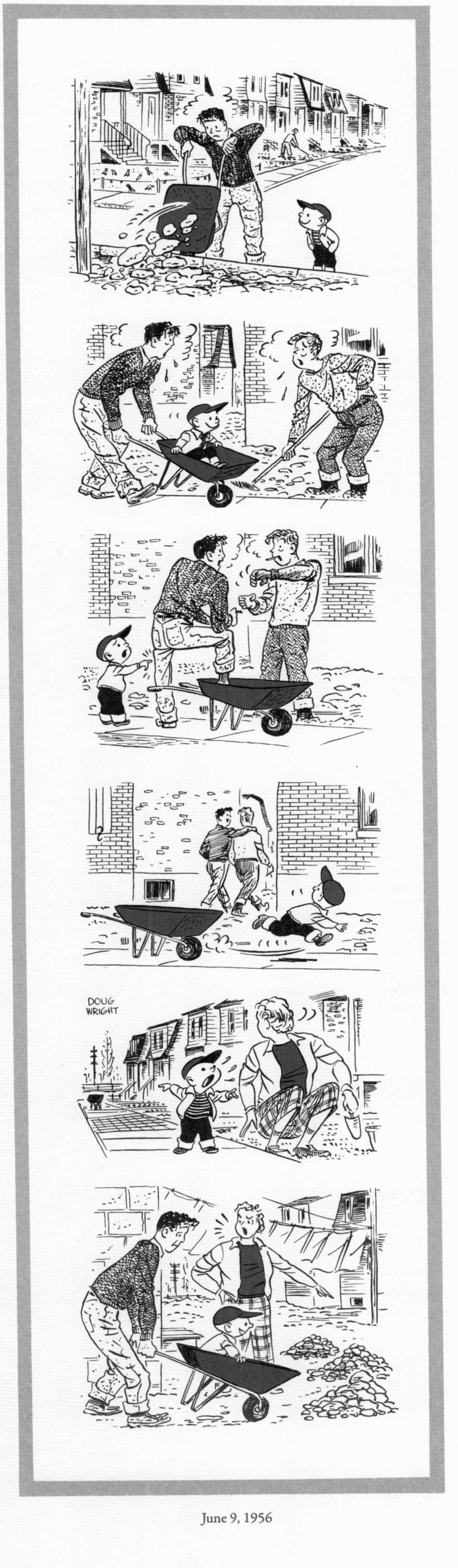
DOUG
WRIGHT

June 9, 1956

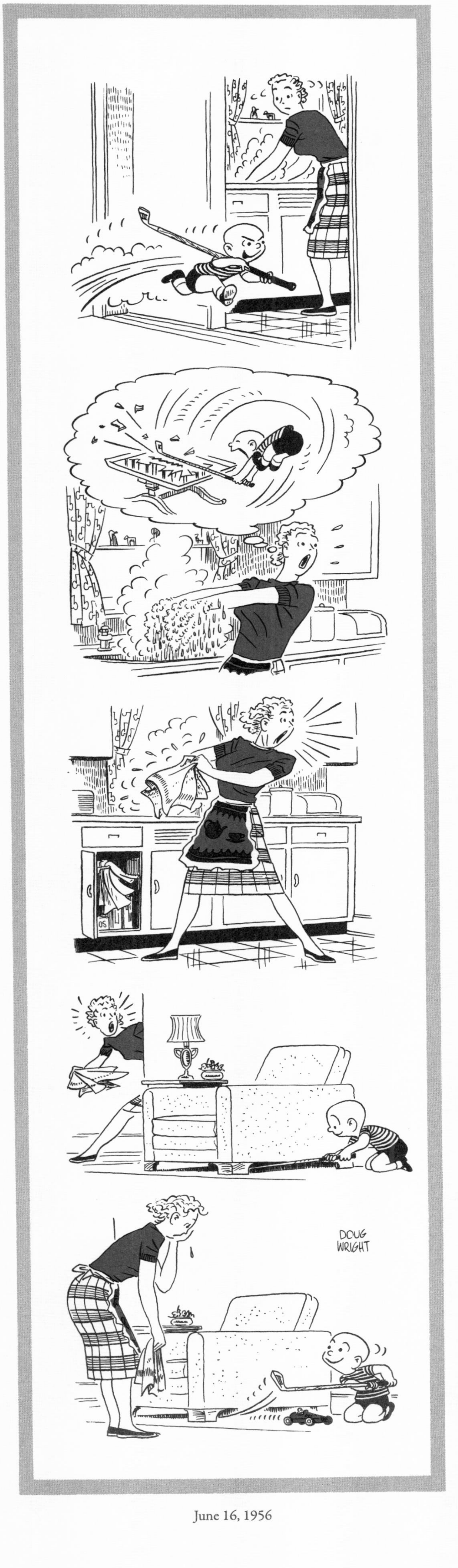
DOUG
WRIGHT

June 16, 1956

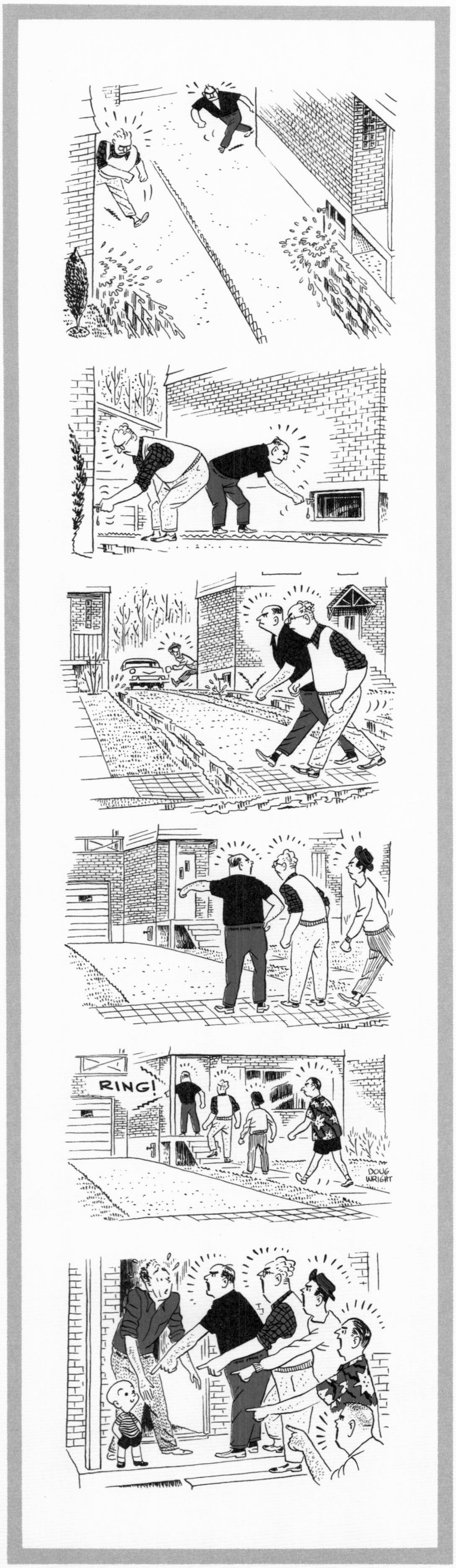
RING!
DOUG WRIGHT

June 23, 1956

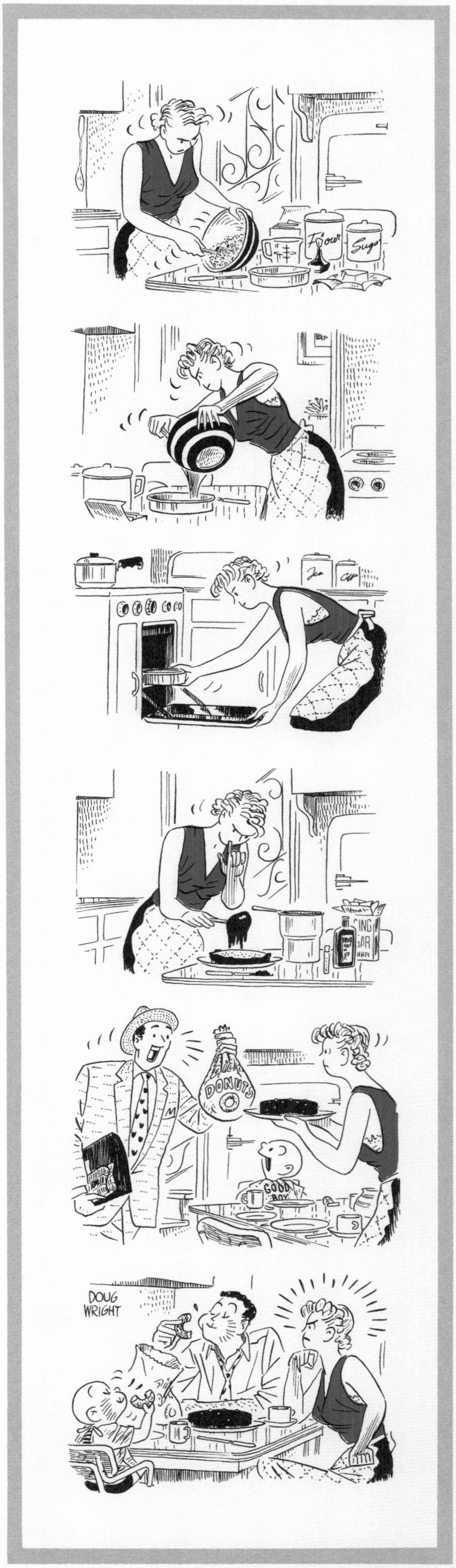
DONUTS
GOOD BOY
DOUG WRIGHT

June 30, 1956

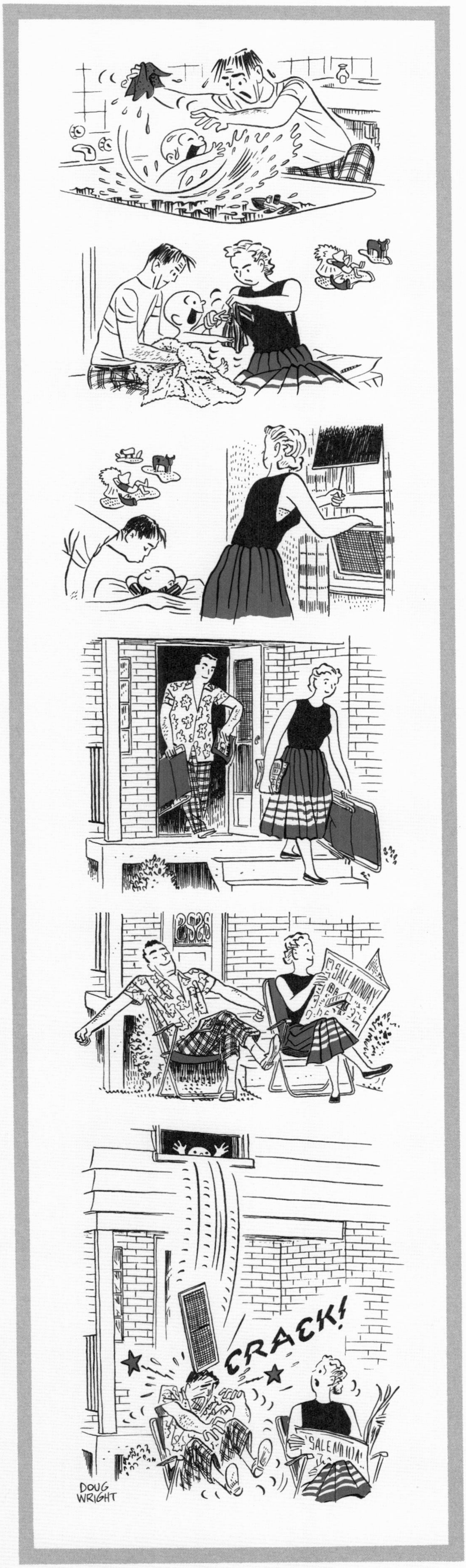
SALE MONDAY!
CRACK!
SALE MONDAY!
DOUG
WRIGHT

July 28, 1956

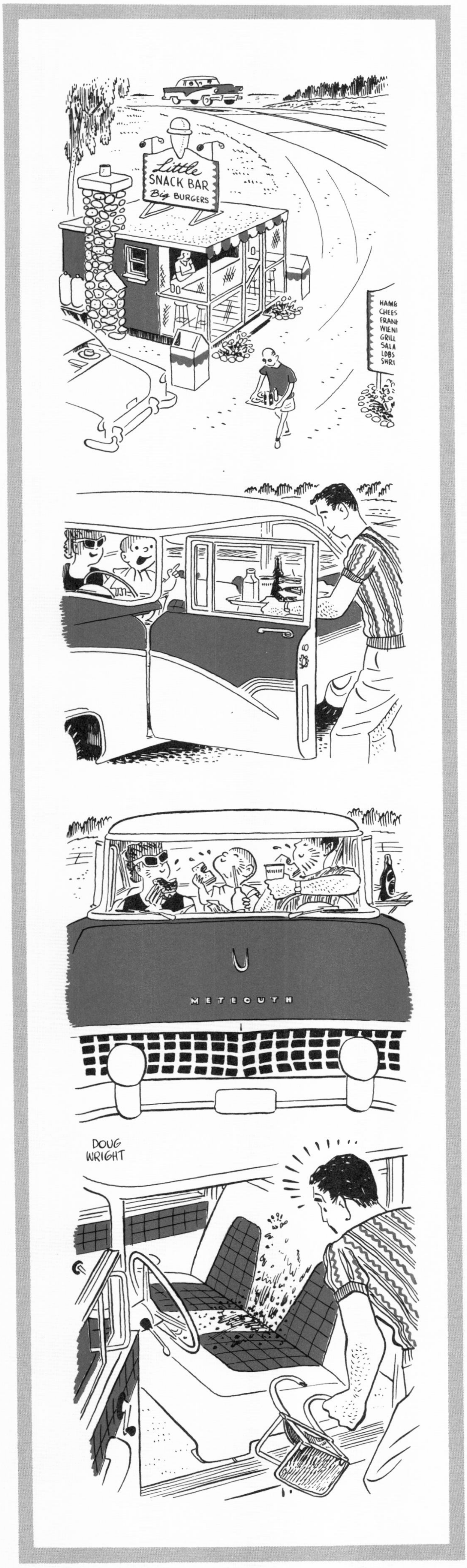
Little
SNACK BAR
Big BURGERS
METEOUTH
DOUG
WRIGHT

August 11, 1956

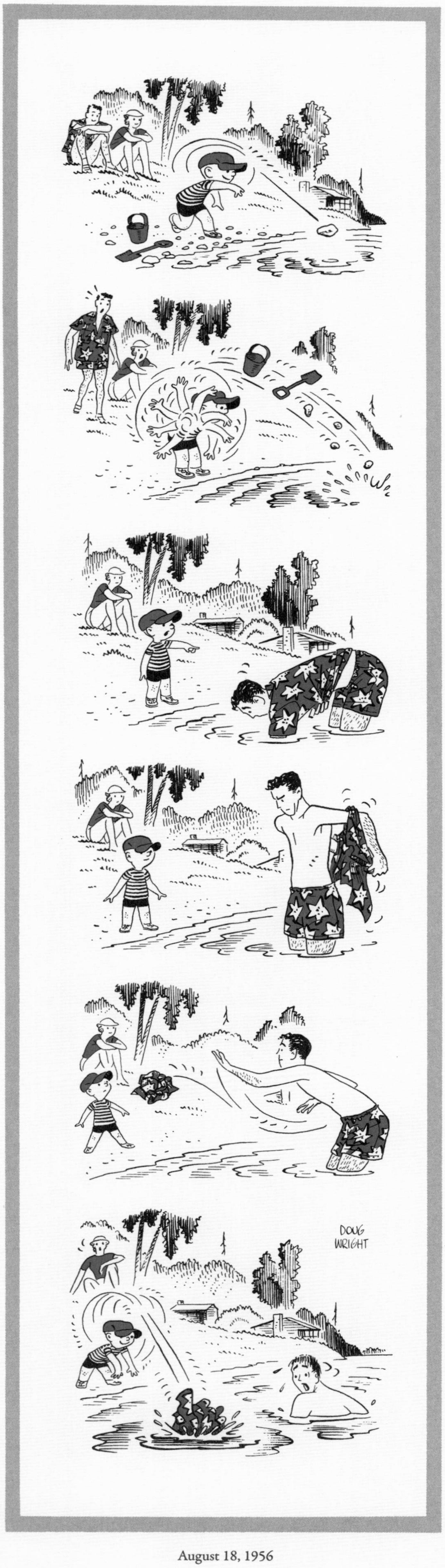
DOUG WRIGHT

August 18, 1956

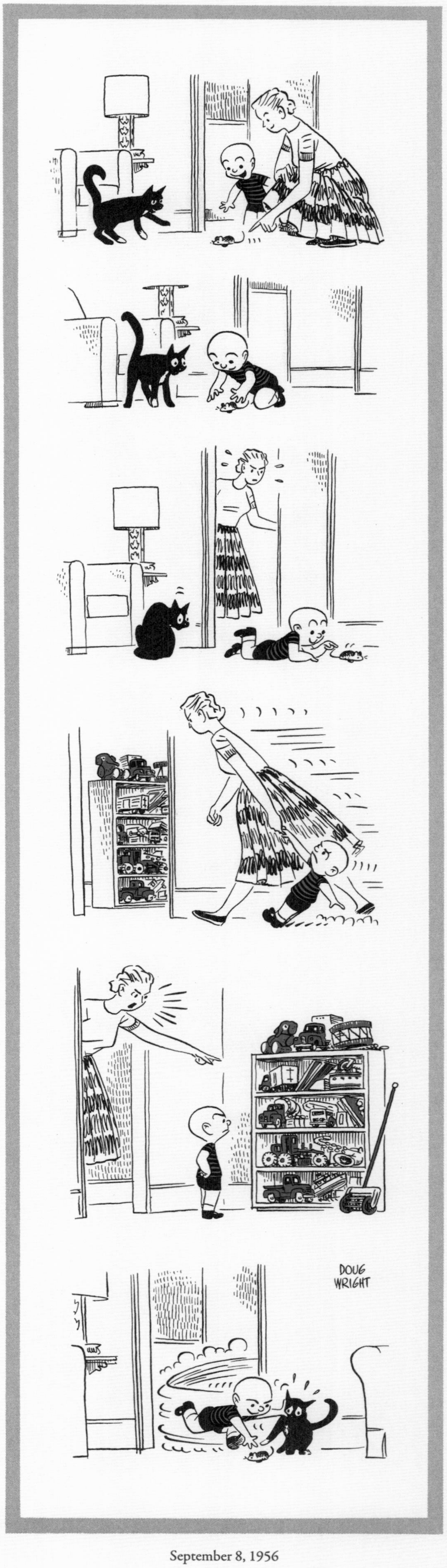
DOUG WRIGHT

September 8, 1956

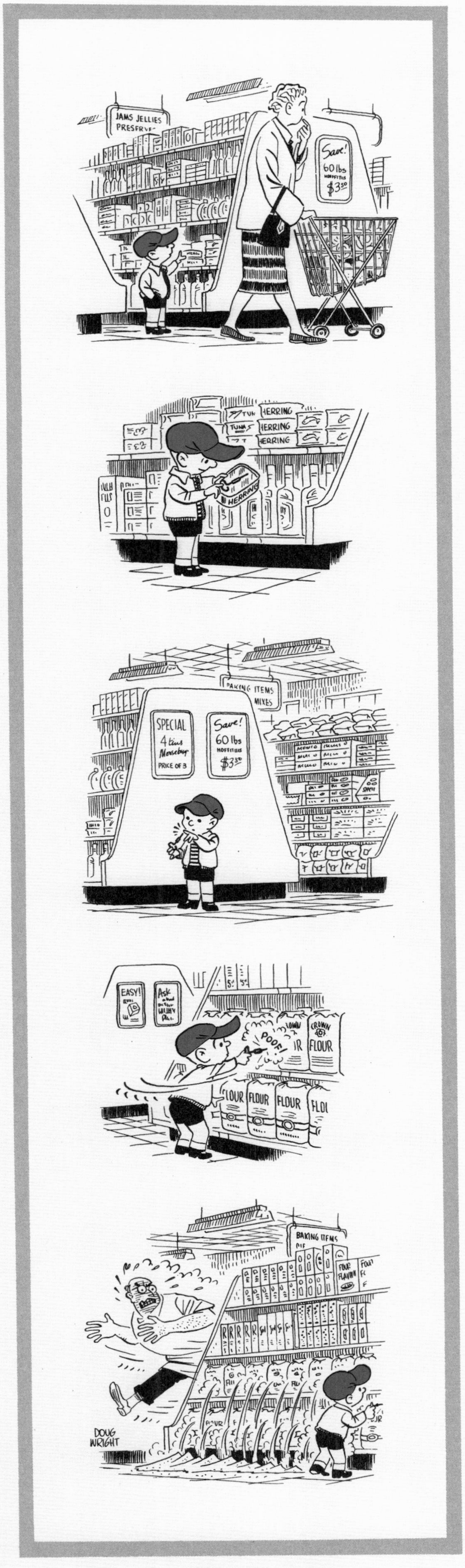
JAMS JELLIES
Save!
60 lbs
$3.50
HERRING
HERRING
SPECIAL
4 tins
PRICE OF 3
Save!
60 lbs
$3.50
MIXES
EASY!
Ask
POOF!
CROWN
FLOUR
FLOUR
FLOUR
FLOUR
BAKING ITEMS
DOUG WRIGHT

September 22, 1956

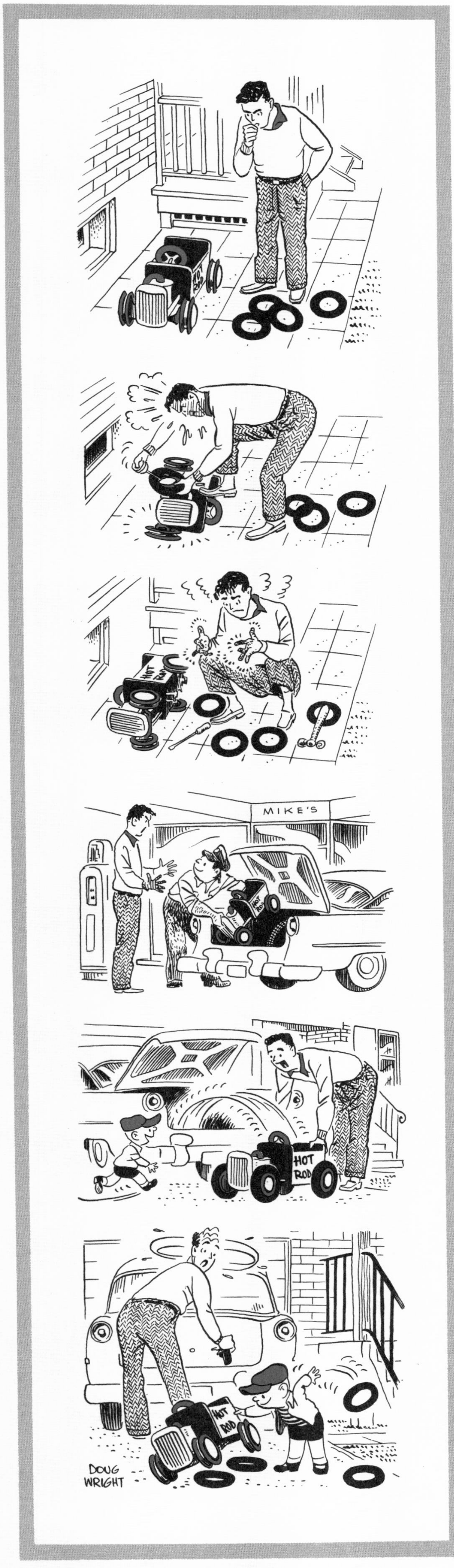
MIKE'S
HOT ROD
HOT ROD
DOUG WRIGHT

September 29, 1956

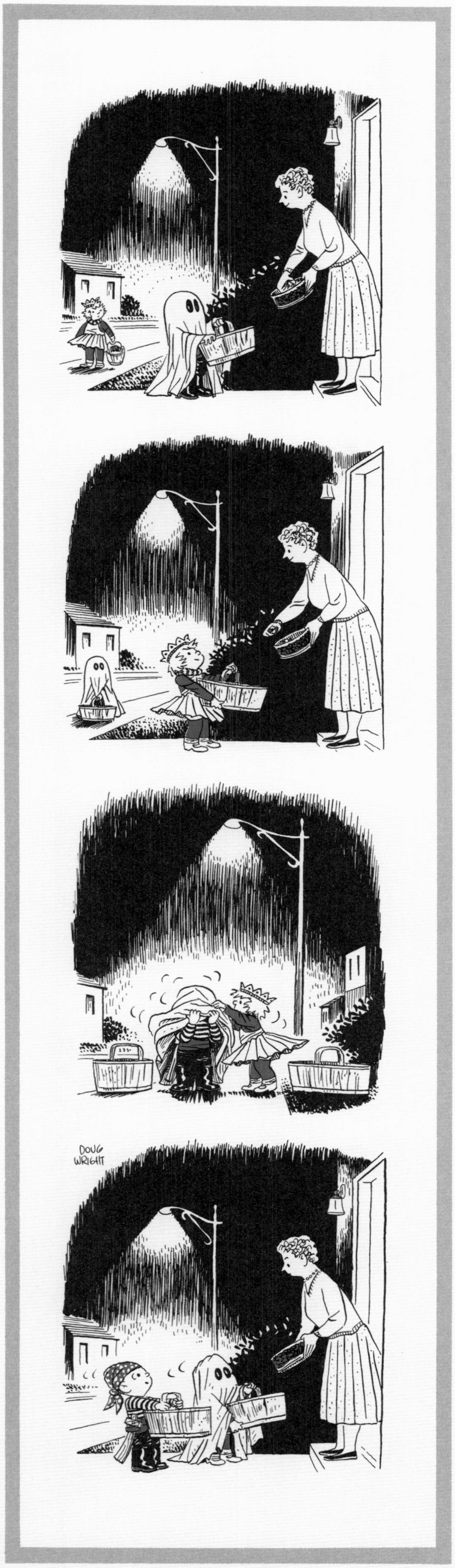
DOUG
WRIGHT

October 27, 1956

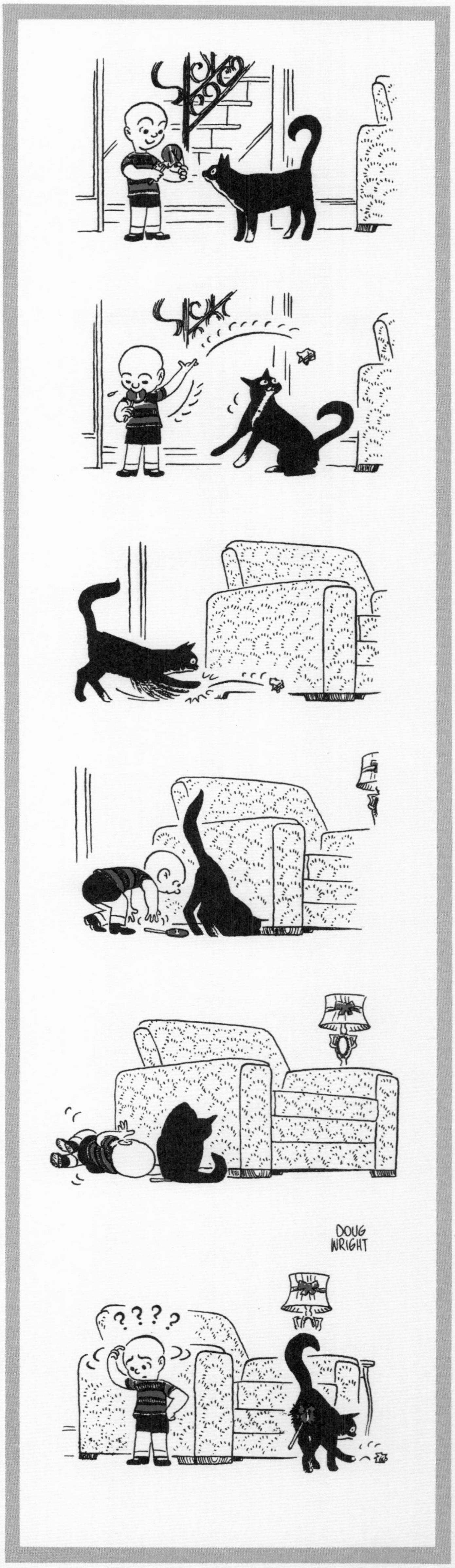
DOUG
WRIGHT
????

November 10, 1956

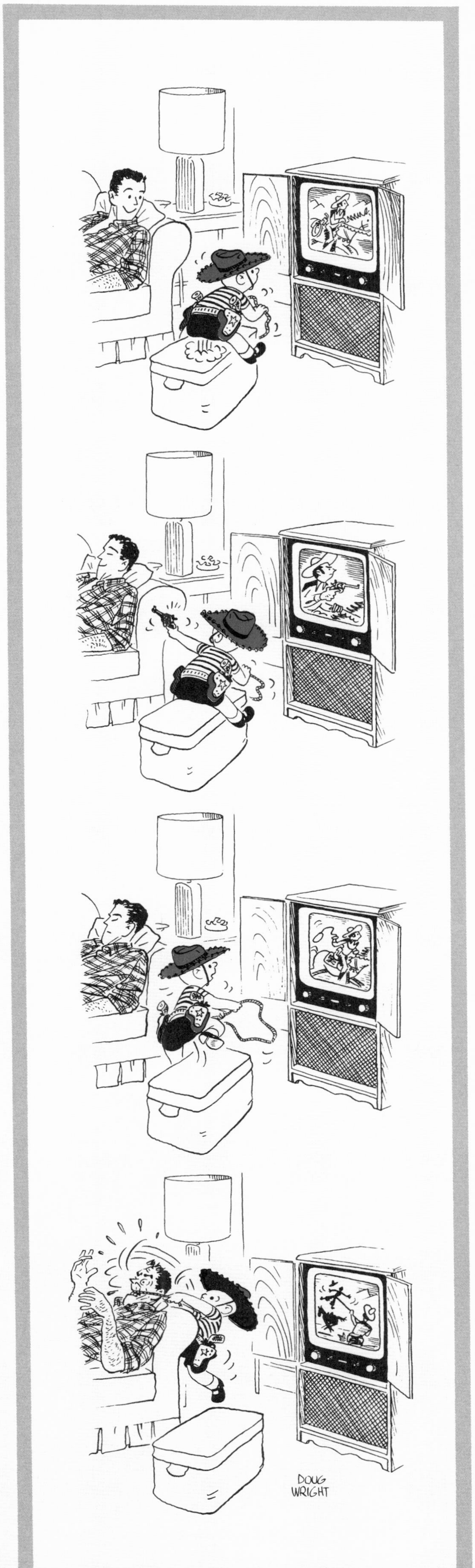
DOUG
WRIGHT

November 17, 1956

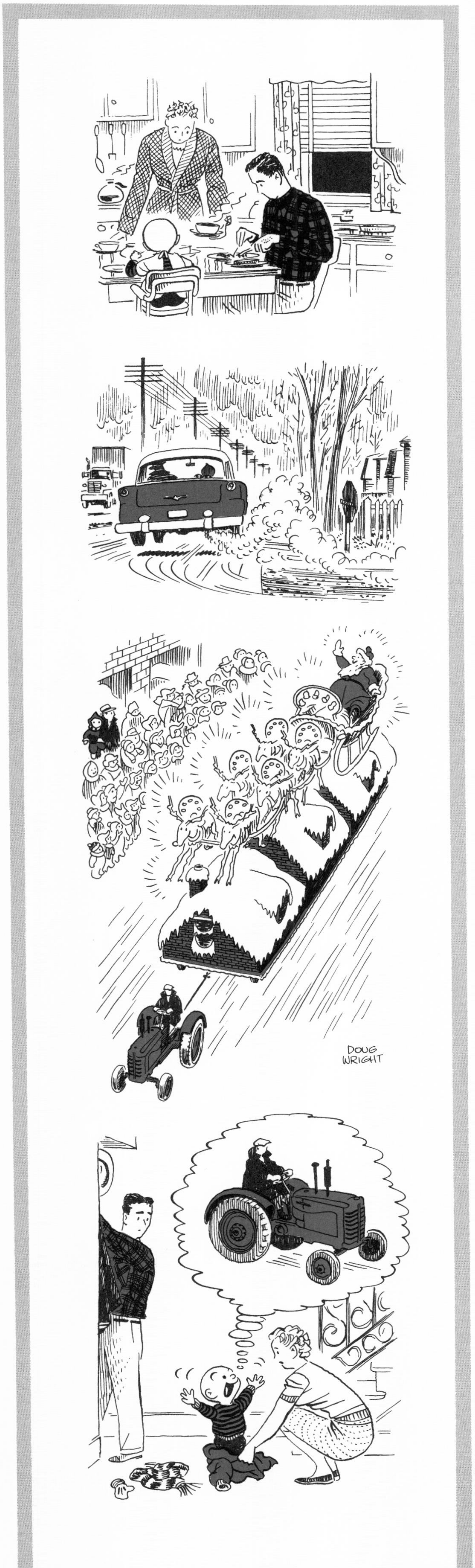
DOUG
WRIGHT

November 24, 1956

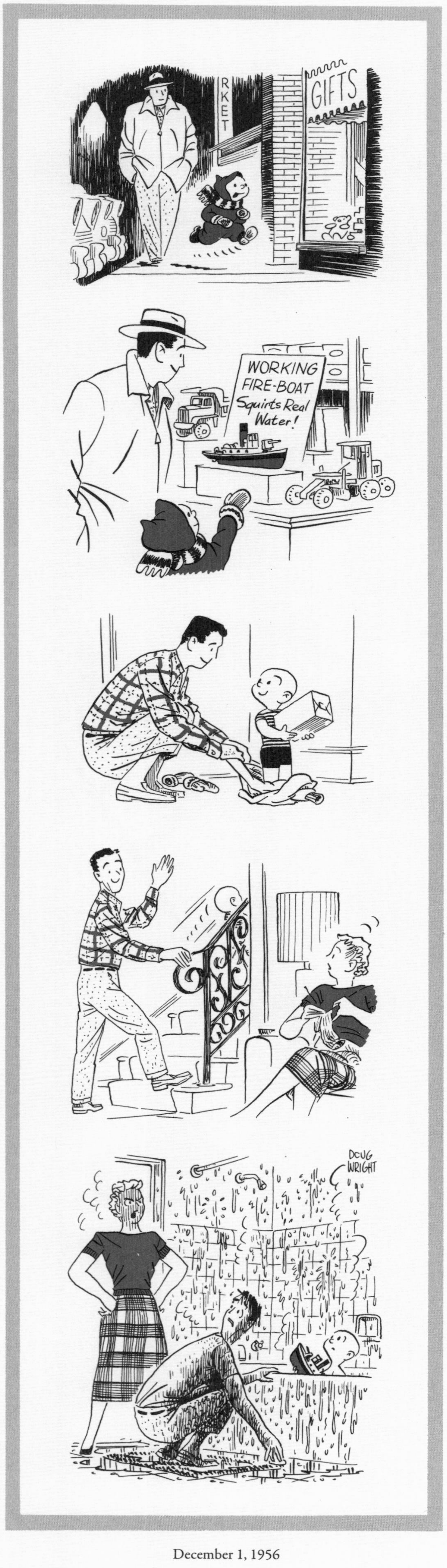
RKET
GIFTS
WORKING
FIRE-BOAT
Squirts Real
Water!
DOUG
WRIGHT

December 1, 1956

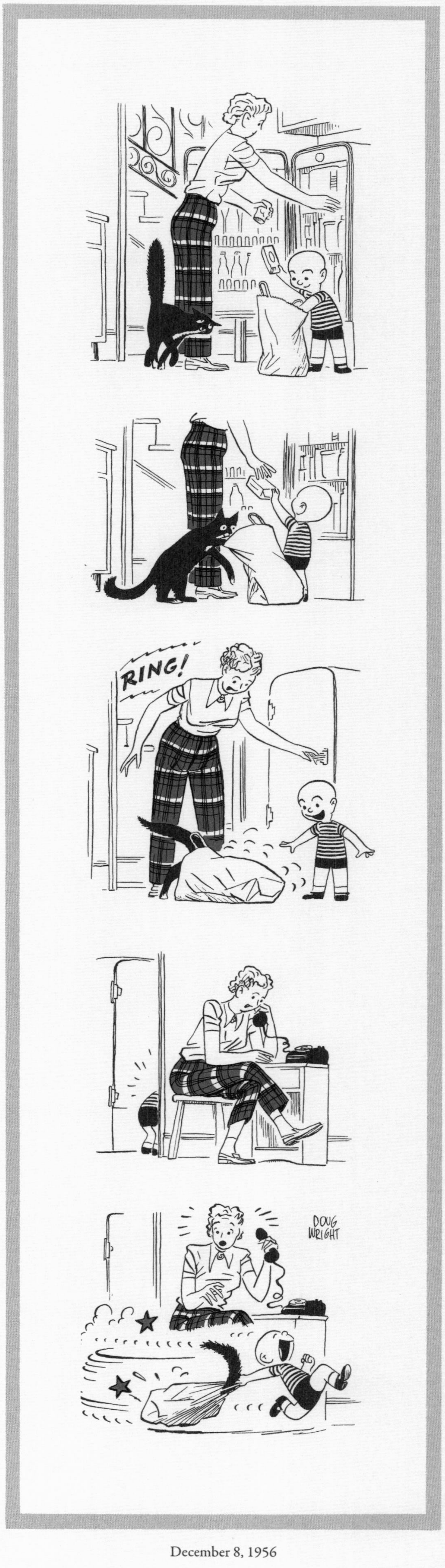
RING!
DOUG
WRIGHT

December 8, 1956

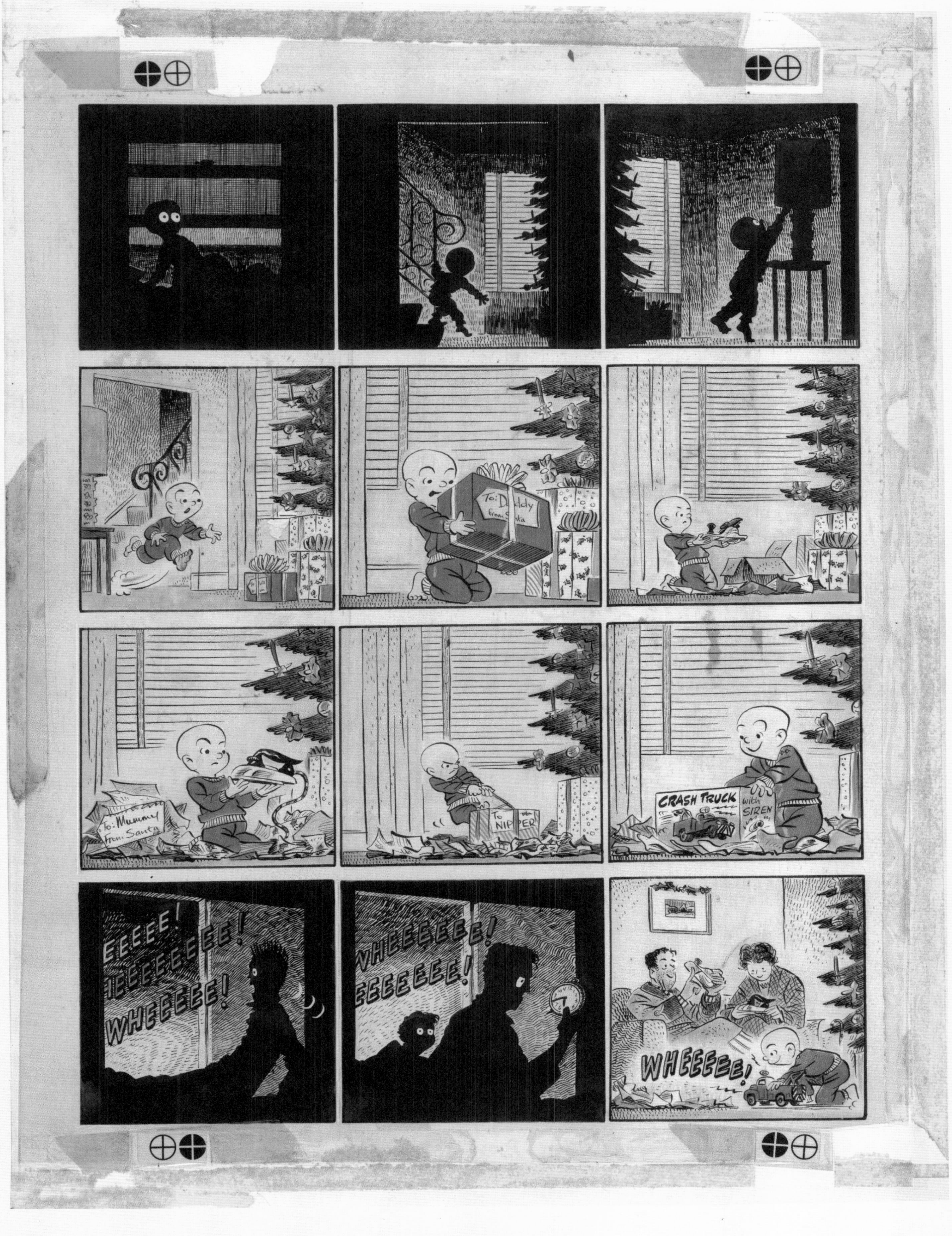
To: Daddy from Santa
To: Mummy from Santa
To NIPPER
CRASH TRUCK with SIREN
EEEEE! EEEEEEEE! WHEEEEE!
WHEEEEEEE! EEEEEEE!
WHEEEEE!

December 29, 1956

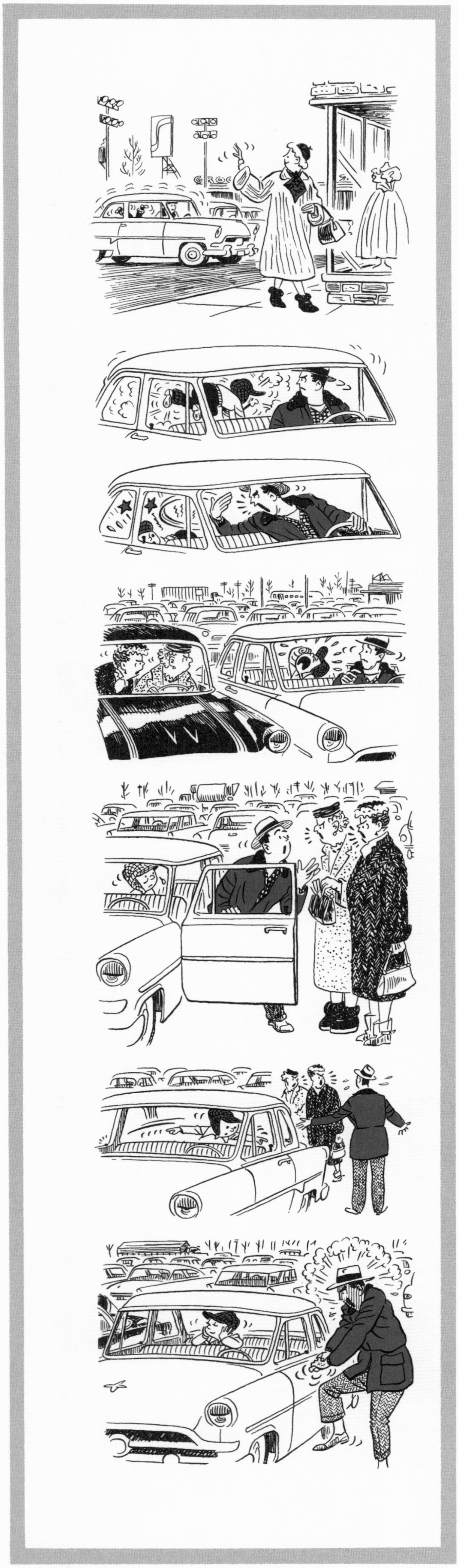

January 5, 1957

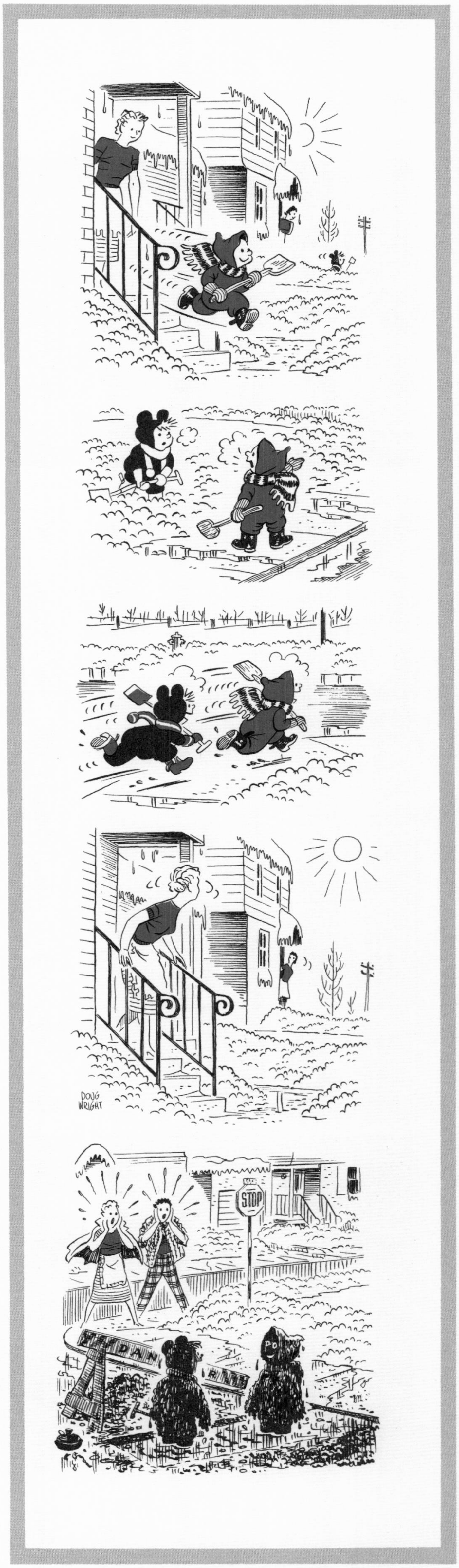
DOUG WRIGHT
STOP

January 12, 1957

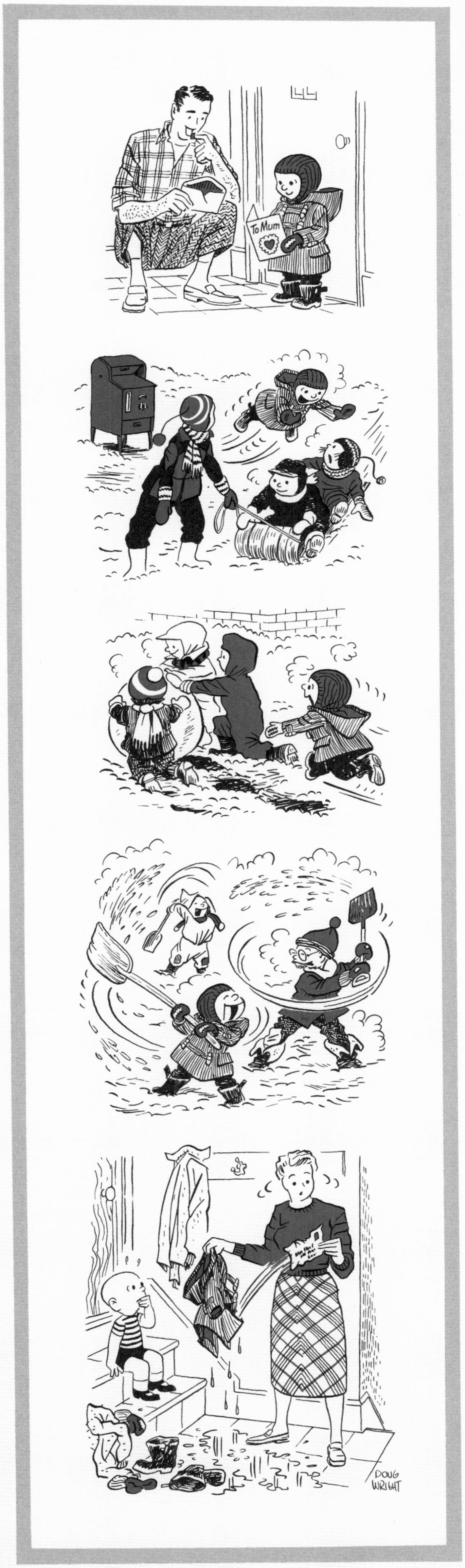
To Mum
DOUG WRIGHT

February 16, 1957

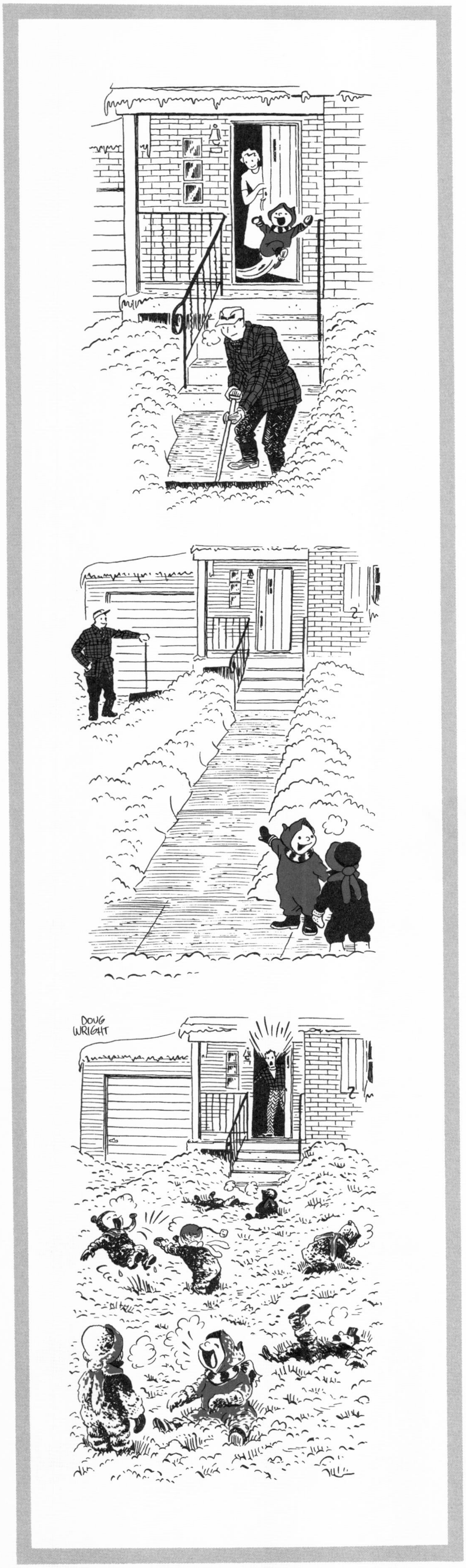
DOUG WRIGHT

February 23, 1957

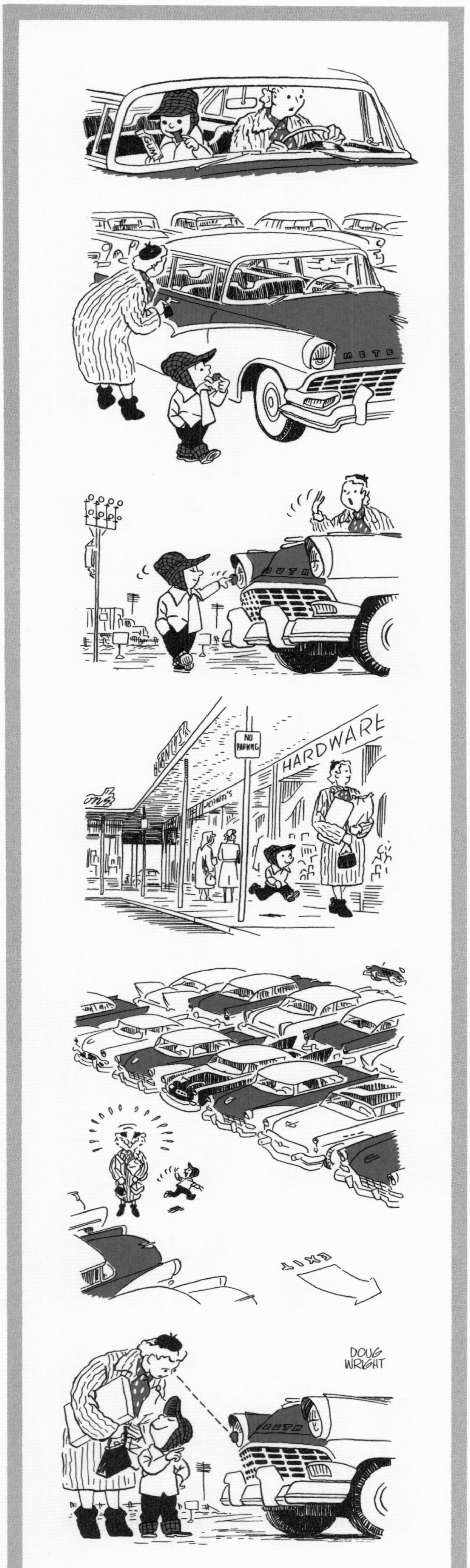
HARDWARE
DOUG WRIGHT

March 2, 1957

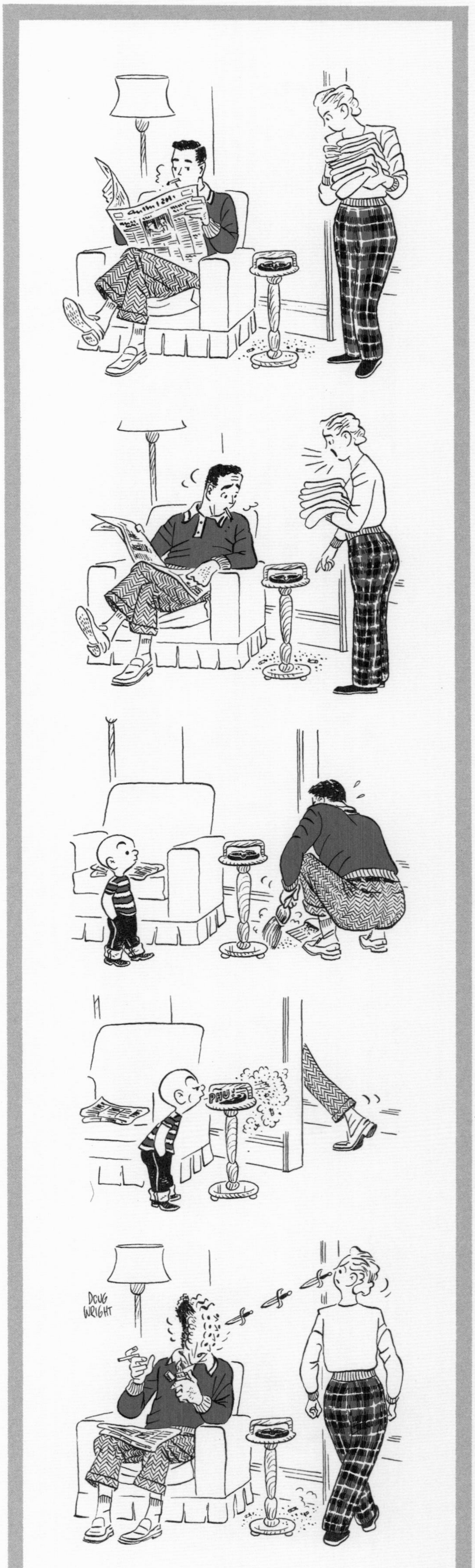
DOUG WRIGHT

March 9, 1957

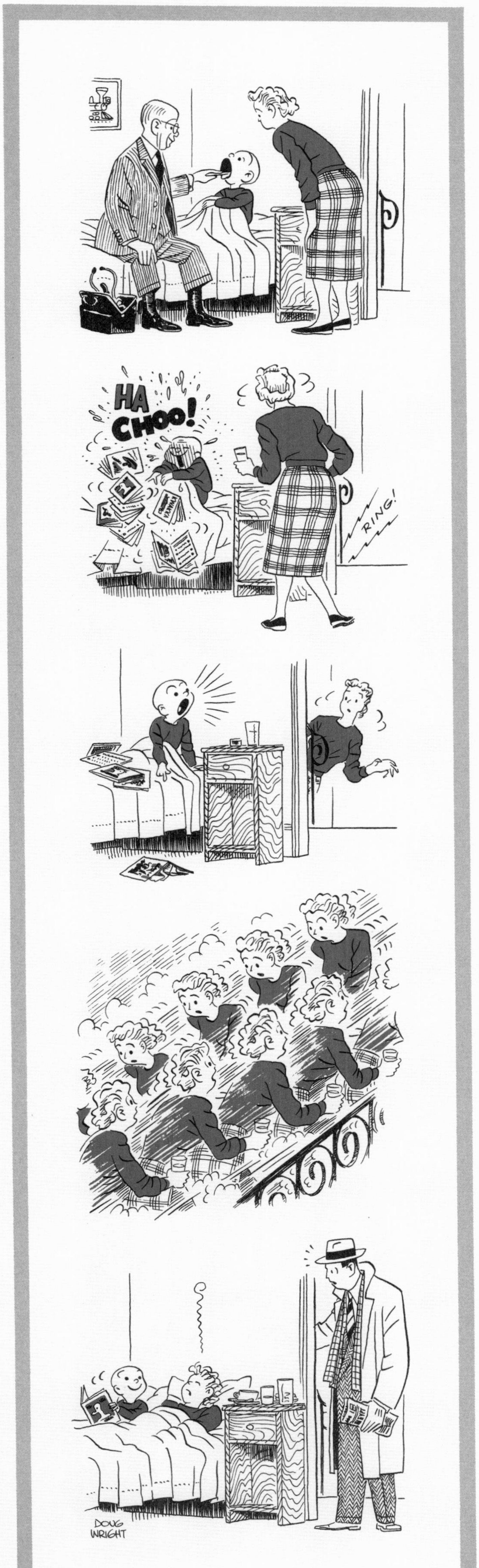
HA CHOO!
RING!
DOUG WRIGHT
March 16, 1957

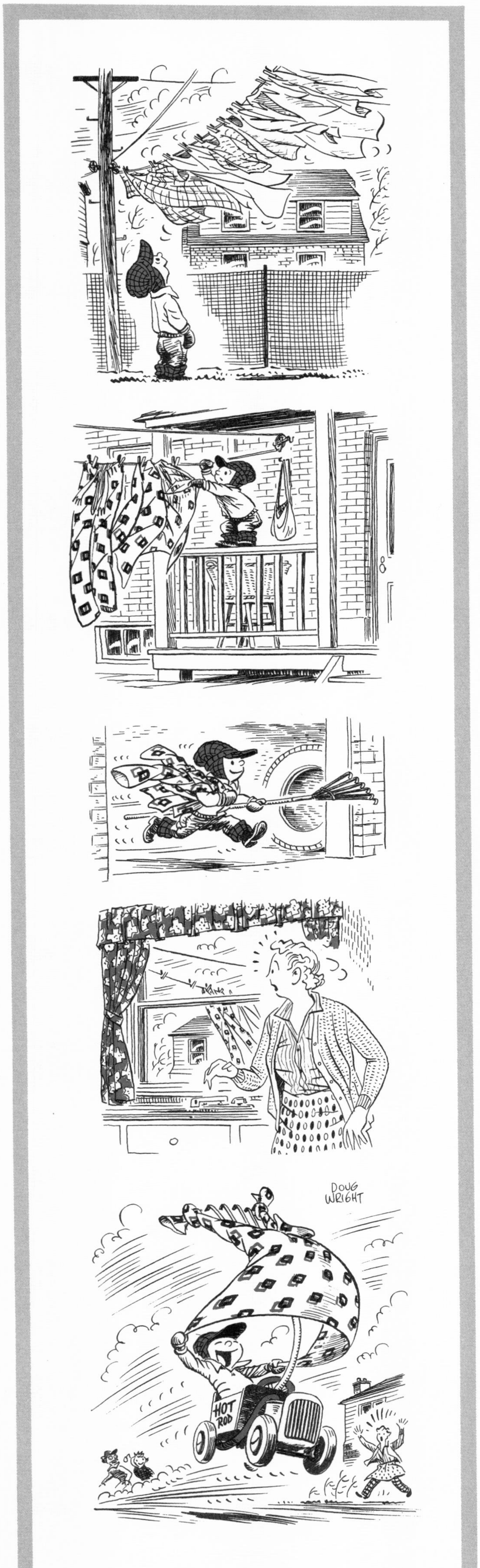
DOUG WRIGHT
HOT ROD
March 23, 1957

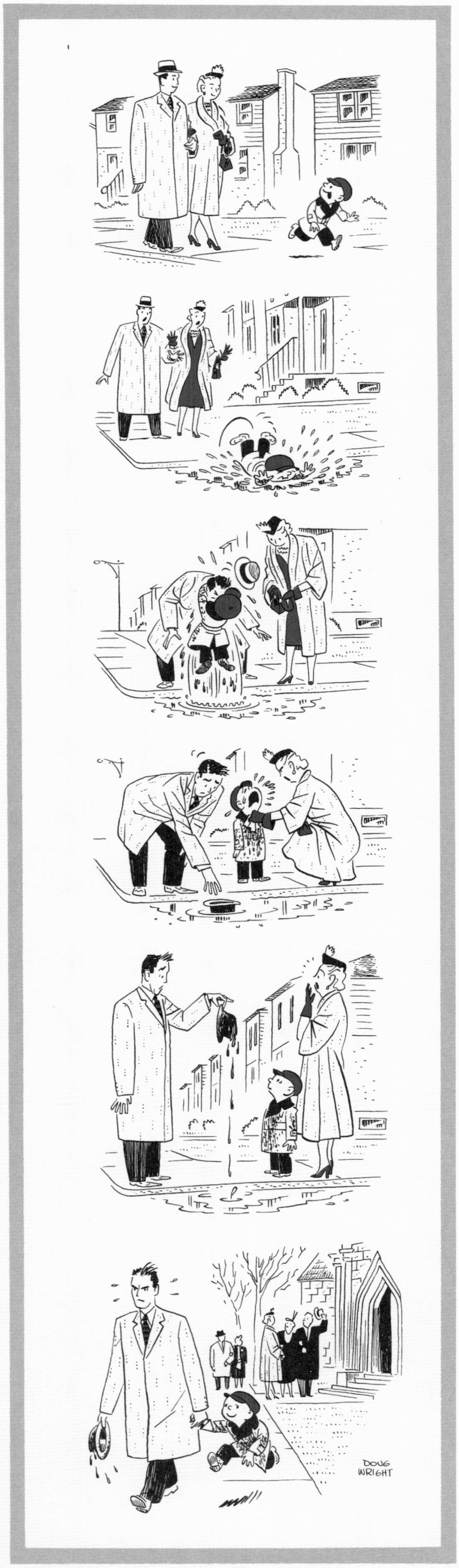
DOUG
WRIGHT

April 20, 1957

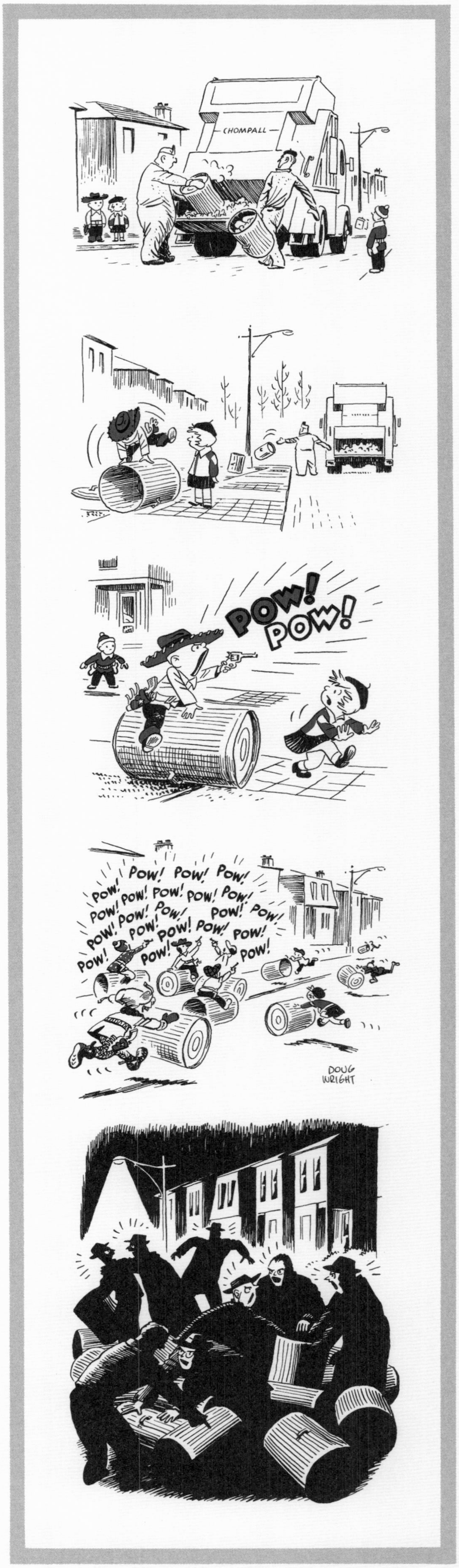
CHOMPALL
POW!
POW!
POW! POW! POW! POW! POW! POW! POW! POW! POW! POW! POW! POW! POW! POW! POW! POW! POW! POW! POW! POW! POW! POW!
DOUG
WRIGHT

April 27, 1957

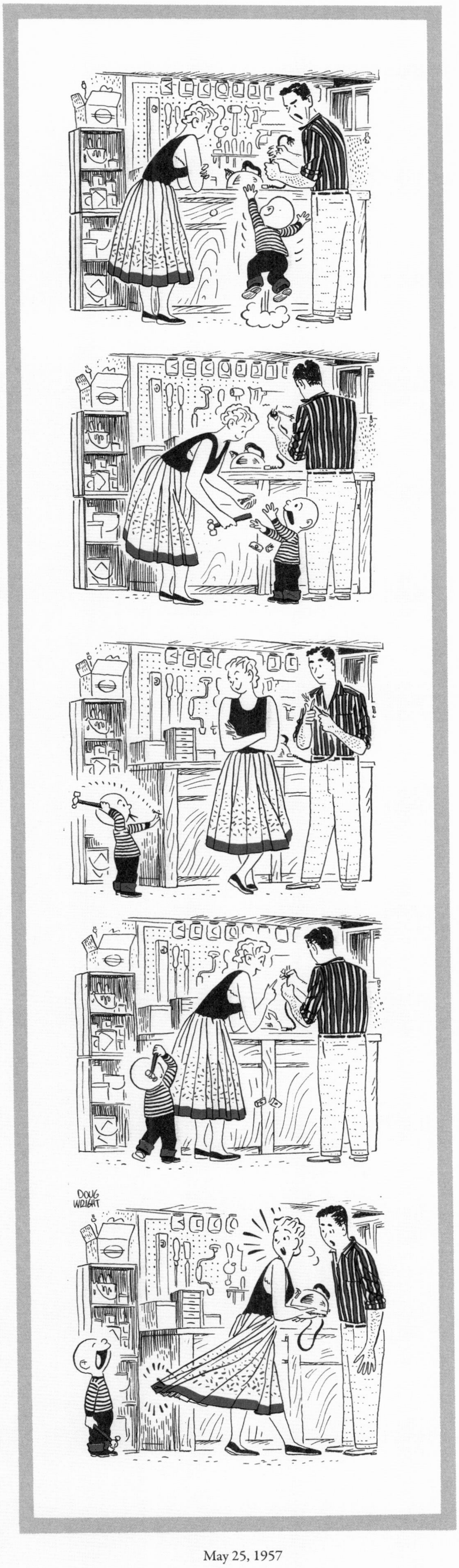
DOUG WRIGHT

May 25, 1957

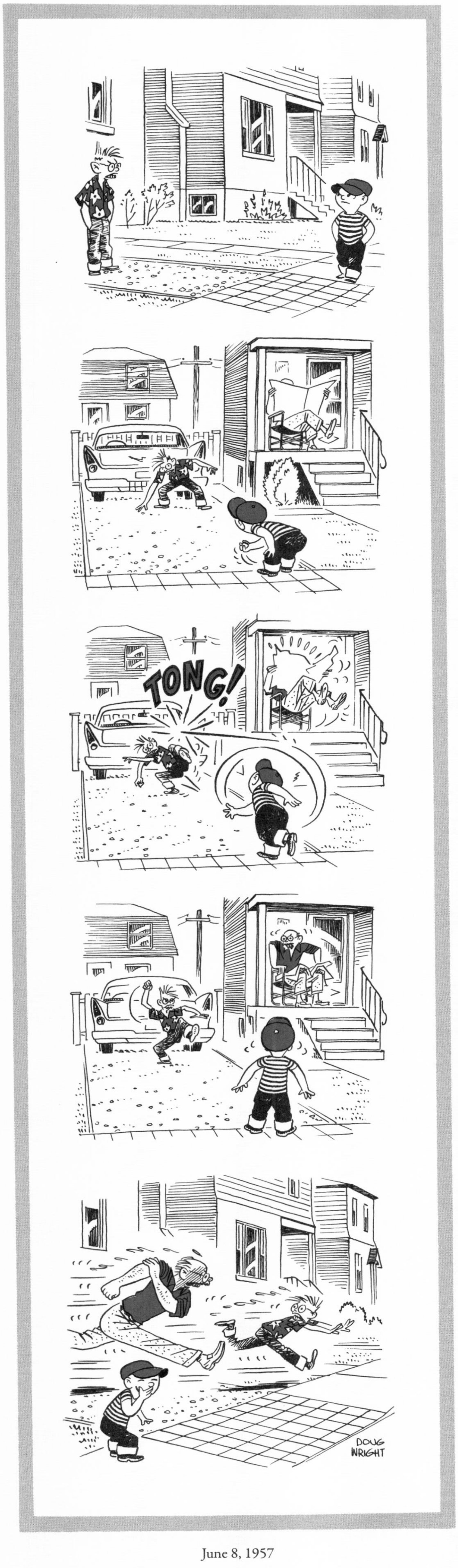
TONG!
DOUG WRIGHT

June 8, 1957

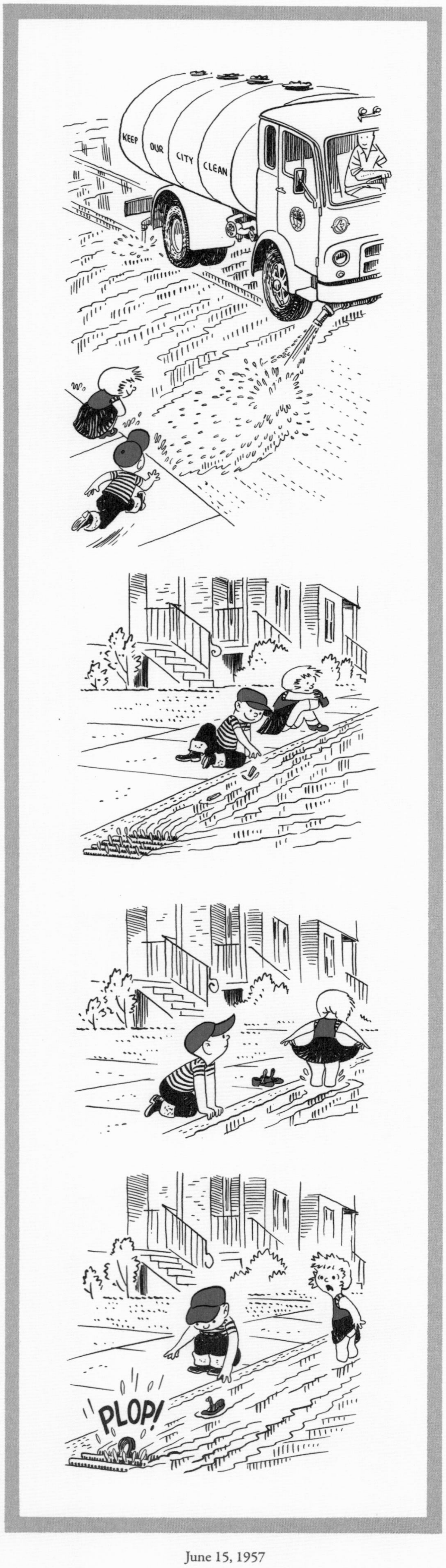
KEEP OUR CITY CLEAN
PLOP!

June 15, 1957

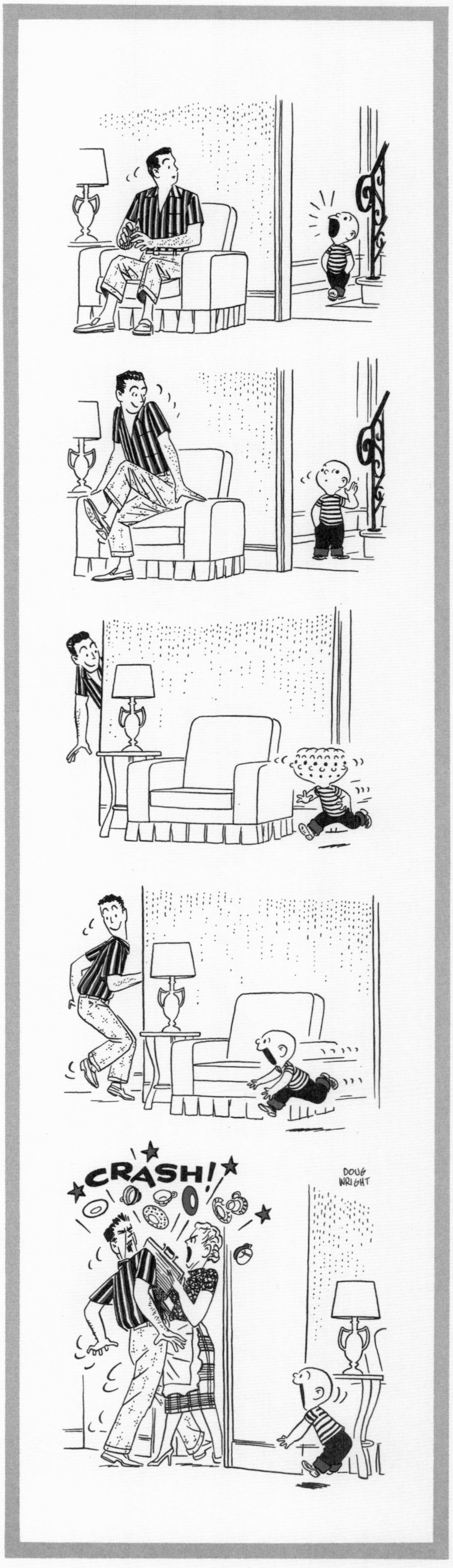
CRASH!
DOUG WRIGHT

June 22, 1957

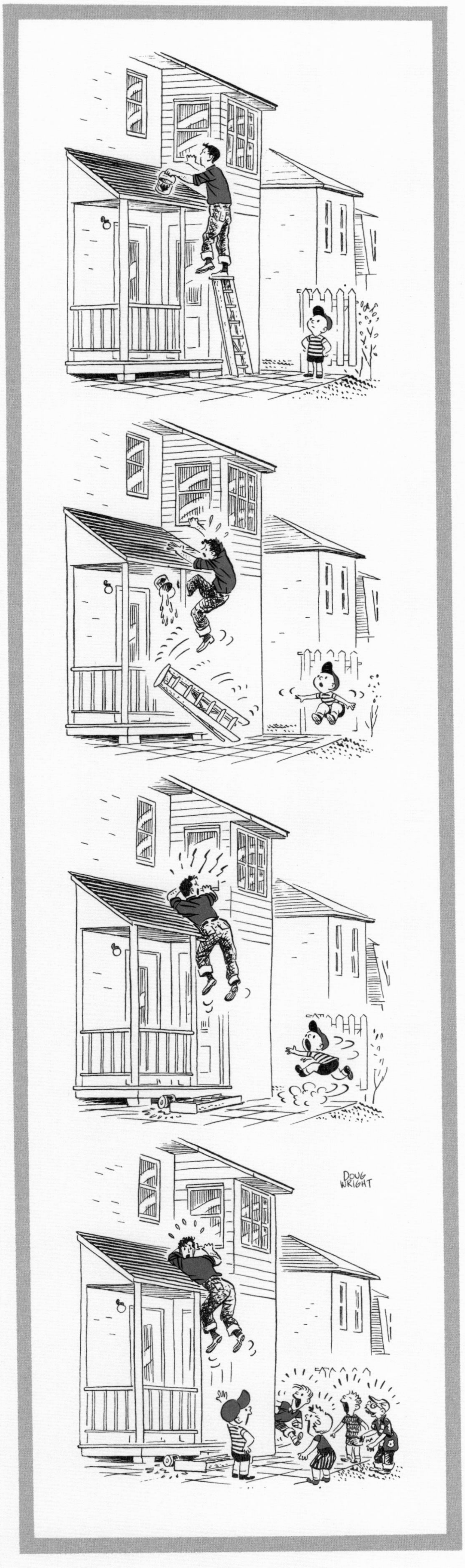
DOUG WRIGHT

June 29, 1957

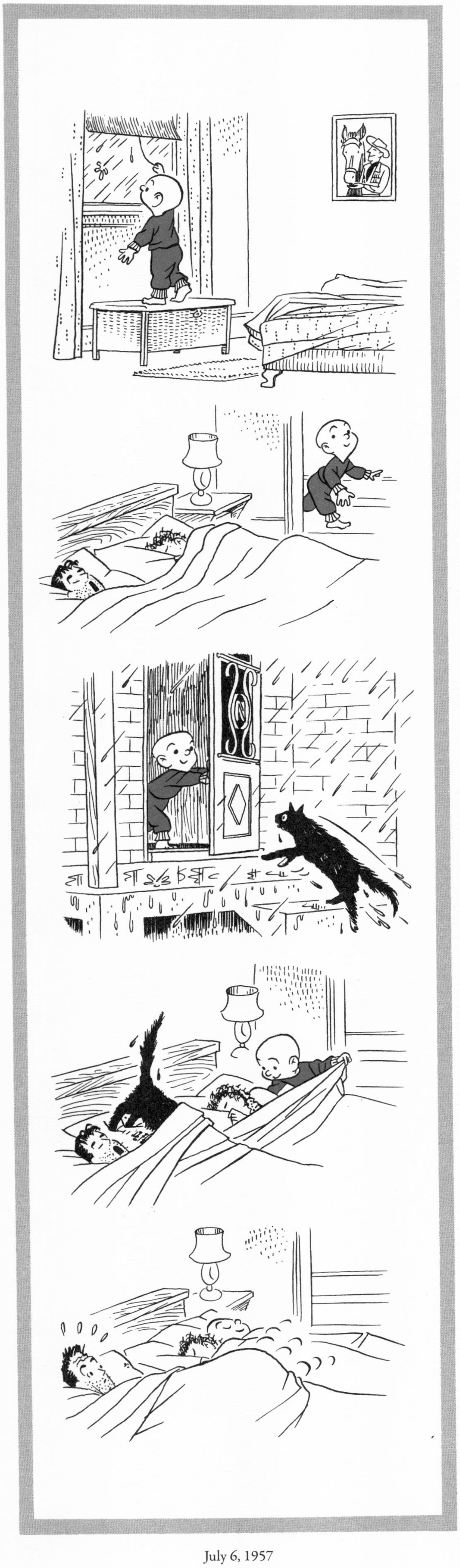

July 6, 1957

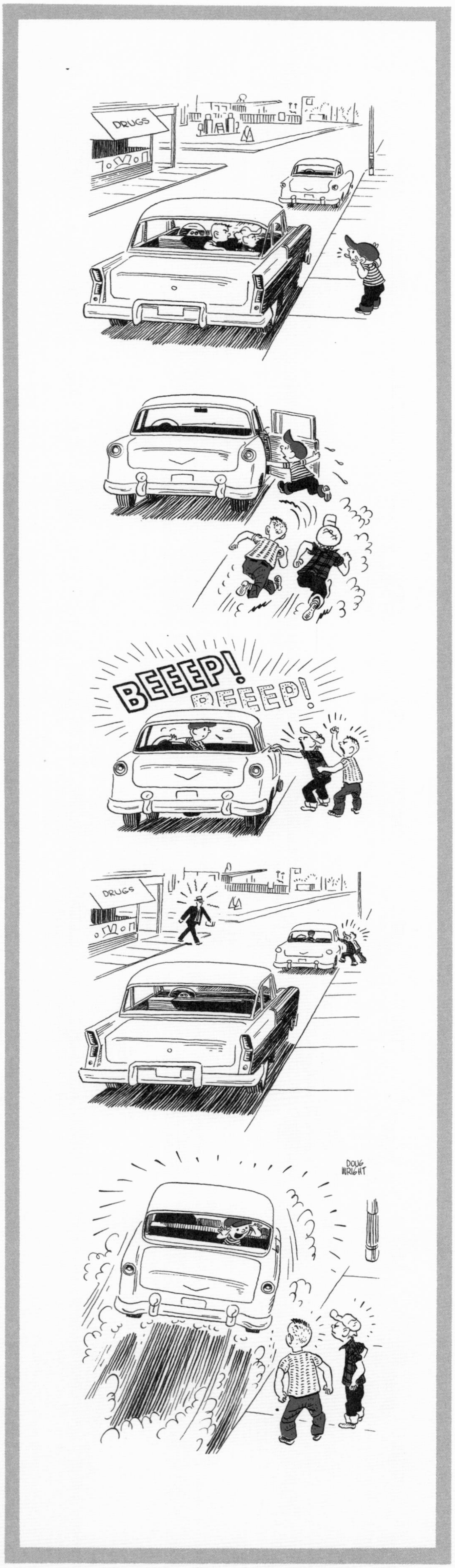
DRUGS
BEEEP! BEEEP!
DRUGS
DOUG WRIGHT

July 13, 1957

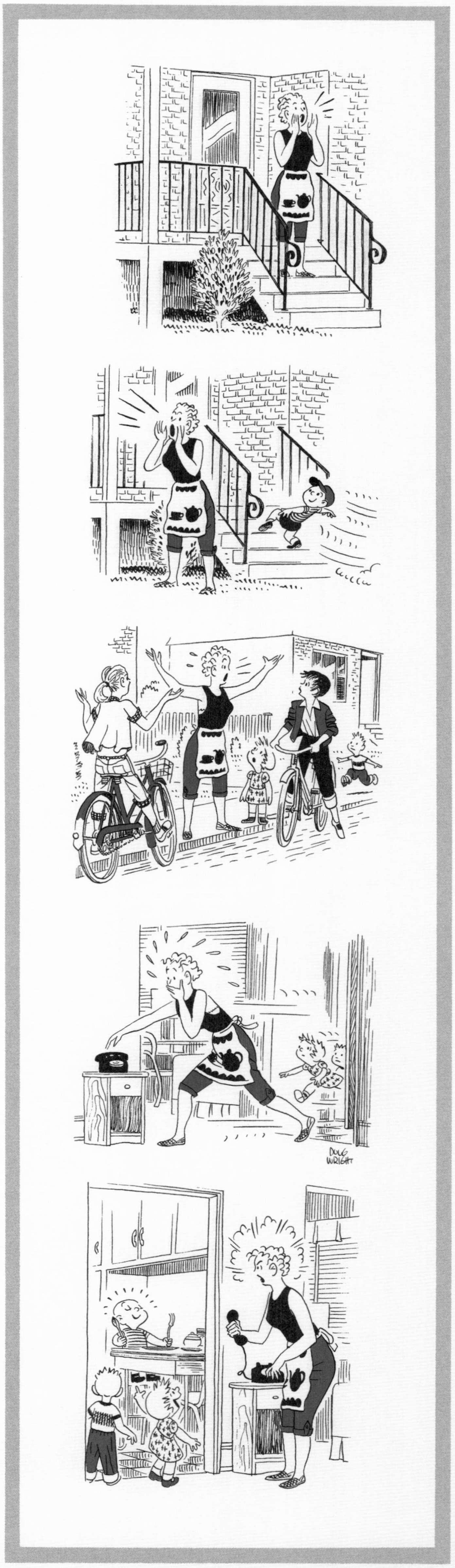
DOUG WRIGHT

July 20, 1957

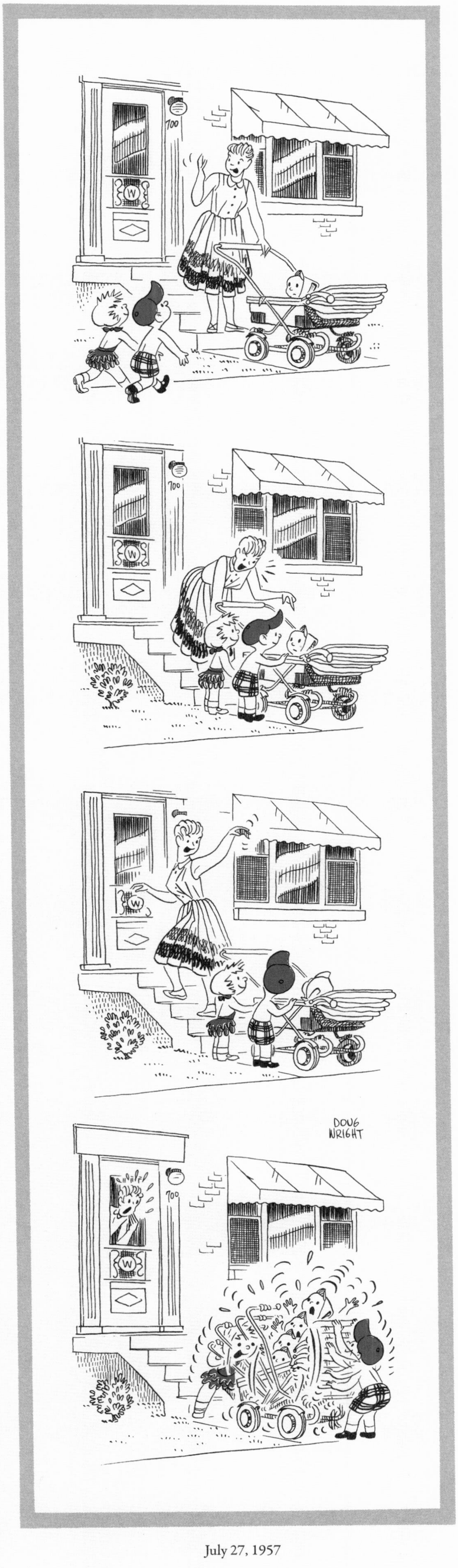
700
DOUG
WRIGHT

July 27, 1957

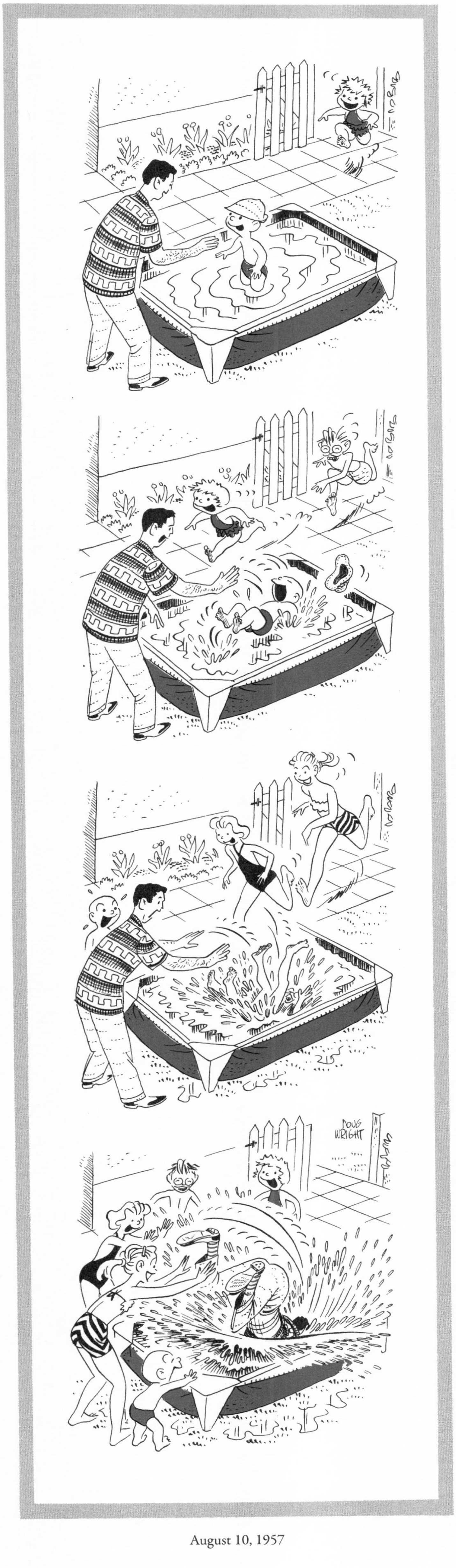
DOUG
WRIGHT

August 10, 1957

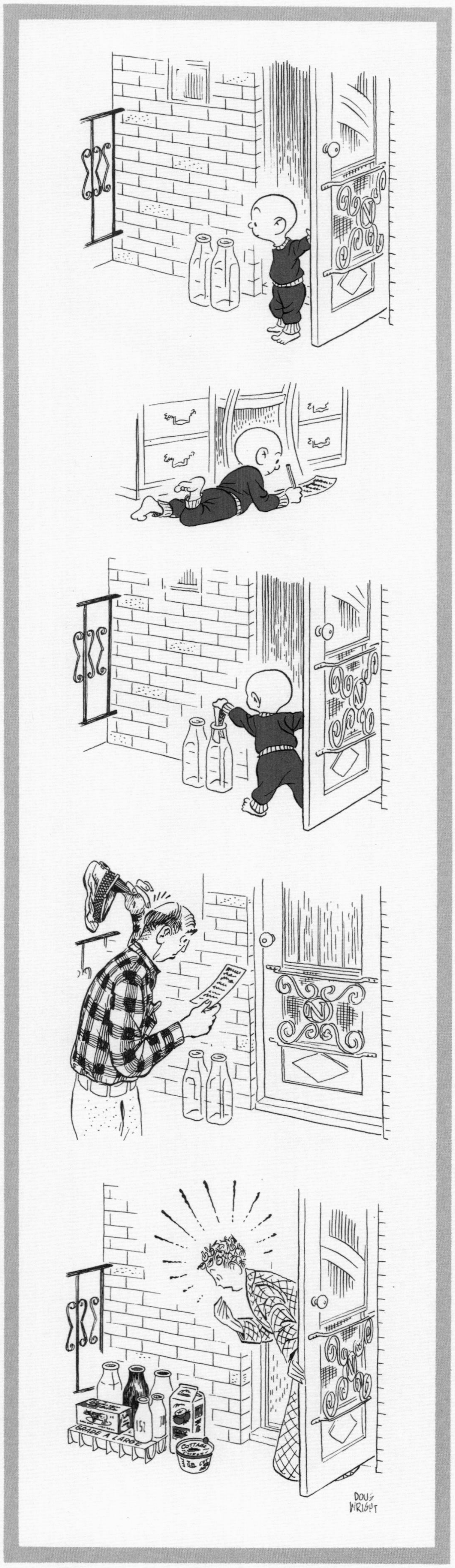
DOUG WRIGHT

September 7, 1957

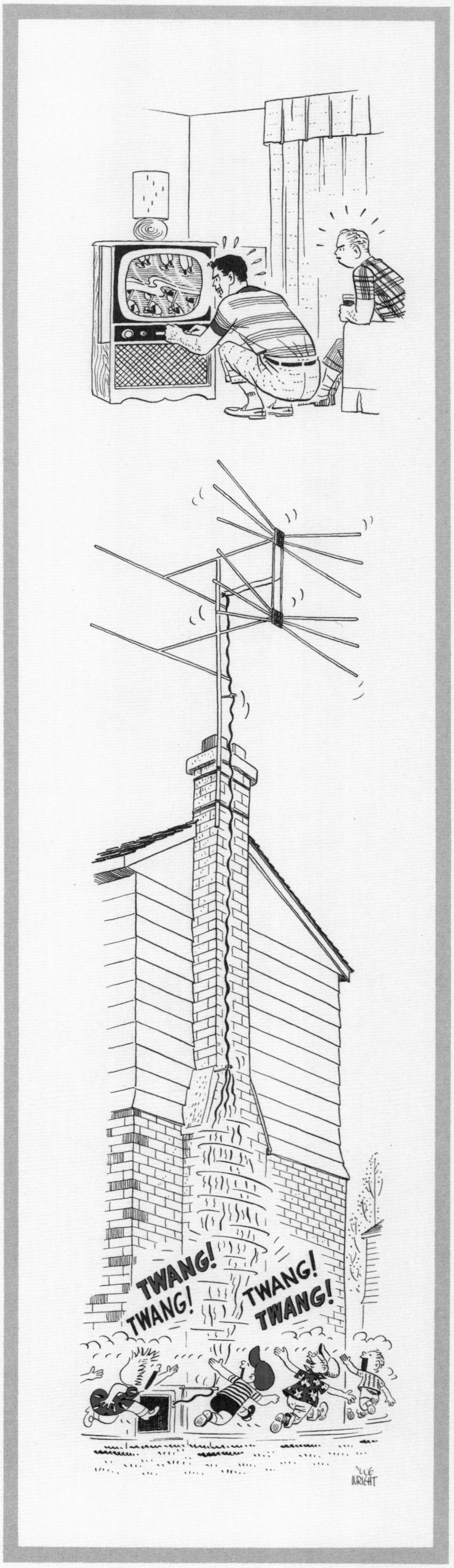
TWANG!
TWANG!
TWANG!
TWANG!
DOUG WRIGHT

September 28, 1957

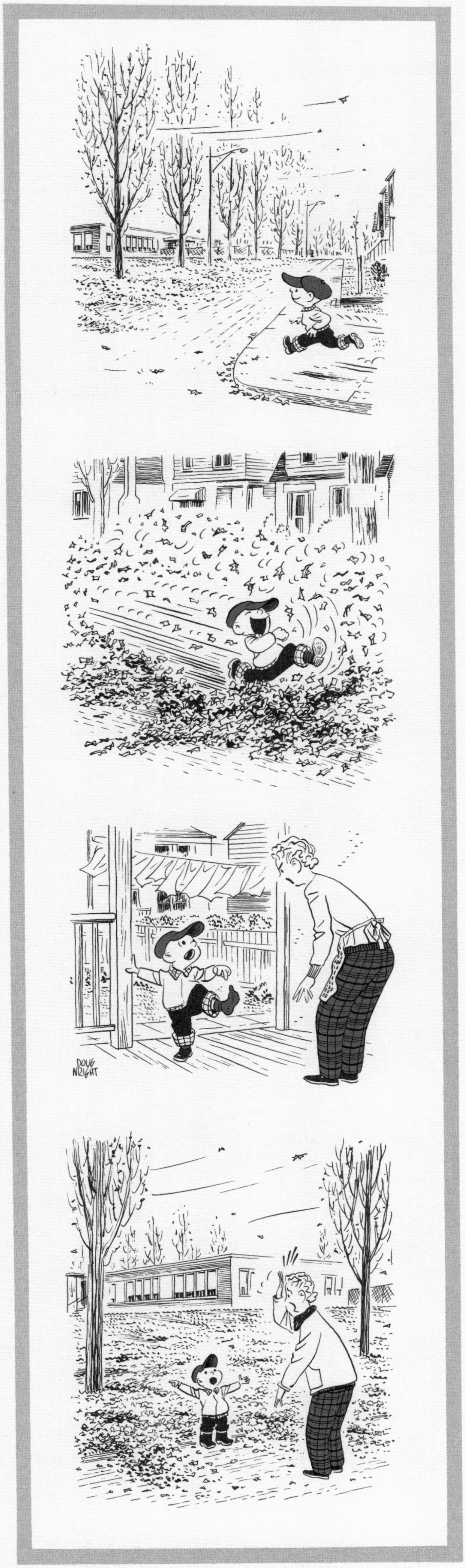
DOUG WRIGHT

October 12, 1957

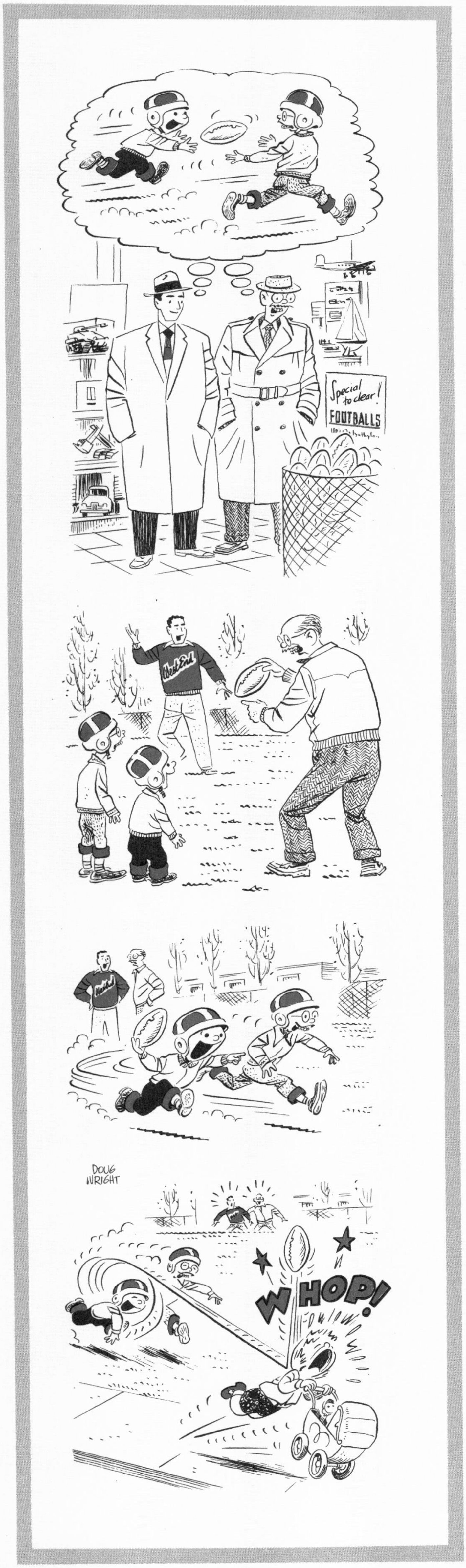
Special to clear!
FOOTBALLS
DOUG WRIGHT
WHOP!

October 19, 1957

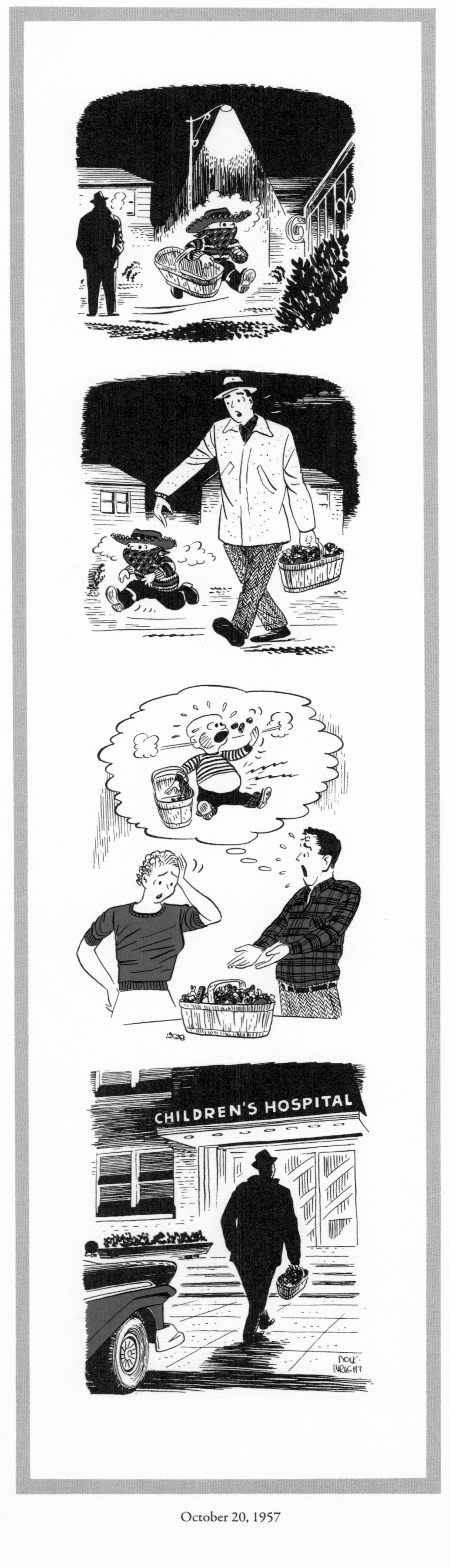
CHILDREN'S HOSPITAL
DOUG WRIGHT

October 20, 1957

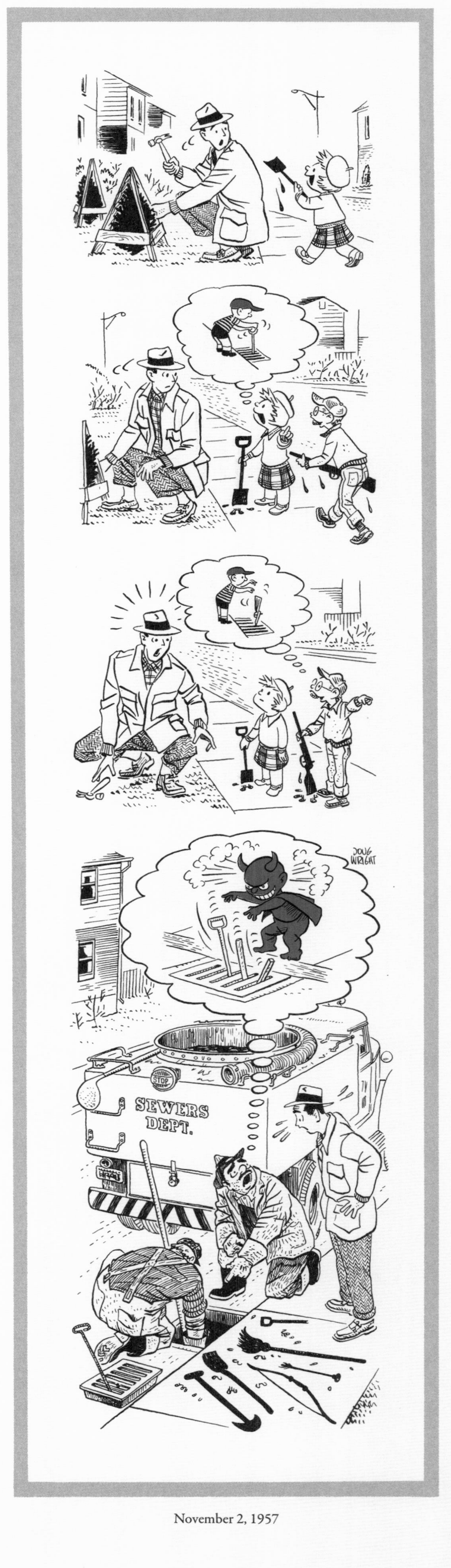
DOUG WRIGHT
STOP
SEWERS DEPT.

November 2, 1957

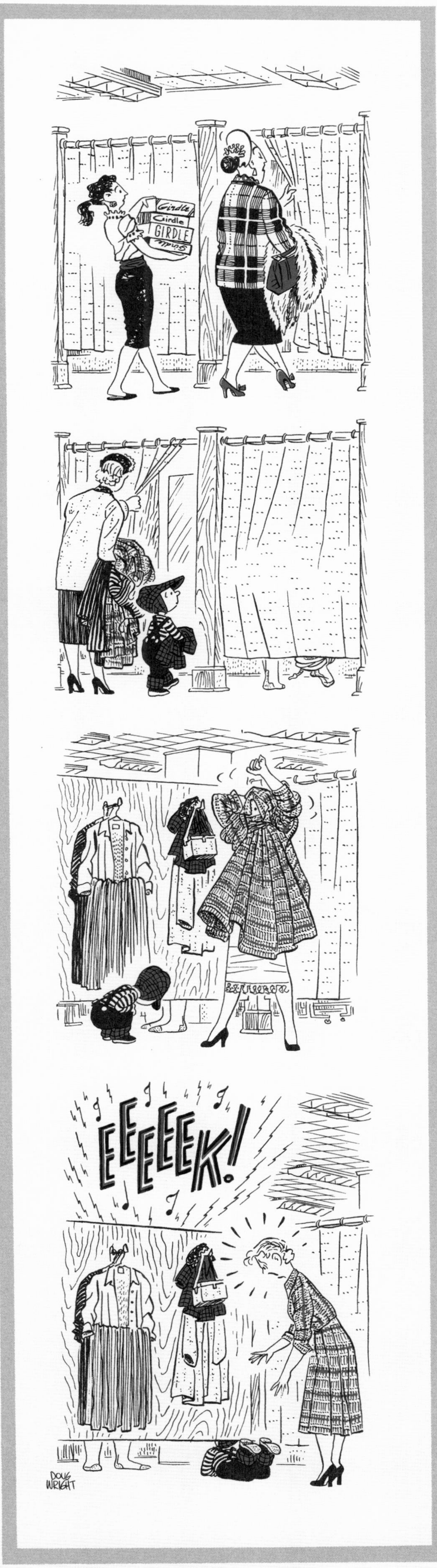

Girdle
Girdle
GIRDLE
Girdle
EEEEEK!
DOUG WRIGHT

November 16, 1957

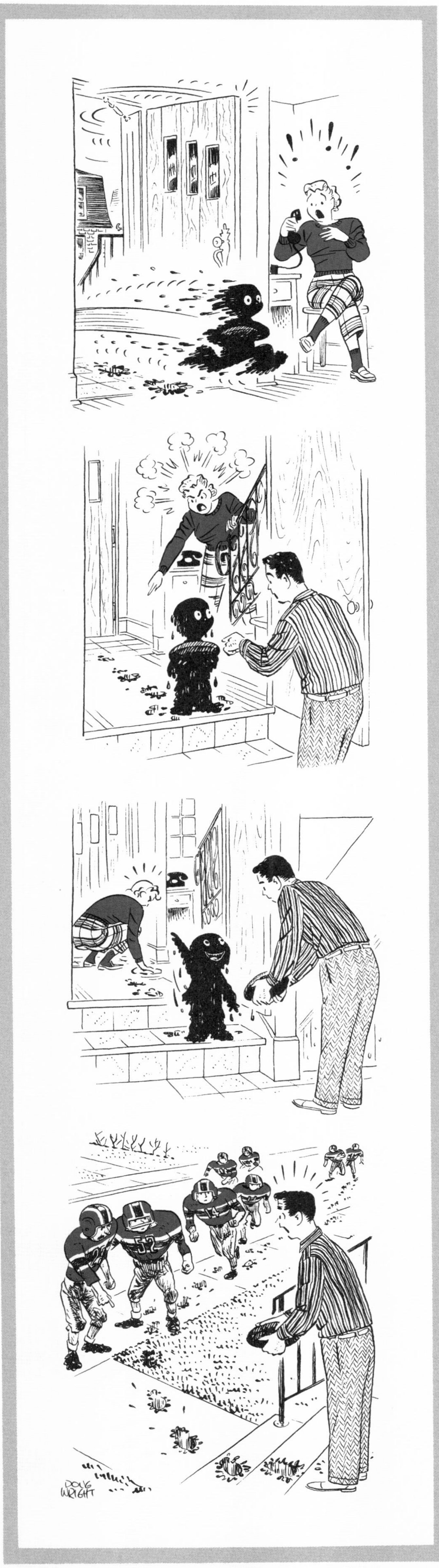

DOUG WRIGHT

November 23, 1957

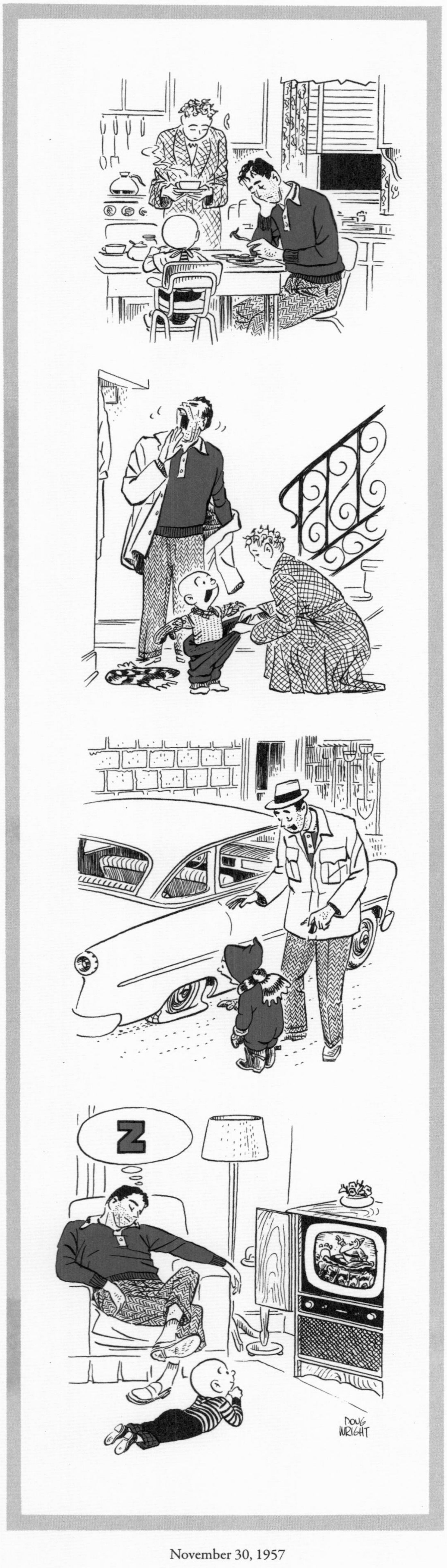
Z
DOUG WRIGHT

November 30, 1957

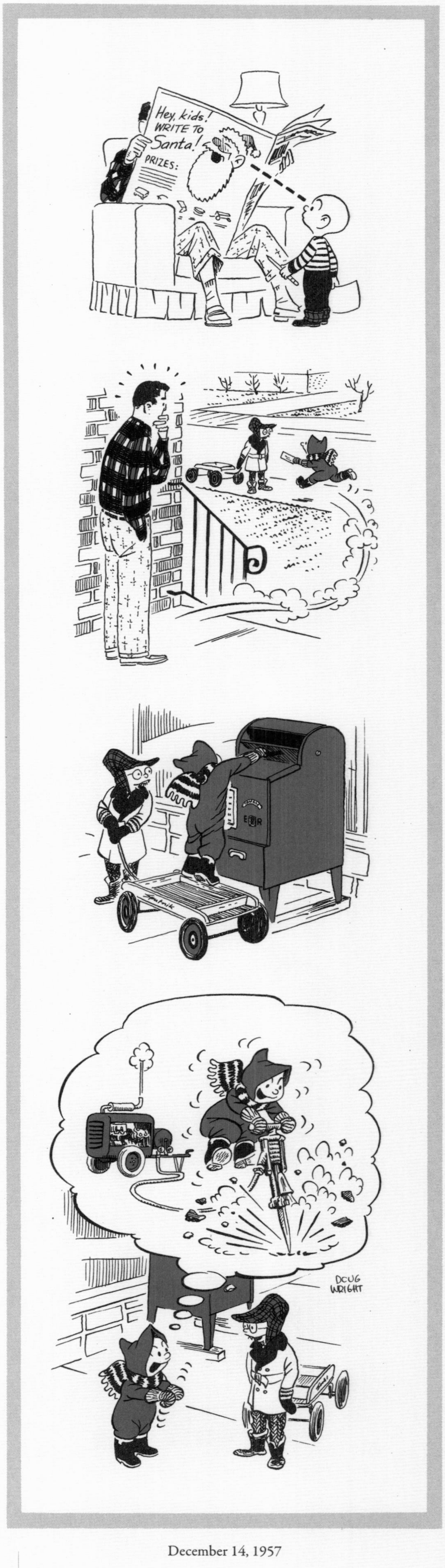
Hey, kids!
WRITE TO
Santa!
PRIZES:
DOUG WRIGHT

December 14, 1957

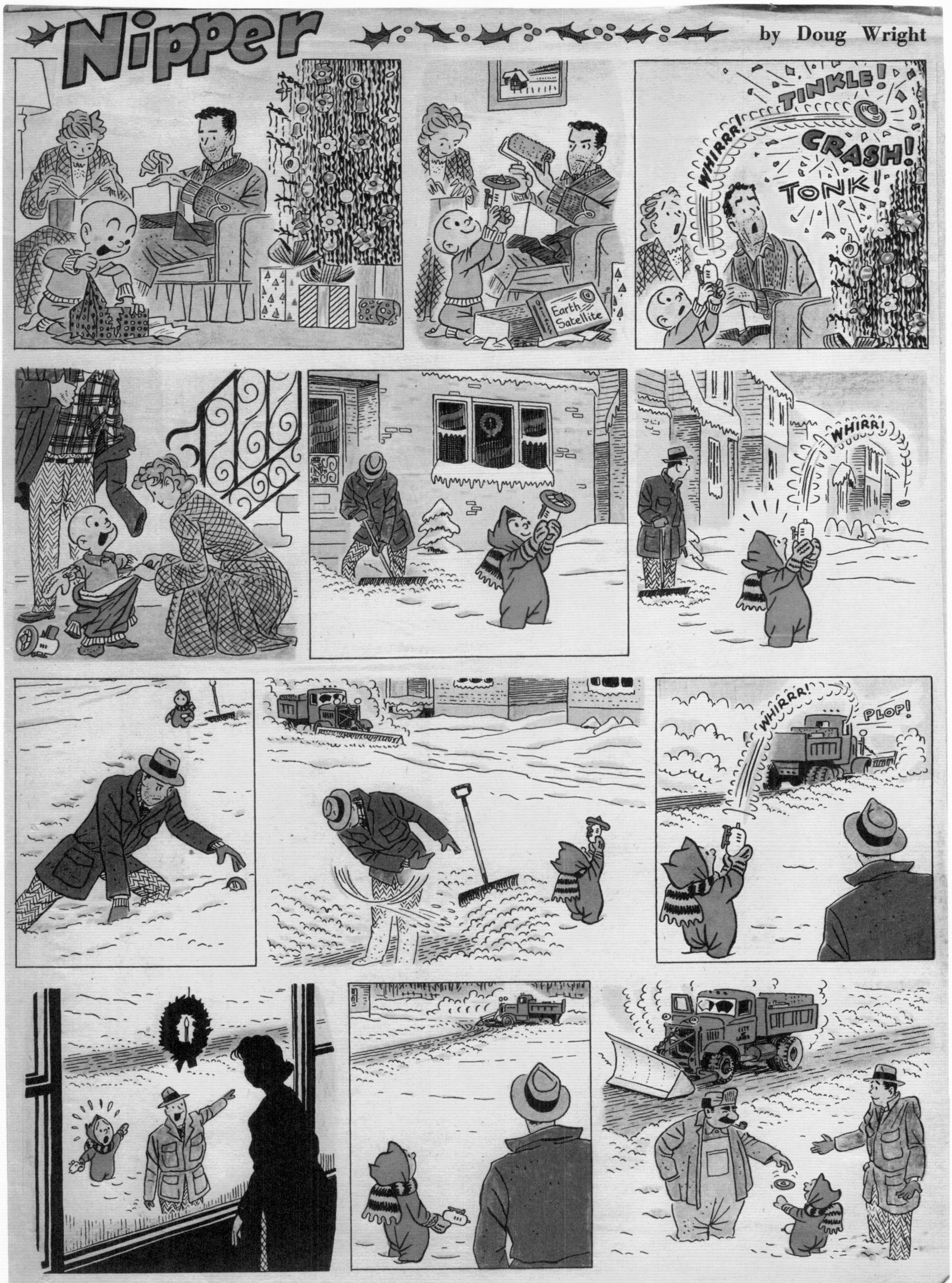
Nipper
by Doug Wright
Earth Satellite
WHIRRR!
TINKLE!
CRASH!
TONK!
WHIRR!
WHIRRR!
PLOP!
26
WEEKEND Magazine Vol. 7 No. 51, 1957

December 21, 1957

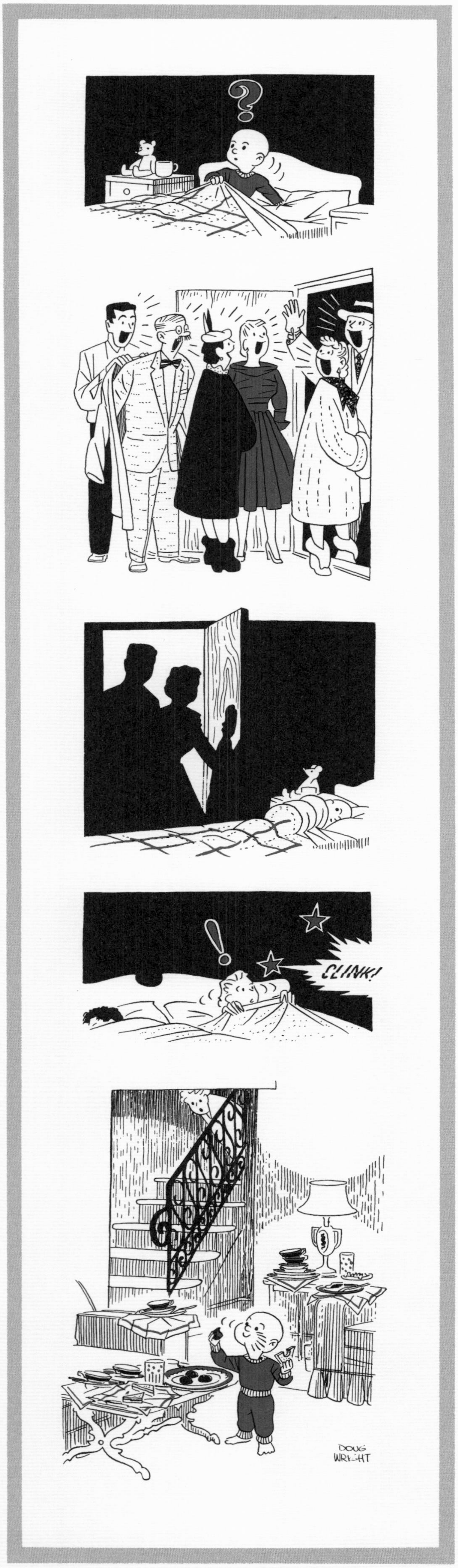
?
CLINK!
!
DOUG WRIGHT

December 28, 1957

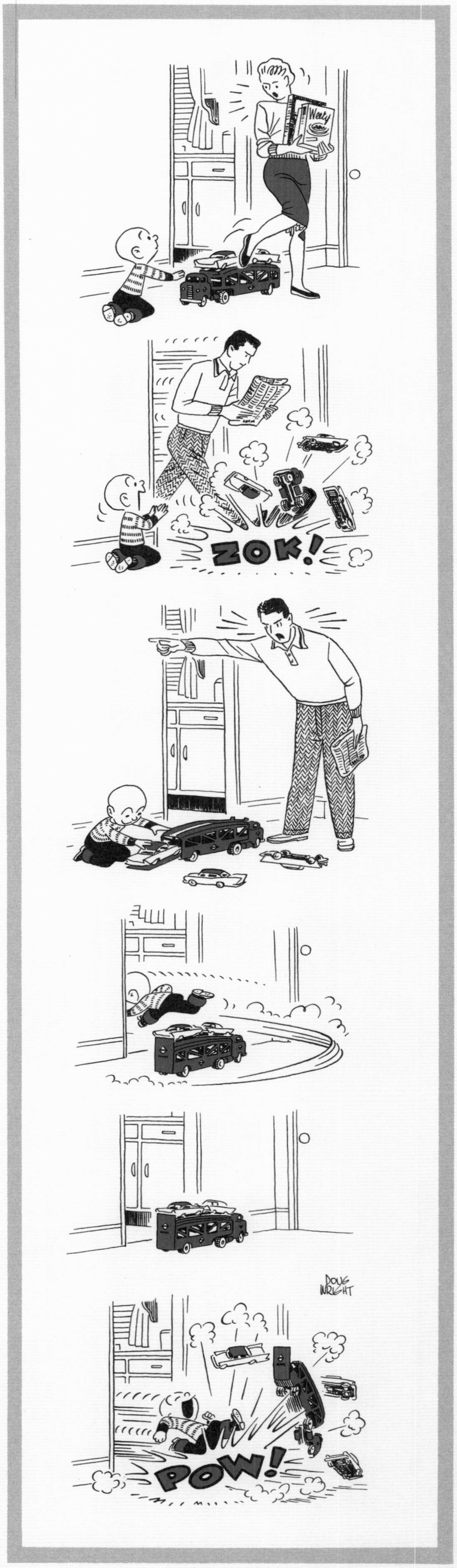
ZOK!
DOUG WRIGHT
POW!

January 18, 1958

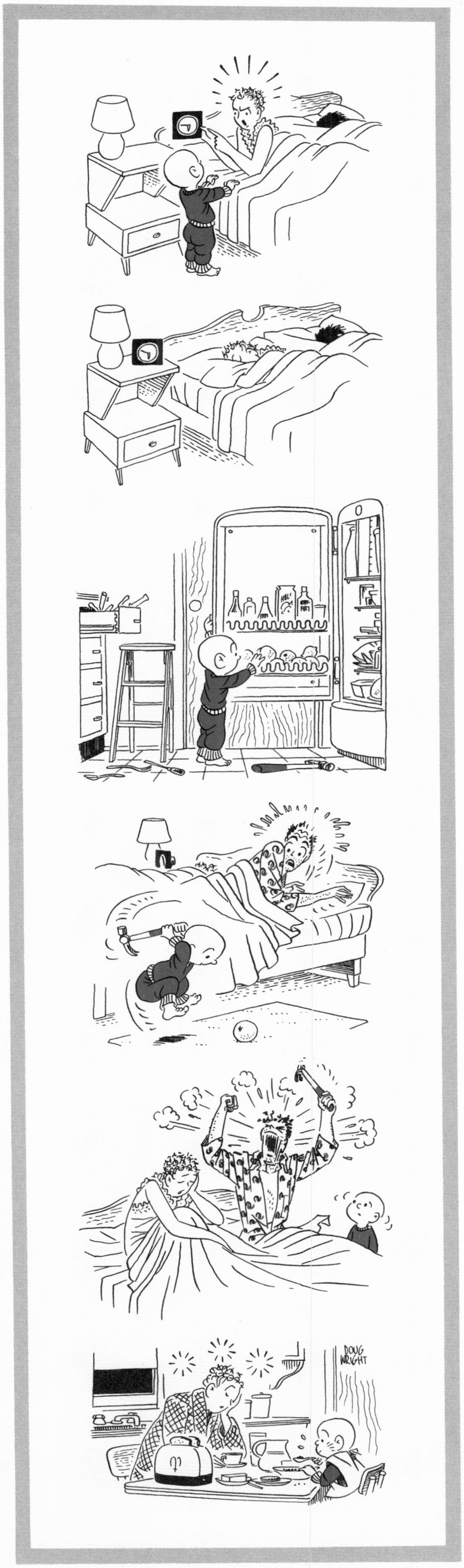
DOUG WRIGHT

February 1, 1958

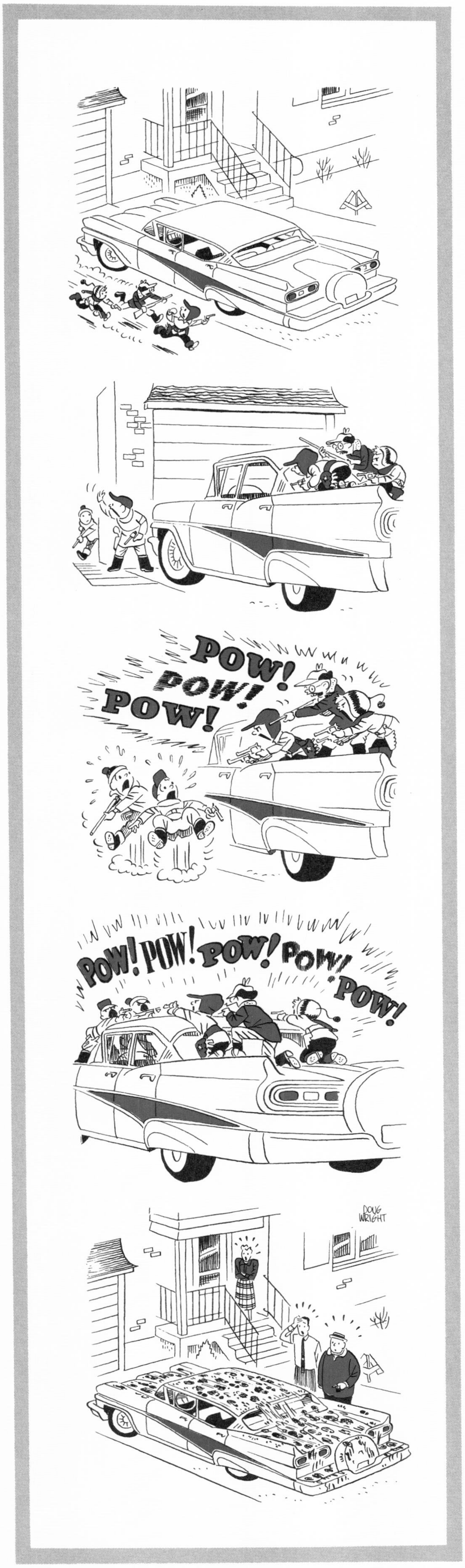
POW!
POW!
POW!
POW! POW! POW! POW! POW!
DOUG WRIGHT

March 1, 1958

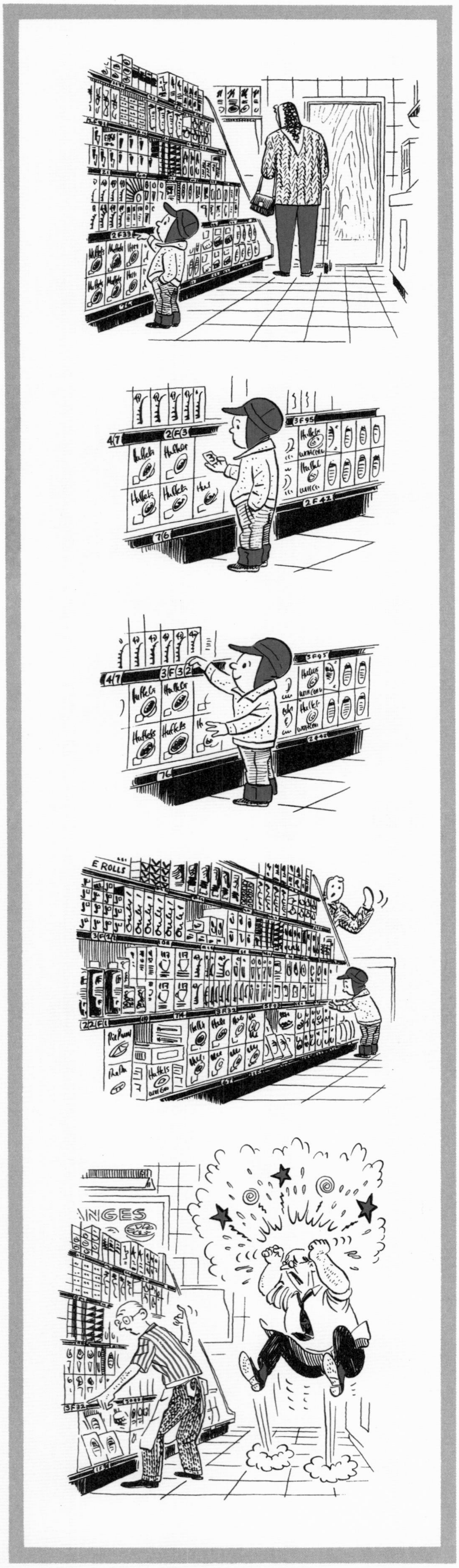

March 8, 1958

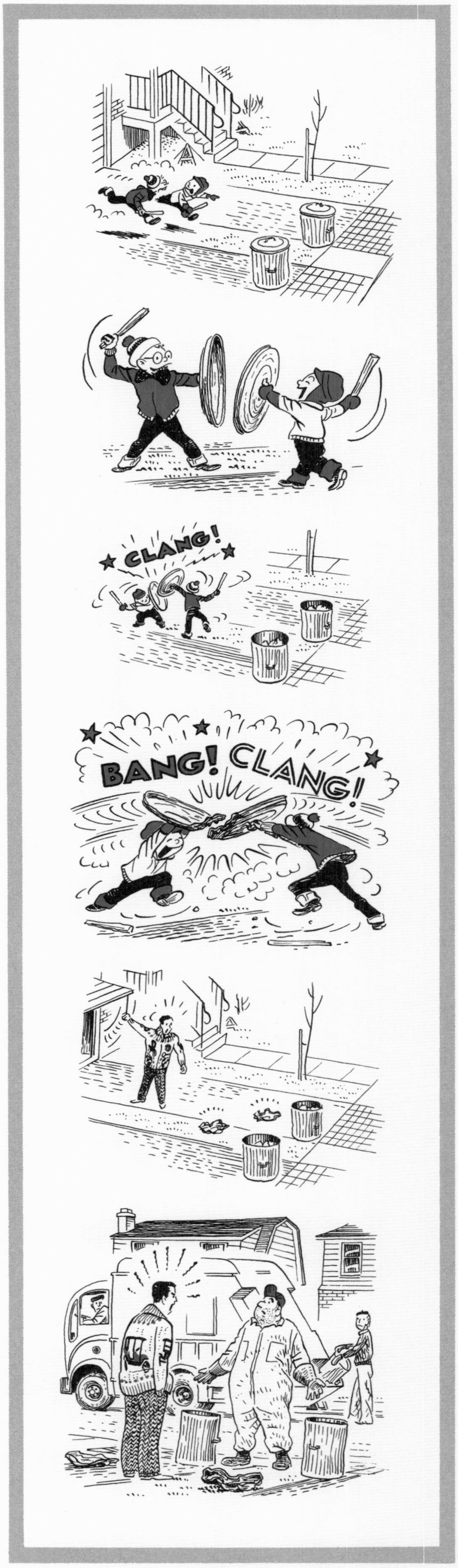
CLANG!
BANG! CLANG!

March 15, 1958

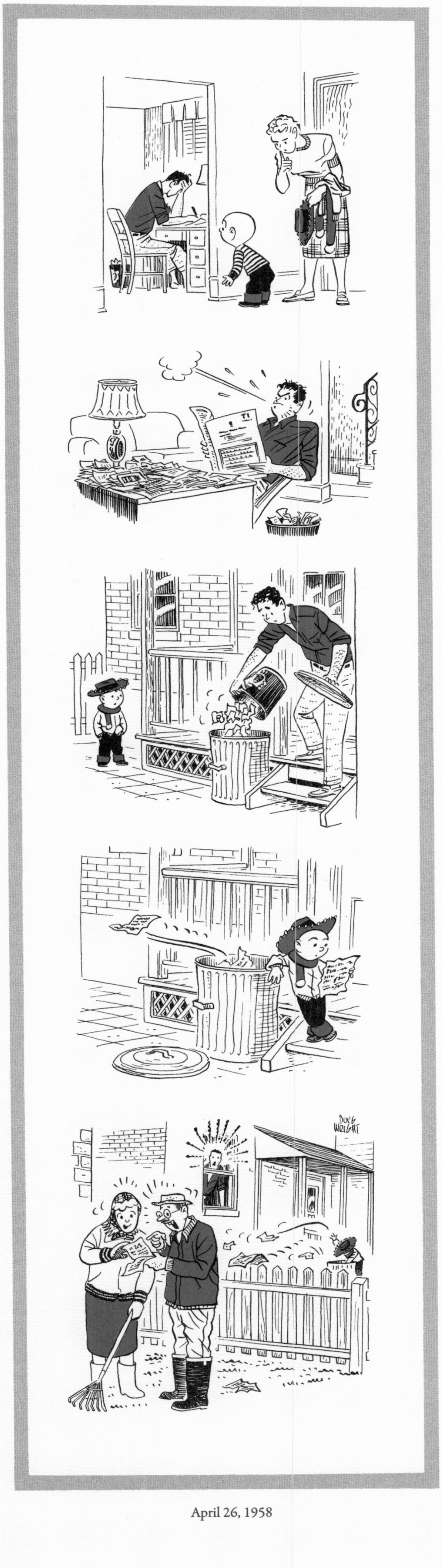
DOUG WRIGHT

April 26, 1958

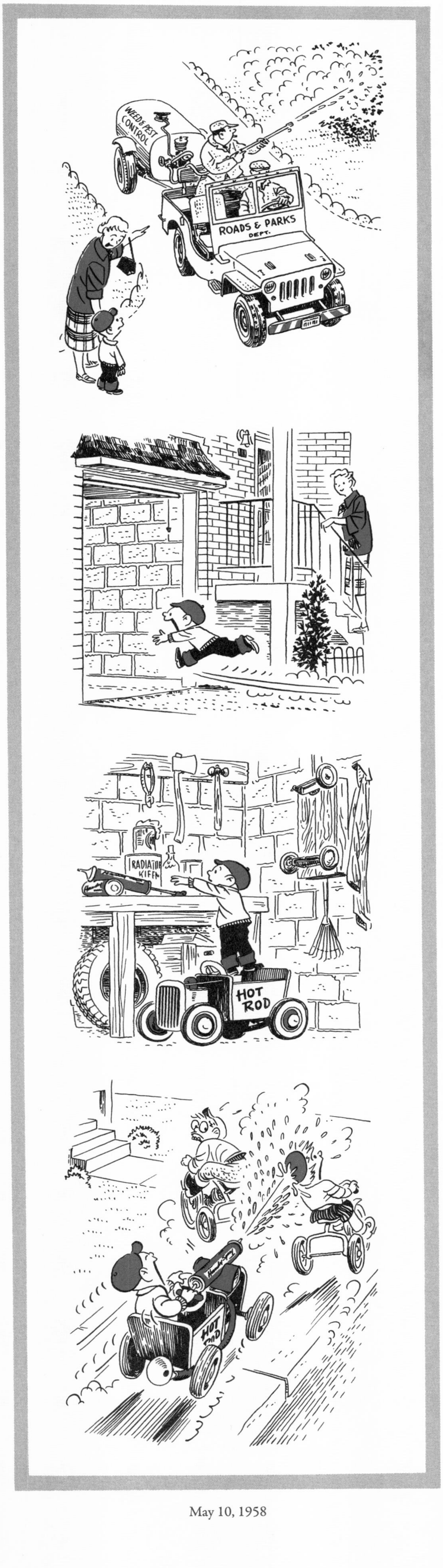
ROADS & PARKS DEPT.
HOT ROD

May 10, 1958

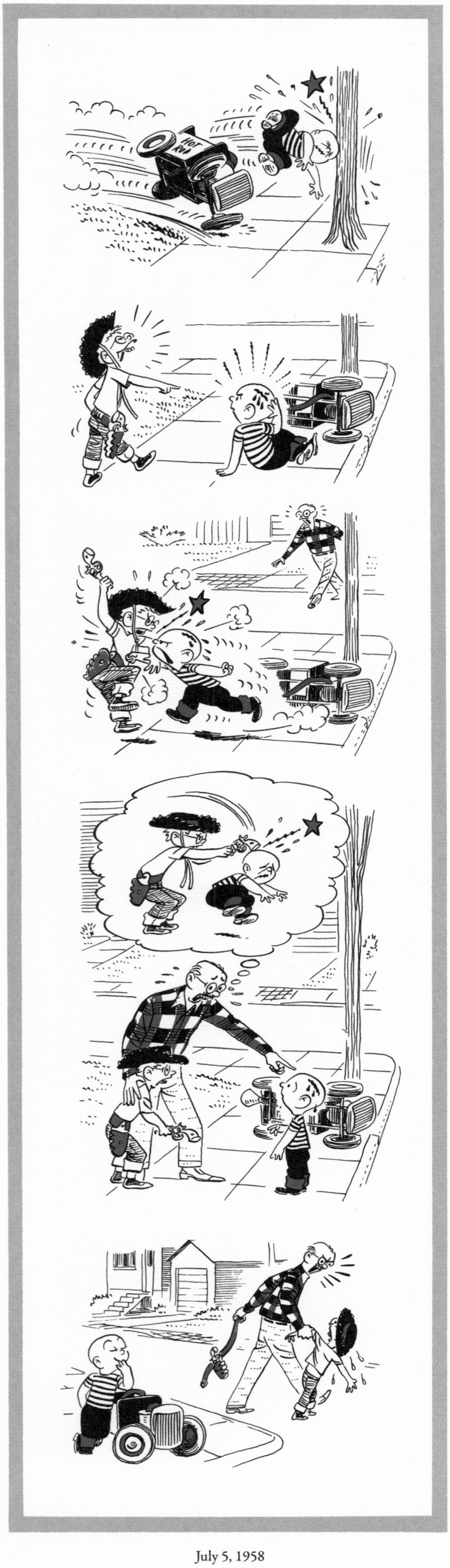

July 5, 1958

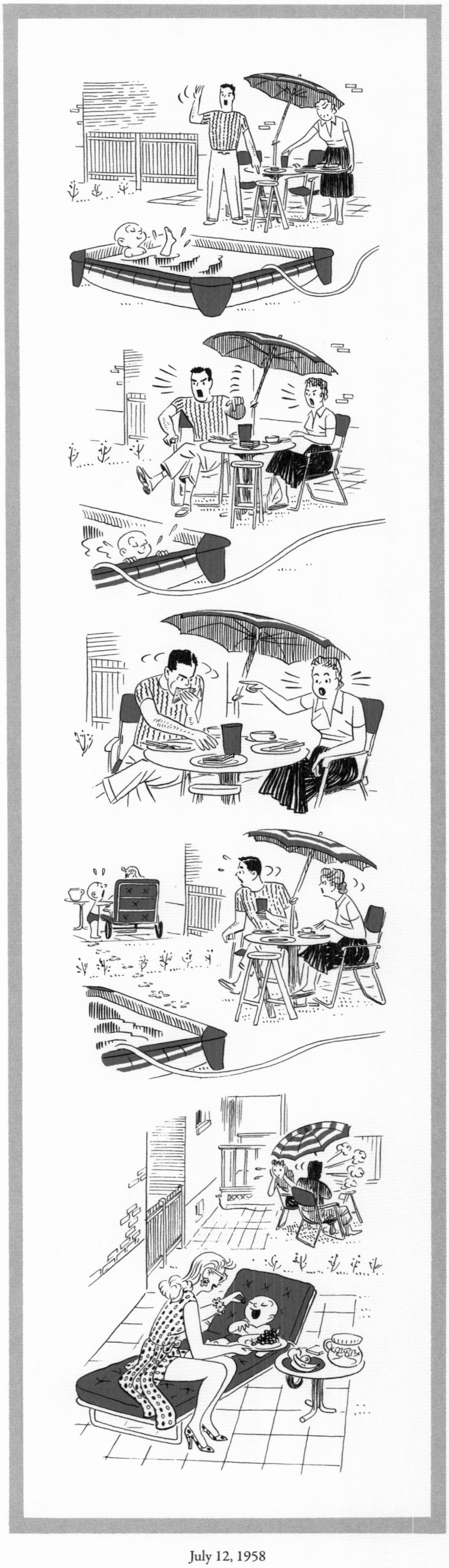

July 12, 1958

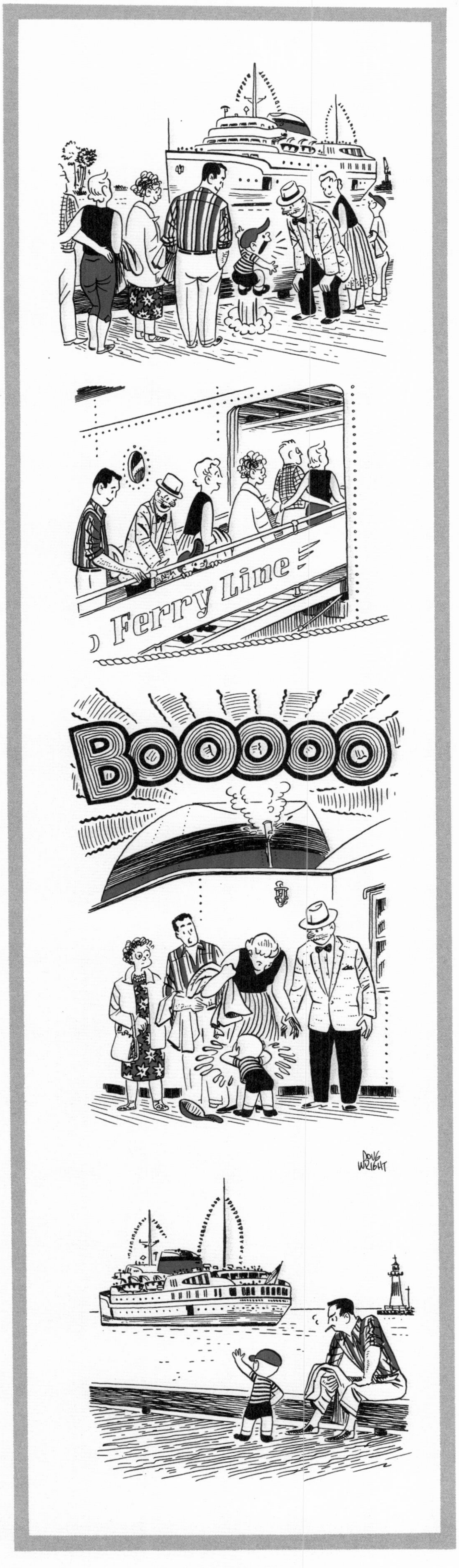
Ferry Line
BOOOOO
DOUG WRIGHT
August 2, 1958

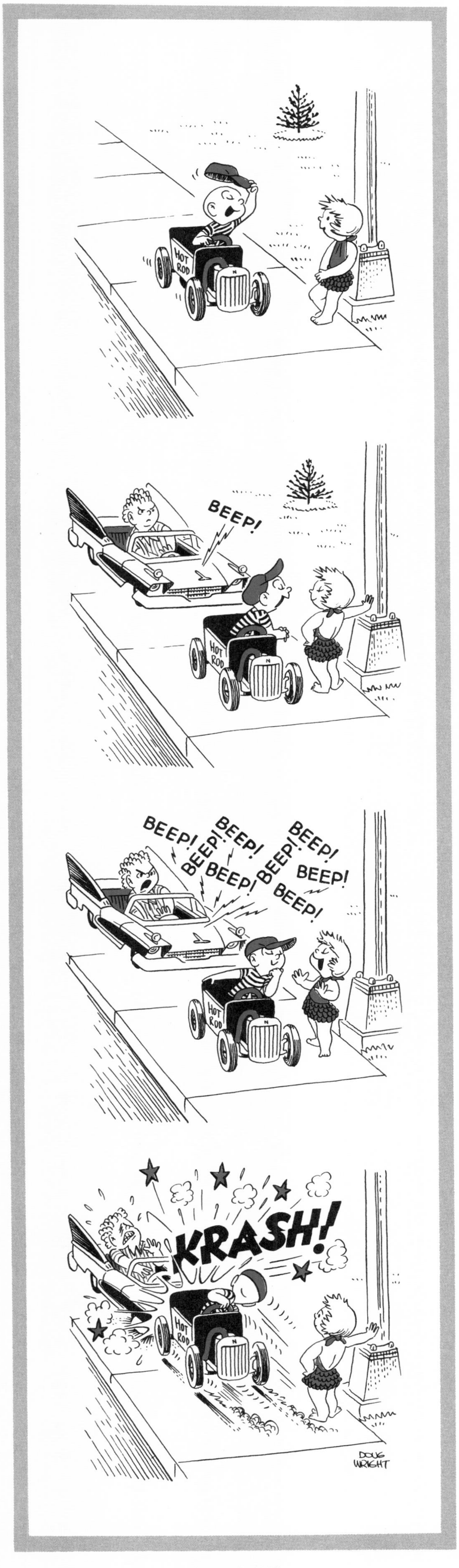
HOT ROD
BEEP!
BEEP! BEEP! BEEP! BEEP! BEEP! BEEP! BEEP! BEEP!
KRASH!
DOUG WRIGHT
August 9, 1958

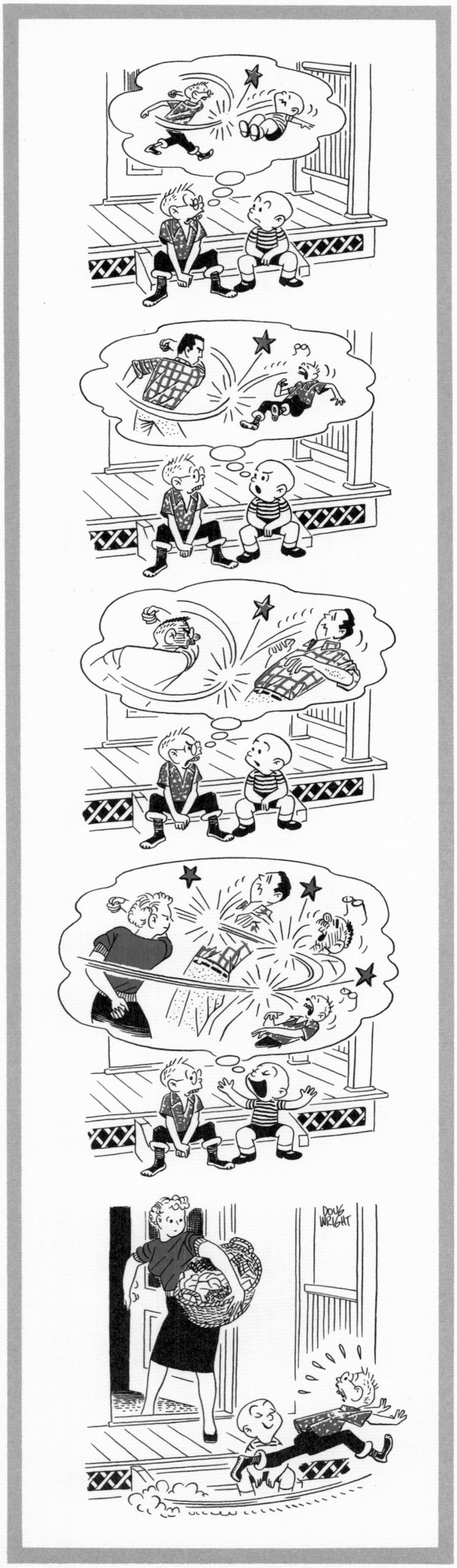
DOUG WRIGHT

August 23, 1958

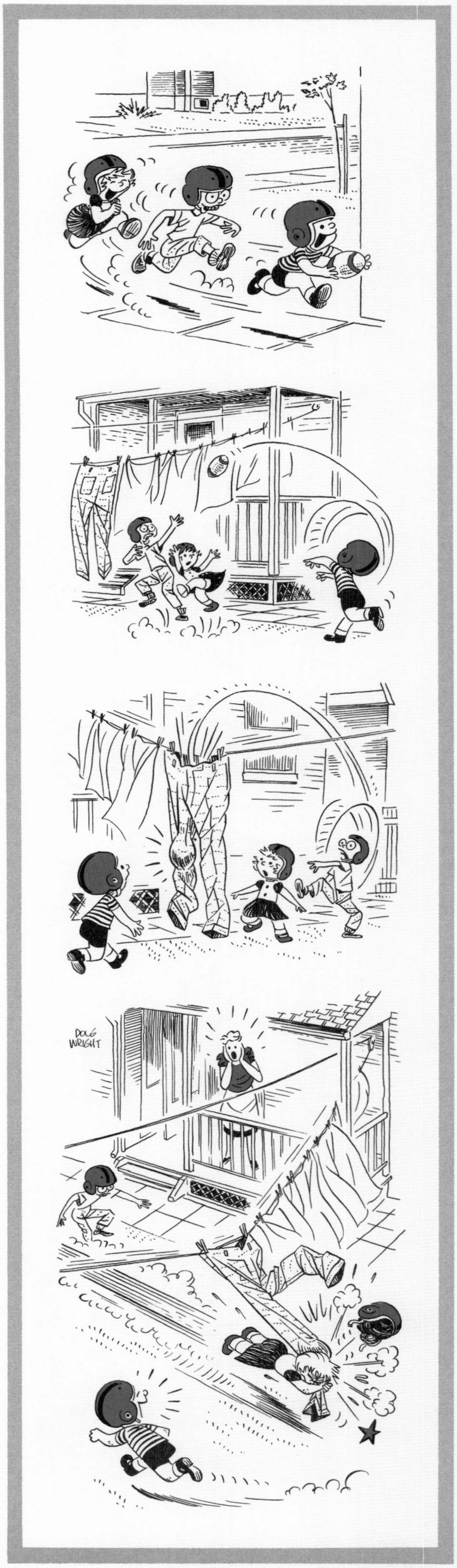
DOUG WRIGHT

September 6, 1958

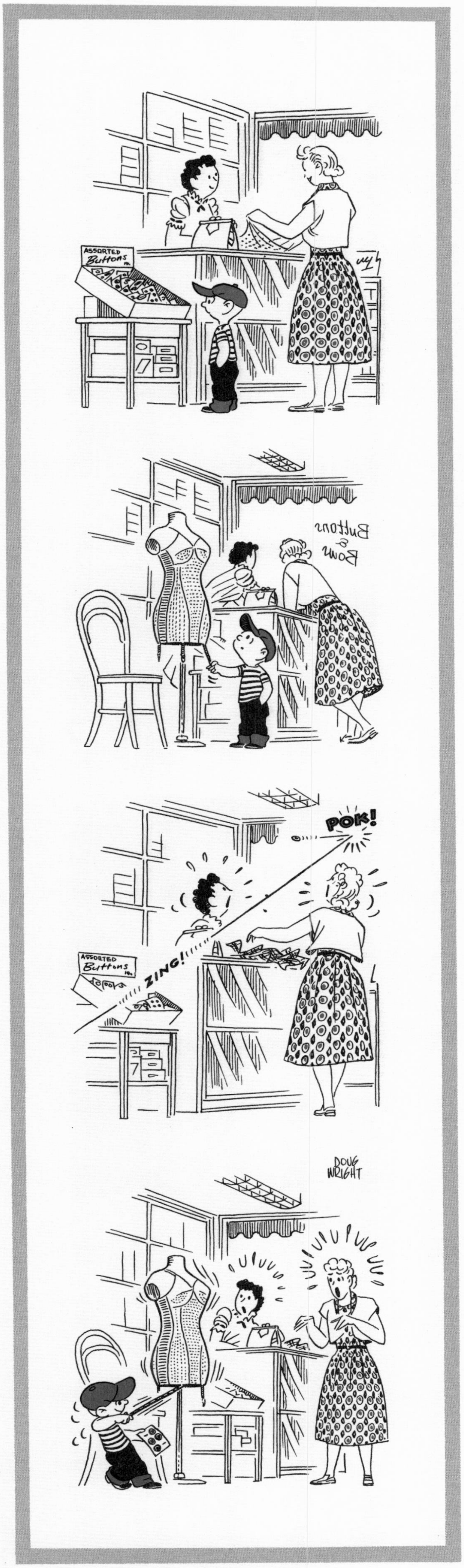
ASSORTED Buttons
Buttons & Bows
POK!
ZING!
ASSORTED Buttons
DOUG WRIGHT

September 27, 1958

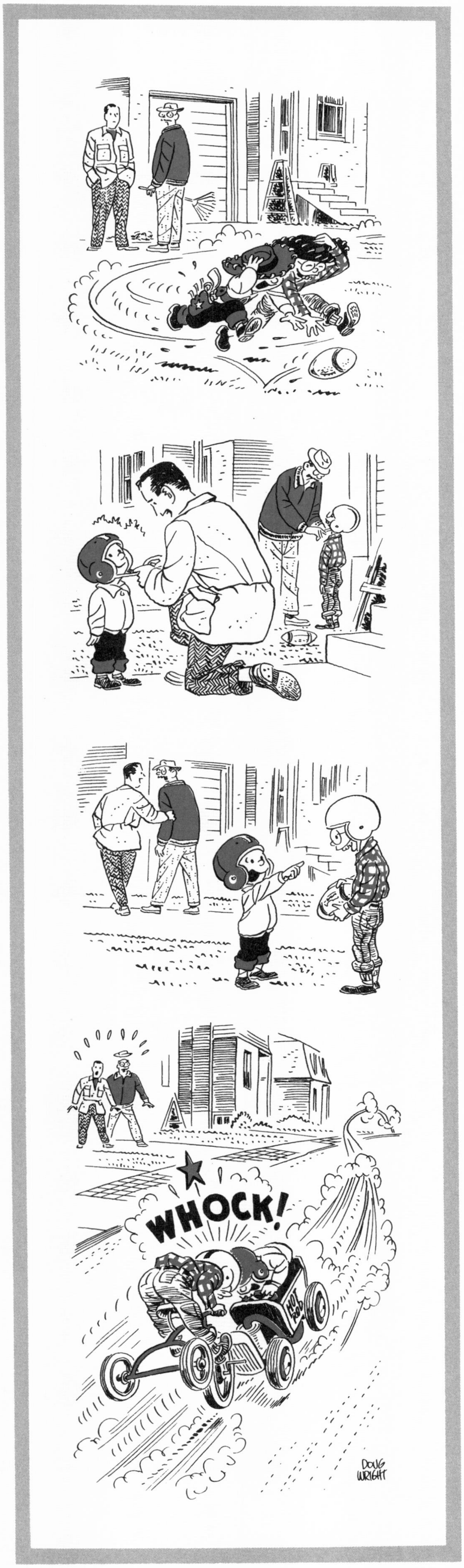
WHOCK!
DOUG WRIGHT

October 25, 1958

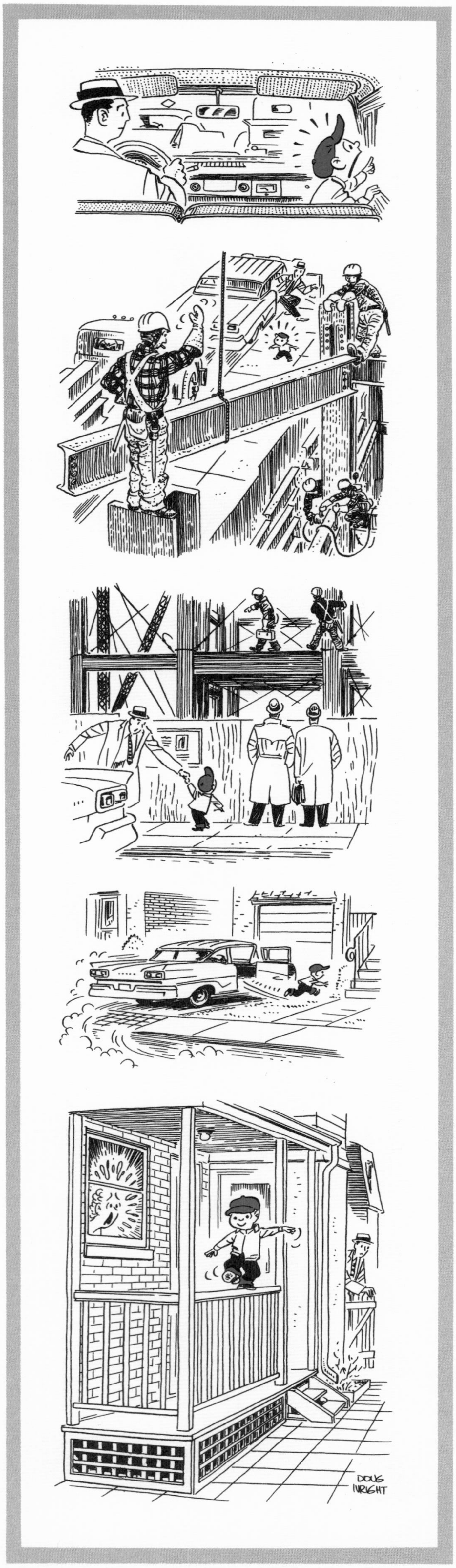
DOUG
WRIGHT

November 8, 1958

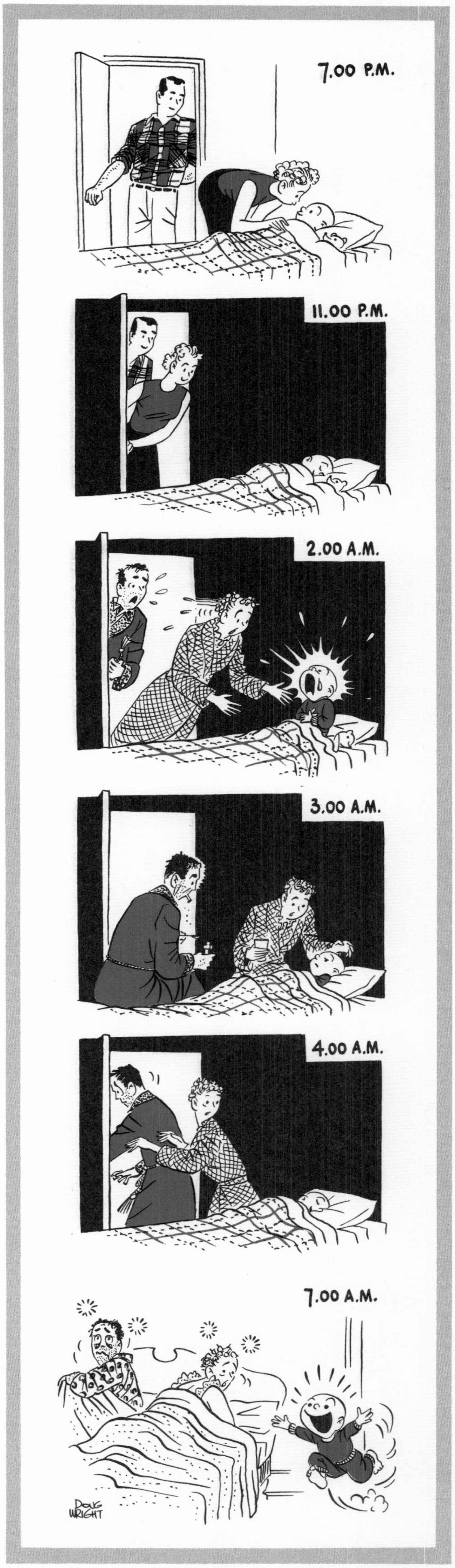
7.00 P.M.
11.00 P.M.
2.00 A.M.
3.00 A.M.
4.00 A.M.
7.00 A.M.
DOUG
WRIGHT

December 6, 1958

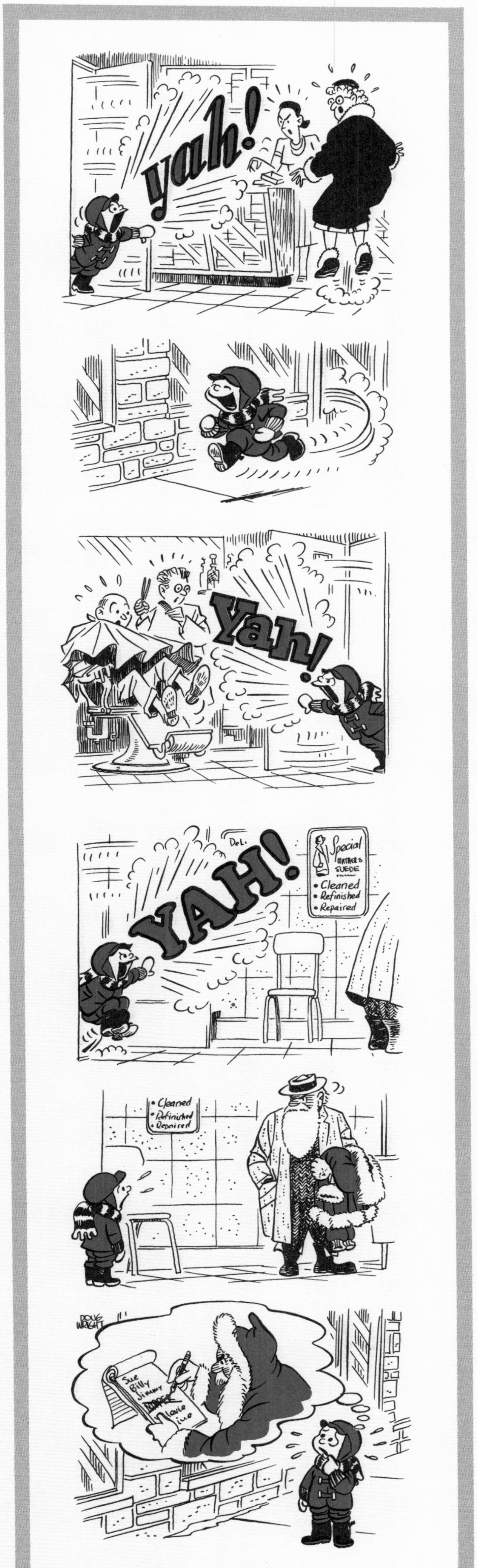
yah!
Yah!
YAH!
Special
LEATHER & SUEDE
• Cleaned
• Refinished
• Repaired
• Cleaned
• Refinished
• Repaired
DOUG WRIGHT
Sue
Billy
Jimmy

December 13, 1958

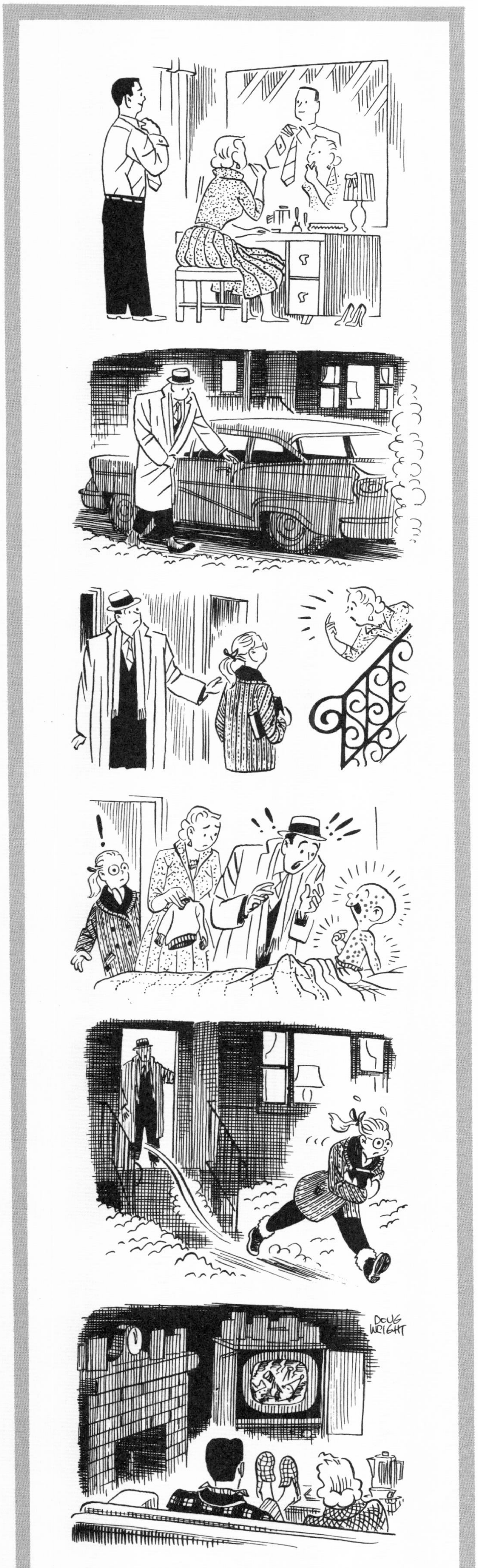
DOUG WRIGHT

December 20, 1958

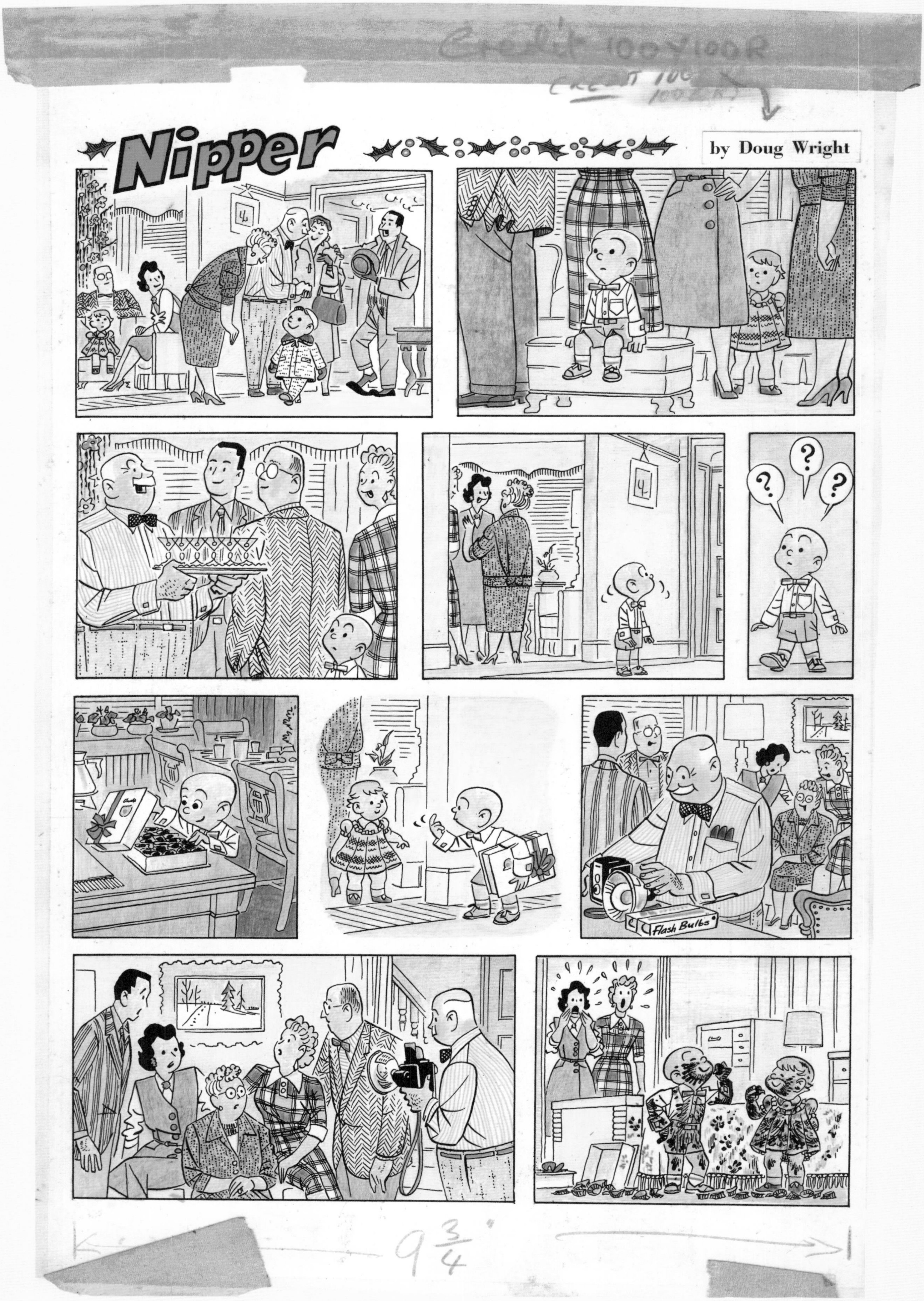

Credit 100Y100R
CREDIT 100Y 100R
Nipper
by Doug Wright
?
?
?
Flash Bulbs
9 3/4

December 27, 1958

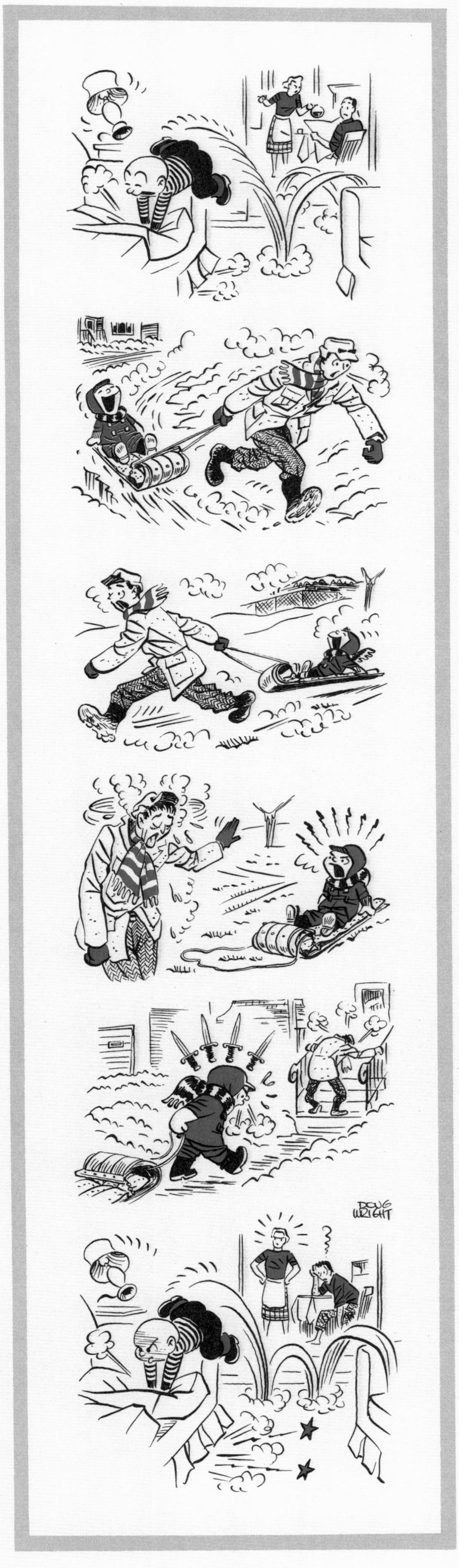
DOUG WRIGHT
February 7, 1959

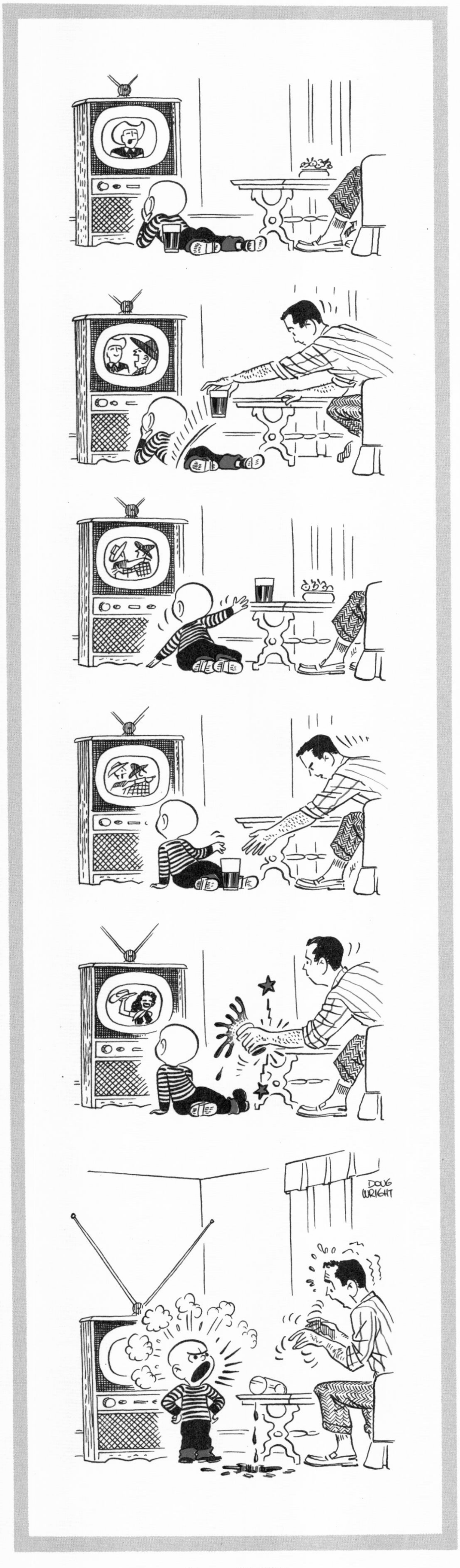
DOUG WRIGHT
February 21, 1959

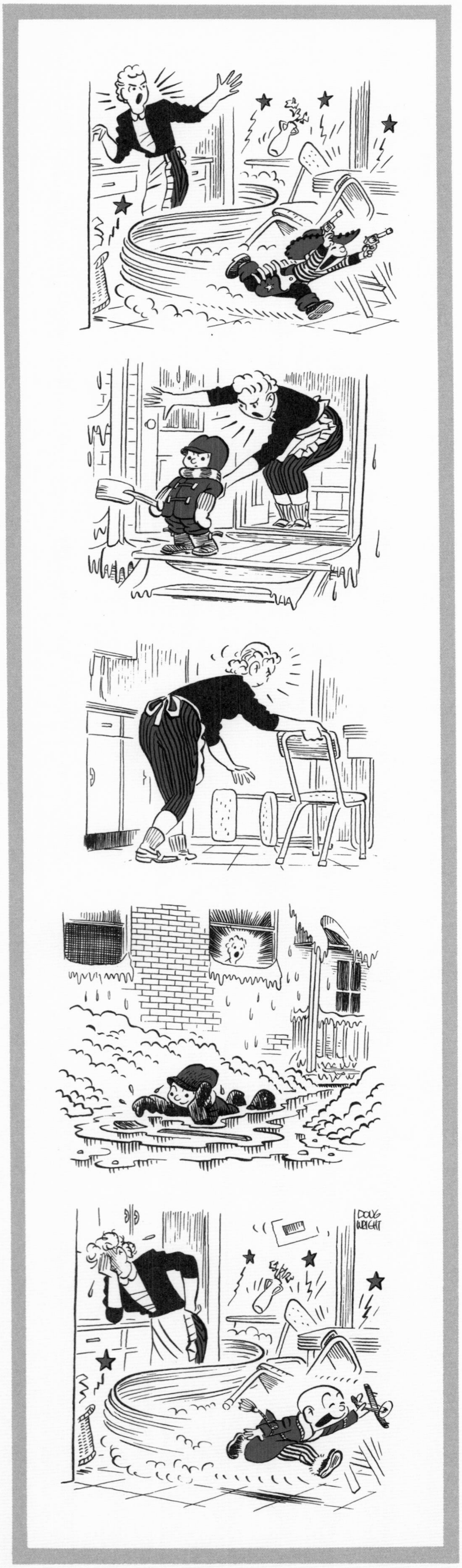
DOUG
WRIGHT

February 28, 1959

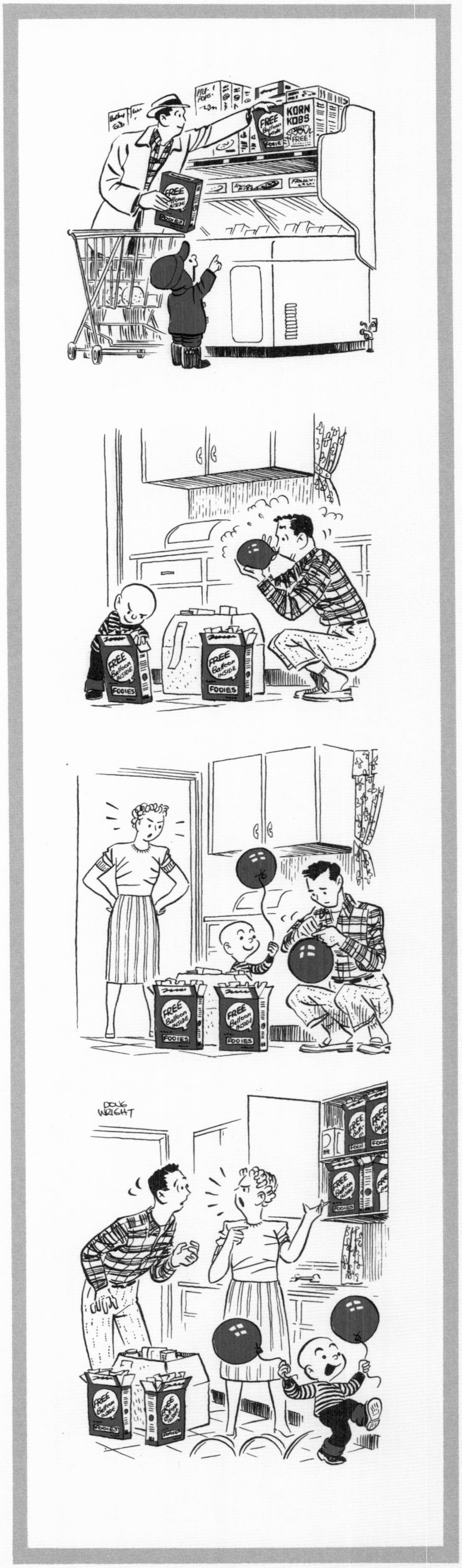
KORN
KOBS
FREE
Balloon
INSIDE
FOODIES
DOUG
WRIGHT

March 7, 1959

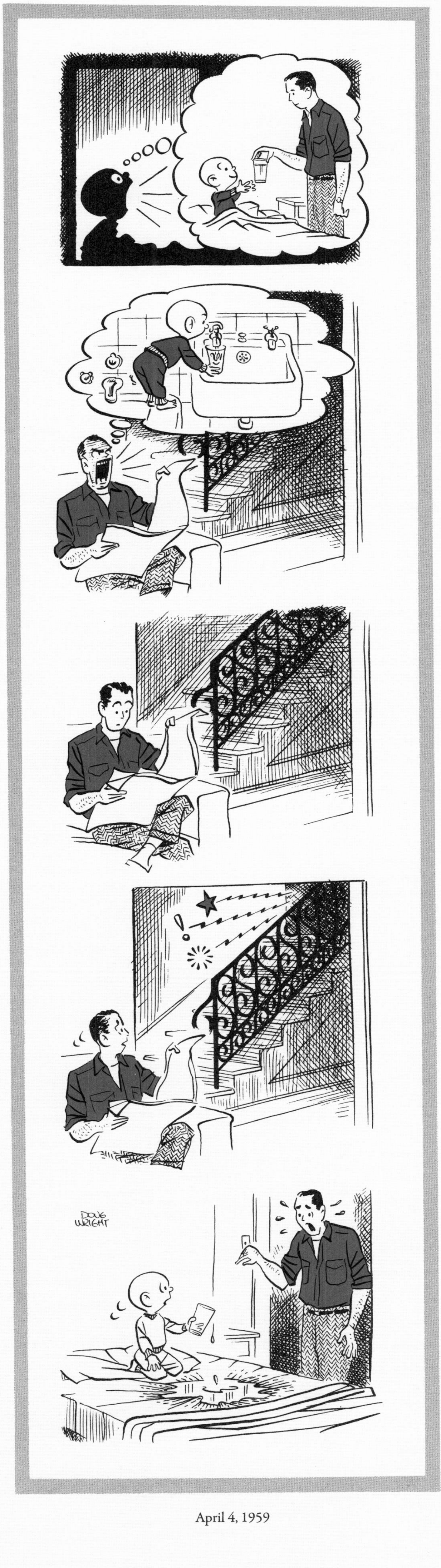
DOUG WRIGHT

April 4, 1959

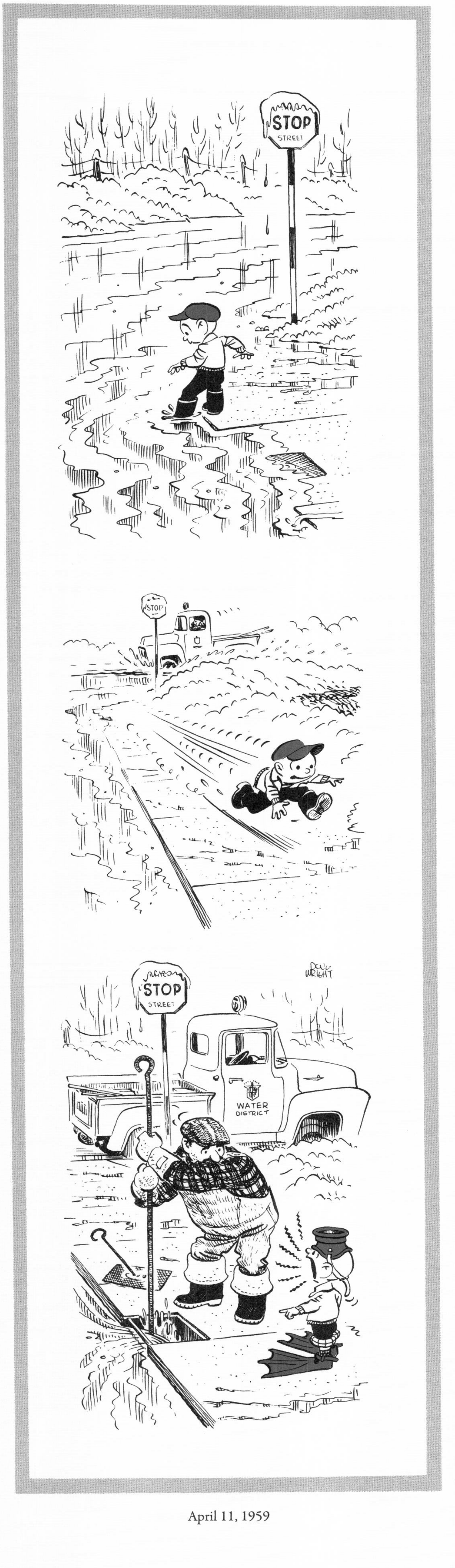
STOP
STREET
WATER DISTRICT
DOUG WRIGHT

April 11, 1959

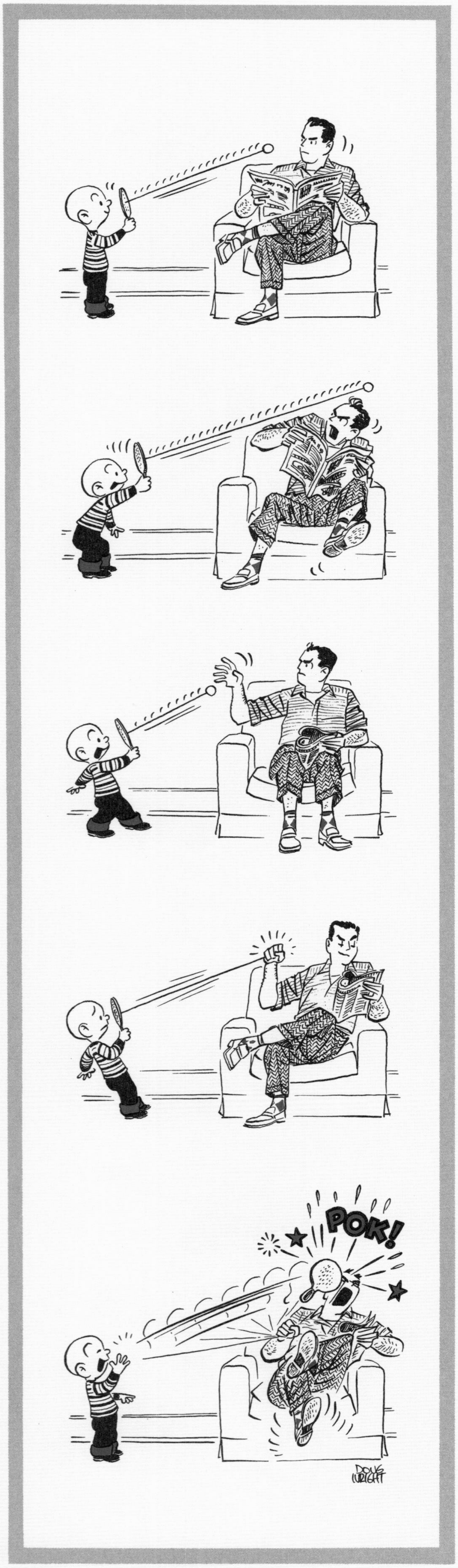
POK!
DOUG WRIGHT

April 25, 1959

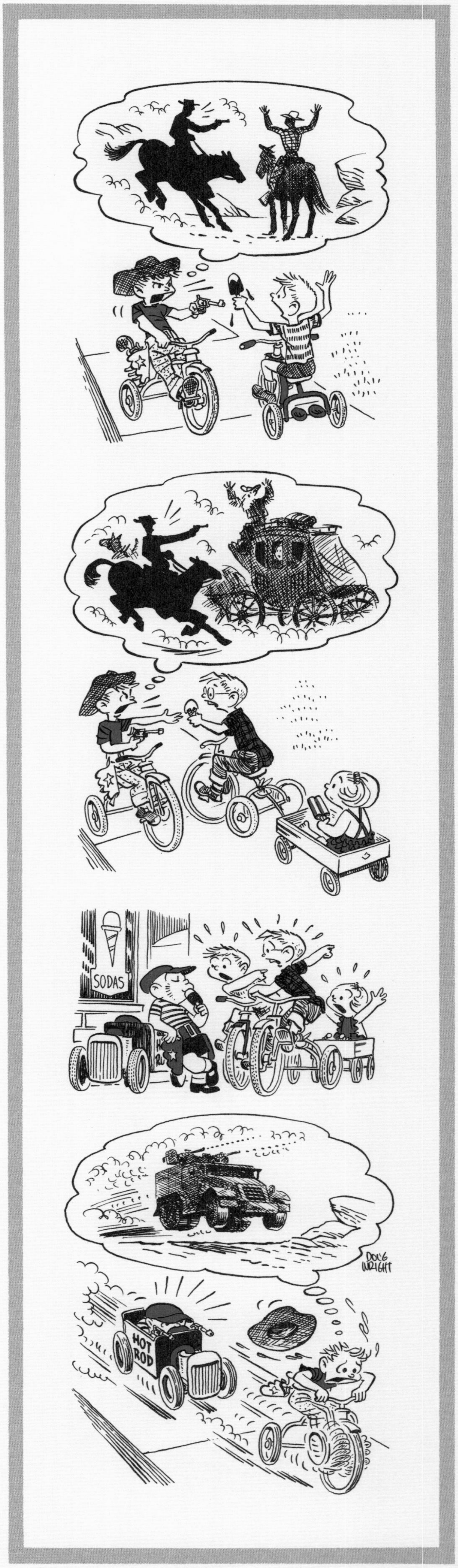
SODAS
DOUG WRIGHT
HOT ROD

June 13, 1959

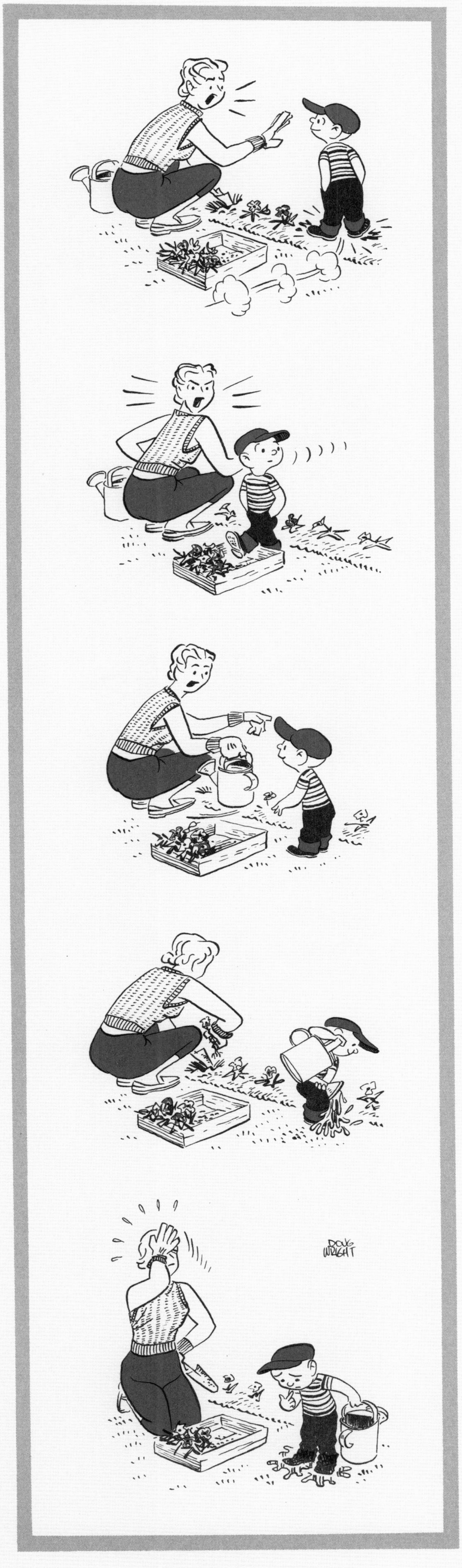
DOUG WRIGHT

June 20, 1959

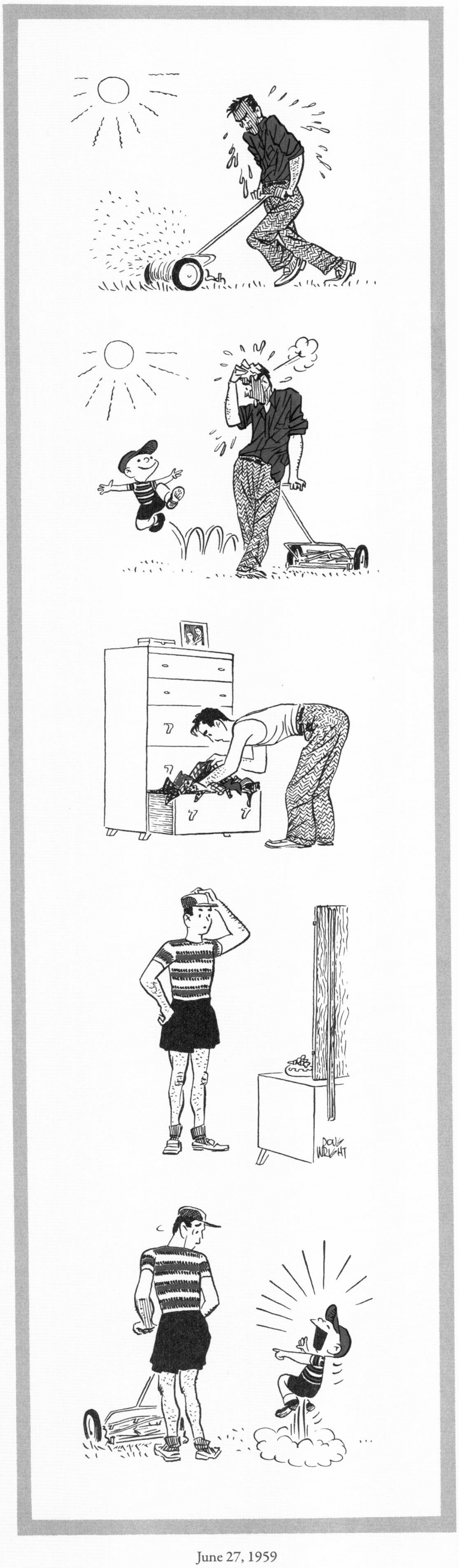
DOUG WRIGHT

June 27, 1959

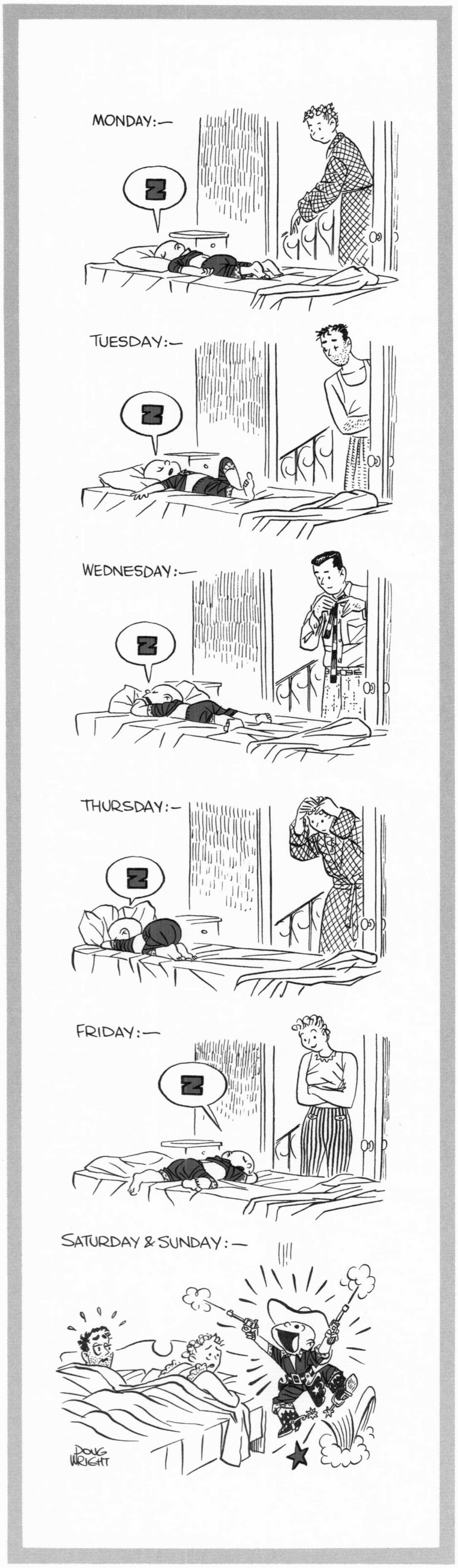
MONDAY:—
Z
TUESDAY:—
Z
WEDNESDAY:—
Z
THURSDAY:—
Z
FRIDAY:—
Z
SATURDAY & SUNDAY:—
DOUG WRIGHT

July 11, 1959

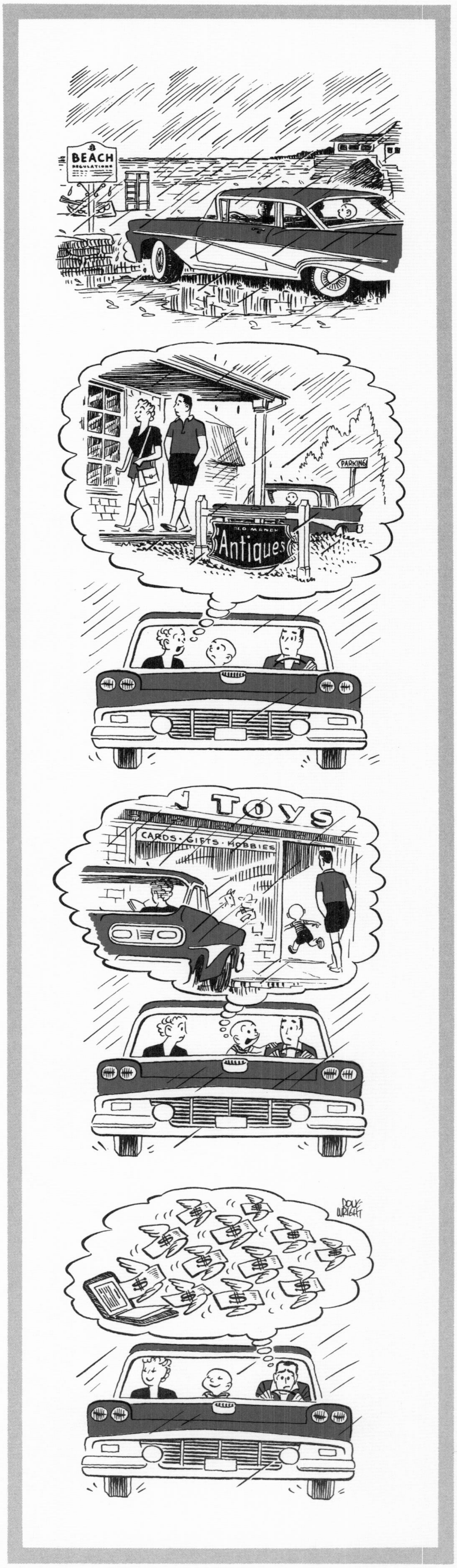
BEACH
PARKING
Antiques
TOYS
CARDS · GIFTS · HOBBIES
DOUG WRIGHT

August 1, 1959

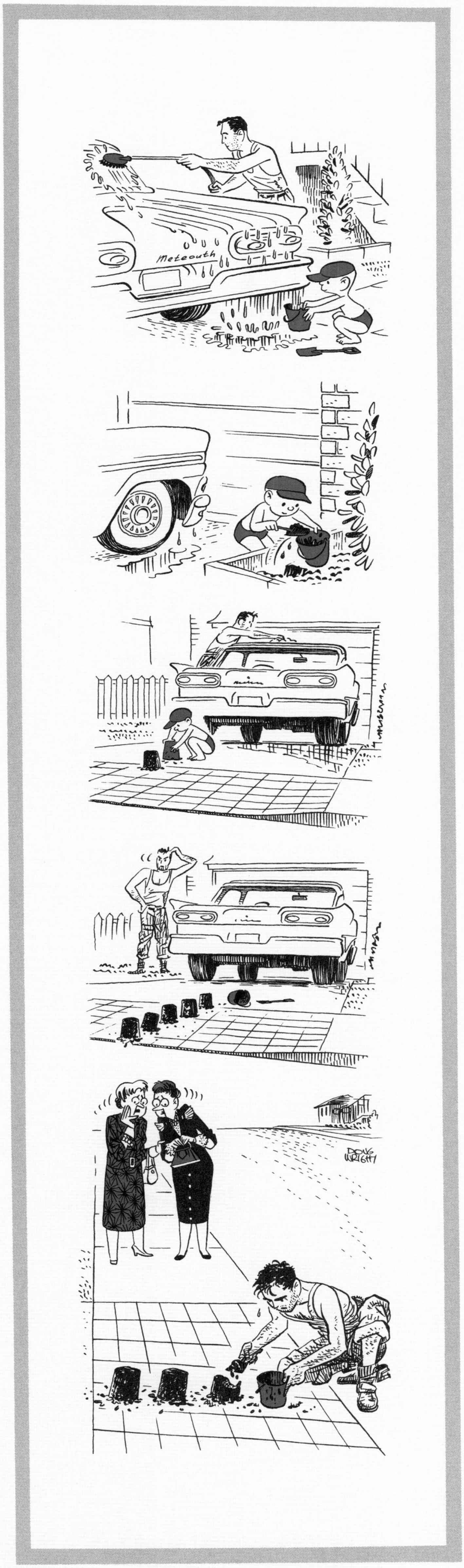
Meteouth
DOUG WRIGHT

August 8, 1959

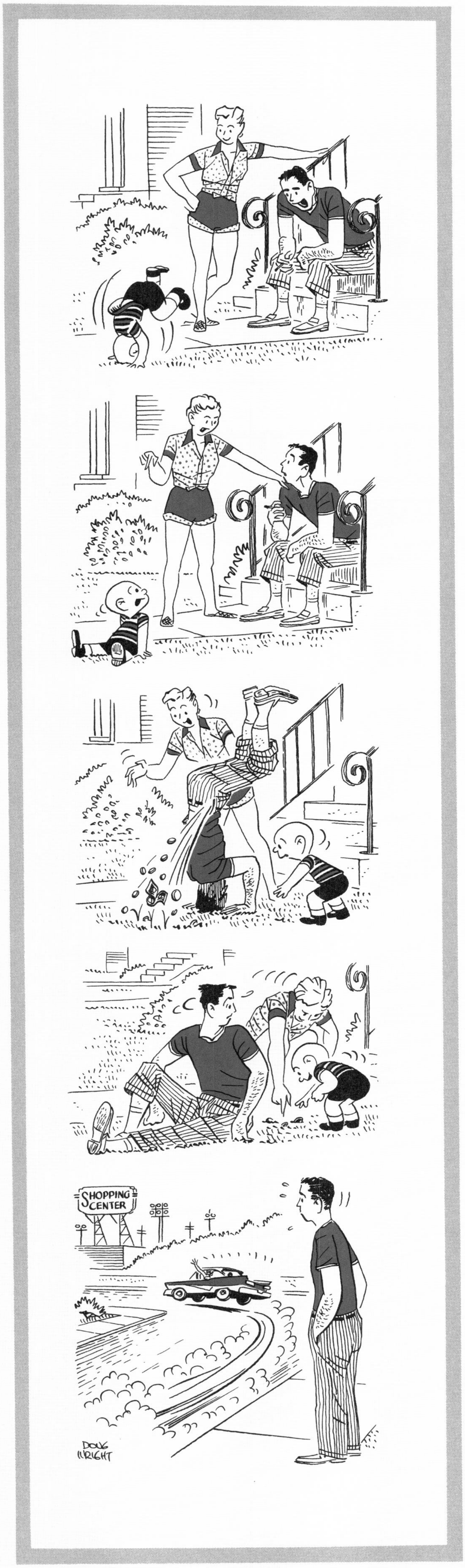
SHOPPING CENTER
DOUG WRIGHT

August 22, 1959

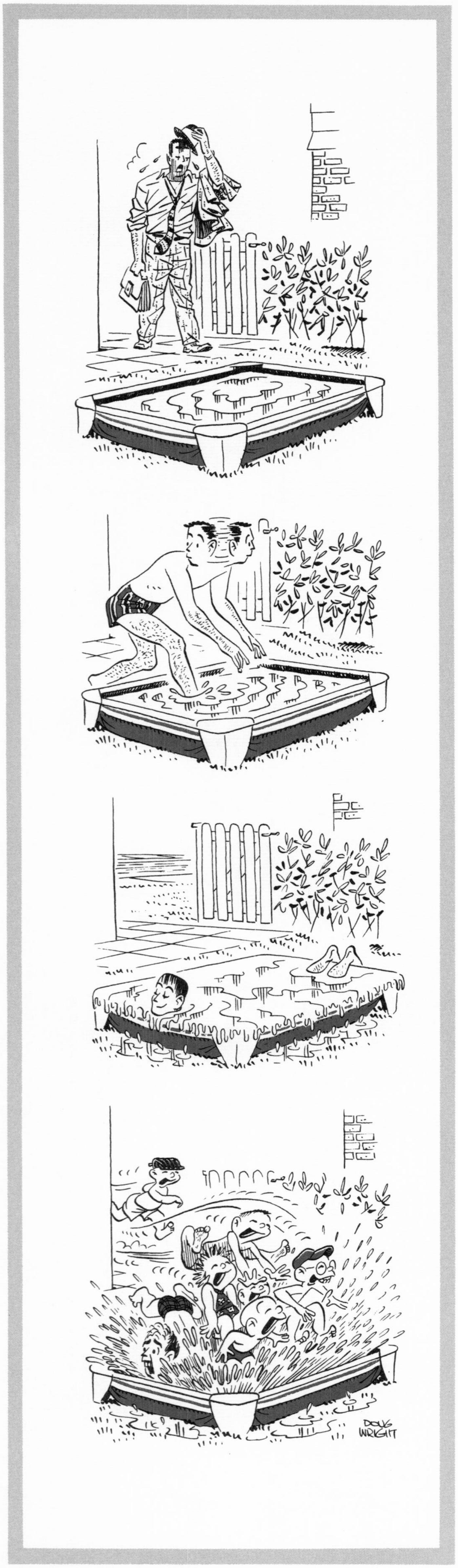
DOUG WRIGHT

August 29, 1959

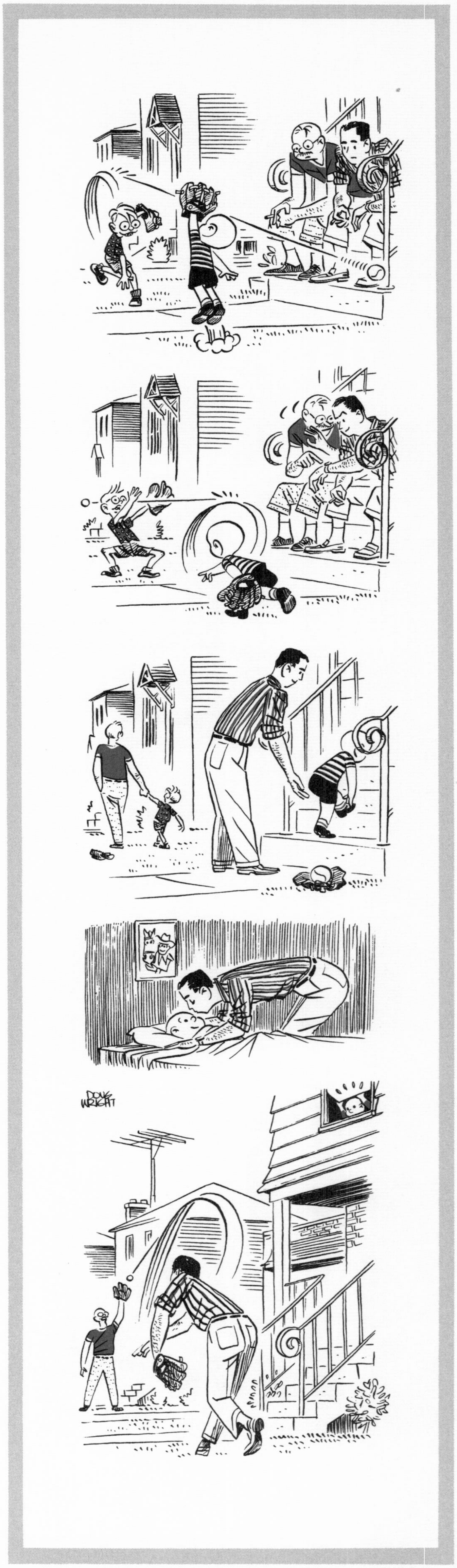
DOUG WRIGHT

September 19, 1959

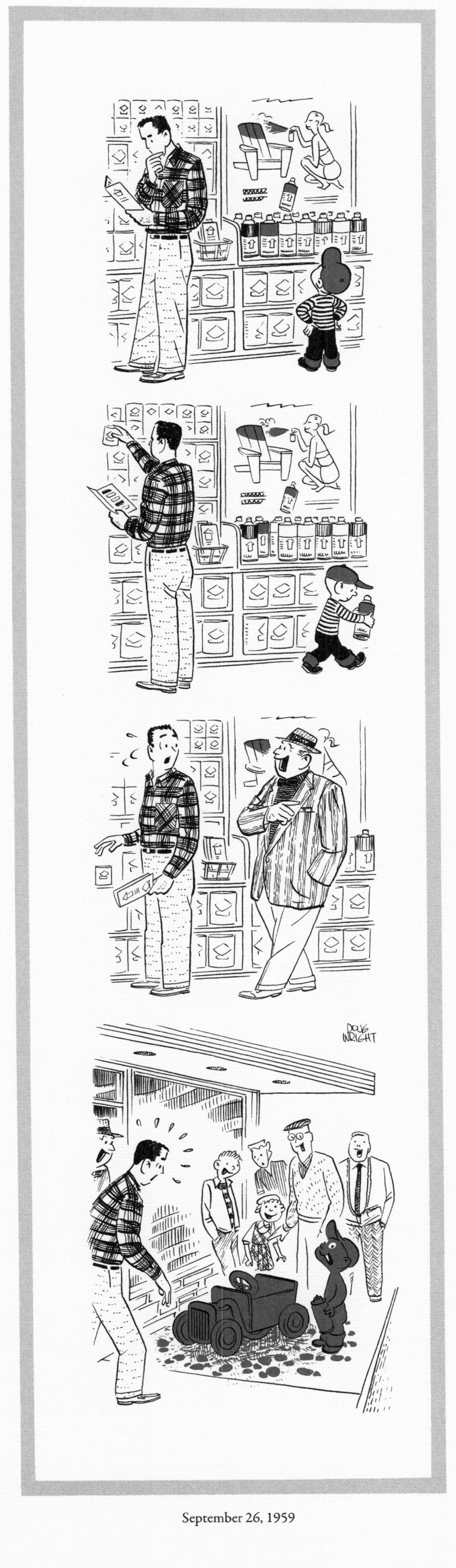
DOUG WRIGHT

September 26, 1959

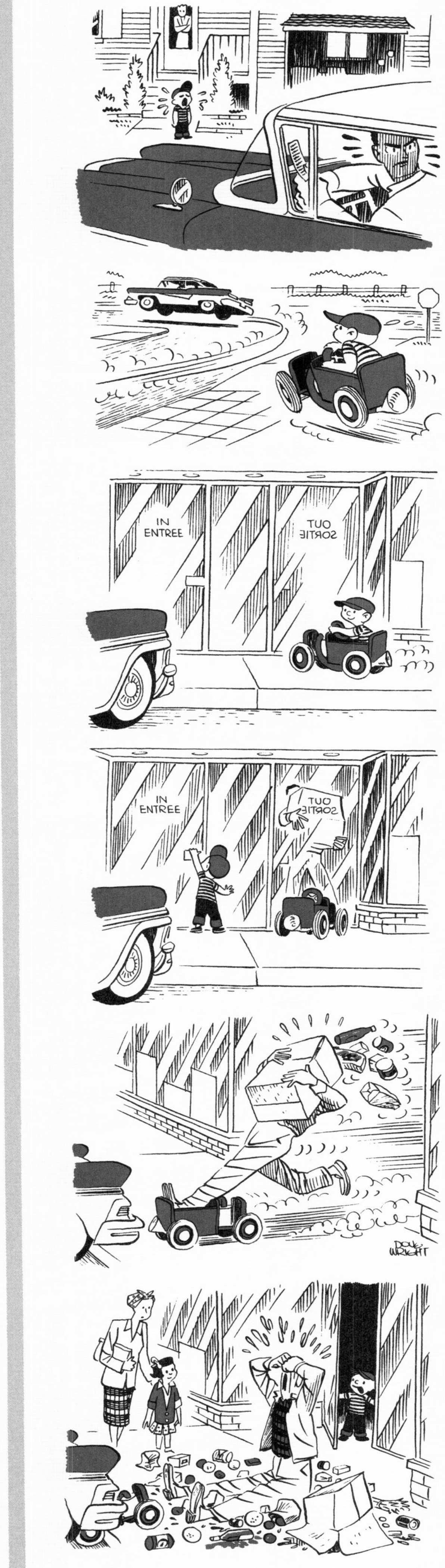
IN
ENTREE
DOUG WRIGHT

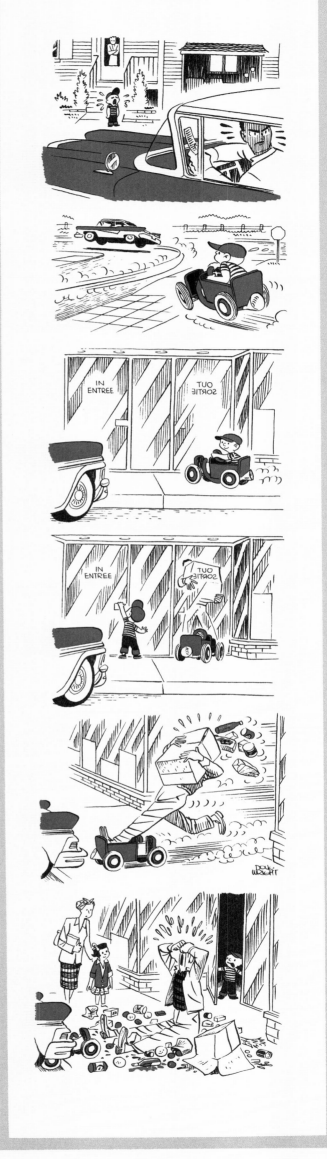

October 3, 1959

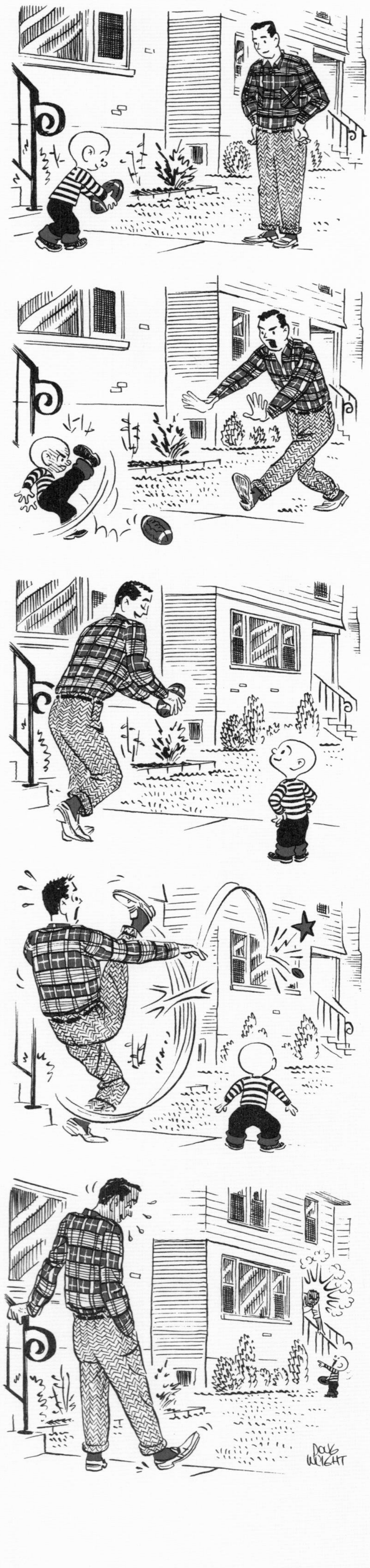
DOUG WRIGHT

October 10, 1959

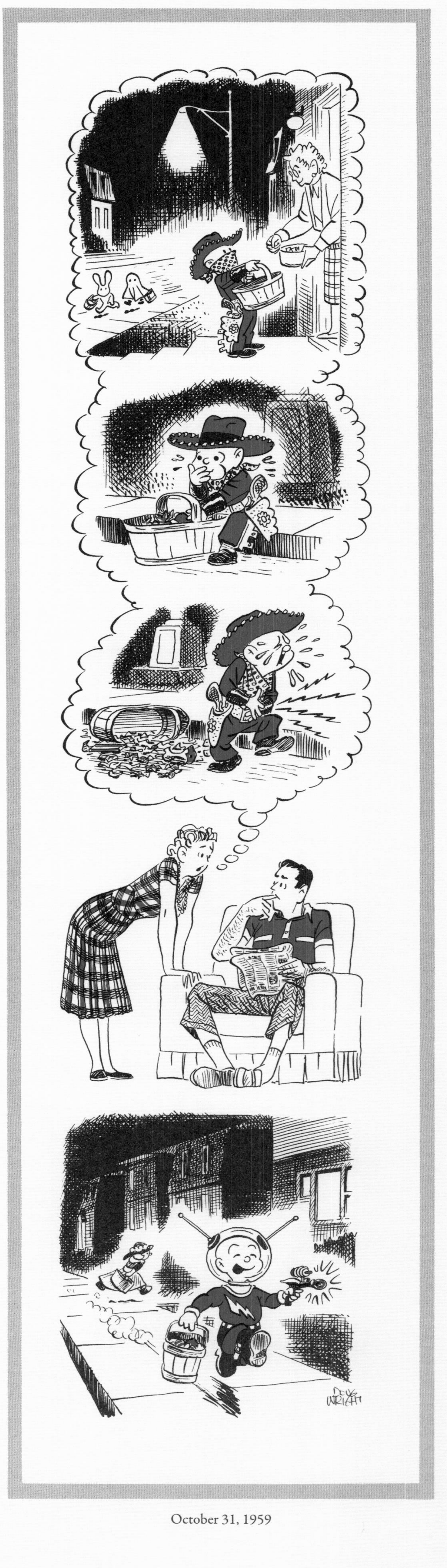
DOUG WRIGHT

October 31, 1959

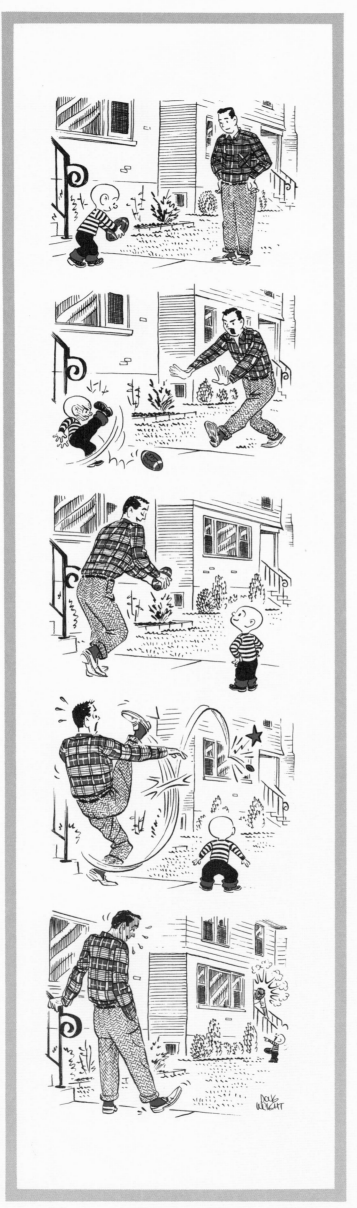

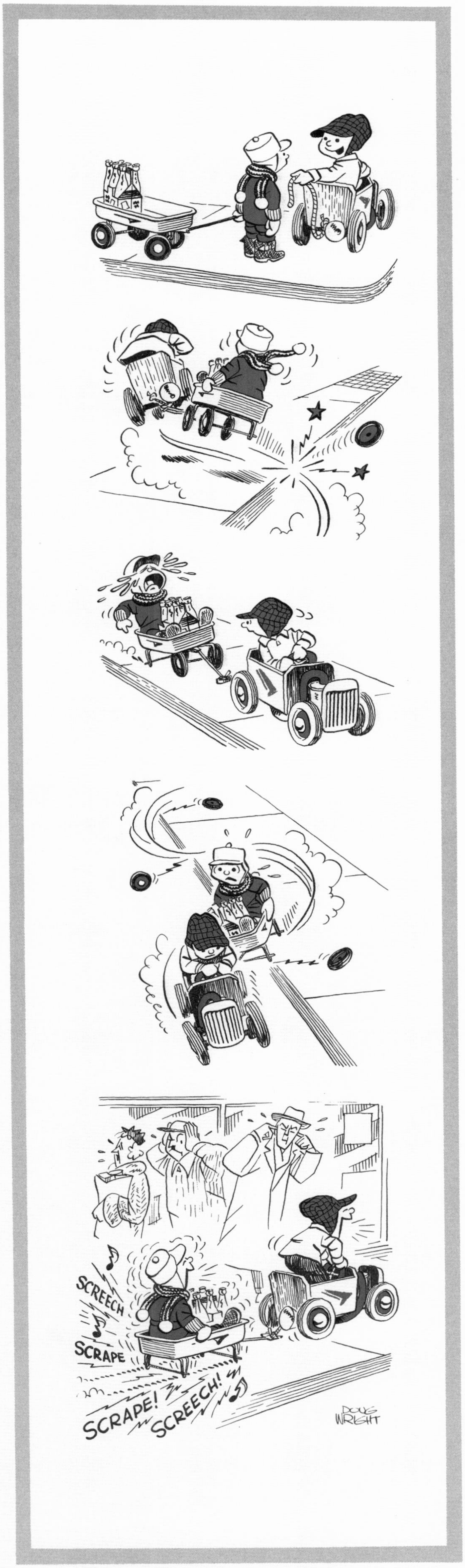
SCREECH
SCRAPE
SCRAPE!
SCREECH!
DOUG WRIGHT

November 7, 1959

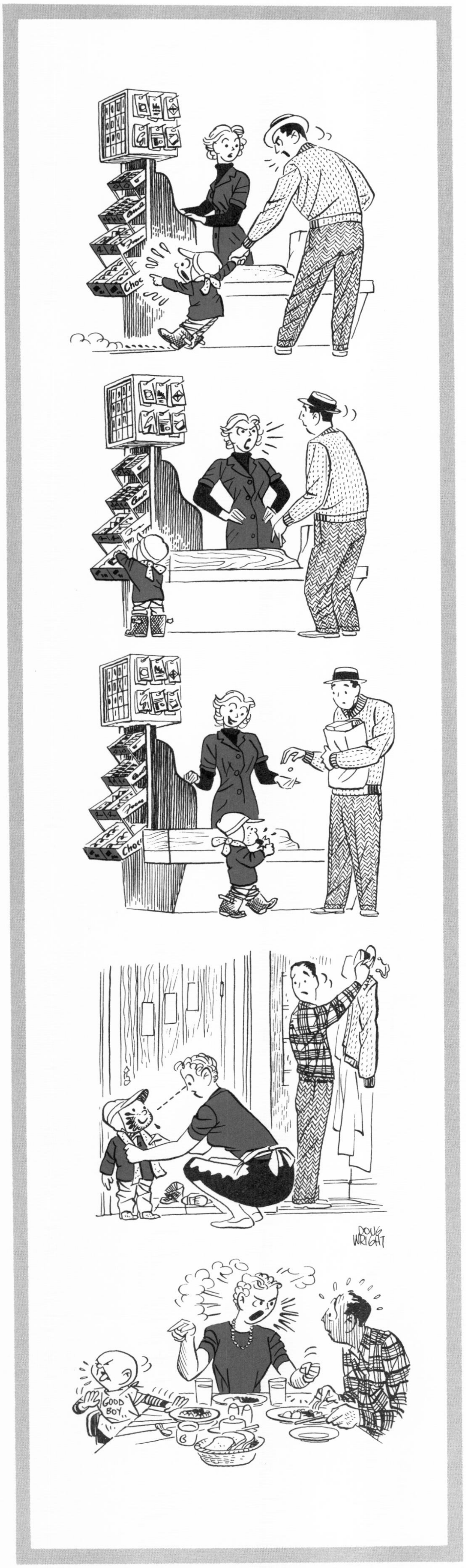
Choc
Choc
DOUG WRIGHT
GOOD BOY

December 19, 1959

Nipper

WEEKEND Magazine Vol. 9 No. 51, 1959

December 26, 1959

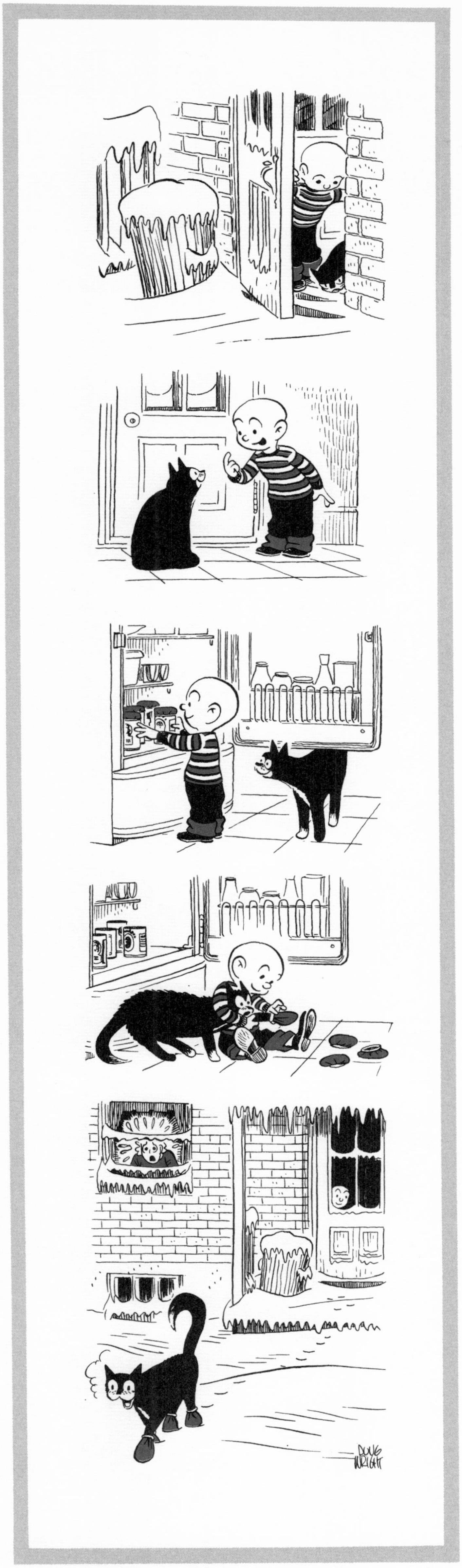

DOUG WRIGHT

January 9, 1960

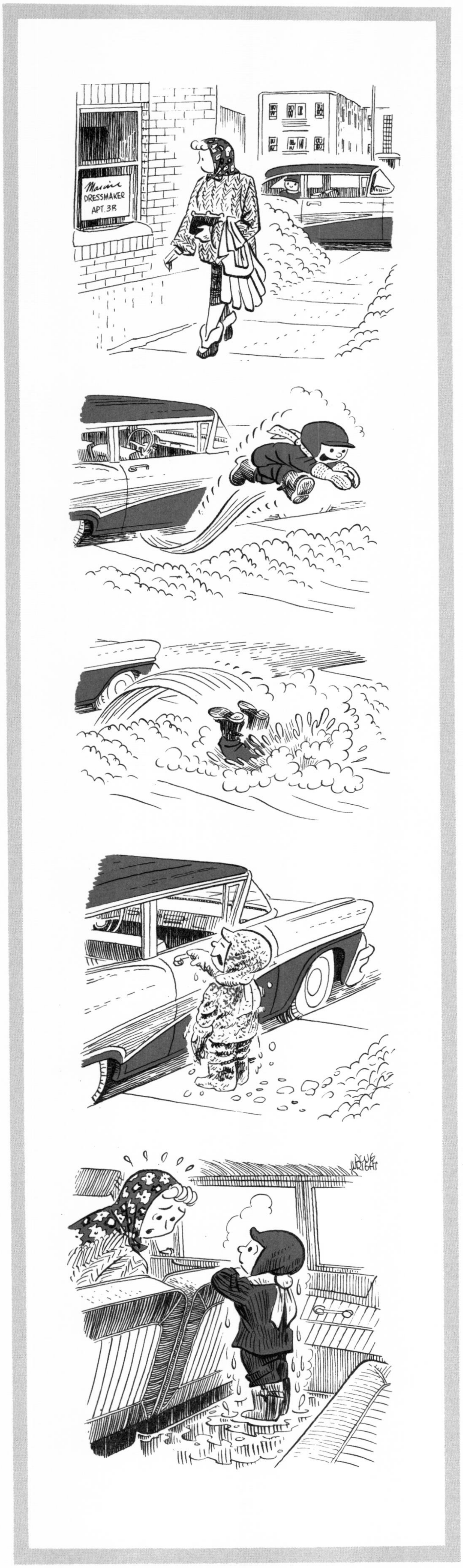

Maxine
DRESSMAKER
APT. 3B
DOUG WRIGHT

January 23, 1960

February 13, 1960 (a)

...and this one didn't. Why was it rejected? Perhaps the editors didn't like Nipper sending a valentine to a boy? Or perhaps it was simply that the strip was too confusing?

February 13, 1960 (b)

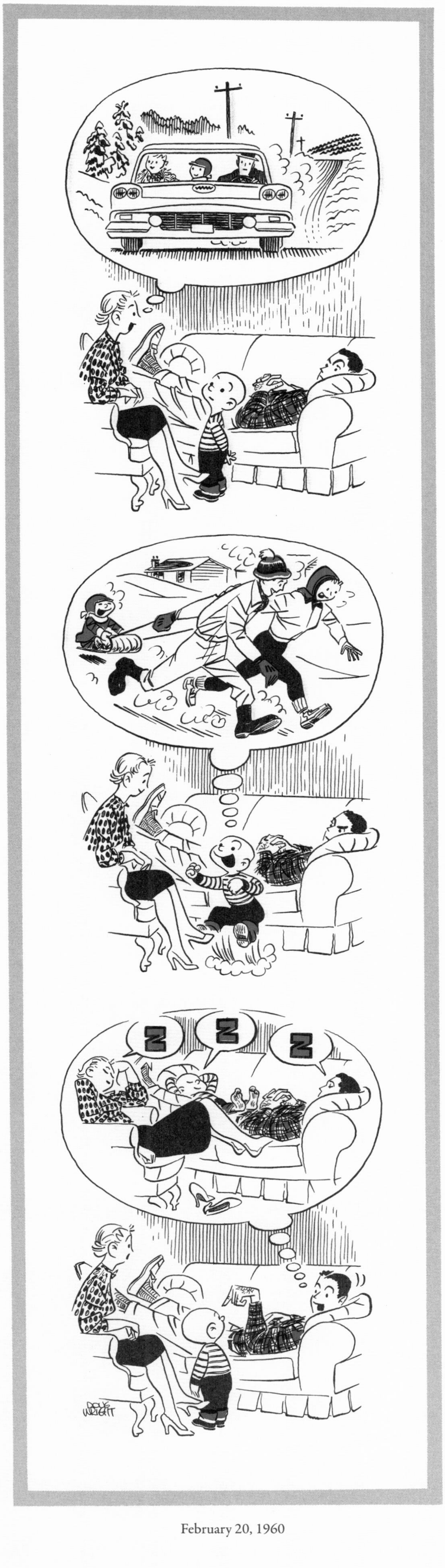

Z
Z
Z
DOUG WRIGHT

February 20, 1960

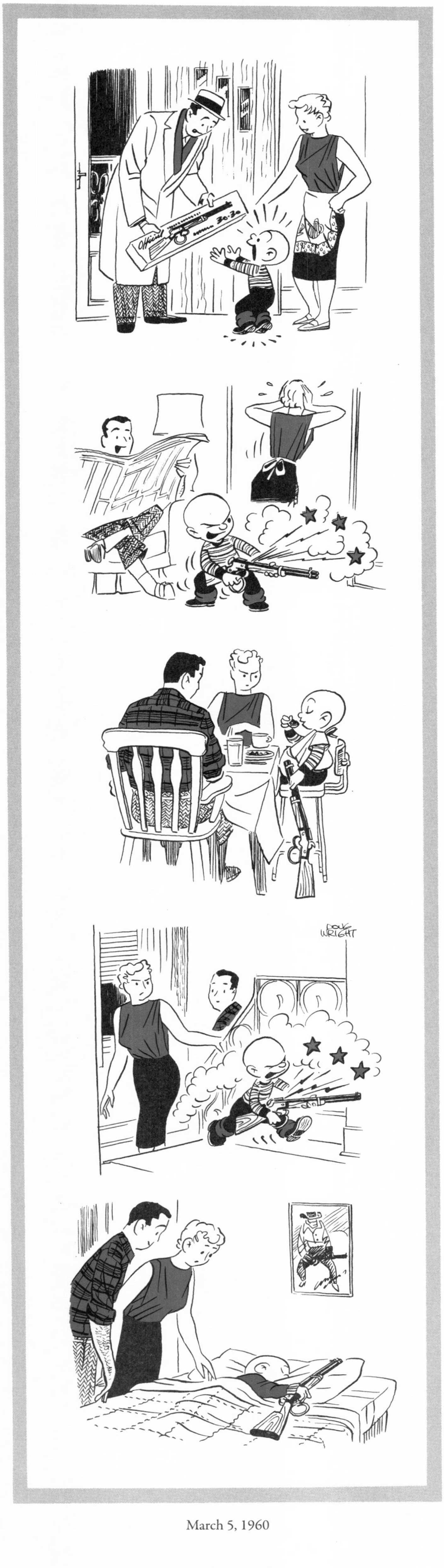

Official
30-30
DOUG WRIGHT

March 5, 1960

The first mention of an important development in Nipper's world.

March 19, 1960

March 26, 1960

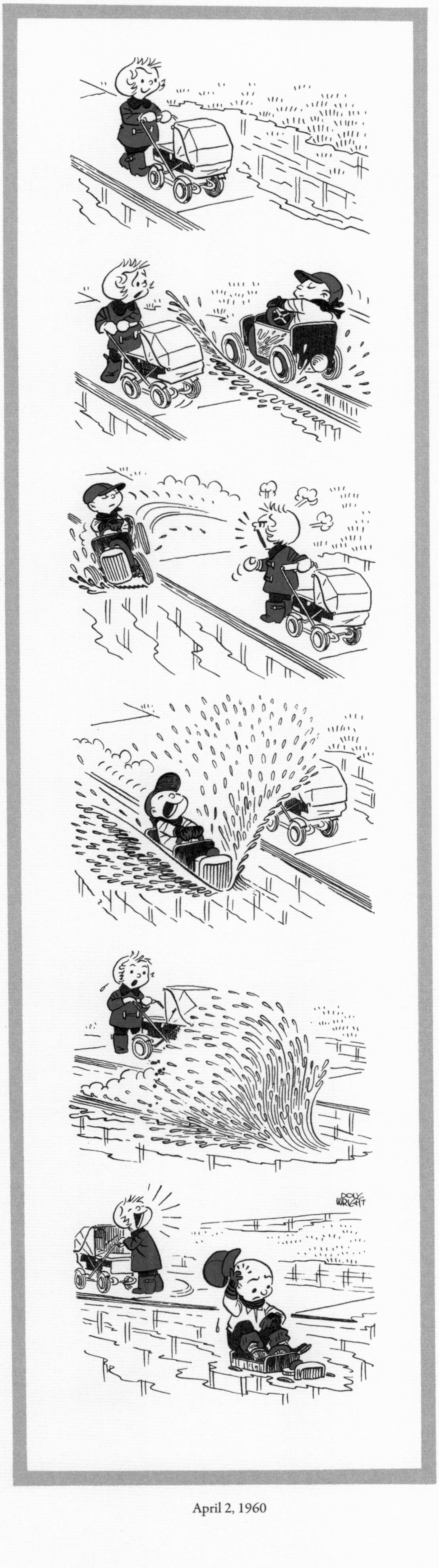
DOUG WRIGHT

April 2, 1960

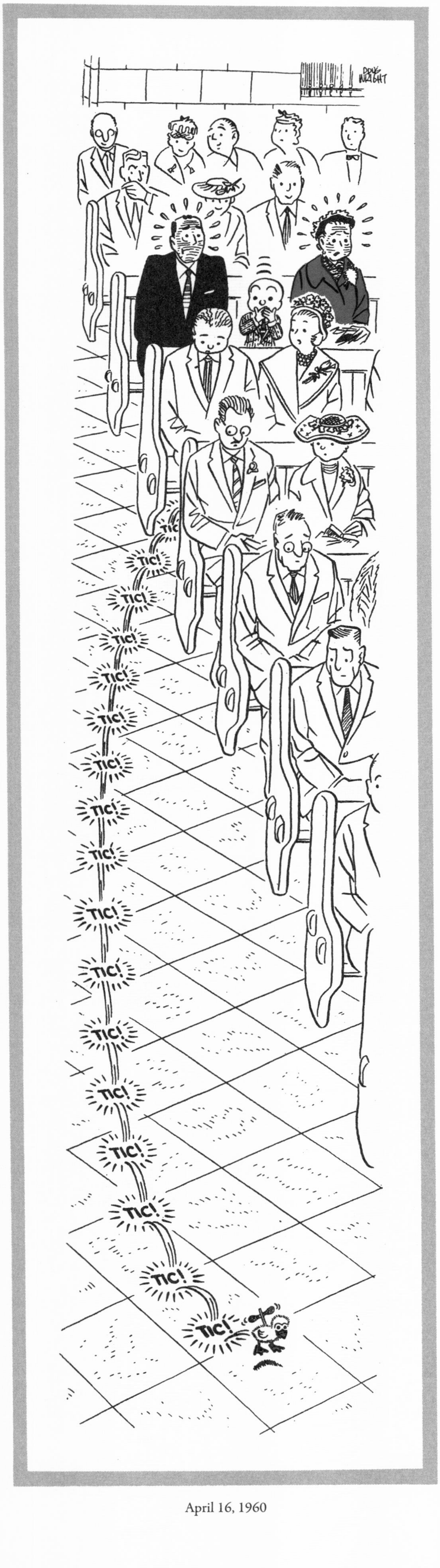
DOUG WRIGHT
TIC!
TIC!
TIC!
TIC!
TIC!
TIC!
TIC!
TIC!
TIC!
TIC!
TIC!
TIC!
TIC!
TIC!
TIC!
TIC!
TIC!

April 16, 1960

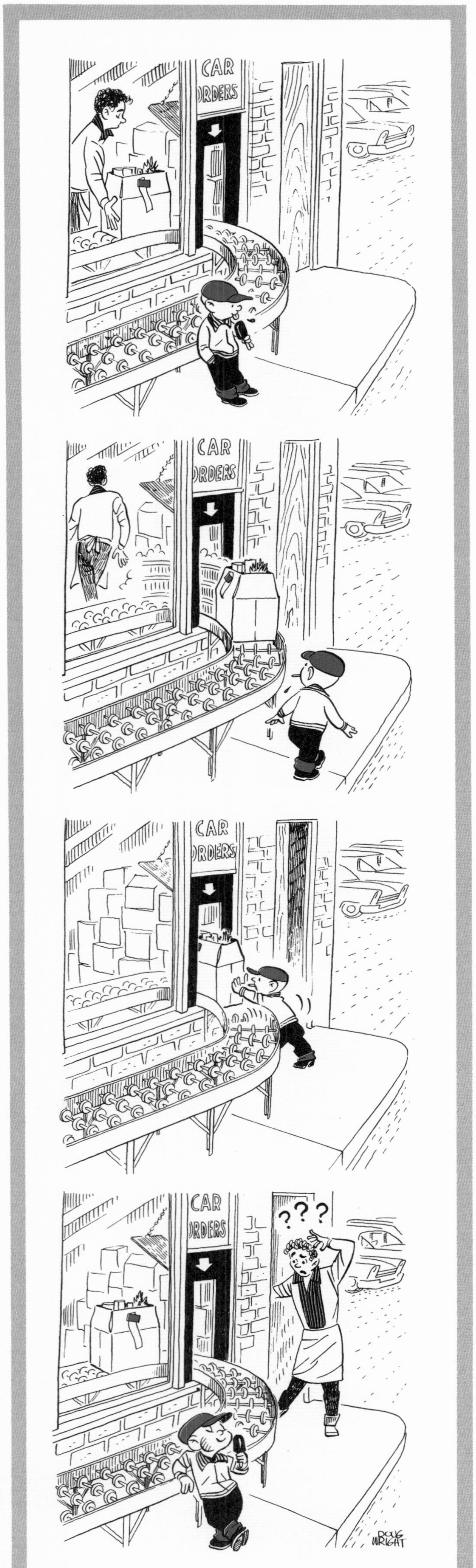
CAR
ORDERS
DOUG WRIGHT

April 30, 1960

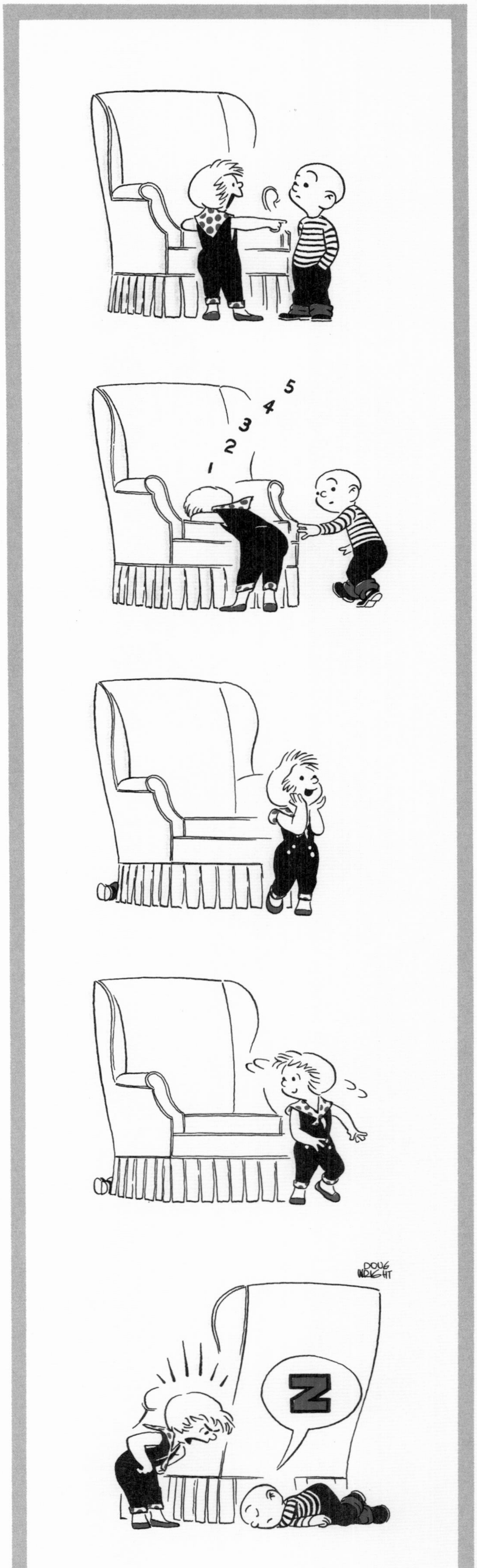
1
2
3
4
5
Z
DOUG WRIGHT

May 4, 1960

Is this the first depiction of an obviously pregnant woman in a nationally published comic strip in North America?

June 11, 1960

June 18, 1960

June 25, 1960

July 2, 1960

The younger sibling comes home from the hospital and the final element of the strip is set in place for the next decade—the peak years of the strip.

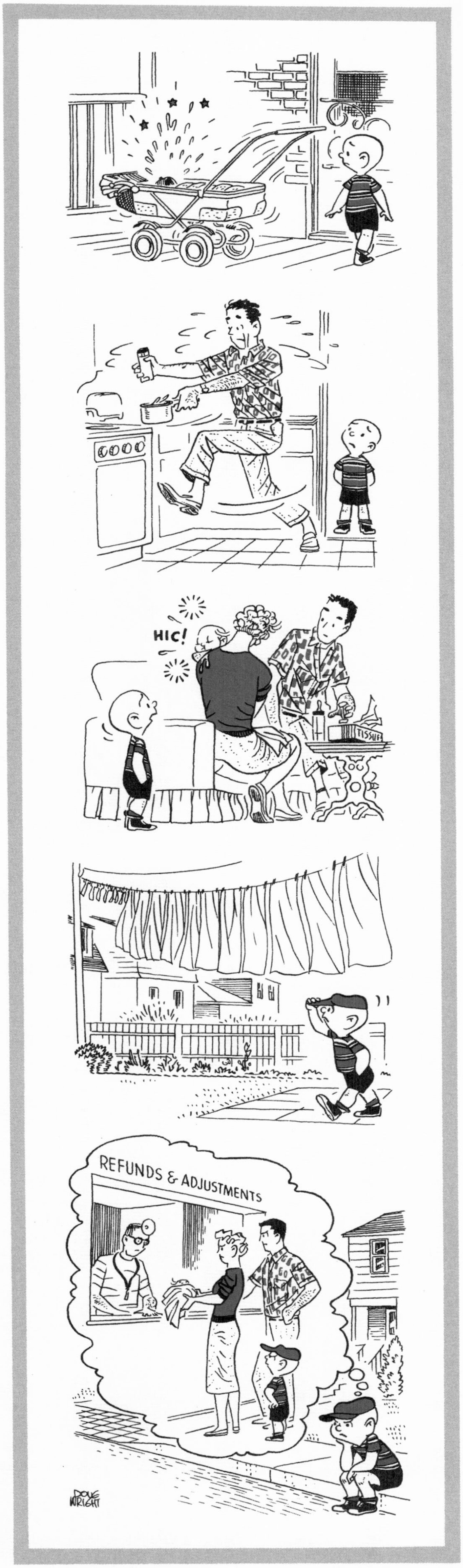
HIC!
TISSUE
REFUNDS & ADJUSTMENTS
DOUG WRIGHT

July 9, 1960

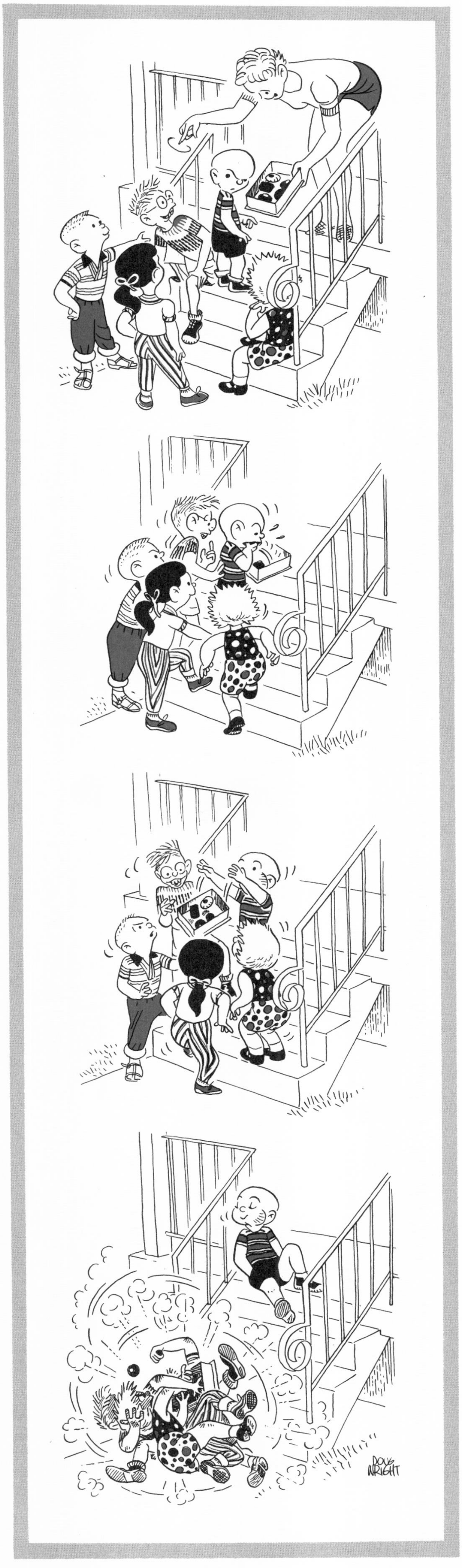
DOUG WRIGHT

July 16, 1960

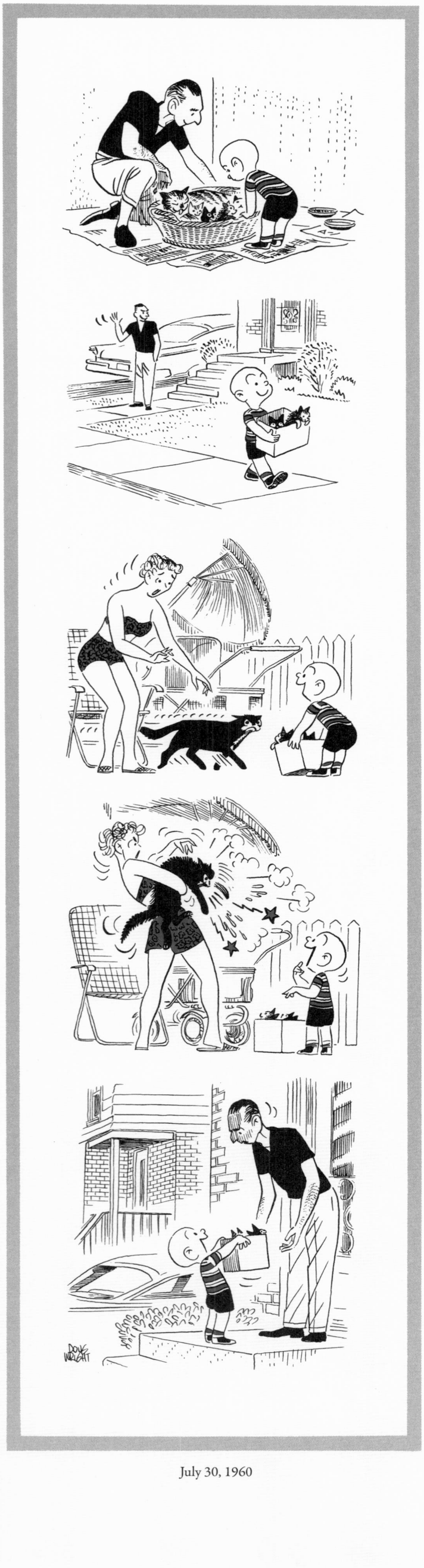

July 30, 1960

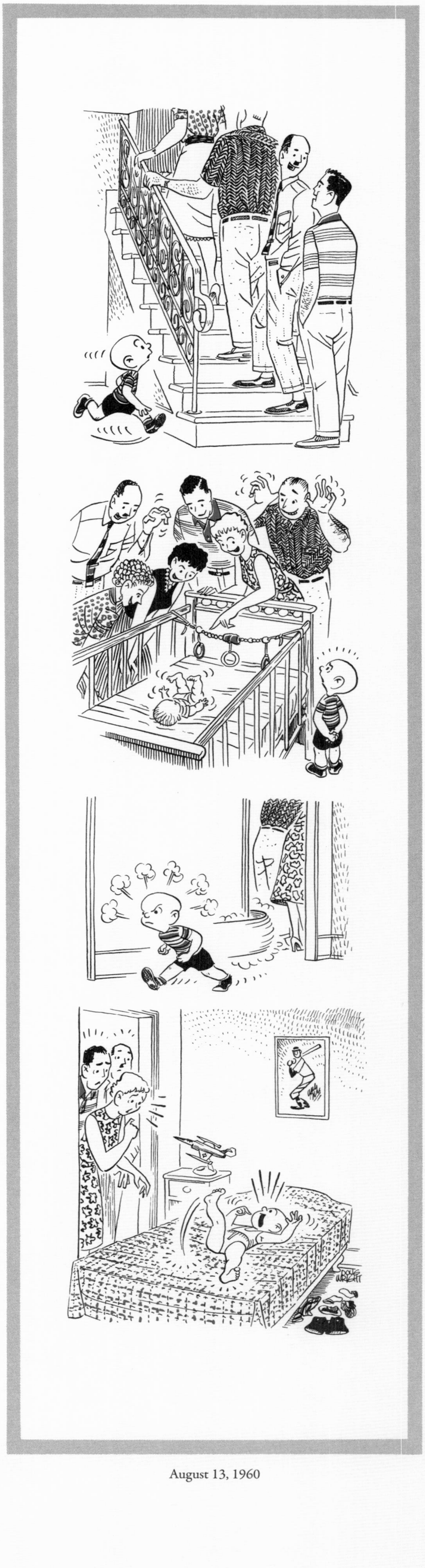

August 13, 1960

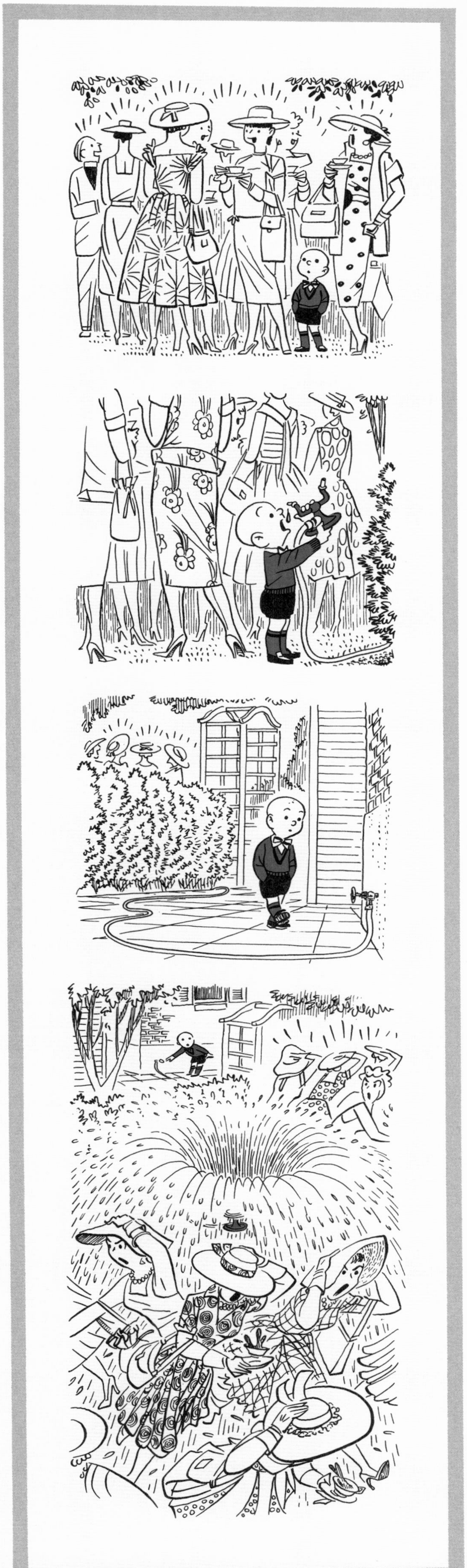

September 3, 1960

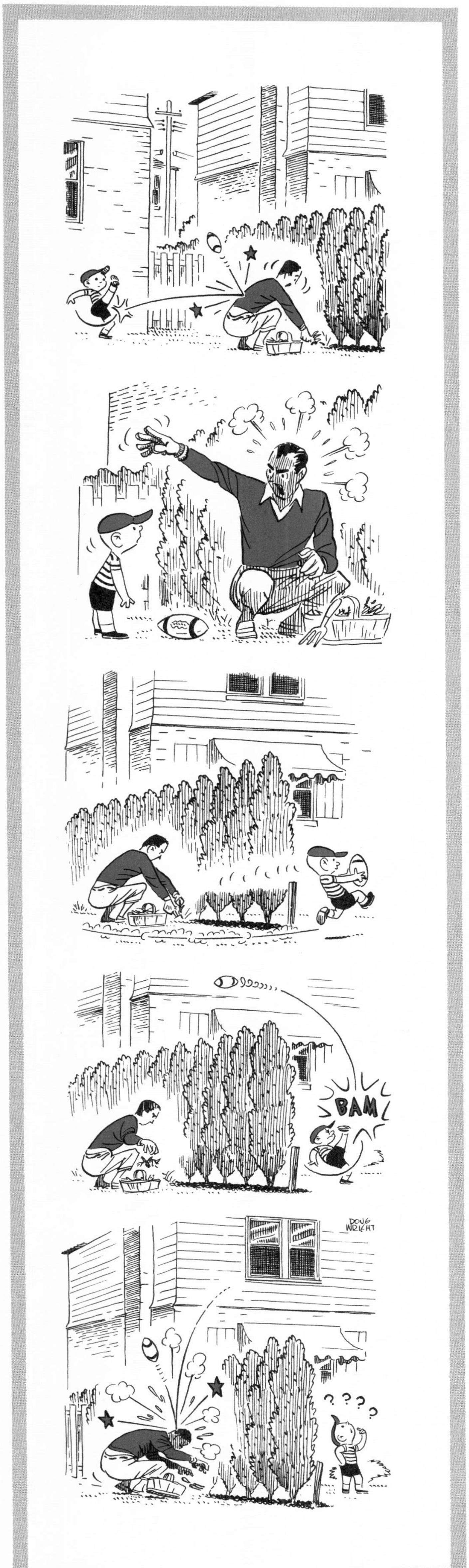
BAM
DOUG WRIGHT

September 10, 1960

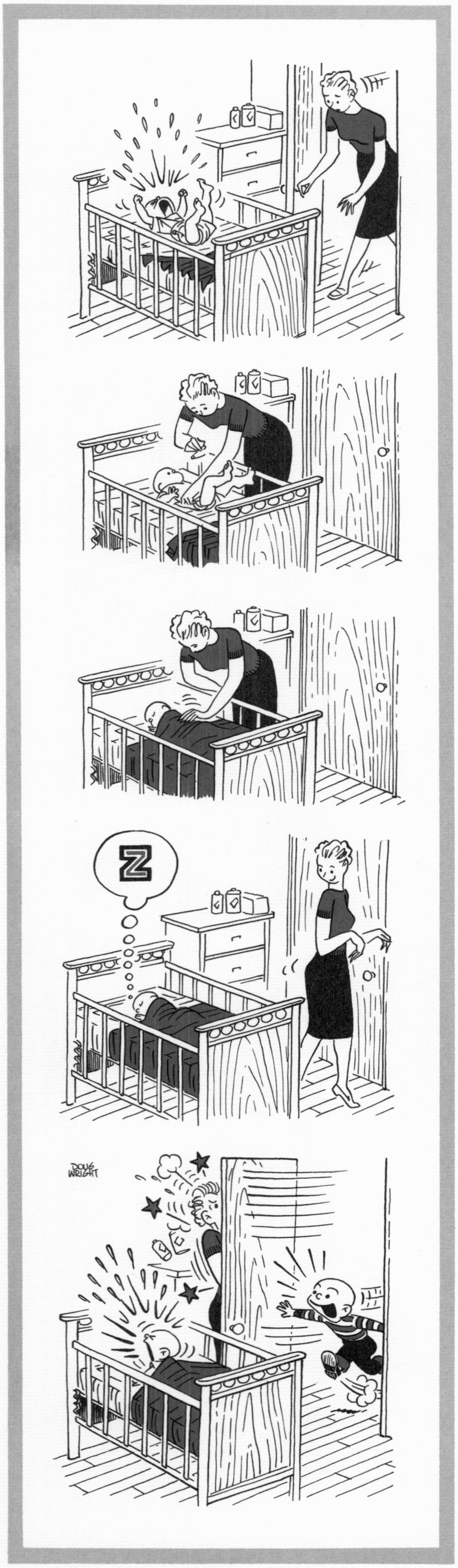
Z
DOUG WRIGHT
October 15, 1960

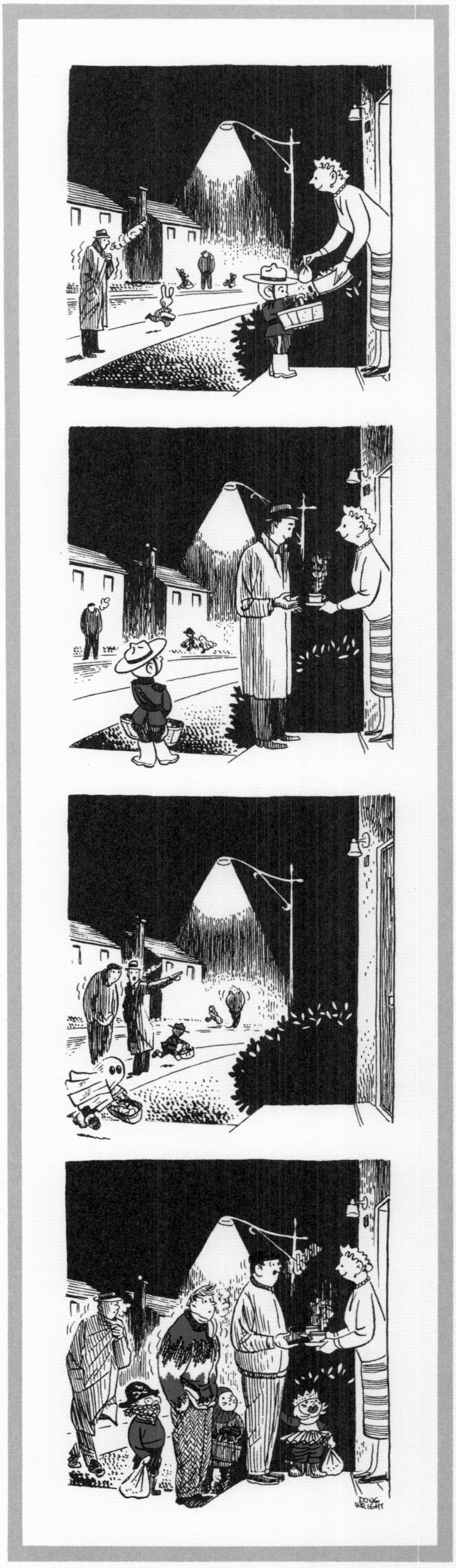
DOUG WRIGHT
October 29, 1960

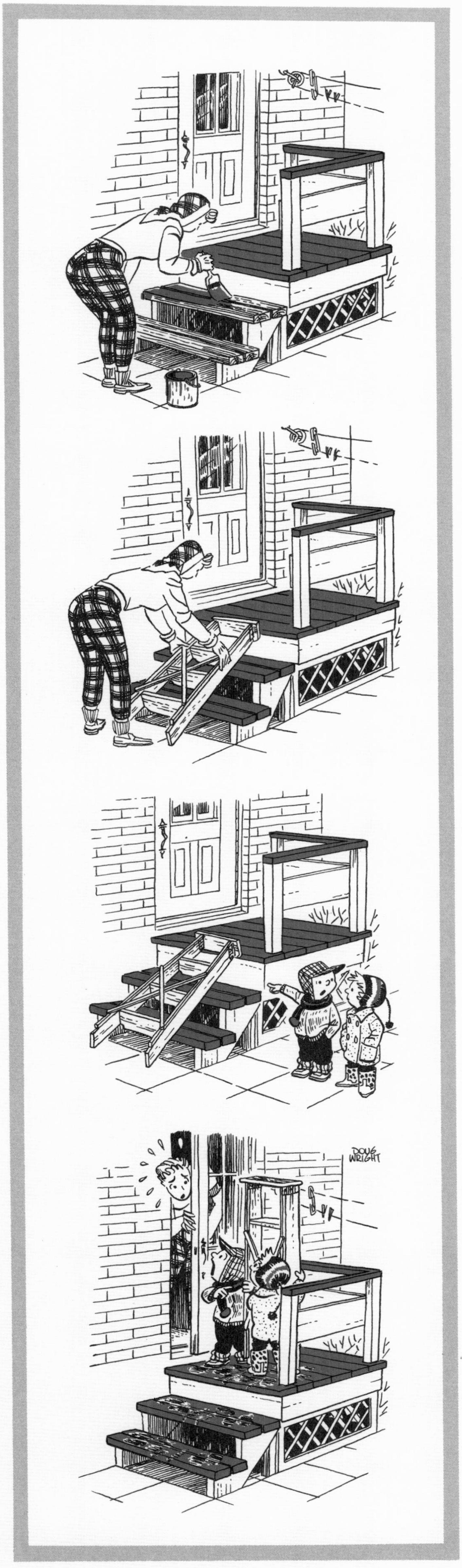
DOUG WRIGHT

November 5, 1960

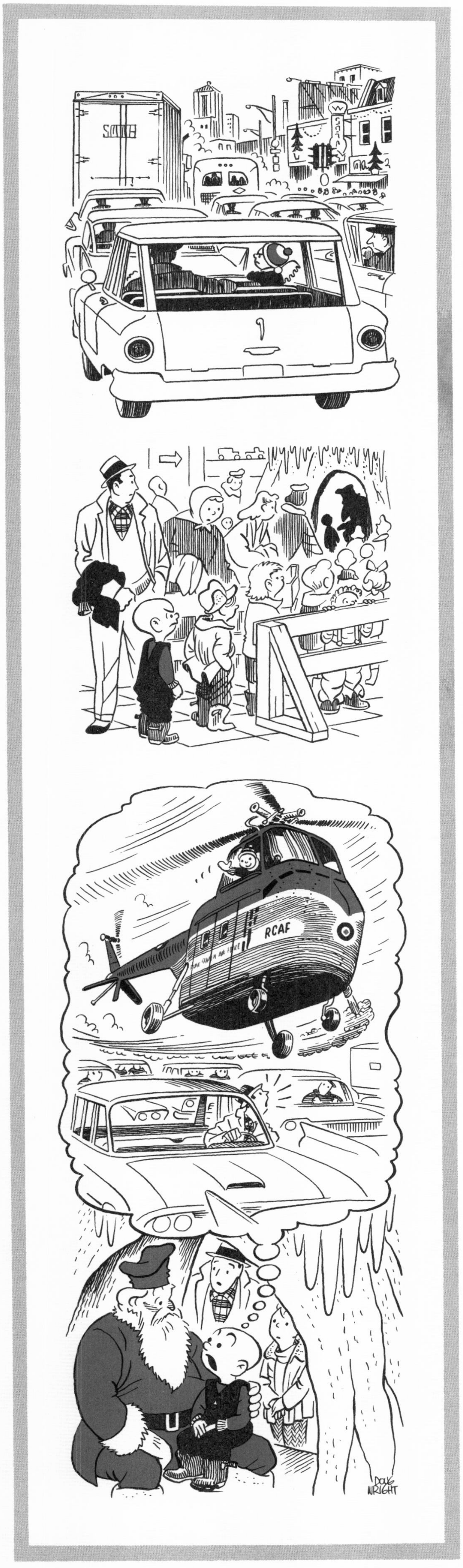
RCAF
DOUG WRIGHT

December 17, 1960

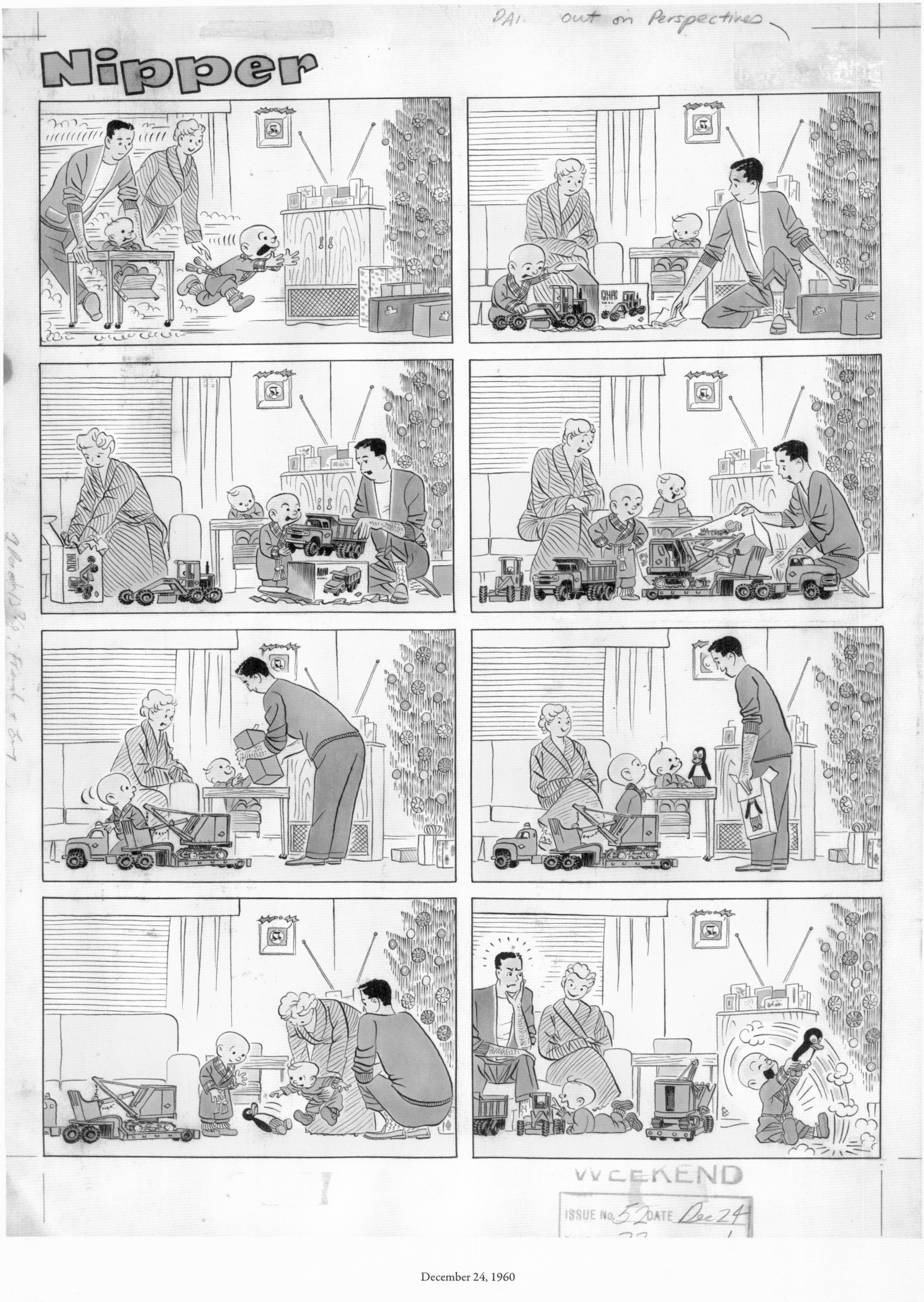
Nipper
DA1. out on Perspectives
WEEKEND
ISSUE No. 52 DATE Dec 24

December 24, 1960

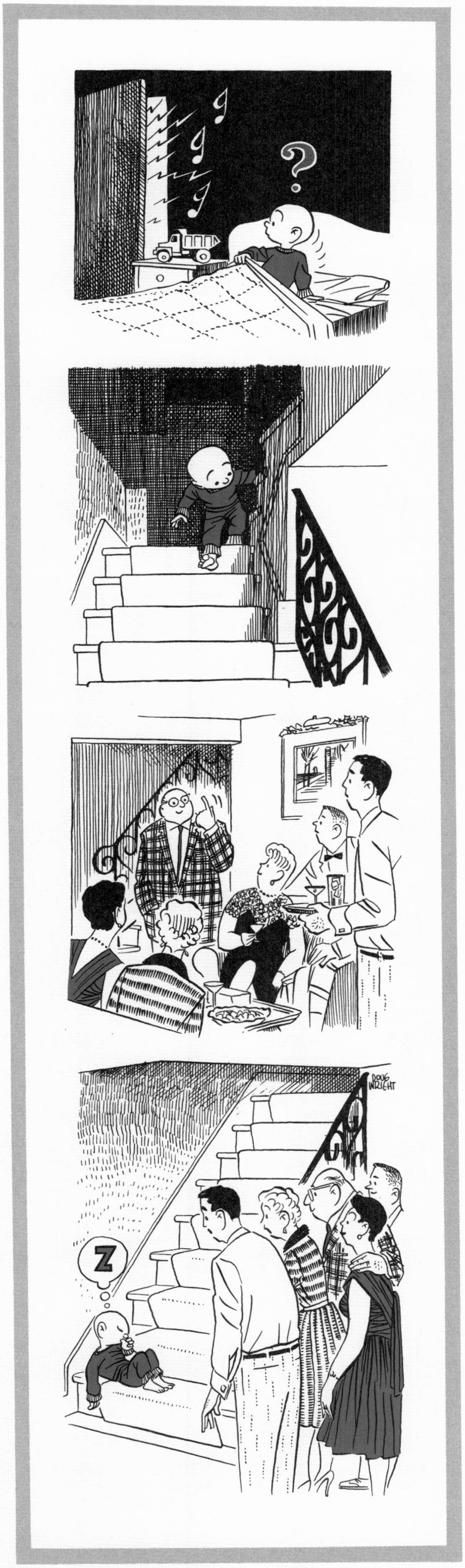
DOUG WRIGHT
Z

December 31, 1960

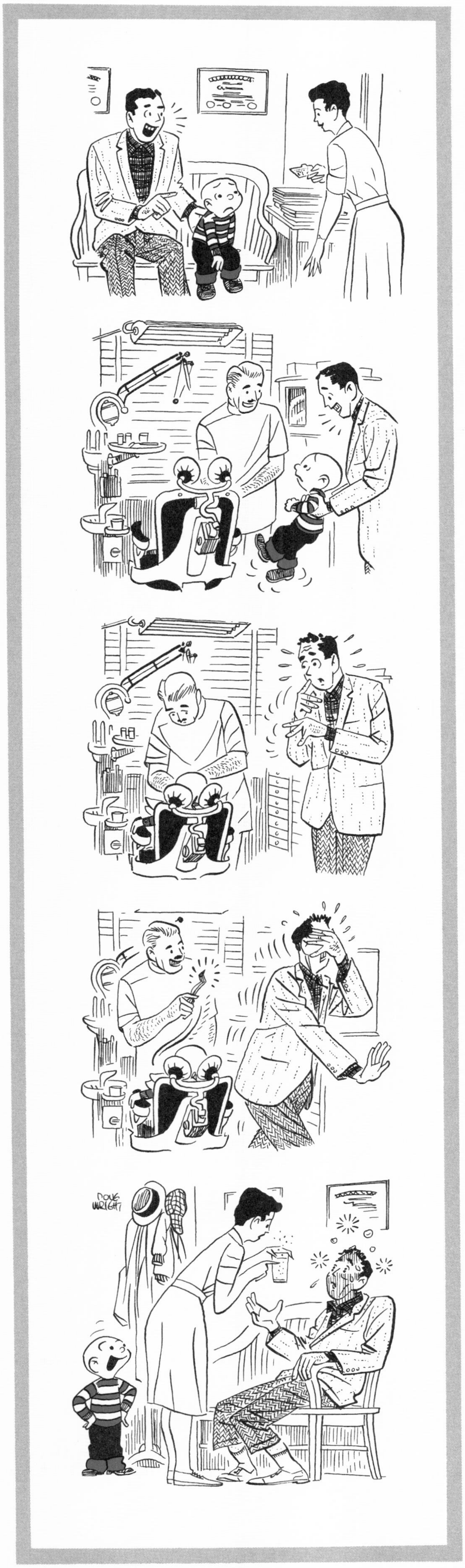
DOUG WRIGHT

January 14, 1961

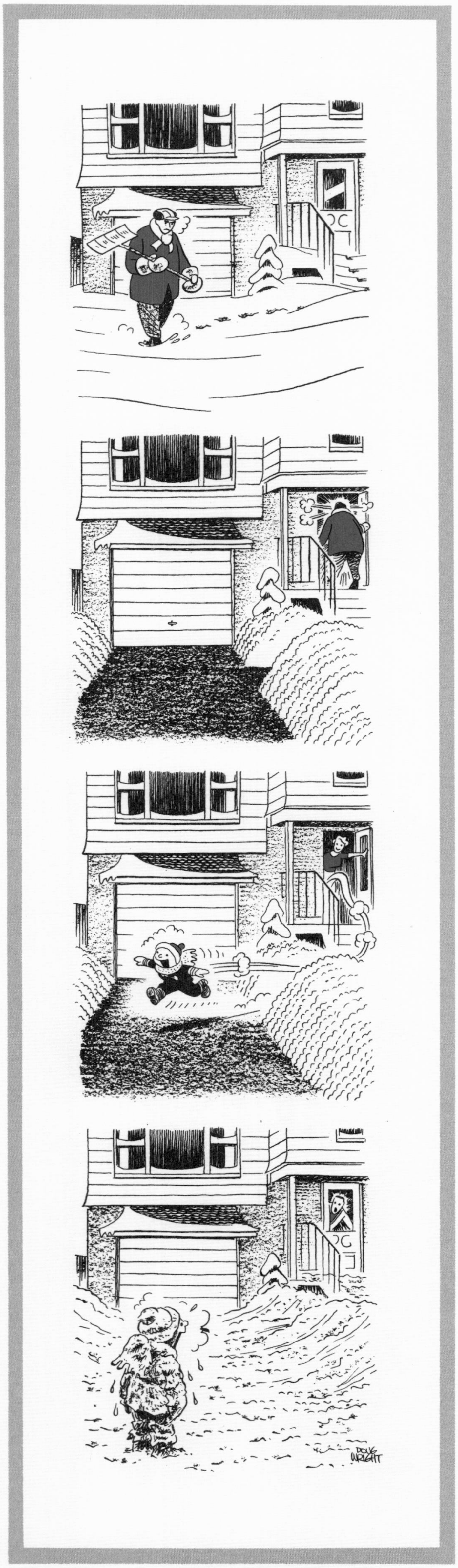

February 18, 1961

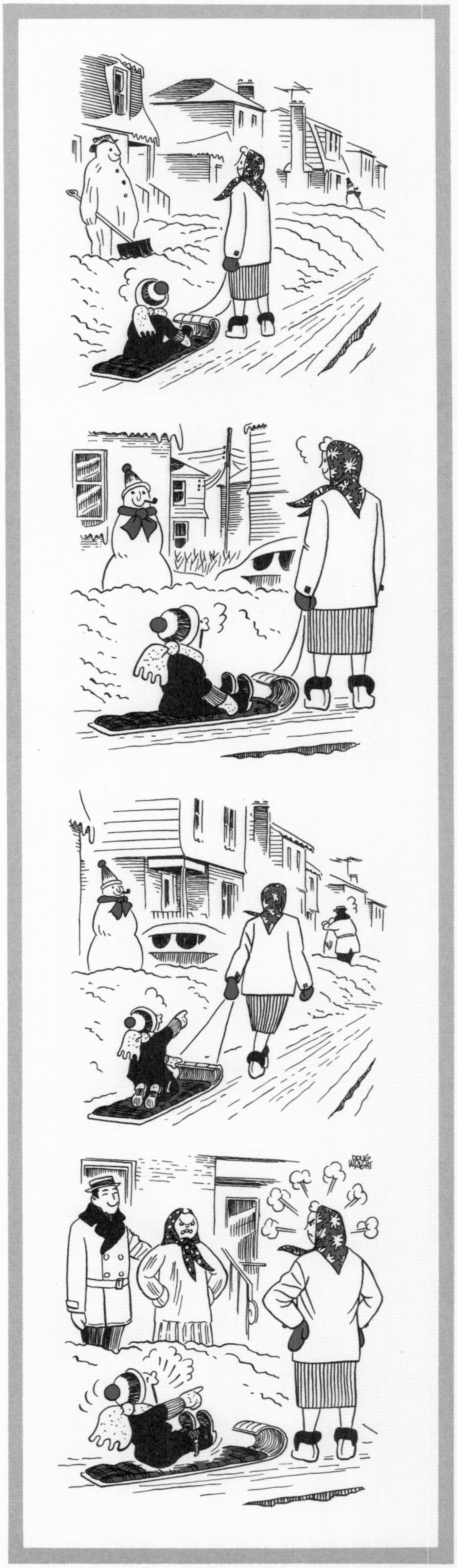

February 25, 1961

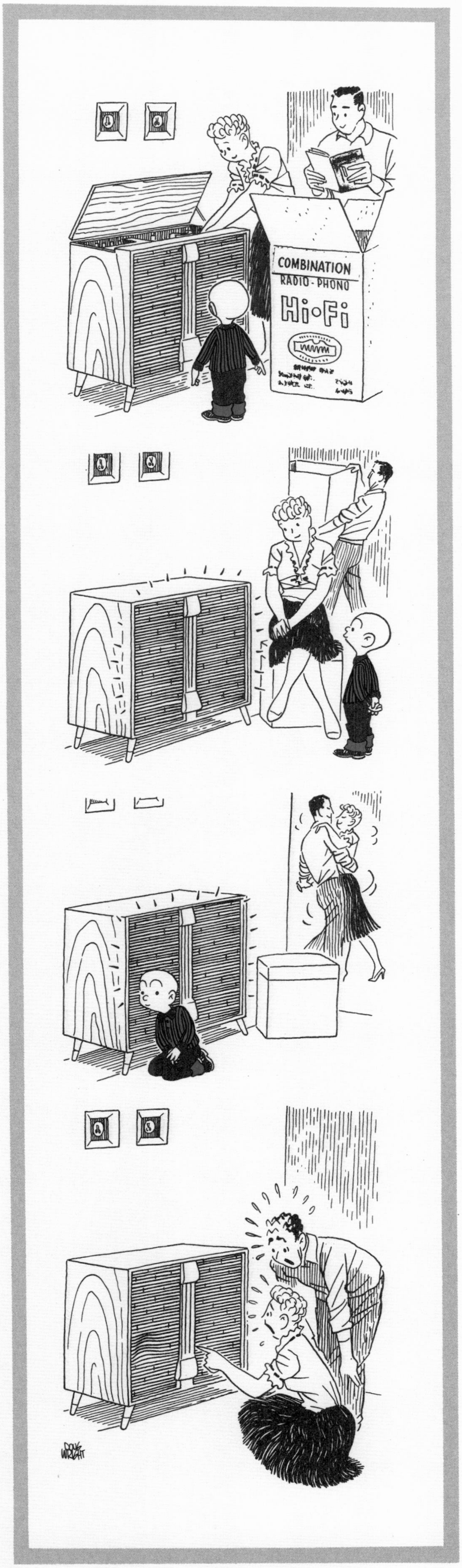
COMBINATION
RADIO-PHONO
Hi-Fi
DOUG WRIGHT

March 4, 1961

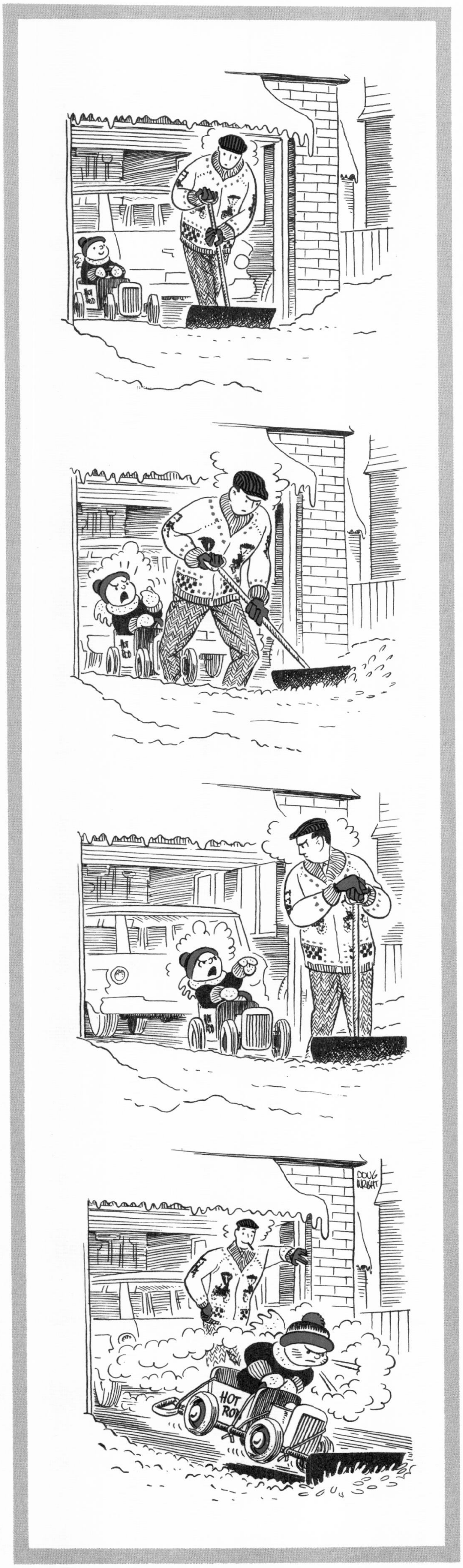
DOUG WRIGHT
HOT ROD

March 18, 1961

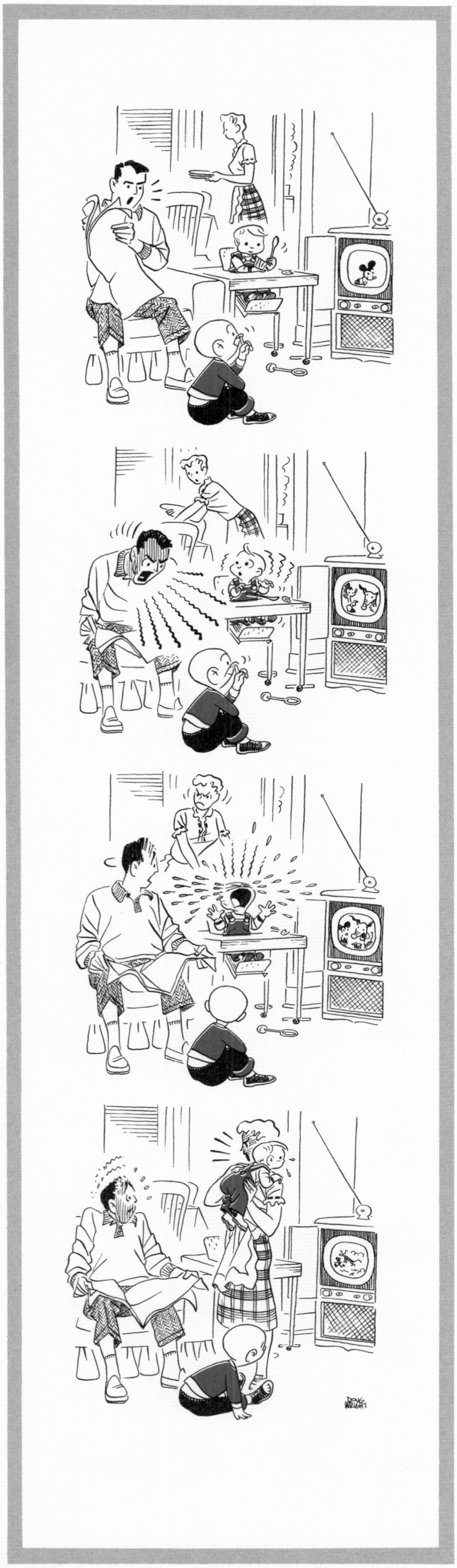

April 2, 1961

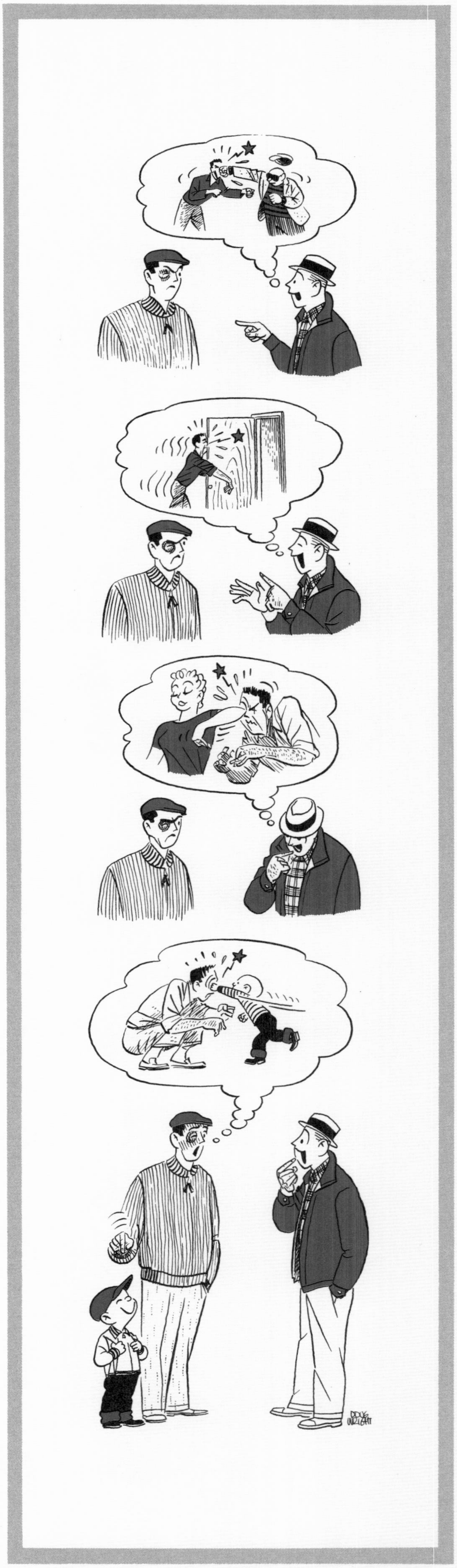

April 22, 1961

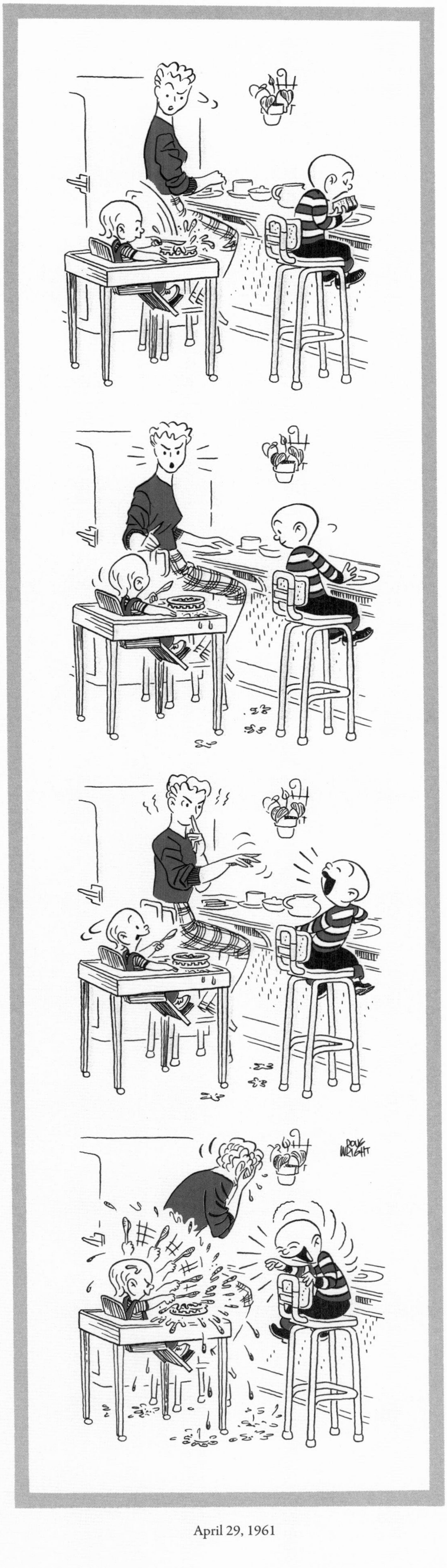

April 29, 1961

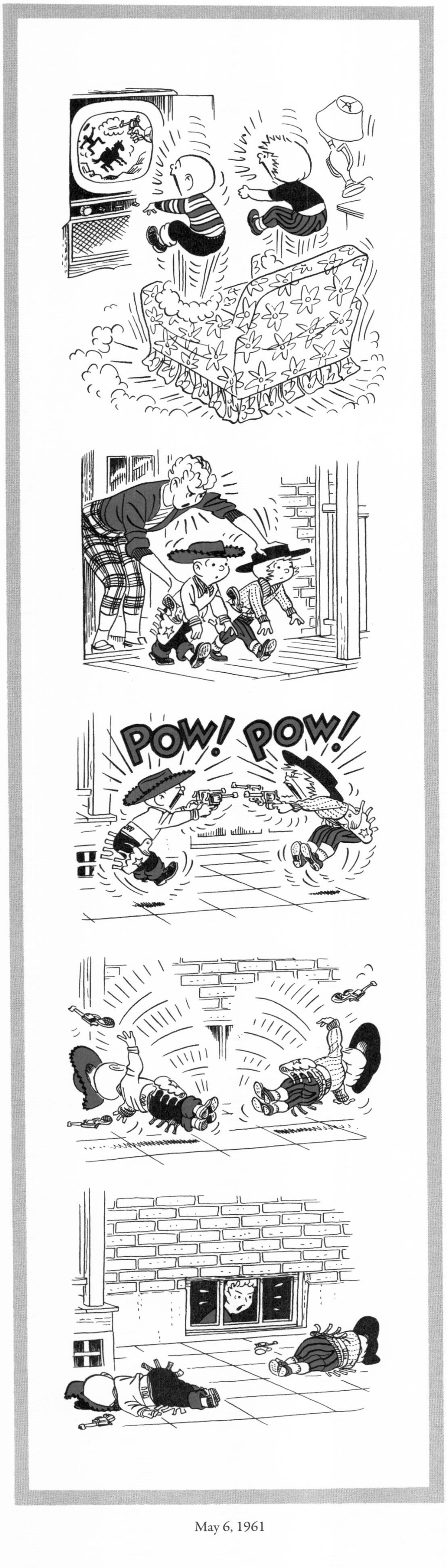
POW! POW!

May 6, 1961

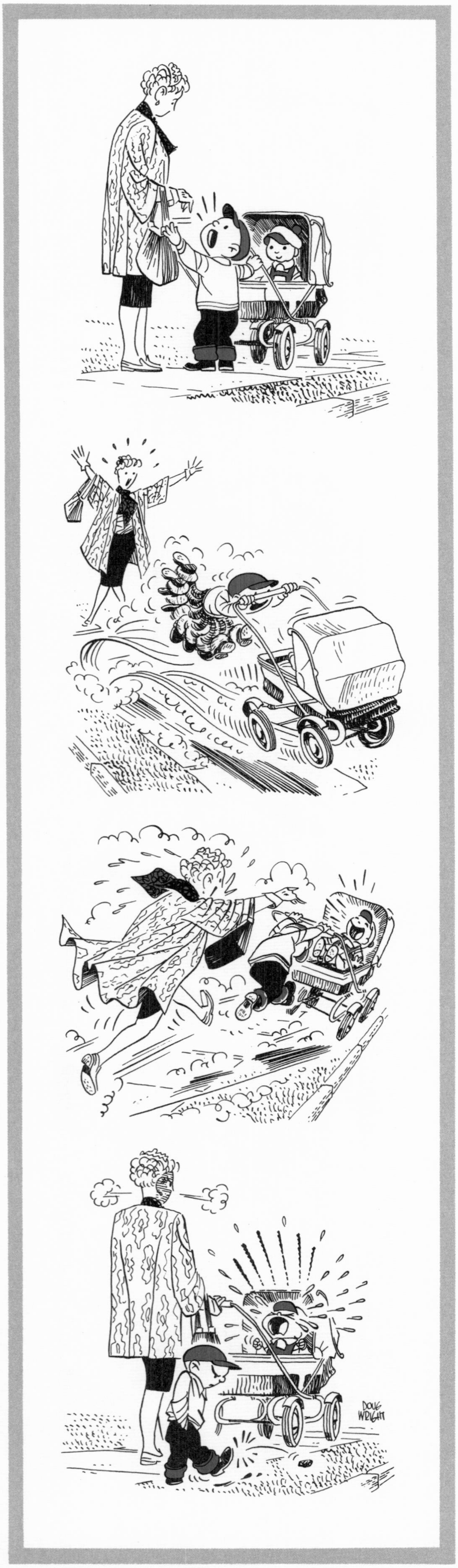
DOUG WRIGHT

May 20, 1961

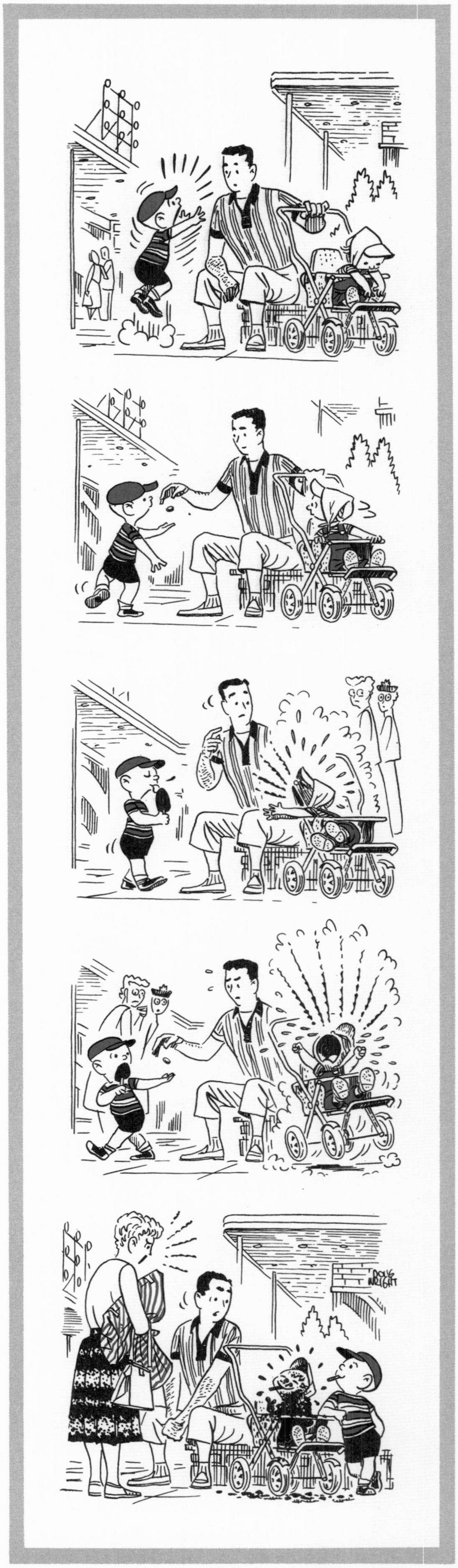
DOUG WRIGHT

July 1, 1961

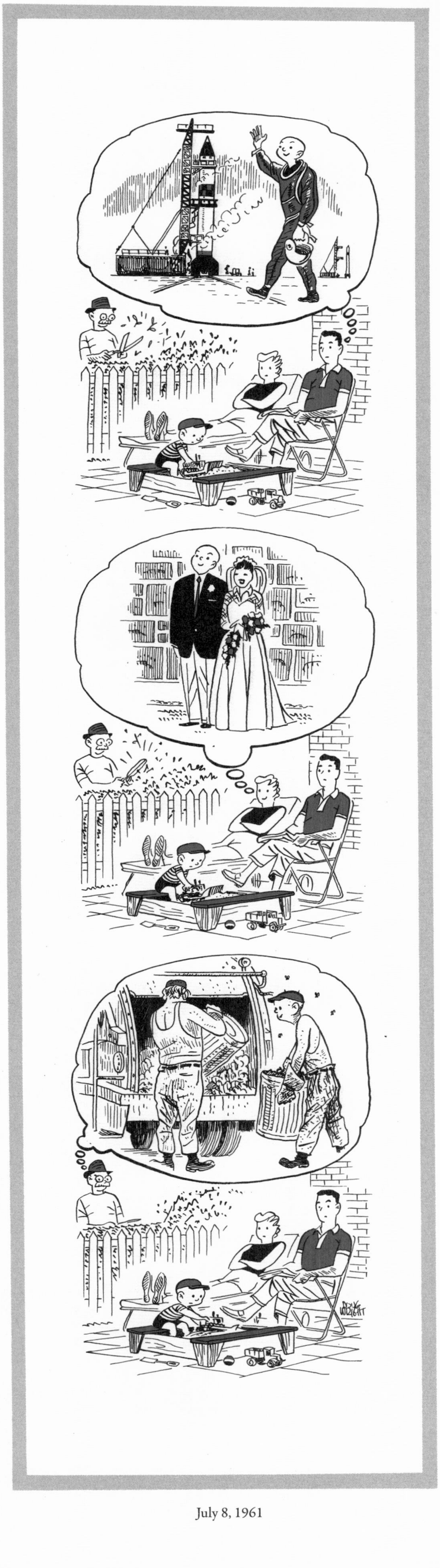
DOUG WRIGHT

July 8, 1961

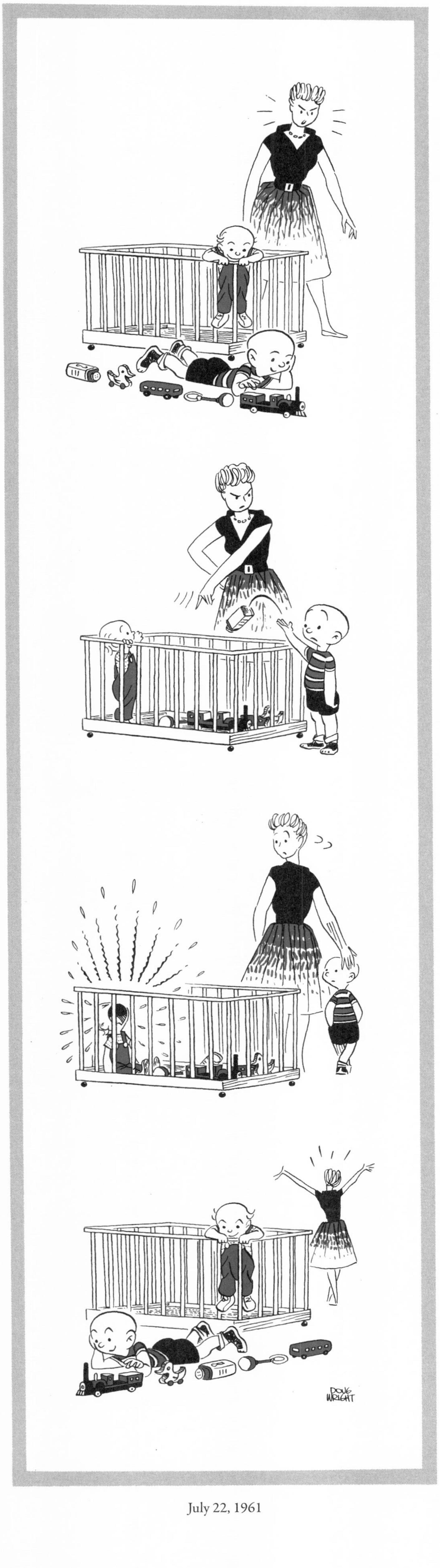
DOUG WRIGHT

July 22, 1961

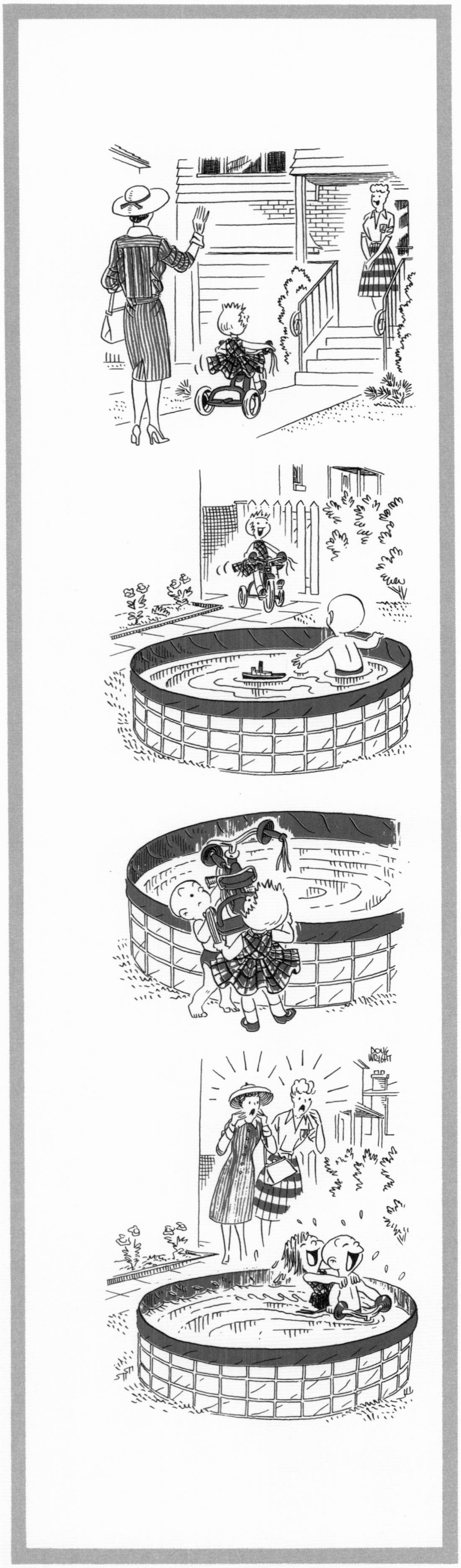
DOUG WRIGHT

August 12, 1961

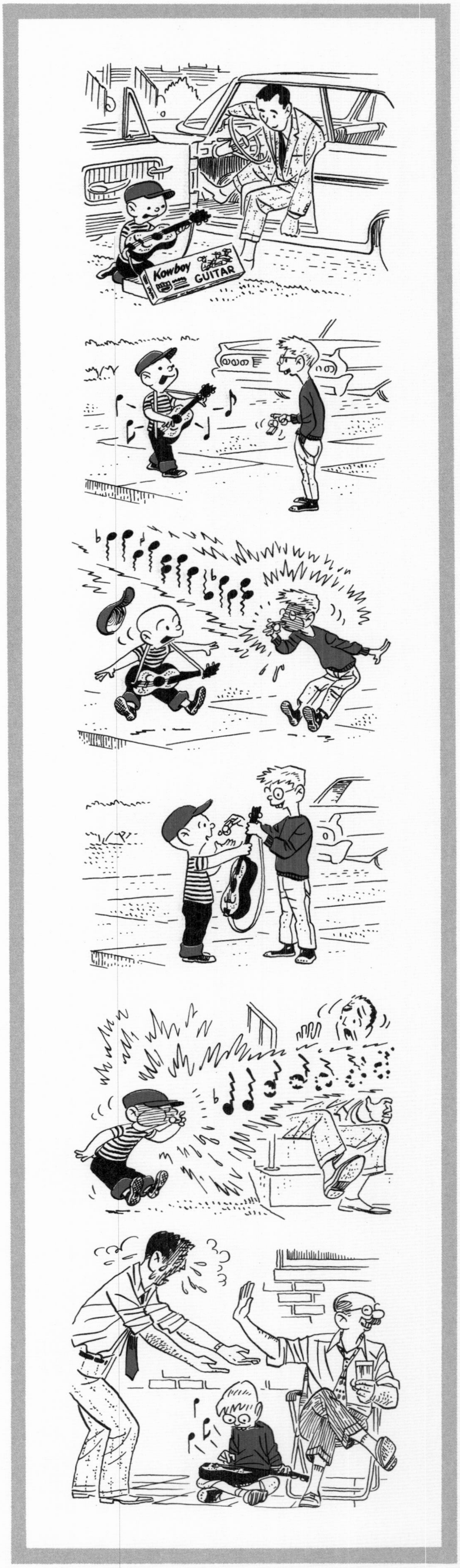
Kowboy
GUITAR

September 9, 1961

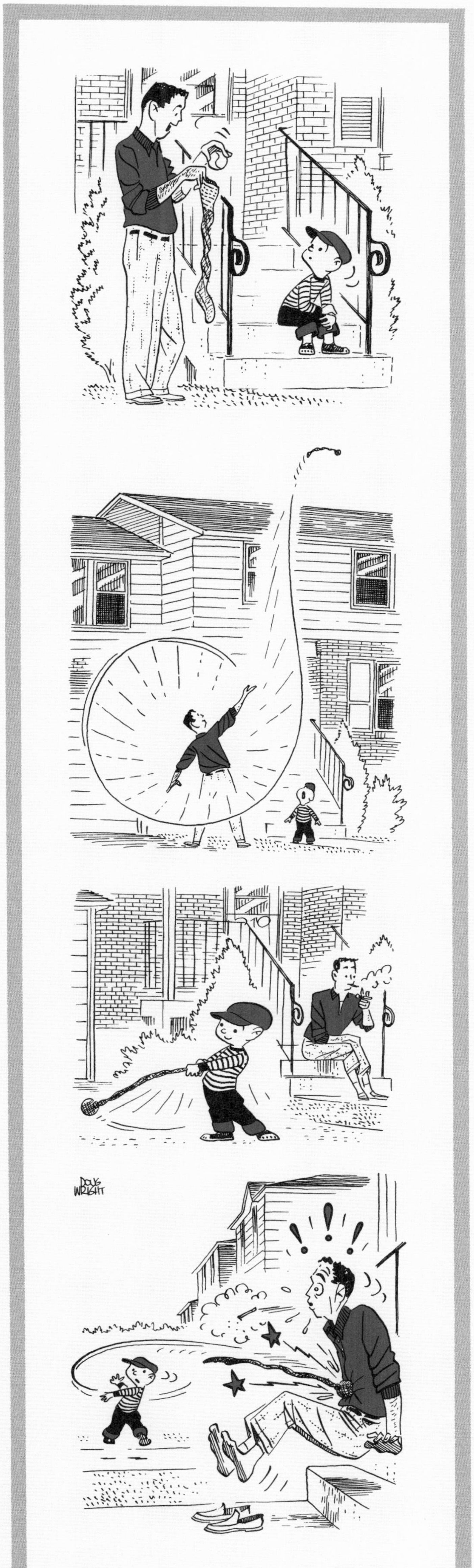
DOUG WRIGHT

September 16, 1961

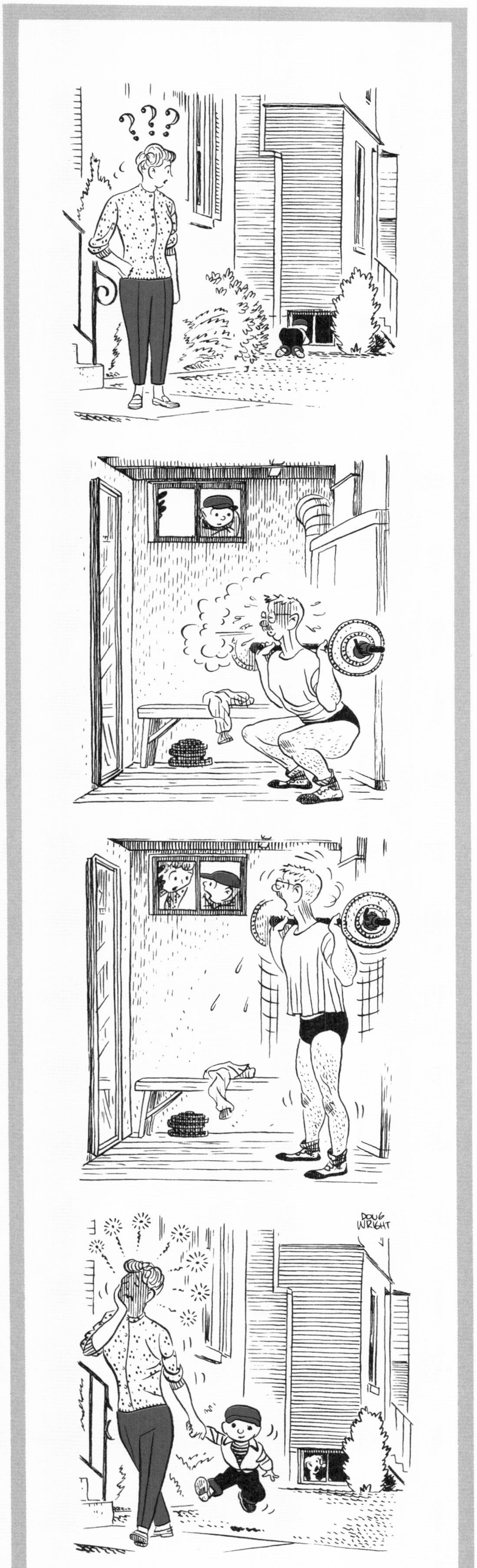
DOUG WRIGHT

September 23, 1961

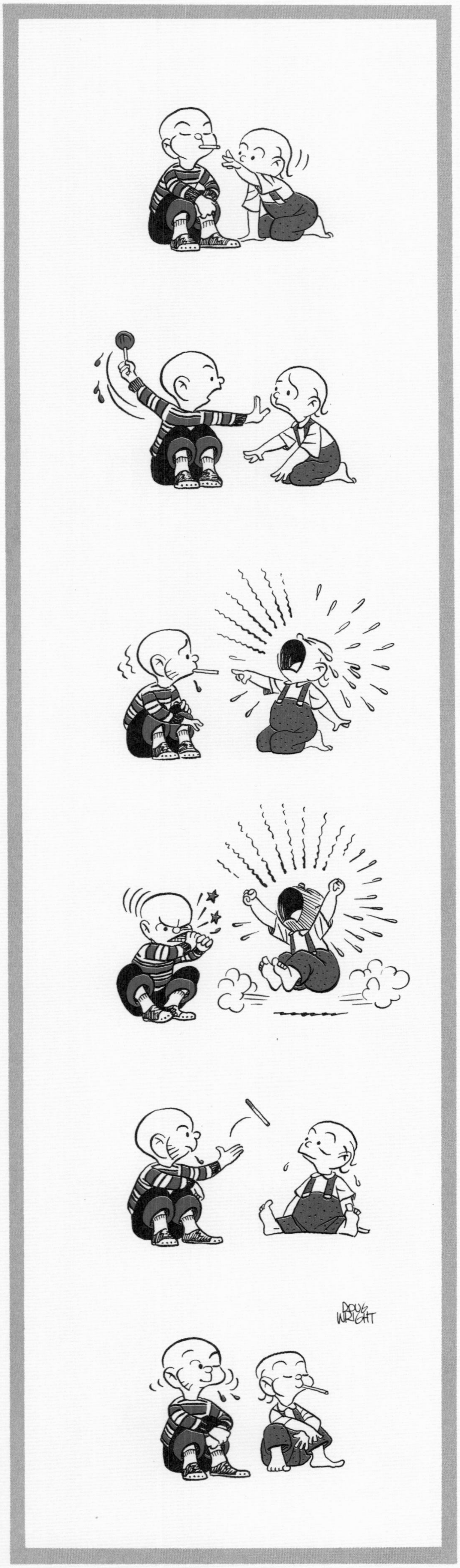
DOUG WRIGHT

September 30, 1961

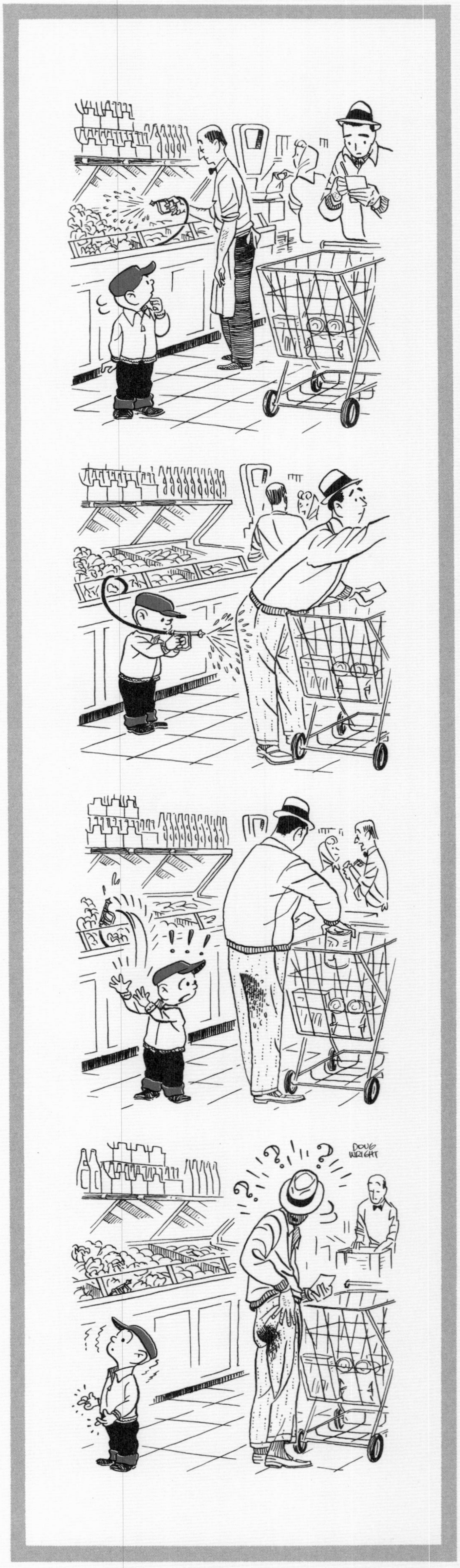
DOUG WRIGHT

October 7, 1961

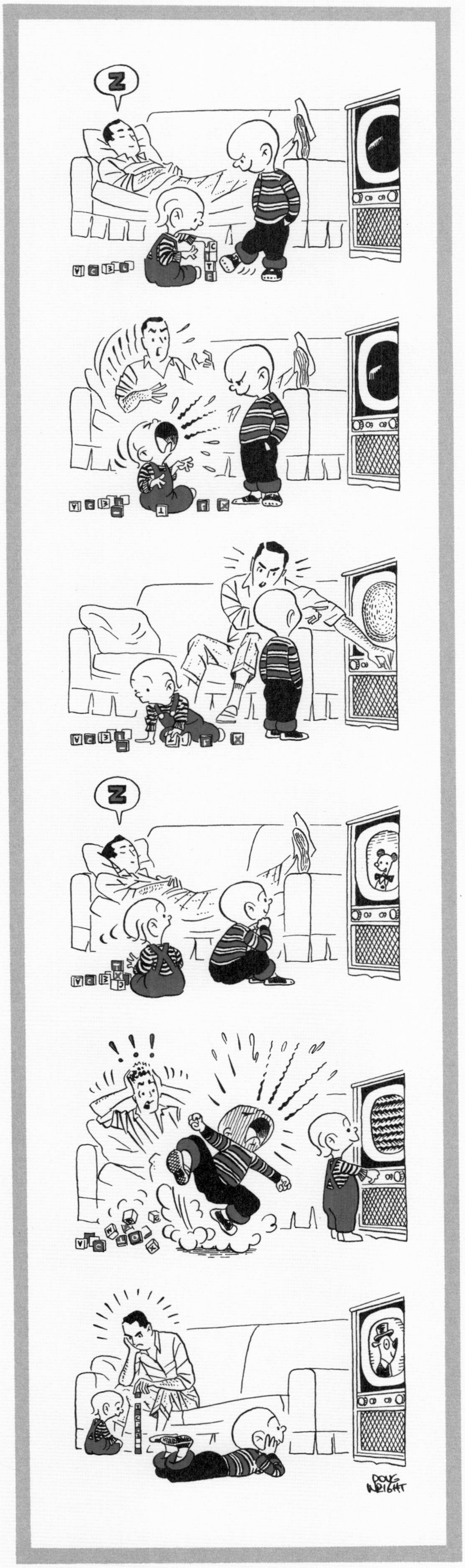

Z
Z
DOUG WRIGHT

October 14, 1961

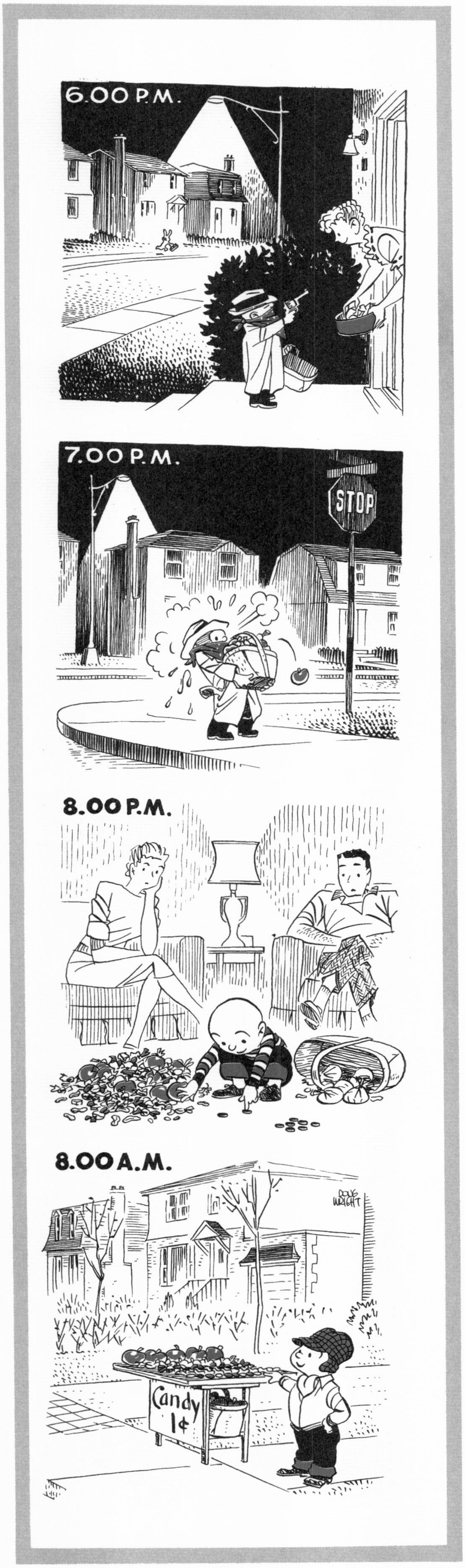

6.00 P.M.
7.00 P.M.
STOP
8.00 P.M.
8.00 A.M.
DOUG WRIGHT
Candy 1¢

October 20, 1961

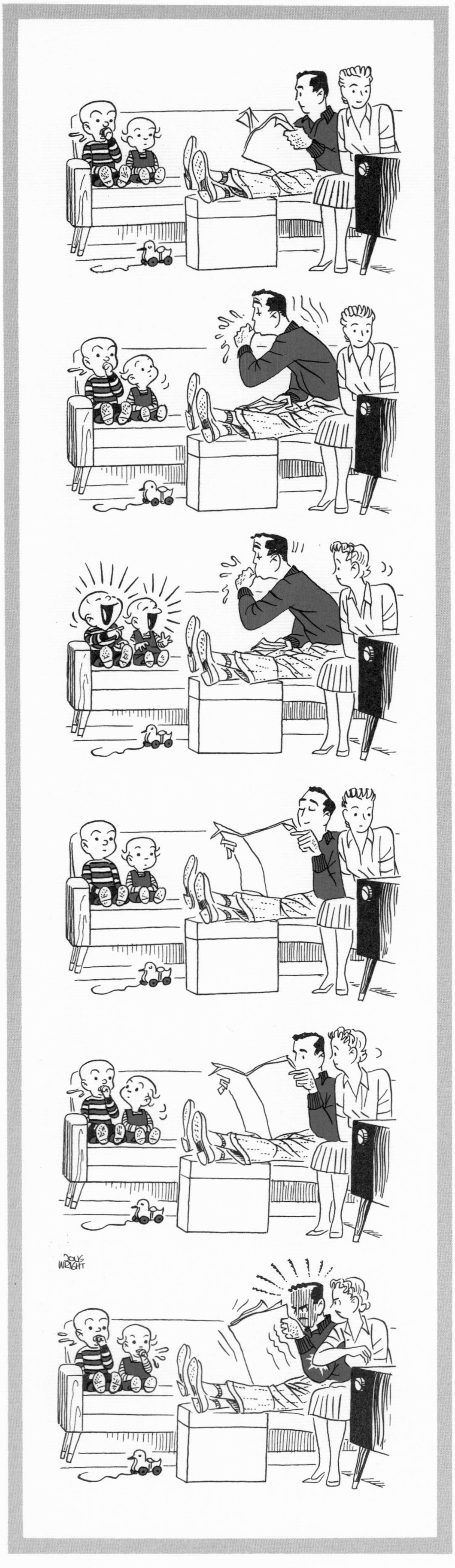
DOUG WRIGHT

November 4, 1961

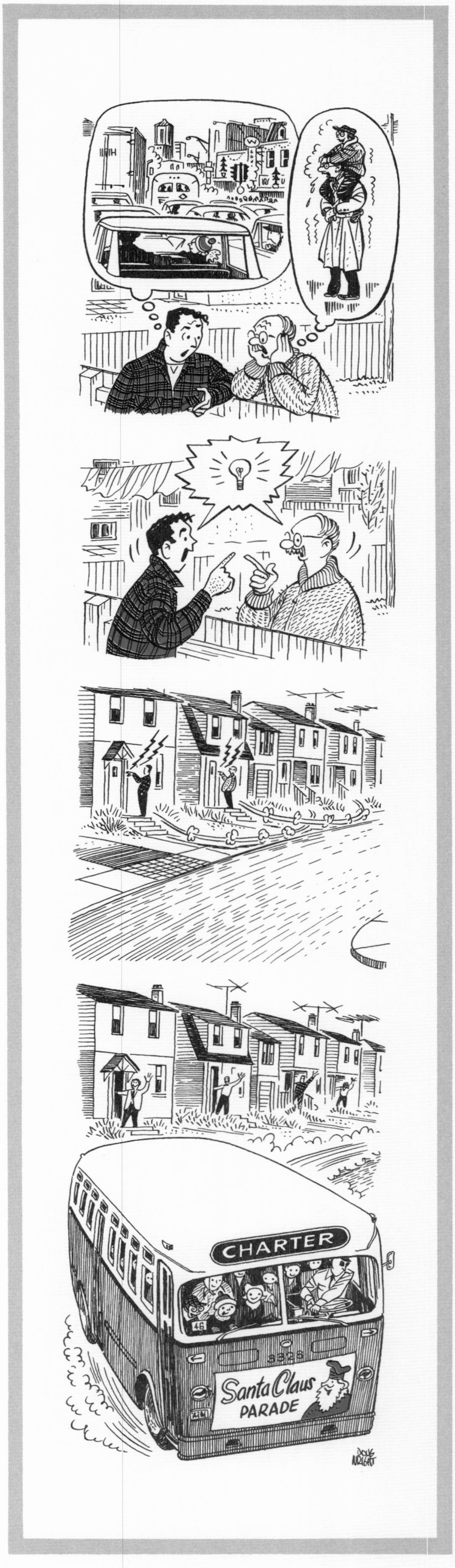
CHARTER
Santa Claus
PARADE
DOUG WRIGHT

December 2, 1961

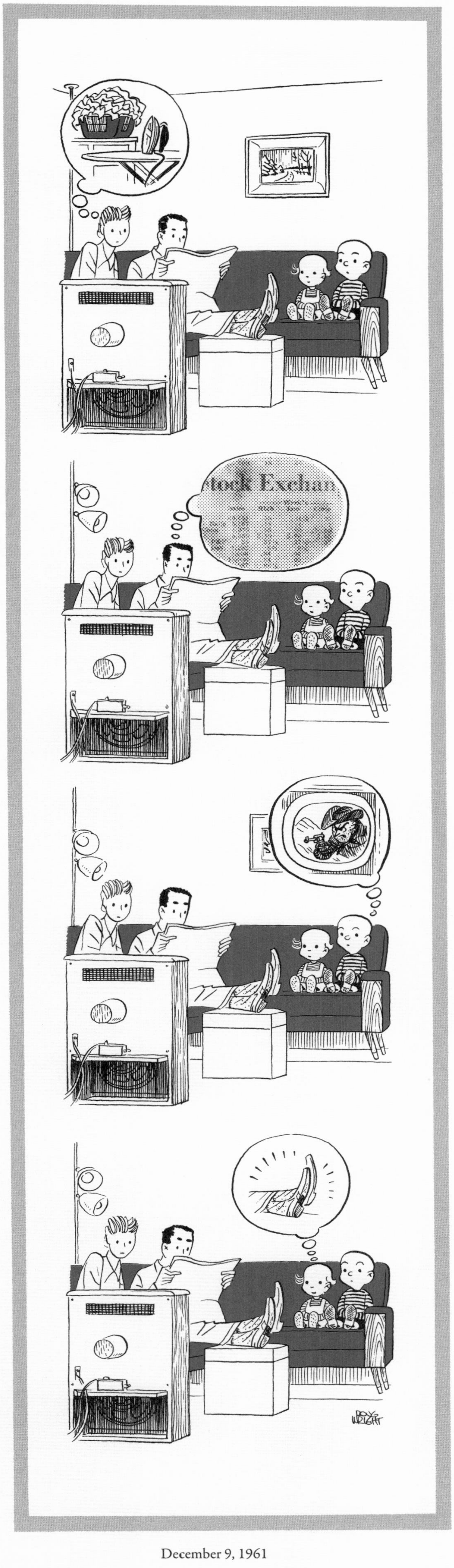
tock Exchan
DOUG WRIGHT

December 9, 1961

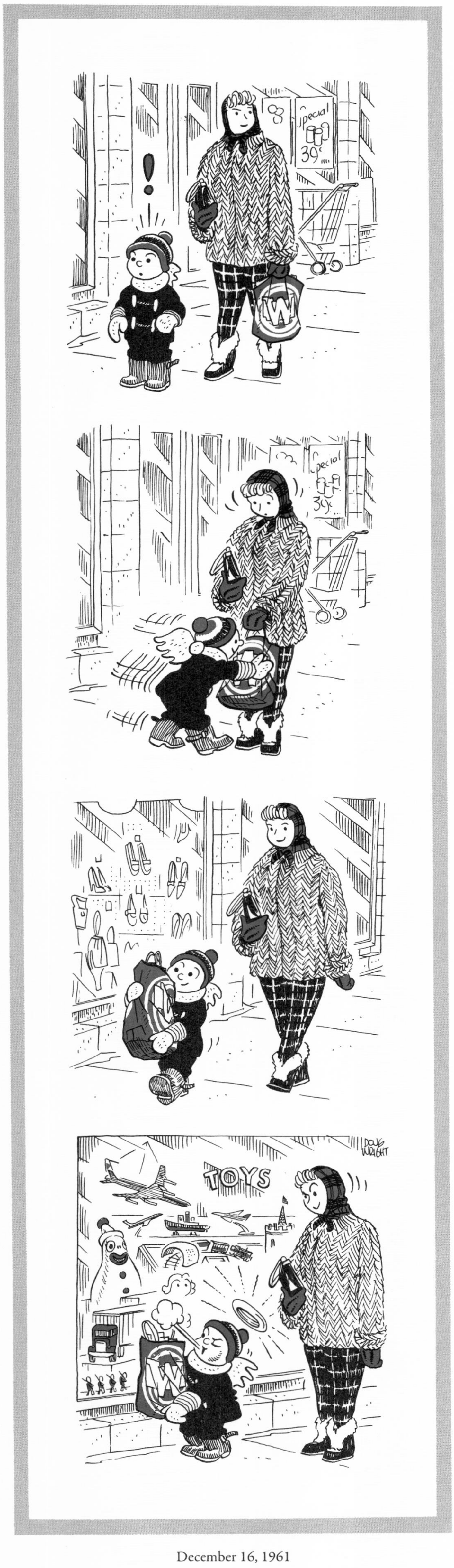
Special
39¢
TOYS
DOUG WRIGHT

December 16, 1961

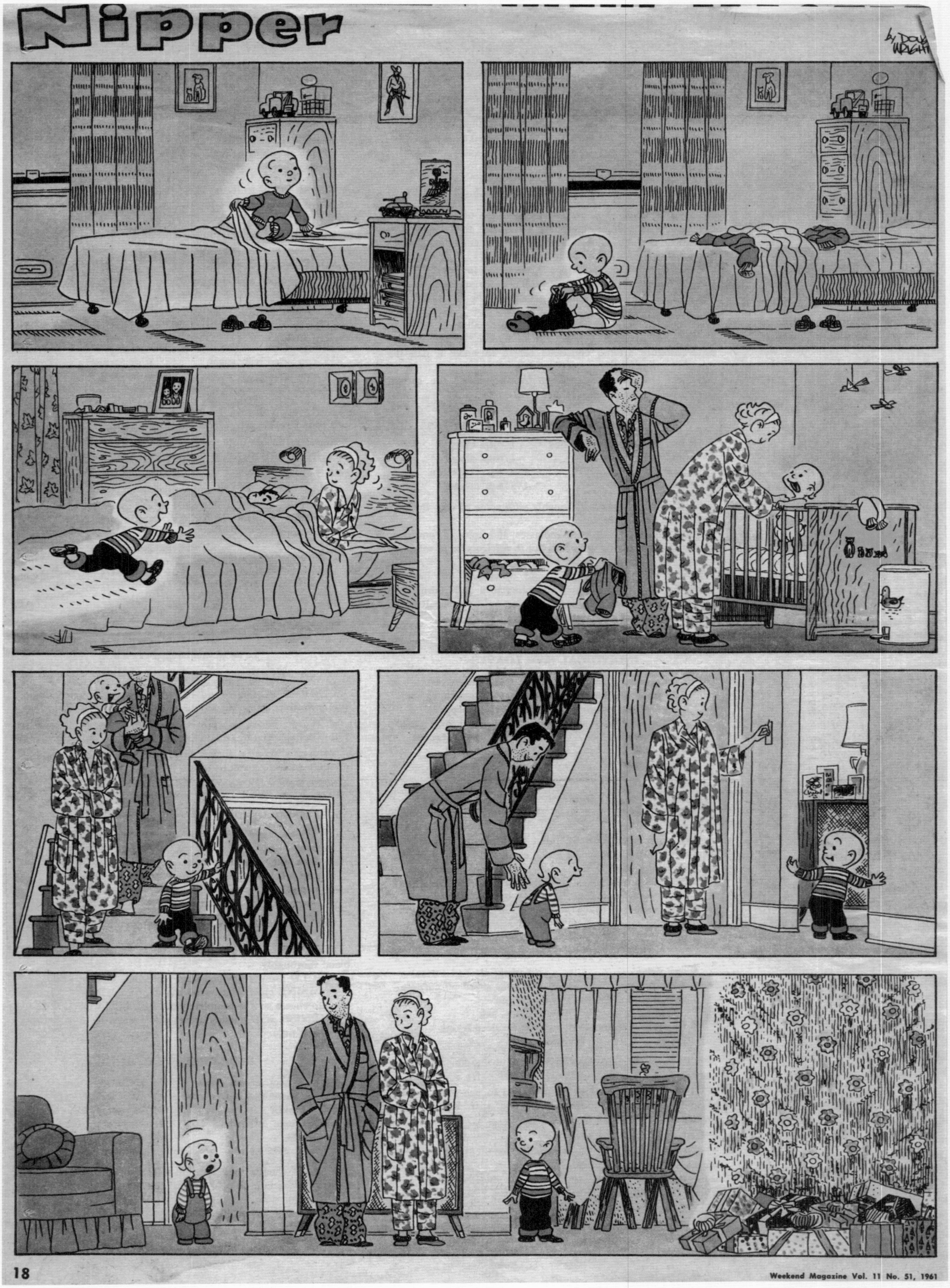
Nipper
18
Weekend Magazine Vol. 11 No. 51, 1961

December 23, 1961

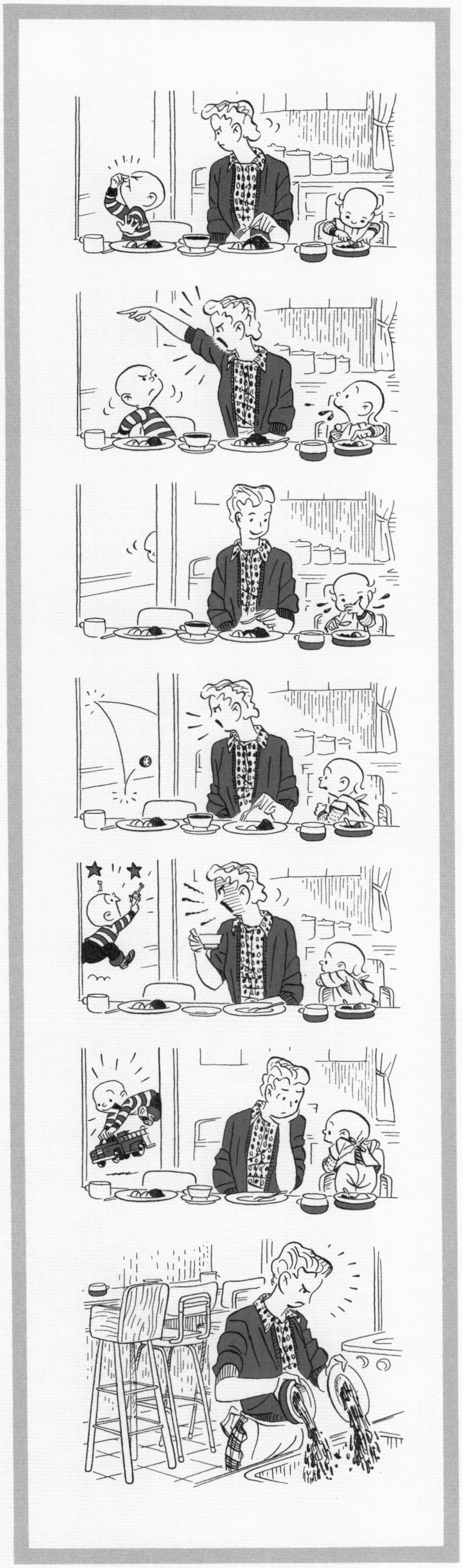
December 30, 1961

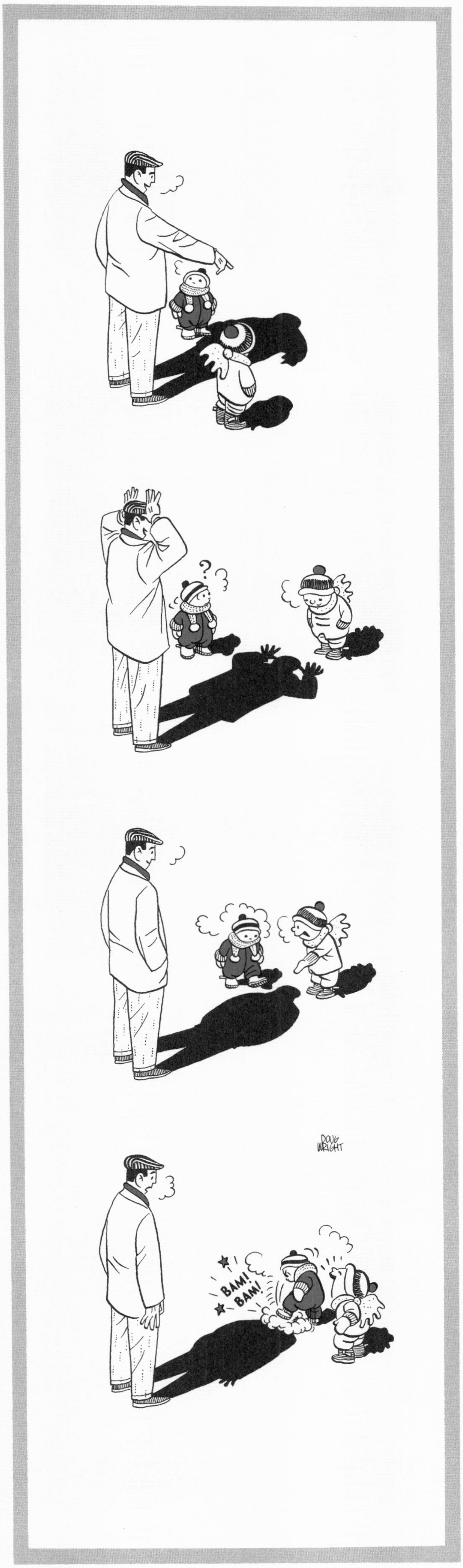
DOUG WRIGHT
BAM! BAM!
January 6, 1962

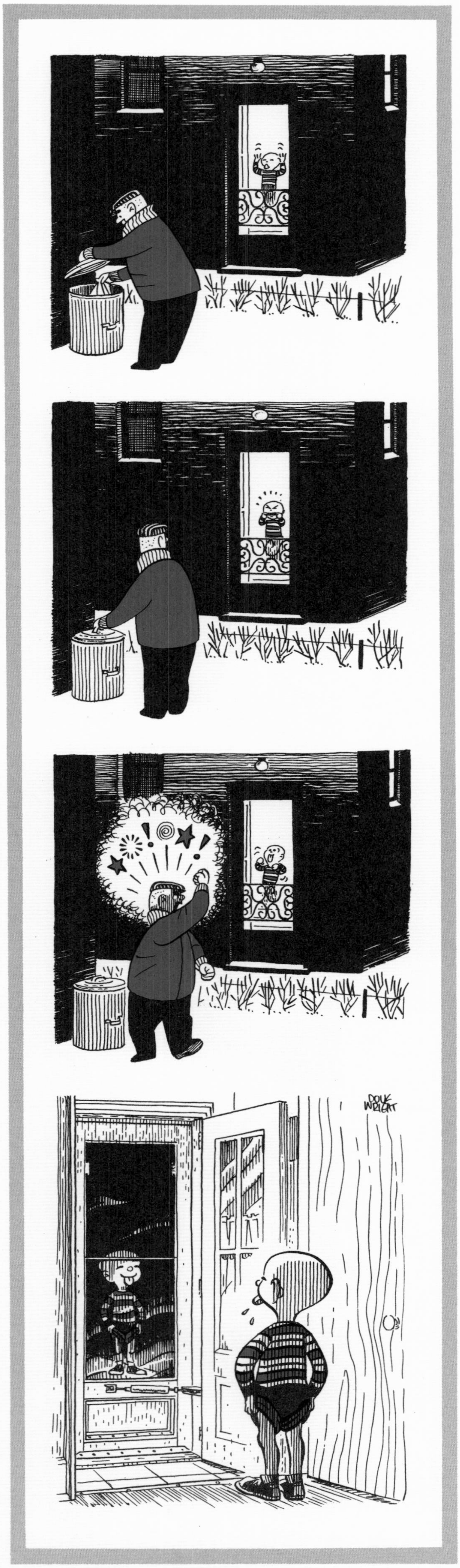
DOUG WRIGHT

January 27, 1962

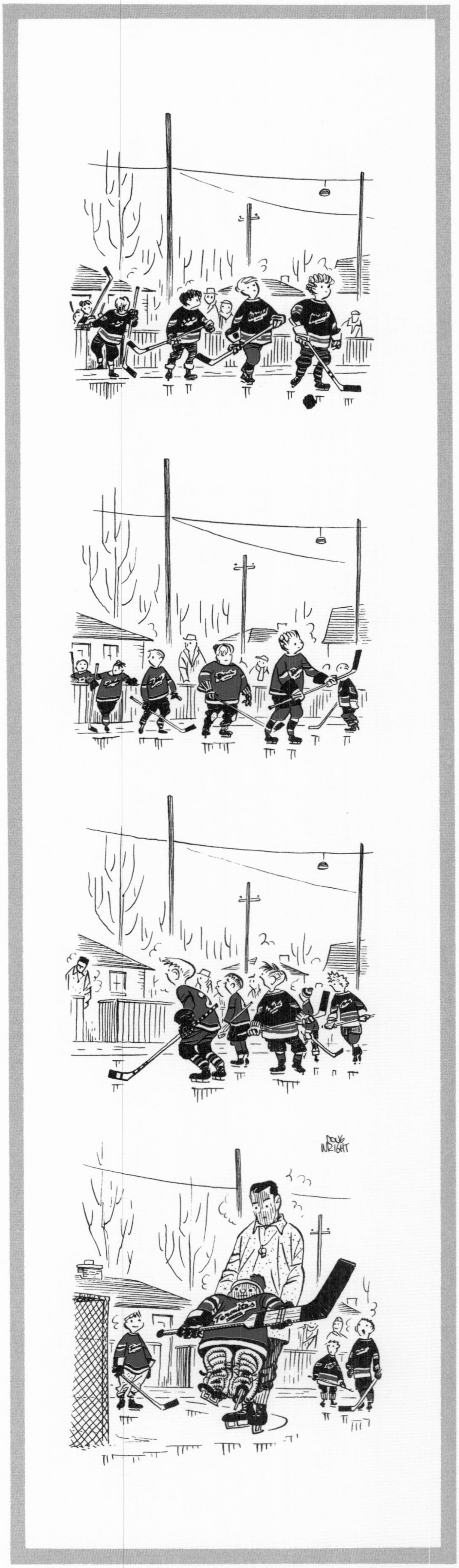
DOUG WRIGHT

February 3, 1962

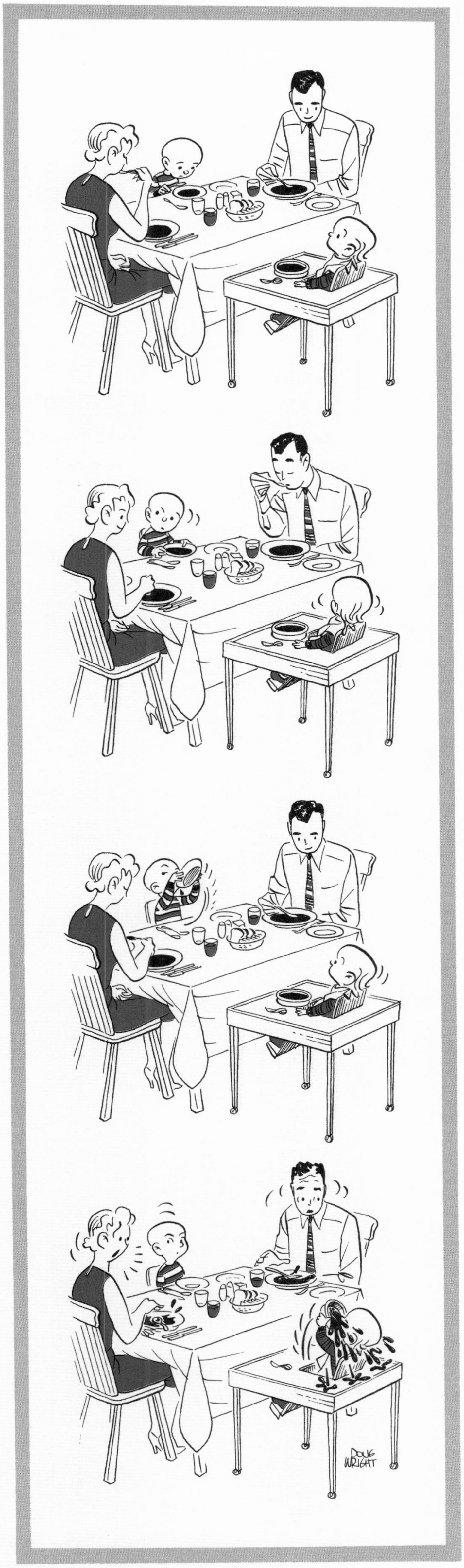
DOUG WRIGHT

February 10, 1962

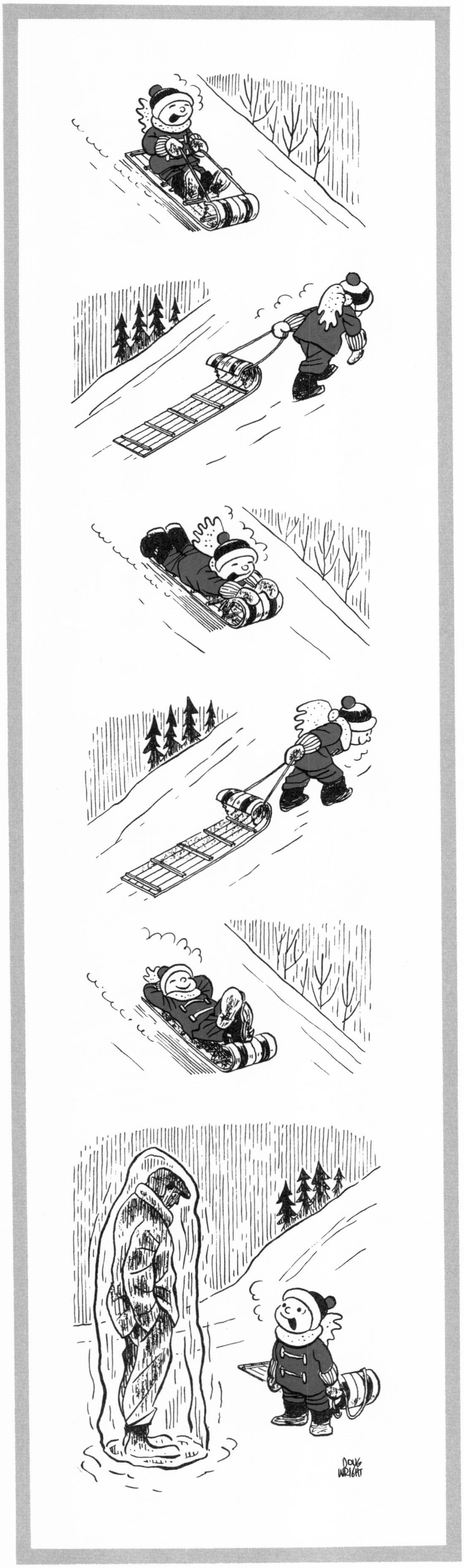
DOUG WRIGHT

February 24, 1962

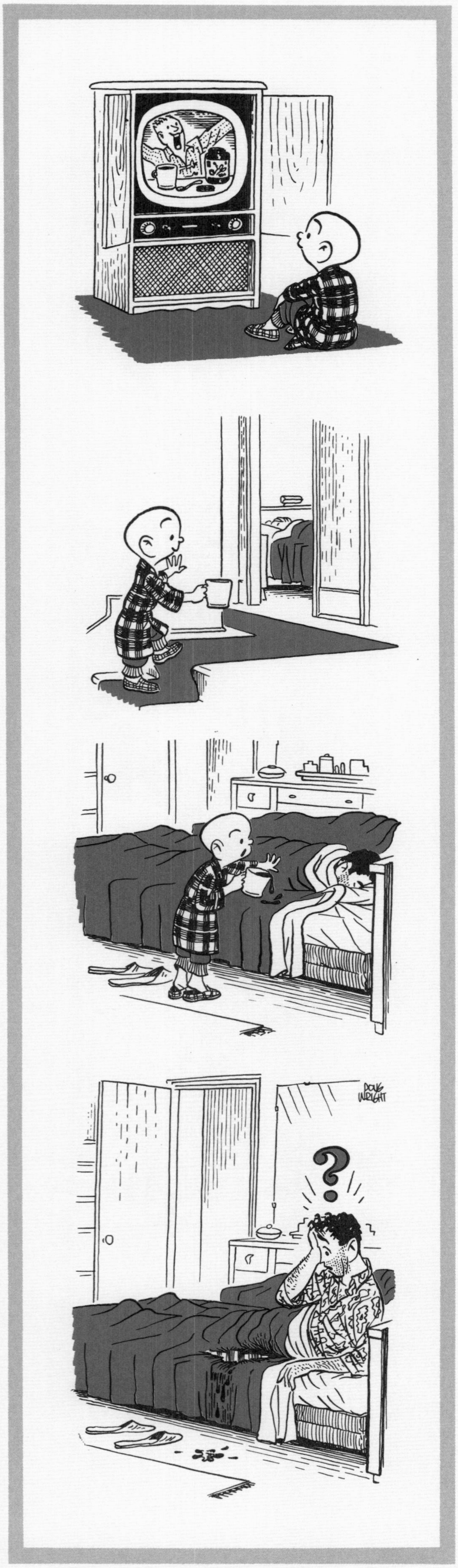
DOUG WRIGHT

March 10, 1962

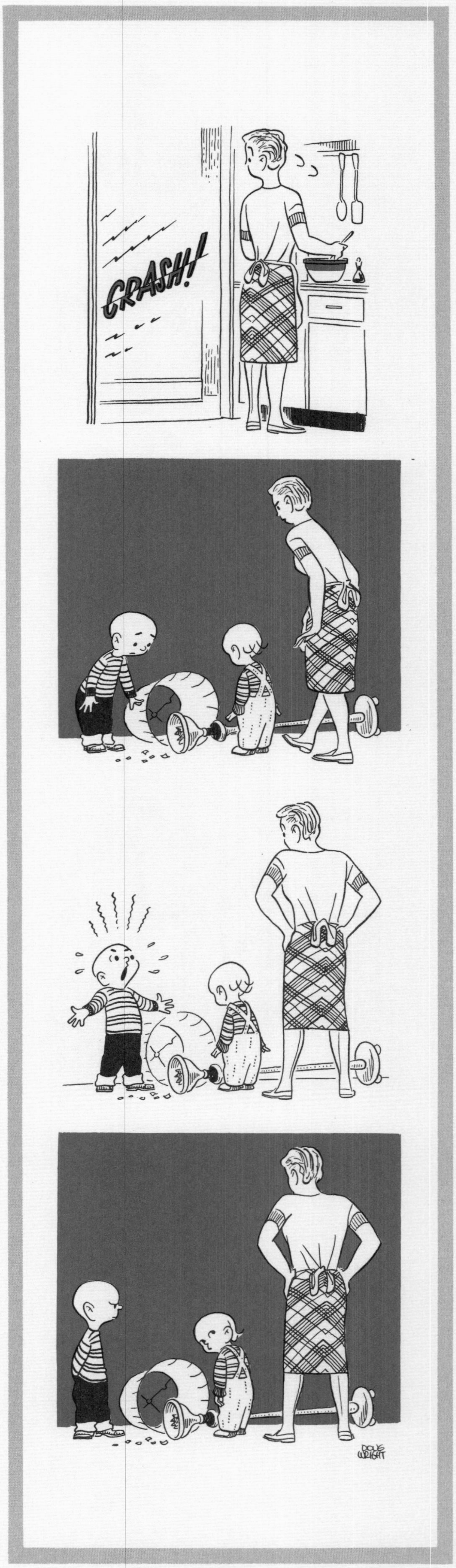
CRASH!
DOUG WRIGHT

April 28, 1962

May 12, 1962

May 19, 1962

Victoria Day fireworks rate a special colour here. Once Wright established red as the strip's colour he only added a second colour on the rarest of occasions.

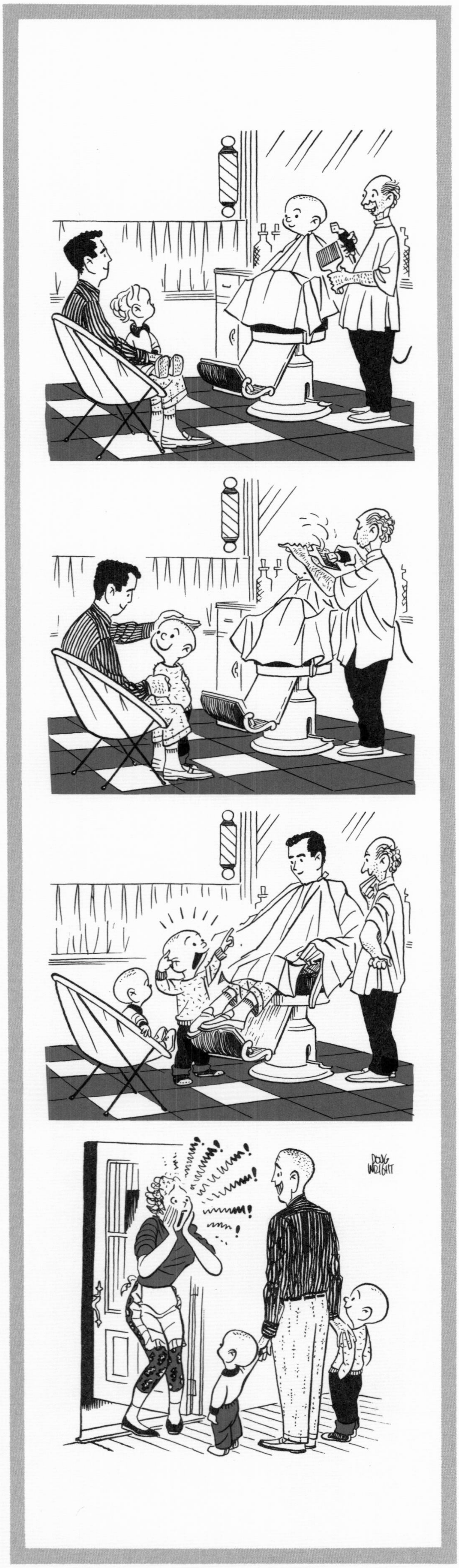
DOUG WRIGHT

May 26, 1962

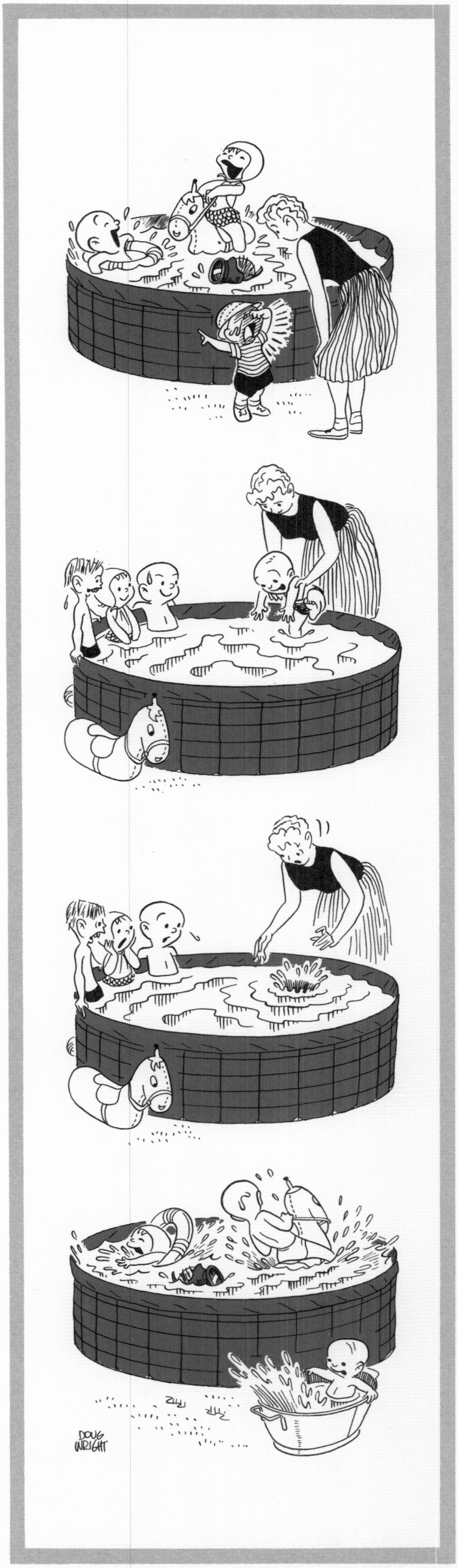
DOUG WRIGHT

June 16, 1962

July 28, 1962

August 11, 1962

Atypically, here and above, Wright employs a single horizontal panel for the strip. This actually anticipates a change in the strip's format. From here on, most likely due to editorial space demands, Wright begins to design his strip so that it can be run horizontally or vertically.

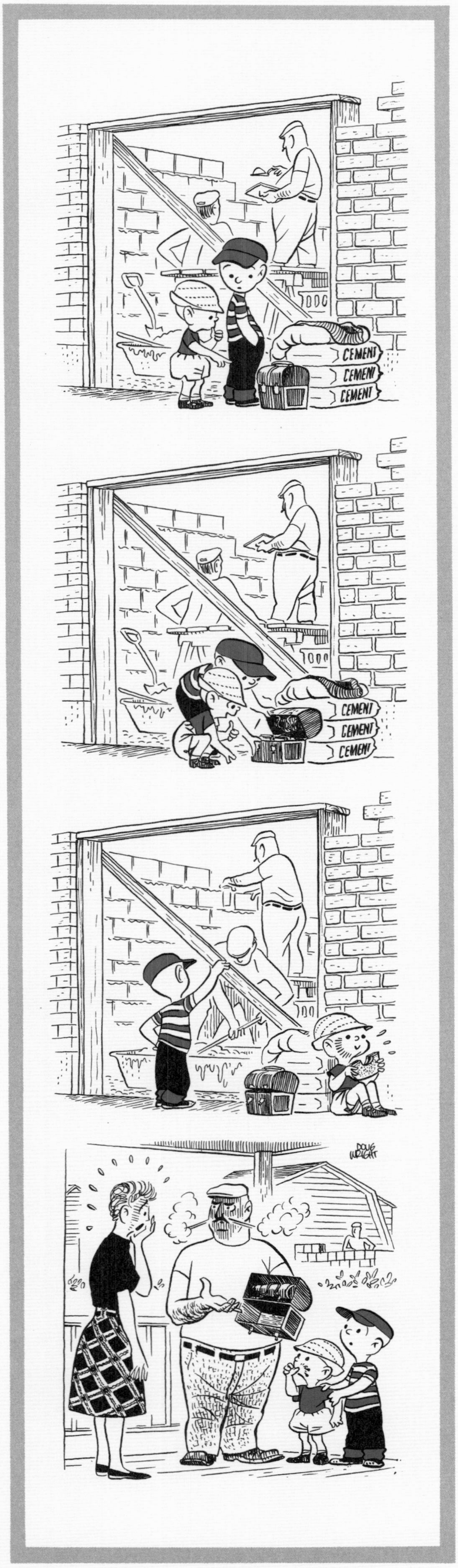
CEMENT
CEMENT
CEMENT
CEMENT
CEMENT
CEMENT
DOUG WRIGHT

August 4, 1962

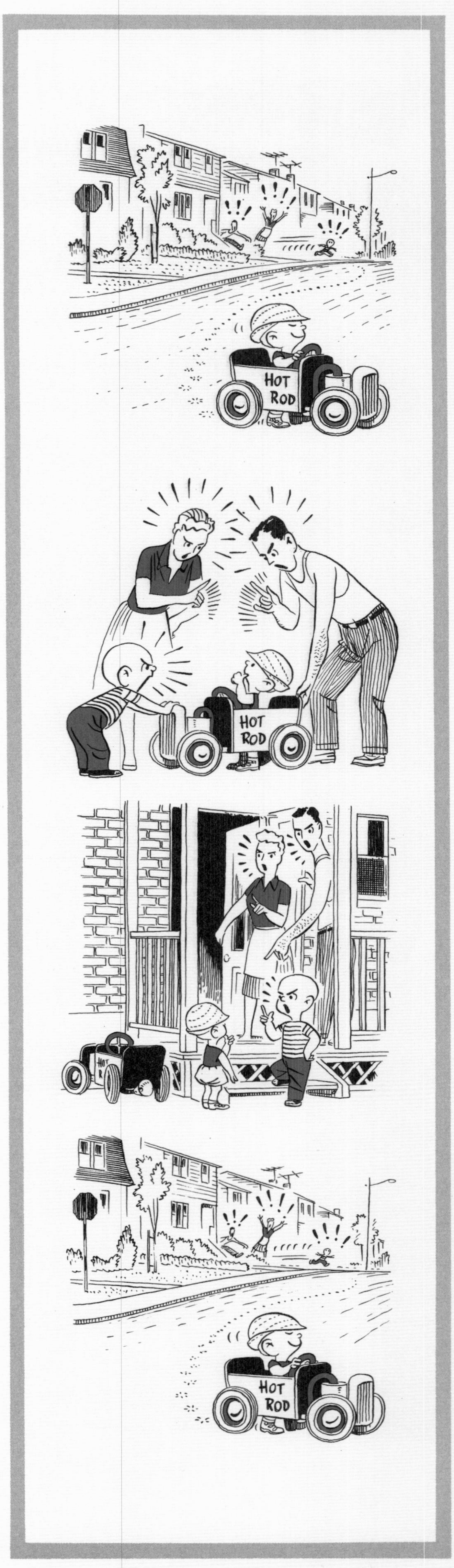
HOT ROD
HOT ROD
HOT ROD

August 18, 1962

October 20, 1962

November 17, 1962

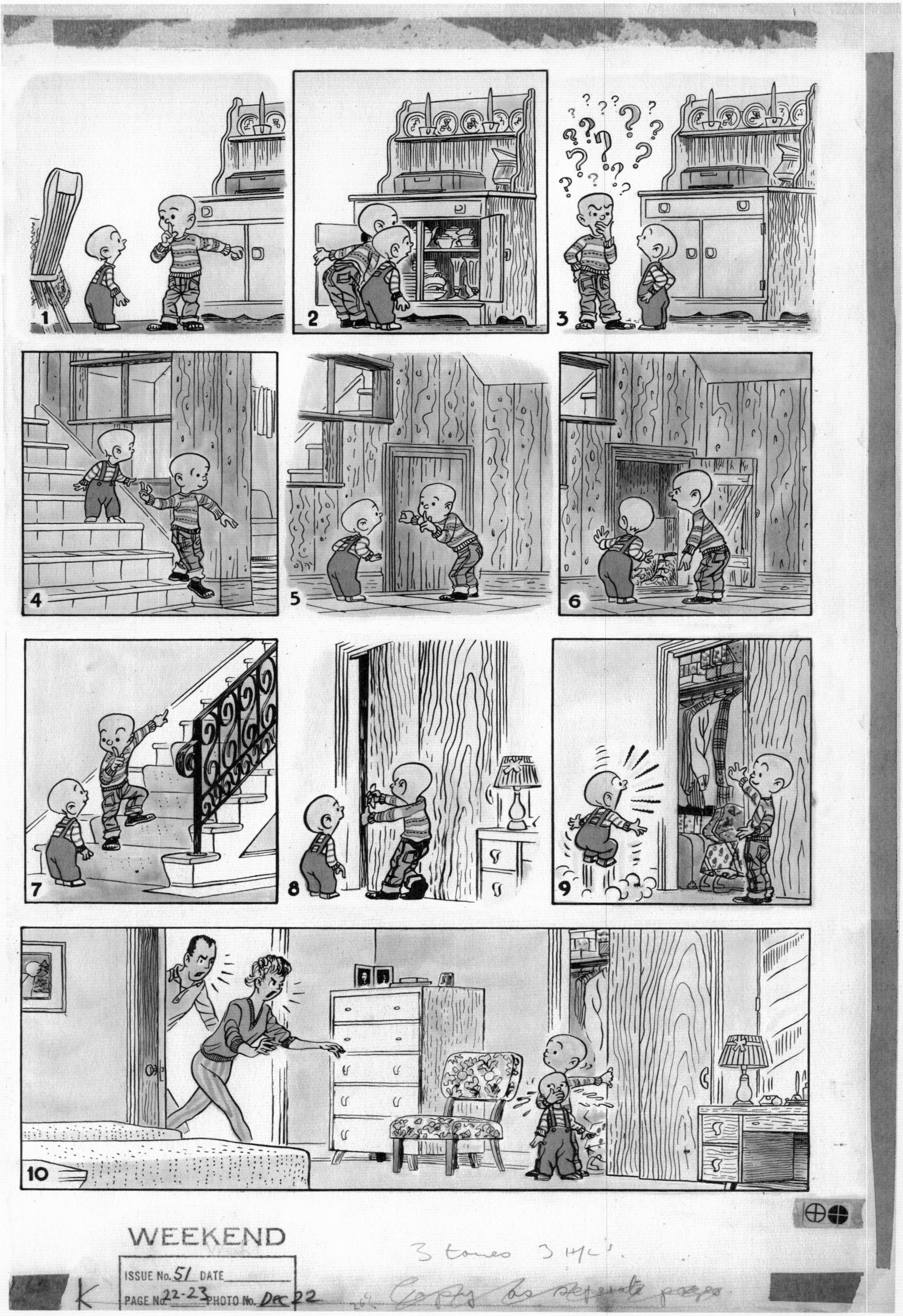
WEEKEND
ISSUE No. 51 DATE
PAGE No. 22-23 PHOTO No. Dec 22
3 tones 3 H/C's
Copy as separate pages

December 22, 1962

SPECIAL THANKS TO
THE WRIGHT "BOYS,"
BILL, JIM AND KEN WRIGHT,
FOR THEIR HELP AND SUPPORT
WITH THIS PROJECT.

A FEW NOTES ABOUT THE EDITORS

BRAD MACKAY is an Ottawa–based writer and journalist who has worked for the *National Post* and the CBC. His youthful infatuation with comics—fed by the unholy trinity of *Peanuts, Batman* comics and *Mad* magazine—survived into adulthood, where it now regularly finds a productive outlet in articles for the *Globe and Mail*, the *Toronto Star*, CBC Arts Online, *THIS* magazine and *Toronto Life*. He is also the director of The Doug Wright Awards for Canadian Cartooning, which he co–founded with Seth in 2004.

SETH is the cartoonist behind the comic book series *Palookaville*. Currently in its 18th year, *Palookaville* will be soon relaunched as a hardcover series, where it will continue to feature *Clyde Fans*, along with other stories, artwork, and subjects of related interest to Seth. His books include *It's A Good Life, If You Don't Weaken, Bannock, Beans, and Black Tea, Wimbledon Green*, and the above–mentioned *Clyde Fans: Book One*. One volume of his sketchbooks has appeared under the title *Vernacular Drawings* and another will likely appear within the following few years. His books have been translated into six languages. As a book designer he has worked on a variety of projects including the recent Penguin edition of *The Portable Dorothy Parker*. He is the designer of the 25–volume series *The Complete Peanuts* and the upcoming *John Stanley Library*. His comics, drawings, and installations have been exhibited throughout the world in a variety of group and solo shows. In 2005 he was the subject of a solo exhibition at the Art Gallery of Ontario, which showcased the first public display of his model city DOMINION. As an illustrator he has produced commercial works for almost all of the major Canadian and American magazines, including numerous cover and interior pieces for the *New Yorker*. Seth is the subject of an upcoming NATIONAL FILM BOARD documentary. Recently his story, *George Sprott (1894–1975)*, was serialized in the *New York Times Magazine* and is now available from Drawn & Quarterly in expanded form as a book. He lives in Guelph, Ontario with his wife and two cats and appears to rarely leave the basement.